Contents

Acknowledgements

Hodder Education would like to thank the reviewers of the book for their invaluable input:

Chapter 3 The Sociology of Families was reviewed by **Dr Alison Lamont**, a Lecturer in Sociology and Criminology at the University of Roehampton. She has co-convened the Families and Relationships Study Group and Conference Stream of the British Sociological Association since 2016.

Chapter 4 The Sociology of Education was reviewed by **Dr Michael Ward**, a Lecturer in Social Sciences at Swansea University. His work centres on the performance of working-class masculinities within and beyond educational institutions. He has written numerous peer-reviewed journal articles, book chapters and reports, and is the author of the award-winning book *From Labouring to Learning: Working-class Masculinities*. Michael is the editor of *Boyhood Studies: An Interdisciplinary Journal*.

Chapter 5 The Sociology of Crime and Deviance was reviewed by **Dr Anthony Ellis**, Lecturer in Sociology and Criminology at the University of Salford.

The whole book was reviewed by **Dr Nadena Doharty**, a sociologist of education working in the School of Education at the University of Sheffield. Nadena read her undergraduate degree in Sociology and Politics and postgraduate degree in International Relations at Goldsmith's College, University of London. After a PGCE specialising in Sociology and Politics, Nadena earned her PhD at the University of Keele.

We would also like to thank **Nadine White**, HuffPost UK, for her feedback on the previous edition of this book, which was invaluable when revising the new edition.

1 The sociological approach

Key learning

You will be able to:
- explain what sociology is and how the discipline developed over time.

KEY TERMS

Culture customs, ideas and practices of a particular society or group

Evidence-based when findings are based on the data collected

Norms informal rules that influence social behaviour

Objective judgements that are not influenced by personal prejudices

Role patterns of behaviour expected by individuals in different situations, e.g. student and teacher

Social construct patterns of behaviour based on the norms and expectations of a society

Society a group of people with a common culture – the term is often used to describe nation states, e.g. British society

Values important beliefs held by individuals and social groups

What is sociology?

Definition

The simplest definition of sociology is the 'science of society', but this definition leaves us with more questions than answers. Is sociology really a science and, if so, what makes it a science? Can we even agree what society is? It may be more helpful to start with a clearer understanding of what sociologists have been trying to achieve.

Sociologists want to understand why people behave as they do when they come together in groups. They ask questions about things that people often take for granted but which are of huge importance to the way in which we live our lives. There is nothing new about the attempt to better understand human behaviour, but in the more distant past people often relied upon ways of thinking that were passed down from one generation to the next and often expressed those ideas in superstitious terms, for example particular behaviours could be the actions of gods and demons. Sociology as an objective evidence-based and systematic study of human behaviour has its origins in our more recent past.

History

Philosophers such as Plato and Confucius, and medieval scholars such as Ibn Khaldun, an Arab Islamic scholar in the fourteenth century, are early key figures in sociological reasoning and analysis. In terms of how sociology came to be a subject of study, this could be said to have begun with the violent events of the French Revolution (1789–99). This was a point in time when European societies began to go through a series of radical changes: political, economic and social. In 1793, most of Western Europe was a place where the vast majority of people worked in agriculture and lived in villages and small towns, ruled by aristocracies (the descendants of a warrior elite whose power came from the ownership of land). By 1900, Europe had been transformed into a place where most people lived in cities and worked in manufacturing industries, ruled by relatively democratic parliamentary systems. In an attempt to understand these changes, some writers and thinkers in Europe began to look for more 'scientific' ways to study the world around them and to move away from old ideas about a 'natural order' to the world, where the authority of rulers came from a special relationship with their God.

The first person to use the term 'sociology' was a French writer, Auguste Comte (1798–1857), although he originally preferred the rather more clumsy term 'social physics'. He believed that sociology was truly a science, in the same way that biology, physics and chemistry are sciences. He was interested in the development of scientific ideas and the relative importance of the different branches of scientific enquiry. Comte believed that ultimately it would be possible to discover and understand 'laws' that governed human behaviour. Modern sociologists, for the most part, tend to see things rather differently, but the idea that sociology is a form of scientific study remains and is an idea to which we will return at a later point in this book.

The sociological imagination

When you look around you what do you see? It may be that you are reading this in a library or at home, but it is also likely that you will be in a classroom. You need to look at the situation in which you find yourself through the eyes of a sociologist; to do so is to use what the American sociologist C. Wright Mills (1916–62) described as 'the sociological imagination'. Let us assume for a minute that you are in a classroom, which from the sociologist's point of view raises a number of interesting questions:

- Who are the different individuals involved in this social situation?
- Do they share a sense of common purpose and is there some sort of unspoken understanding about how they should behave?
- What happens to those individuals who do not wish to conform to the 'rules' that govern this social situation?

From a 'common sense' point of view, in the classroom, teachers teach and students learn. However, this 'obvious' answer fails to give us a real understanding of the complex social interactions that occur in any social situation. Sociologists use a form of specialist 'language' to describe these interactions and to express the complexities that lie beneath a surface reality. To a sociologist, the classroom is a place where norms and expectations govern the behaviour of the individuals involved; school itself is a social construct and the participants (students and teachers) play different roles that reflect the culture and values of the wider society.

Activities

1 Write down a list of your school or college rules from memory. Compare your list with others produced by members of your class. Look for similarities and differences.

2 Ask a member of the science department in your school or college if they consider sociology to be a science. Report back your findings to your sociology class.

Check your knowledge

1 From memory, write a brief definition of sociology. (Check your answer against the definition provided.)
2 Who invented the term 'social physics'?
3 Who used the term 'sociological imagination'?

Extension

Research the life and work of C. Wright Mills. Write a brief summary of his most important ideas.

Summary

- The simplest definition of sociology is the 'science of society'.
- Sociology as an objective and systematic study of human behaviour has its origins in the nineteenth and early twentieth centuries.

KEY TERMS

Consumerism a desire to buy and use consumer products for their use and gratification

New social movements an informally organised group (often very large and sometimes global in reach) who support a particular cause or promote certain interests, e.g. women's rights or environmentalism

Progress belief in the continual improvement of society

Sociological debate discussions between sociologists about how to best understand the nature of society

Unit of consumption the family unit consumes the products of industrial society by purchasing goods and services

Conflict and consensus

▲ In the 1960s and 1970s the car industry in Britain was subject to conflict in the form of many industrial disputes

Sociological debates

You are already aware from reading the first few pages in this book that sociologists have a number of different perspectives on society. Over the next few pages, we will look at a number of sociological debates that have taken place about how best to understand society. Sociology began largely as an attempt to understand change, in particular the sweeping changes that were happening in nineteenth-century society as industrial capitalism and the growth of cities (urbanisation) transformed how people lived their lives. Two different approaches to understanding this process have been taken by Marxists and functionalists.

Conflict perspectives

Marxists believe that different groups within society have very different interests. From a Marxist perspective, conflict is a common and persistent feature of societies throughout history. Marx saw capitalism as an economic system that exploited the labour of workers and oppressed them. Further change (the next epoch in history) would occur when the conflicts and contradictions at the heart of capitalism caused it to disintegrate, leading to the emergence of a fairer and more equal society.

Marxism is associated with the idea of revolutionary change; a revolution is a mass social movement that creates a major process of reform. Given that those in positions of power are unlikely to give up their power voluntarily, political revolutions usually involve violence and the outcomes can be dangerously unpredictable. Marxism is not the only conflict perspective. For example, feminism also emphasises the conflicting interests of different groups in society such as between men and women.

Consensus perspectives

Durkheim in the nineteenth century and American sociologist Talcott Parsons (1902–79) in the first half of the twentieth century developed functionalist ideas about society as a system. (Society from this point of view can be compared to a machine or the human body.) From their perspective, all the various parts of society were interrelated and human behaviour was governed by rules. Those rules were based on shared values and social life was only possible when order was maintained. Functionalism as a theory did not pretend that society was free from conflict, but conflict was seen as a temporary passing phase. The important common interests of the members of society would ensure that order was restored and society survived. In other words, a value consensus (agreement) existed. In the 1950s, Parsons believed that the members of American society shared common values that helped to maintain the capitalist economic system. For example, many people in the USA at that time were experiencing greater material prosperity and wanted to achieve an ever-improving standard of living (more consumer goods, more comfortable homes). The education system and the family helped to underpin that shared value of **consumerism**. The family had become a **unit of consumption** (buying the cars, washing machines and televisions produced by industry) while the education system produced the workforce required to maintain ever-increasing productivity.

Alternative points of view

Both functionalism and Marxism are 'grand theories' (see pages 16–19) about how society works. Both have their roots in nineteenth-century society and both have at their heart ideas about **progress**. From a functionalist perspective, society works for the benefit of all by ensuring future stability, peace and prosperity. Functionalism emphasises continuity rather than change, but it still embraces the idea of social progress as societies move from simple to more complex structures. From a Marxist perspective, progress comes about as the result of revolutionary change that ultimately produces a fairer and more equal society free from exploitation and oppression. However, nineteenth- and early twentieth-century ideas about 'progress' have been challenged by some social theorists who see change as arbitrary, accidental and unpredictable. For example, British society has experienced political changes and **new social movements** with a variety of agendas. These include a return to selective secondary education (grammar schools), 'Brexit' (leaving the European Union) and student-led protests in February 2019 that emphasise the need to protect the Earth and conserve its natural resources.

Link

Refer to the sections on functionalism and Marxism on pages 10–13 and 16–19 for more details.

Activities

1 Do you believe that a value consensus exists in British society? If so, what are those values? Organise a class debate with arguments for and against.
2 Write a paragraph to explain what functionalist sociologists meant when they described the family as a unit of consumption.

Extension

Watch Michael Moore's documentary Capitalism: A Love Story (2009). Extracts are available online.

Check your knowledge

1 Why is feminism described as a conflict perspective?
2 What do sociologists mean when they talk about 'a value consensus'?
3 What do sociologists mean when they talk about 'consumerism'?

Summary

- Marxism and feminism are conflict perspectives; they see different groups in society with conflicting interests.
- Functionalists see a value consensus; conflict is only a passing phase.
- Marxism and functionalism both share ideas about progress, an idea that has been challenged by some social theorists.

KEY TERMS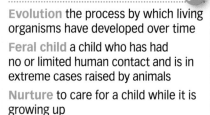

Evolution the process by which living organisms have developed over time

Feral child a child who has had no or limited human contact and is in extreme cases raised by animals

Nurture to care for a child while it is growing up

Primary socialisation the process of social learning that takes place within the family during a child's early years

Secondary socialisation a process of social learning that takes place outside the family, e.g. school, employment and mass media

Sociobiology the scientific idea that human behaviour has evolved

Socio-economic class a type of social stratification based on economic factors (different types of employment, e.g. manual and non-manual) and various social factors linked to an individual's economic position

Culture and nature

▲ To what extent are men culturally expected to be interested in sport?

What is culture?

Sociologists use the term 'culture' to describe the total way of life of a society: its language, history, traditions, customs and practices. Different cultures have different symbols, rituals and ways of expression and this can include differences between groups based on factors such as social class or religious belief. To a sociologist, whether you like to go to an art gallery or spend your time watching football might reveal something about your socio-economic class, but both the art gallery and the football match are simply different aspects of the same culture.

What is nature?

Sociologists use the term 'nature' to refer to the natural state of the world before humanity starts to transform it. As soon as human beings cut down a tree and turn it into a building or an item of furniture, that building or piece of furniture becomes a cultural object; it is no longer in its 'natural' state. Sociologists are particularly interested in how much of what makes us human is due to nature and how much is due to nurture. (Sociologists tend to emphasise the importance of the primary and secondary socialisation we experience throughout life.) In general terms, sociologists focus their attention on the way that society works rather than the influence of biology (nature) on human behaviour.

Nature versus nurture

Sociologists do not believe that social behaviour in humans is innate (something they are born with); in other words, we have to learn to be human beings. We are nurtured by our parents and through our primary socialisation experiences we learn the basics of language and how to behave in society. Cases of feral children confirm that if a child is deprived of normal human contact in early life, they will be incapable of normal social responses. However, when normal human contact is restored, sympathetic support and training can enable the child to make enormous progress.

One famous case involved a child referred to as 'Isabelle'. In the 1930s, Isabelle was discovered in the USA living with her deaf and mute mother. For much of the time, she had lived in a dark room shut away from the rest of the family, apparently to hide the shame they felt at her illegitimate birth. When she was first discovered, Isabelle showed only fear and hostility and at first it was thought that she might be deaf and have severe learning difficulties. But within nine months of her discovery, she was speaking, could identify words and sentences on the printed page, could add to ten and retell a story after hearing it. Eventually, Isabelle was able to attend school and participate in normal activities with other children. Those of you who have younger relatives might be able to observe the same process of primary socialisation and 'language building' that enabled Isabelle to enter human society.

Sociobiology

Sociobiologists take a rather different view of human behaviour; they base their ideas on the work of the nineteenth-century scientist Charles Darwin (1809–82) who developed the theory of evolution. Sociobiologists go further than Darwin because they believe that it is not only physical characteristics that evolve, but also behaviour. Sociobiologists believe that human behaviour is governed by genetic instructions, particularly the impulse for humans to pass on their genes to future generations. Some scientists have even gone so far as to suggest that there might be such a thing as a 'gene for crime'. In 2014, a scientific study of 900 criminals in Finland suggested that up to 10 per cent of all violent crimes could be explained by a particular type of gene. However, sociologists remain sceptical of attempts to reduce human behaviour to biological impulses or genetic inheritance. For example, sociologists suggest that even gender cannot be seen as natural and inevitable, and that different cultures have very different attitudes towards masculine and feminine behaviour. The assumption that women are somehow 'naturally' submissive and caring has far more to do with cultural values and beliefs than biology. In Russia during the Second World War (1939–45), women served in combat units and as fighter pilots, whereas in twenty-first-century Britain women have only recently been allowed to take on frontline roles in the armed forces.

Activities

1 Write a paragraph to explain the difference between sociology and sociobiology.
2 Write down ten words to describe men and ten words to describe women. (Make careful choices, avoid using any language that might cause offence and, if you have any doubts about whether a word can be used, ask your teacher.) If you are working in a mixed group, compare the lists produced by male and female students. Hold a class debate to discuss how far these words reflect cultural assumptions about masculinity and femininity.

Summary

- Sociologists emphasise the importance of culture and socialisation.
- They are sceptical about attempts to reduce human behaviour to biological impulses or genetic inheritance.

Extension

Research the ideas of social Darwinism and eugenics. Can you explain why these ideas are inaccurate and controversial?

Check your knowledge

1 What do sociologists mean when they use the term 'culture'?
2 What do sociologists mean when they use the term 'feral children'?
3 What do sociobiologists believe about human behaviour and do sociologists agree with them?

Key learning

You will be able to:

- explain who Durkheim was and the sort of world he lived in
- describe his contribution to the development of sociology.

KEY TERMS

Anomie the breakdown of norms governing accepted social behaviour

Crime any form of behaviour that breaks the law

Deviance any form of behaviour that does not conform to dominant norms, ranging from behaviours that are simply disapproved of to criminal actions

Division of labour the separation of any form of work into various component parts, all of which are relatively simple. In industry, this allows employers to use cheaper unskilled or semi-skilled workers

Functionalism a sociological perspective that attempts to explain social structures by reference to the role that they perform for society as a whole

Emile Durkheim: life and times

Born in France during the nineteenth century, Emile Durkheim (1858–1917) is regarded as one of the founders of modern sociology. He was considered to be a brilliant student and graduated with a degree in philosophy (the history of ideas), although his main interest was in the scientific study of society. He completed his studies in Germany, where he found an intellectual world that was more sympathetic to his interest in the new discipline of sociology. Although Durkheim recognised the importance of Comte's work and ideas, he believed that sociology needed to be more scientific and his approach can be described as laying the foundations for functionalism.

France in the middle of the nineteenth century was going through a period of radical change. Largely as a consequence of the disruption caused by the French Revolution (1789–99) and Napoleonic Wars (1803–15), France had been slow to move away from an economy that depended on agriculture and to develop its manufacturing industries. However, by the time Durkheim was born in 1858, France was rapidly catching up with near neighbours in Europe (Britain and Germany). The population was increasing, modern transportation systems (railways) were being built and many French citizens lived in expanding cities, where they found employment in trade and manufacturing industry. Durkheim believed that it would be possible to use the knowledge gained from scientific study to improve society.

Important ideas

Durkheim argued that crime was a natural and inevitable part of human life. He observed that crime was more common in advanced industrialised societies, but believed that this only became a problem if the crime rate was too high. He held to the view that social change began with some form of deviant behaviour and that a certain amount of change was important if society was to remain healthy.

Durkheim saw the division of labour as a generally positive feature of modern society. He believed that specialised workers needed to co-operate in order to produce a range of finished products and that, in the process, they would become interdependent on each other. This interdependence would, in turn, lead to the development of rules that provide a framework for future co-operation, reinforcing social solidarity. However, Durkheim recognised that under certain circumstances the rapid expansion of industrial society could create anomie – a situation where, for some individuals, the normal rules of behaviour break down and they no longer feel themselves to be a part of the wider society, leading in turn to high rates of suicide and industrial unrest. For Durkheim, education, and, in particular, the teaching of history, provided an important link between the individual and society, developing a sense of belonging and responsible behaviour towards the wider social group.

One of Durkheim's best-known works is concerned with the study of suicide. His methods clearly illustrate his scientific approach; using suicide statistics from a number of European countries he was able to demonstrate patterns. For example, he found that suicide was more common in Protestant countries and that the suicide rate actually went down during times of political upheaval. He then went on to identify social factors associated with this type of extreme behaviour.

Activities

1 Identify three important ideas that Durkheim contributed to sociology. Arrange them in order of importance and then explain your reasons.
2 Write a short paragraph explaining why Durkheim can be regarded as one of the founders of modern sociology.

Check your knowledge

1 From memory, list three important changes to life in nineteenth-century France. (Check your answer against the information provided.)
2 Did Durkheim see the division of labour as a positive or negative feature of society?
3 What did Durkheim discover about the suicide rate during times of political upheaval?

Extension

Can Durkheim's ideas about crime and deviance help us to explain the life of Nelson Mandela? You will need to do some further research in order to complete this activity.

Summary

● Emile Durkheim is regarded as one of the founders of modern sociology.
● One of his best-known works is a study of suicide. His methods clearly illustrate his scientific approach; using suicide statistics he was able to identify sociological factors associated with this type of extreme behaviour.

Key learning

You will be able to:
- explain who Marx was and the sort of world he lived in
- describe his contribution to the development of sociology.

KEY TERMS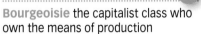

Bourgeoisie the capitalist class who own the means of production

Capitalism a system of economic organisation in which businesses are owned by private individuals who profit from the labour of the workers they employ

Communism Karl Marx believed that a future ideal communist society would be one in which the community would own all property and there would be no social classes

Communist Manifesto a political pamphlet outlining the principles of communism

Economics the study of the production and consumption of goods and services

Left wing political beliefs that emphasise social equality, e.g. socialism

Liberalism a political belief in systems of government in which the rights and freedoms of the individual are protected by laws and a constitution

Proletariat a term used by Marx to describe all the workers who do not own the means of production

Wealth material resources owned by individuals, e.g. property, savings and businesses

Working class members of society who are engaged in some form of manual work

Karl Marx: life and times

Karl Marx (1818–83) spent much of his life writing about the changes to nineteenth-century society brought about by the Industrial Revolution. He came from a comfortable middle-class background and after attending university in Berlin, where he studied economics and philosophy, he worked as a newspaper editor. His involvement in the liberal politics of the day got him into trouble with the government of Prussia, which is now part of modern Germany (Germany did not become a completely unified nation until 1871). Eventually, Marx left Germany and went to live in France. During this period in his life,

his left-wing political beliefs developed and eventually, in 1848, Marx published the Communist Manifesto, a document which he wrote with the help of his friend Friedrich Engels (1820–95). The ideas contained in the manifesto emphasised the need for a fairer and more equal communist society, which Marx believed would result from a political revolution. People in positions of power naturally came to regard his ideas as dangerous, at a time when revolutionary movements were gaining support in a number of European countries.

In 1849, after more problems with the authorities and further travels around Europe in an attempt to avoid these problems, Marx came to live in England, where he remained for the rest of his life. Marx and his family were supported by Friedrich Engels, who managed a cotton factory that his family owned in Manchester, and by Marx's work as a journalist. Marx wrote about many things, a lot of the time concerning economic issues, but his writing was always full of sociological ideas.

Important ideas

Marx had a very different view of society to Durkheim. For Marx, the most important cause of social change was conflict between the social classes, which he believed to be a feature of all economically developed human societies. He called this idea the materialist conception of history. Simply put, human beings need to produce things in order to survive: food, shelter and clothing. How they produce those things varies over time. For example, in Europe during the Middle Ages, land was the most important factor; a class divide existed where a minority owned the land (what a Marxist would describe as the means of production) while the majority worked on it to produce the food and other materials needed to survive.

Following the Industrial Revolution, an economic system that Marx called capitalism developed. Marx believed that this system was very different to previously existing forms of production as it was based on money (capital) rather than land. Industrial capitalism had the capacity to produce enormous amounts of goods that could be sold at a vast profit to huge numbers of people. Those who owned the means of production, the mines and the factories, became a new capitalist ruling class bourgeoisie with power concentrated in their hands. They exploited the labour of their workers, the working class (or proletariat) who were the great majority of the population, who created all the wealth but received little in return for their labour. There was a small middle class (or 'petty bourgeoisie'), who managed the businesses owned by the capitalist class, but who were still members of the proletariat. Therefore, Marx believed that conflict (essentially revolutionary political change) was inevitable in order to create a more just and equal society in which everyone received a fair share of the wealth that their labour created.

Das Kapital (*Capital, Volume 1*) was published in 1867, the first of a three-volume work, most of which would only be published after Marx had died. Although he was relatively unknown during his own lifetime, Marx's work has had a lasting effect on politics, economics and sociology. At one time during the twentieth century, vast numbers of people in Eastern Europe, Russia, China, Asia and South America were ruled by governments that claimed to be inspired by his ideas.

Activities

1 Draw up a chart to compare the most important ideas of Durkheim and Marx.
2 Write a short paragraph explaining why the ideas of Karl Marx might still be considered to be controversial.

Extension

Research the life and work of Friedrich Engels.

Check your knowledge

1 What did Marx do for a living after he finished his university studies?
2 Who helped Marx financially and co-authored the Communist Manifesto?
3 What book did Marx publish in 1867?

Summary

- Karl Marx spent much of his life writing about the changes to nineteenth-century society brought about by the Industrial Revolution.
- Although Marx was relatively unknown during his own lifetime, his work has had a lasting effect on politics, economics and sociology.

You will be able to:
- explain who Weber was and the sort of world he lived in
- describe his contribution to the development of sociology.

KEY TERMS

Authority a form of power in which people willingly obey commands that they believe to be lawful

Establishment in sociology, the term is generally used to describe dominant elites (superior groups) who hold power and authority

Immigration the movement of individuals or a group of people from one part of the world into another, e.g. people who leave their country of origin to live in another country

Nationalism a strong belief in the importance of a particular nation state

Objective approach sociologists who attempt to study the social world without allowing their personal values to influence the outcome of their research

Protestant work ethic the moral and spiritual virtue of individual effort and hard work

Rationalisation the efficient organisation of society based on rational legal authority, technical and scientific knowledge

Max Weber: life and times

Max Weber (1864–1920) was born in Germany and, like Marx and Durkheim, became concerned about the changes taking place in society. He was a brilliant student with an interest in economics, law, philosophy and history. But, unlike Marx, Weber was much more of an **establishment** figure, working as a lawyer, acting as a consultant to the government of the day and writing from a **nationalistic** perspective about issues such as Polish **immigration**. Eventually, Weber became a Professor of Economics, but after the death of his father in 1897 he suffered from depression and eventually gave up his university post.

As his health recovered, Weber focused more on sociological ideas, publishing in 1904 *The Protestant Ethic and the Spirit of Capitalism*. This became one of his most famous sociological studies and clearly demonstrates Weber's interest in the role that religion had to play in society, even though he was not personally religious. In 1907, he co-founded the German Sociological Association. As a sociologist, he believed that an **objective approach** to the study of human society was possible. At the outbreak of the First World War (1914–18), Weber volunteered for military service but, like many men who served in that terrible war, he became dissatisfied and opposed policies such as unrestricted submarine warfare. After the defeat of Germany, Weber served in the German delegation at the Paris Peace Conference. He was involved in the drafting of a new German constitution and the foundation of the liberal German Democratic Party. Germany was in chaos at the end of the war, with violent confrontations between supporters of different political groups. Weber was a critic of those with more extreme left-wing views, particularly those who supported the idea of a communist revolution.

Important ideas

Weber was influenced by the ideas of Marx, but he rejected Marxist ideas about history and did not believe that class conflict was the most significant cause of social change. He believed that people's ideas and values were more important than their social class. For example, he saw workers as far more differentiated, in terms of factors like qualifications, status, skills and power. In his most famous work, Weber links the development of capitalism to religious beliefs; he argues that in societies where Protestantism was the dominant religion, work became associated with moral and spiritual values, hard work and individual effort became a morally virtuous act whereas idleness was to be condemned as 'sinful'. This belief system can be described as the Protestant work ethic and Weber believed it to be an important explanation of how and why capitalism developed first in Protestant parts of Europe and later from Protestant descendants of migrants to what became the USA.

Weber also developed important ideas about the nature of power and authority, which continue to have an influence on modern sociology. Weber believed that there were three distinct types of authority:

1 Charismatic authority, for example that of the Church and religious leaders.
2 Traditional authority, for example the medieval feudal system which linked land ownership to aristocratic status (aristocrats owned the land on which the peasant farmers worked).
3 Legal or bureaucratic authority, for example the legal framework of modern states.

Weber described the development of modern societies based on scientific knowledge, technology and bureaucratic systems of government as rationalisation. In other words, he believed that the social and economic life of modern society should be based on knowledge and organised in the most efficient way possible, as compared to past societies based on irrational superstitious beliefs that the authority of rulers, for example, came directly from their special relationship with their God.

Activities

1 Draw up a chart to compare the ideas of Weber and Marx.
2 Write a short paragraph about the Protestant work ethic. Do you think this idea has any relevance to modern British society?

Extension

Research Weber's ideas about social class and add them to your comparison chart.

Check your knowledge

1 What did Weber do for a living after he finished his university studies?
2 What did Weber help to found in 1907?
3 From memory, list the three types of authority described by Weber. (Check your answer against the list provided.)

Summary

- Max Weber, like Marx and Durkheim, became concerned about the changes taking place in society.
- Weber was influenced by Marx, but he rejected some of his ideas.
- Weber believed that the social and economic life of modern society should be based on knowledge and organised in the most efficient way possible.

KEY TERMS

Functional prerequisites the basic needs of society

Institutions important parts of the structure of society maintained by social norms

Social order how society is constructed and maintained

Value consensus beliefs that are commonly shared by a particular social group

An introduction to functionalism

Theories about society

How does society work? Why do people behave in certain ways when they come together in groups? These are fundamental questions to all sociologists and, from the nineteenth century onwards, sociologists have developed increasingly sophisticated ideas to explain how society works and why people behave as they do. Grand theories, like functionalism, are all-embracing sets of ideas that provide sociologists with a broad framework from which to approach these fundamental questions. Some of these theories are less fashionable than they once were and many modern sociologists have moved away from the idea that just one big set of ideas can be used to explain everything that happens in society. However, it would be unwise for any student of sociology to dismiss a particular idea simply because it is unfashionable or because another set of ideas seems to be more relevant to the way we live now. Such theories tell us not only about the history and development of sociology, they also continue to help us gain meaningful insights into the social world.

▲ Everyone in a school knows their role and what is expected of them

What is functionalism?

Functionalism is the oldest of the 'grand theories' that we will study. Durkheim's view of society can broadly be described as 'functionalist' because he had the idea that society can be understood scientifically and that human behaviour is governed by a set of understandable 'laws' designed to preserve the 'health' of the wider society. A more modern version of these ideas developed in the USA in the 1930s (although most prominently in the 1950s), with Parsons taking a leading role. Simply put, functionalists argue that society cannot be understood as a series of isolated component parts. For example, if you want to understand the education system, you need to consider how it contributes to maintaining the wider society. These ideas are sometimes described as a 'consensus theory' because functionalists see society as based on shared values.

Functionalists believe that human relationships are governed by rules that reflect the values of society and that those rules and values are then turned into sets of roles and norms. In other words, we should all know how to play our part in the social world, how to behave and what is expected of us. These rule-governed social relationships then become the framework or structure of society. The family, the education system and the political system are all parts of this structure, referred to by functionalists as the institutions of society. If we look closely at the school, we can see this pattern – teachers and students, administrative, catering and maintenance staff, the head teacher and the board of governors all have their role to play and should know what is expected of them. From a functionalist perspective, if the school performs well, it does so because it helps to maintain the wider society, providing, for example, a future workforce equipped with the skills that society needs and, at the same time, helping to ensure that common values are shared.

The functionalist perspective on society has a number of key principles:

- All societies have certain basic needs that must be satisfied if they are to survive and prosper. These are called functional prerequisites and include such basic things as producing enough food and housing for the population.
- Functionalists see society as a system made up of interconnected parts like a machine. If society is going to survive and prosper, the various parts have to work together and, if they fail to do so, society will break down. From a functionalist perspective, the 'machine' of society works when a value consensus exists, or, in other words, a general agreement among the members of society about the important values that they hold in common.
- Functionalists believe that society needs order and stability if it is to survive and prosper; the maintenance of the social order depends upon effective socialisation and social control, with the members of society working together within a framework of common values.

Activities

1 Create a 'mind map' (or spider diagram) of important functionalist ideas about society.
2 Write a short paragraph to explain what functionalists mean when they talk about the basic needs of society. How well do you think these needs are being met in Britain today?

Extension

Research the life and work of Talcott Parsons.

Check your knowledge

1 Why has functionalism been described as a 'consensus theory'?
2 Was Durkheim a functionalist?
3 Who developed functionalist ideas in 1950s America?

Summary

- Functionalists argue that society cannot be understood as a series of isolated component parts.
- Functionalists believe that human relationships are governed by rules that reflect the values of society and that those rules and values are then turned into sets of roles and norms.

Key learning

You will be able to:
- explain what Marxism is
- explain what Marxist sociology is.

KEY TERMS

False consciousness the mistaken belief that capitalist society is basically fair and opportunities are open to all (see ruling class ideology)

Forces of production the materials, technology and knowledge required to produce the goods that society needs

Infrastructure the class structure that forms the basic foundation of society

Means of production the resources from which wealth is derived, such as land, factories, etc. Ownership of these defines the ruling class

Ruling class ideology the ideas and beliefs of the ruling class

Superstructure the cultural and political aspects of society built upon the foundation of the infrastructure, e.g. government and political systems

Link

For more information on Marxism, see pages 12–13.

An introduction to Marxism

▲ Workers undertaking repetitive tasks in a factory

What is Marxism?

Since his death in 1883, the ideas of Karl Marx have been interpreted and re-interpreted by generations of political theorists, economists and sociologists. They have inspired people to try to bring about social change and have been considered a dangerous threat to Western democracy. Marxism has a common origin in the ideas of Karl Marx, but it has developed in many different ways; it can be used to describe a political system, an approach to economic theory and, most significantly for our purposes, a sociological perspective. It has been described as a 'conflict theory' because it emphasises the conflict in interests and power differences between the social classes.

What is Marxist sociology?

Marxist theory begins with an important insight into the workings of society. Marxists see all societies as class societies, with class determined by the relationship to the means of production (the resources from which wealth is derived). Those who own the means of production, such as land in a feudal society or factories under capitalism, are the dominant class who exploit the subordinate class. From a Marxist perspective, the whole of human civilisation is based on a series of historical developments from one exploitative society to the next. Humanity evolved from simple bands of hunter gatherers to become farmers, merchants and eventually industrialists (owners of industries) as the means of production changed. At each stage in this process different forms of class exploitation developed. For example, the feudal lords owned the land, but it was peasants who worked on it; under capitalism the bourgeoisie ruling class own the factories and mines, but those working within them create all the wealth. Marxists describe the technology, materials and knowledge required by workers to add value and transform capital into products for sale as the forces of production.

The forces of production, and the social relationships based on the class structure dependent upon them, then become what Marxists refer to as the infrastructure of society or, to put it another way, its foundations. Every other aspect of society, including the government and legal systems, the education system, beliefs and values are all part of what Marxists call the superstructure of society. When there are changes in the means of production, for example due to an industrial revolution, this also produces changes in government and legal systems. At the heart of this process Marx saw a contradiction; he believed that, because of class conflict, all societies were basically unstable and would eventually fail. They were unstable because they depended upon one group in society, those with power and wealth, exploiting those who were powerless and poor. The aristocracy who owned the land in the Middle Ages exploited the labour of the landless poor. Under capitalism, the bourgeoisie factory owners exploit the labour of the working class.

Therefore, Marx saw history as a series of epochs, or time periods, with each major change in history being brought about by class conflict. The peasants overthrew feudalism, which became replaced by capitalism. Capitalism changed both the way in which people worked (in factories for wages) and the relationship was still one of exploitation between workers and the bourgeois ruling class. Forced into wage slavery, Marx described workers as alienated from everything – even themselves. Consequently, this fundamental change in the means and forces of production introduced a new class-based system of exploitation in the modern world. Marx predicted that this capitalist world would eventually fail because of the same inbuilt contradiction: the rich continue to exploit the labour of the poor. His vision was that this contradiction would only be resolved by a revolution, which would produce a fairer and more just society, with common rather than individual ownership of the means of production – a communist society working for the benefit of all and not just the privileged few. Only then would society be classless.

Marxist sociology focuses on analysing and understanding the relationships that exist between the different classes in society. Marxists believe that ruling class ideology (the widely circulated ideas and beliefs of the powerful elite in society) prevents many ordinary working people from really understanding the nature of society. These ideas create what Marxists call false consciousness (the mistaken belief that capitalist society is basically fair and that real opportunities are available to all).

Activities

1 Make a list of three important Marxist ideas and then arrange them in order of importance. Compare your list with others produced by members of your class. Look for similarities and differences, and then try to explain and justify your choices.

2 Marx and Weber never met, but Weber was inspired by some of Marx's ideas, even though he did not agree with all of them. Write a letter beginning 'Dear Karl', outlining some of your key disagreements with Marx. Write a reply beginning 'Dear Max', explaining why you are right and he is mistaken (you can then try this exercise in reverse).

Extension

Did Russia under the leadership of Joseph Stalin become the ideal communist world that Marx hoped for? Do some research and write a paragraph to summarise your conclusions.

Summary

- Marxists describe the technology, materials and knowledge required to satisfy basic needs as the forces of production, and believe that human civilisation is based on a series of historical developments in these forces of production.
- Marxist sociology focuses on analysing and understanding the relationships that exist between the different groups in society.

Check your knowledge

1 Is Marxism a 'conflict' or a 'consensus' theory?

2 What are the 'forces of production'?

3 What do Marxists mean when they talk about 'ruling class ideology'?

Key learning

You will be able to:
- explain what interactionism is.

KEY TERMS

Labelling a label as applied to an individual influences both their behaviour and the way that others respond to them

Master status is a status which overrides all other features of a person's social standing; the characteristic that shapes how a person sees themselves and how others perceive them

Negotiation the process by which an individual changes the reactions of others or shapes their own role

Self-concept the idea an individual has of the kind of person that they think they are

Self-fulfilling prophecy when an individual accepts the label that has been given to them by others and acts accordingly

An introduction to interactionism

▲ Interactionism is based on everyday encounters

What is interactionism?

Interactionism is different to functionalism and Marxism because it focuses not on the big picture, how the 'social system' shapes human behaviour, but rather on small-scale human actions. Think back to your first day at secondary school or college. How did you feel about this event? Did you understand what you had to do or was everything confusing and seemingly designed to make you feel anxious and inadequate? After time passed, how did your feelings about school or college change? From an interactionist perspective, all social actions are meaningful to the individuals involved. However, simply because they occupy the same location in time does not mean that different individuals attach the same meaning to the events that they experience. Neither are meanings fixed and unchanging; the insecure new student can and most probably will become the confident and experienced senior. Talk to some of your fellow sociology students about recent classes that you have all attended, compare notes on your experiences and look for different interpretations of events that you witnessed.

Interactionists believe that how individuals react to certain situations, like a new student entering a school or college for the first time, will depend at least in part on their self-concept. The idea of the self is a picture that we carry around inside us of the person we think we are and it develops as a result of our interactions with others. This idea is closely linked to interactionist ideas about the process of labelling. Returning again to the idea of the new student, what happens if they compensate for feelings of inadequacy by becoming aggressive and unco-operative? The label of 'problem student' can soon be applied by teachers and fellow students. This label can then become a master status. The student's sense of self centres upon their idea that they are badly behaved – it is what they expect to be and what others expect of them. A **self-fulfilling prophecy** can develop; our student becomes what they think they should be at least in part as a consequence of the label that has been applied to them by others.

However, it is by no means inevitable that our new student will go down this particular path and accept the label of 'problem student'. Interactionist sociologists believe that people have 'free will' and that they are not forced to behave according to social norms; they choose to do so or choose not to do so. Interactionists believe that a process of **negotiation** occurs. The badly behaved student does not have to follow some pre-set route and they may successfully change the view that others have of them. This idea of negotiation can be applied in other circumstances. For example, functionalists see roles as defined by the social system – the system expects certain behaviours from students and teachers and those expectations reflect the norms and values of society. Interactionists, on the other hand, do not see this in such clear-cut terms. From their perspective, roles are often not at all clearly defined and individuals can negotiate and re-negotiate how those roles will be performed; the teacher as lecturer or mentor, the student as pupil or colleague.

Some sociologists are critical of interactionist ideas. For example, it can be argued that by focusing on the detail of small-scale human interactions the significance of the 'bigger picture' can be ignored. Schools and colleges, to follow our example, do not exist in a historical vacuum. As many teachers and students will probably be well aware, government policies towards education are constantly changing and these policies can have a very significant impact upon the individuals involved. Government policies, in turn, reflect changing social and economic circumstances. The forces that drive historical change have not disappeared and should not be forgotten.

Activities

1 Try an experiment: when someone that you know well asks a simple question, ask them for clarification. For example, if they ask how you are, then ask them to be more specific. Be prepared for them to become a little annoyed with you and, when they do, explain that it is an experiment to underline the importance of the shared cultural assumptions upon which human interactions are based.

2 Write a paragraph to defend interactionism from the criticism that it ignores the 'bigger picture', for example by failing to appreciate the importance of socio-economic class.

Extension

Research the life and work of the following key interactionists: George Herbert Mead (1863–1931) and Howard Becker (1928–).

Summary

- Interactionism focuses on small-scale human actions.
- From an interactionist perspective, all social actions are meaningful to the individuals involved. However, simply because they occupy the same location in time does not mean that different individuals attach the same meaning to the events that they experience.

Check your knowledge

1 What do sociologists mean when they use the term 'labelling'?

2 What do sociologists mean when they use the term 'master status'?

3 What do sociologists mean when they use the term 'self-fulfilling prophecy'?

KEY TERMS

Equal pay and sex discrimination laws laws introduced in Britain in the 1970s to stop gender-based discrimination (now incorporated into the Equality Act 2010)

Life history research a type of qualitative research that uses life experiences to provide insights into the workings of society

Patriarchy male domination of society and its institutions

Polygamy the accepted practice in some societies of having more than one spouse at the same time

Polygyny the accepted practice in some societies of men having more than one wife at the same time

An introduction to feminism

▲ The campaign for female equality often involves demonstrations

What is feminism?

Feminists occupy some of the same ground as Marxists and their approach can also be described as a 'conflict theory' in the sense that they see a divided society and believe that one group in society exploits the other. However, for feminists, the most important issue is not the division between capitalists and workers but the division between men and women. Feminists believe that society is essentially patriarchal, in other words it is dominated by men. From a feminist perspective, men get the greatest benefit from family life, while women, having borne the children, provide most of the childcare and domestic labour (even if they also go out to work). Despite laws that should guarantee women equal pay and protection against sex discrimination in employment, men still tend to earn more money and hold more high status positions. In political situations, men are still more likely to occupy the most important roles; Britain has only managed to select two female prime ministers and women did not gain the right to vote on the same basis as men (at the age of 21) until 1928, while equal pay and sex discrimination laws were not introduced until the 1970s. That may seem like a long time ago but in historical terms it is still within living memory.

While feminists all see gender inequality as unjust, there is a growing awareness of differentiation within women both in developed countries like Britain and globally. Feminists highlight the status of women in other societies by emphasising social and cultural differences. For example, in some societies, polygamy prevails, such as in parts of West Africa and most countries in the Middle East where polygyny (where a man can have multiple wives) is relatively common. The United Nations estimates that more than 200 million girls and women alive today have been subjected to Female Genital Mutilation (FGM) in 30 countries in Africa, the Middle East and Asia where it is concentrated. There is no country in the world where women's average earnings are the same as men's.

Some feminists hold very radical views on how to bring about an end to the exploitation of women, while others are more moderate (sometimes referred to as liberal feminists). Those who occupy the more moderate position argue that it is important to recognise that not all women are disadvantaged at work and that increasing numbers of women in Europe and the USA are now occupying senior positions in business, the law, politics and even the military. They also do not believe that all husbands exploit their wives. In the past, the idea that the husband should be the one to put their career on hold in order to provide childcare would have seemed ridiculous, whereas in Britain today it is increasingly an option that many couples will consider. However, it is important to recognise that the status position of women in most of Europe and the USA is not necessarily the same in other cultures. Even among women in countries like Britain, the degree to which they experience inequality can be quite variable, shaped by factors like class, ethnicity and age. Religion has often been used as a mechanism to justify the oppression, or domination, of women and in some cultures belief systems are still used to deny women access to education and to constrain their freedom to follow a career, even to deny them the opportunity to drive a car or to move about freely outside their home. In many cultures, male violence including the threat of sexual assault is still used to control women and limit their lives.

There is also truth in the idea that sociology has in the past neglected the contribution of women to society. Until the 1970s, senior sociologists were mostly men and much of their research was focused on the lives of other men. Women, if they were considered at all, were seen primarily as wives and mothers. Since the 1970s, thanks to feminism, this situation has changed with women now occupying prominent academic positions and pioneering not only new areas of research (for example, the study of women and crime) but also developing qualitative methods such as life history research. There are feminists who would also describe themselves as Marxists and they argue that the exploitation of women's unpaid domestic work and the under-payment of women in employment is a feature of capitalism. Capitalist employers benefit from the creation of a new generation of workers, from the unpaid domestic support provided for their male workers and from the exploitation of female labour in the workforce.

Activities

1 Some feminists argue that the family is the main institution of patriarchy. Can you explain why they might think this?
2 Visit the website of the Fawcett Society (www.fawcettsociety.org.uk/) and do some research. Create a poster to illustrate some of the key points that you discover.

Summary

- For feminists, the most important issue is the division in society between men and women.
- Feminists believe that society is essentially patriarchal, in other words it is dominated by men.
- Sociology has in the past neglected the contribution of women to society, but this situation has now changed.

Extension

Research the life and work of Harriet Martineau (1802–76), who has been described as the first female sociologist.

Check your knowledge

1 What do feminists mean when they use the term 'patriarchy'?
2 When did women gain the right to vote?
3 When were equal pay and sex discrimination laws first introduced?

Key learning

You will be able to:
- explain New Right ideas
- describe the culture of poverty
- explain the underclass.

KEY TERMS

Anthropology the scientific study of the origins and development of human society

Culture of dependency the idea that social welfare systems encourage people to stay on benefits rather than support themselves through work

Culture of poverty when poverty is seen as inevitable and becomes a way of life

Identity a sense of self (who you believe yourself to be)

Market capitalism an economic system that supports private business in a competitive market

Marketisation of education refers to changes in the late 1980s that made the education system more business-like, based on competition and consumer choice

Neo-liberals and neo-conservatives those who favour capitalism and the free market to allocate resources

Underclass a group of people at the very bottom of the social scale who are dependent on welfare benefits

An introduction to New Right ideas

▲ New Right ideas in the USA are associated with Ronald Reagan who was the president from 1981 to 1989

New Right ideas about society

New Right ideas are often associated with the governments of Margaret Thatcher (1925–2013) in Britain and Ronald Reagan (1911–2004) in the USA during the 1980s. However, the term can also be loosely used to describe more recent neo-liberal and neo-conservative approaches to society. We can identify a number of key ideas associated with this way of looking at society:

- An emphasis on the individual rather than the group.
- A strong support for free enterprise (market capitalism).
- An emphasis on competition and choice as a way of driving up standards in public services such as health care and education.
- Support for a distinctive cultural identity based on the nation state.
- A distrust of 'experts' and the 'establishment'.
- Reduced state provision of welfare benefits.

Among sociologists the New Right is associated with ideas including the culture of dependency, the culture of poverty, the underclass, the marketisation of education, traditional moral standards (for example, support for heterosexual as opposed to same-sex marriage), welfare reform and the importance of the family and traditional gender roles. We can look at two of these ideas in more detail as examples of this perspective.

The culture of poverty

The idea of a culture (or subculture) of poverty was first developed by the American anthropologist Oscar Lewis (1914–70) and was based on his research in South America. Lewis believed that the culture of poverty amounted to a 'design for living' which was passed from one generation to the next. In his research, Lewis recorded that the poor felt helpless to change the direction of their lives and instead focused only on the present. Marital relationships, he claimed, were often unstable with high levels of child abandonment and divorce. The poor, he said, were also unlikely to participate in the wider community, for example by joining trade unions or political parties.

Critics of this theory deny the existence of such a culture and point to alternative research evidence that shows the existence of stable family lives among poor people in South America and relatively high levels of community participation (including political activity). Many sociologists argue that structural factors such as age, education, health and disability are far more important when it comes to explaining why some people in society continue to be poor.

The underclass

Charles Murray (1943–) developed the idea of the underclass and his theories have had some influence on government welfare policies in both the USA and Britain. Murray believes that the members of the underclass are not just poor people; they are also people who behave badly, are unwilling to take jobs that are available to them and are more likely to commit crimes. Murray argues that in the 1980s and 1990s increased numbers of illegitimate births (children born to unmarried parents) were one indication of a developing underclass in Britain. He does not support the idea that relationships between cohabiting parents can be as stable as those between married parents. His argument is that children from unstable (often lone parent) homes are more likely to become involved in antisocial behaviour and less likely to go on to lead productive and successful adult lives. Murray also pointed to a rising crime rate during the 1980s and 1990s as a second indication of a developing underclass; he believes that crime damages community life as people become suspicious of their neighbours and close their doors on the outside world. Finally, Murray believes that a third indication is the way in which young people see welfare benefits as an entitlement and a valid alternative to employment, even when jobs are available. Murray connects the rise of an underclass to welfare systems that he believes remove individual responsibility and encourage irresponsible and antisocial behaviour. He does not argue for drastic cuts in benefits, but rather suggests returning power and responsibility for welfare policies to local communities. Murray also argues for a return to more traditional values, for example encouraging marriage and discouraging lone parenthood.

Murray's ideas have been criticised as based on sweeping generalisations, inadequate research and a misunderstanding of the often very conventional attitudes of those who claim benefits or who become lone parents. For example, sociological research has shown the children of lone parents do not inevitably become lone parents themselves, and that the majority of those who claim benefits do not wish to do so and will seek employment at the earliest opportunity.

Activities

1 Compare the ideas of Oscar Lewis and Charles Murray. Draw up a simple table to illustrate the similarities and differences that you discover.

2 Write a short speech to explain why you believe (or do not believe) that competition and choice can be used to improve standards in health care. You will need to do some research to help with this activity. Try to support a well-structured argument with evidence and attempt to reach clear conclusions.

Extension

Find a copy of the book *The Children of Sanchez* (1961) by Oscar Lewis. Write a short review of the book and discuss your findings with the other members of your sociology class.

Check your knowledge

1 From memory, list the key ideas associated with the New Right. (Check your answer against the list provided.)

2 Who first developed the idea of a culture of poverty?

3 From memory, list the three factors that Charles Murray claimed to be evidence of a developing British underclass. (Check your answer against the information provided.)

Summary

- The term 'New Right' can be loosely used to describe politically right of centre, neo-liberal and neo-conservative approaches to society.
- Among sociologists the New Right is associated with ideas including the culture of dependency, the culture of poverty, the underclass and the marketisation of education.

KEY TERMS

Apartheid the institutionalised system of segregation between races that existed in South Africa from 1948 to 1994

Caste system a form of social stratification based on religion found in India

Discrimination an action based on prejudice, e.g. racial discrimination

Ethnicity a shared cultural identity, e.g. language and customs

Feudal system a form of social stratification based on the ownership of land

Gender a culturally determined identity (masculine or feminine)

Race the classification of people based on apparent physical differences

Social class a type of social stratification based on economic factors

Social stratification the way in which a society is divided hierarchically on the basis of various factors, e.g. class, gender and ethnicity

Social theorists this term can be used to describe sociologists, economists, philosophers and others who think and write about society

Stereotype an unfavourable simplistic image of a group based on the behaviour of a small number of individuals from within that group

Social structures

When we talk about the 'structure' of a building, we are discussing something that has physical substance: wood, brick, concrete and steel. We can see it and we can touch it. The structure can be built and demolished before our eyes. However, when sociologists talk about social structures, they are discussing things that lack the solid substance of the physical world.

However, sociology began with the idea that social structures can be compared to a building in that they contain our behaviour and limit what we, as individuals, are able to do. Durkheim certainly believed that to be true. For example, most societies have some form of social stratification: layered systems that order the social world, placing some individuals in positions of power while others are expected to be obedient citizens or subjects. How these systems are organised changes over time and between different geographical locations. The feudal system in medieval Europe and the caste system in India are examples of different forms of social stratification, one based on the ownership of land and the other on religious beliefs. The class system is another example. To be a member of a particular social class in Britain today has a very real impact on your chances of success in education and employment, and even on your future health and life expectancy.

Our ethnicity and our gender are also examples of social structures. When sociologists talk about ethnicity, they are referring to a complex web of cultural differences that include an individual's language, customs and belief systems. The colour of a person's skin and other physical features are simply a relatively insignificant product of biology. The classification of different races is based on the ideas of early scientists such as Carl Linnaeus (1707–78) and is no longer accepted by modern science. In the biological sense, the physical differences between different individuals, such as their hair, skin, eyes and blood groups, are simply minor variations on a common theme and not markers of intelligence or superiority. We are all human above all else. However, this does not mean that ethnic identities are unimportant. Stereotypes, prejudice and discrimination continue to plague our world and have been widely used as ways of structuring societies. British society had no specific laws to prevent racial discrimination until the Race Relations Act was passed in 1965 and, in South Africa, the apartheid system did not end until 1994. However, just because discrimination on the basis of race (colour, nationality and ethnic or national origins) has been made illegal in some countries, and racial prejudice has become socially unacceptable, does not mean that these have stopped shaping societies. Events in the modern world, such as warfare and acts of terrorism, tend to bring out old fears and prejudices against those perceived to be different and 'outsiders'.

In a similar way, gender and sexuality continue to be used to structure societies. To sociologists, our gender and sexuality is based on social and cultural expectations. However, some social theorists have argued that such matters are mainly shaped by biology, even to the extent of suggesting that this somehow justifies the differential and discriminatory treatment of women, homosexuals and transgendered people. Such a position is incompatible with the equal status given to the protected characteristics as defined in the Equality Act (2010). However, it would also be foolish to pretend that gender- and sexuality-based prejudice and discrimination (such as against women, homosexuals and transgendered people) have disappeared even in societies like Britain, where laws have been passed to prevent actions based on such prejudices. In some cultures, belief systems still place women in an inferior position to men and homosexuality and transgender is outlawed.

Other social structures include families, the education system, religion, age, income wealth and poverty, and the world of work. Most of these structures are discussed further throughout this book.

Activities

1 Write a short paragraph to explain the difference between the idea of race and what sociologists mean by ethnicity.
2 Prepare a presentation for your class based on your research into either the civil rights movement in the USA or apartheid in South Africa.

Extension

Find a copy of *The Bell Curve: Intelligence and Class Structure in American Life* (1994) by Richard Herrnstein and Charles Murray. What makes this book so controversial and what do its critics have to say about it?

Check your knowledge

1 What do sociologists mean when they use the term 'social stratification'?
2 What do sociologists mean when they use the term 'ethnicity'?
3 Who was Carl Linnaeus?

Summary

- Sociology began with the idea that social structures can be compared to a building in that they contain our behaviour and limit what we as individuals are able to do. For example, most societies have some form of social stratification, systems that order the social world.

You will be able to:
- explain what a social process is.

KEY TERMS

Mass media any form of communication media that can reach a large audience, e.g. newspapers, television or various forms of social media

Nature versus nurture a debate about how far human behaviour is a result of life experiences (socialisation) as opposed to biology

Peer group a group of people of similar age and status

Sanction negative sanctions are any form of penalty for unacceptable actions of an individual or group, while positive sanctions (or rewards) are applied for good behaviour

Social control the process by which the members of a society are persuaded to conform to the rules of that society, e.g. the actions of the police who enforce the law (formal) and the disapproval of the other members of society (informal)

Social processes

Sociologists use the term 'social process' to describe the various ways in which human beings are affected by their interactions with others. For example, a human baby is not well equipped to enter the world; it depends on its parents to feed and care for it and to teach it how to communicate with others and become part

▲ Human babies learn how to behave through interacting with their carers

of human society. That may seem an obvious statement to make, but at its heart is an important difference between instinctive behaviour and learned behaviour, or the nature versus nurture debate. Humans have reflexes and needs – simple physical reactions that require no thought or understanding – but these are not the same as instincts. Many animals, on the other hand, will display quite complicated patterns of behaviour, such as mating rituals, without being taught to do so. Human babies have to learn how to behave through the process of primary socialisation; they respond to the approval or disapproval of their carers and learn by copying. This process equips the growing child with the basics of language and an understanding of how to behave in human society. As the child grows into adulthood, it is exposed to a variety of other influences, including the school, the mass media and the peer group. Sociologists refer to these experiences as the process of secondary socialisation.

If the process of primary socialisation fails, the baby may survive and develop if its basic needs are met, but it will not be able to function well in human society. There are a number of examples of so-called feral children in history and literature, together with more recent cases of abused children who, for a variety of reasons, have not experienced an appropriate process of primary socialisation. Romulus and Remus, the mythical founders of Ancient Rome, were said to have been abandoned by their mother and raised by a she-wolf. A more recent and only too real case from the 1990s involved a Ukrainian girl (Oxana Malaya) who was neglected by her alcoholic parents and found care and support from a pack of dogs who apparently 'adopted' her as a young child. When the local authorities discovered this situation, Oxana was sleeping on the floor, barked at social workers and generally behaved like a dog. She was successfully taught how to behave and communicate as a human being, but her intellectual development has been damaged by her experiences as an abused child.

Another example of a social process is **social control**. All cultures have rules that distinguish between what is and is not acceptable behaviour. Sociologists call these rules norms. For example, there are norms about how we dress and how we eat. These norms are enforced through the use of positive and negative **sanctions**; informally, we reinforce behaviour that we approve of by our acceptance of it or by outward expressions of approval. In a similar way, we seek to extinguish behaviour we do not approve of by expressing our dislike for it. Certain norms are so important to the social order that they become formal laws. In these circumstances, individuals who refuse to conform can face more serious sanctions including exclusion from the wider society through the use of prison sentences. In the past and in other cultures, death is the ultimate sanction.

Society's norms reflect the values of a particular culture; a value is a commonly held belief that something is important. In Europe and the USA, democratic government, the rights of the individual, free speech and tolerance have often been given as examples of important values. Traditionally, religion has played an important part in the process of social control. From a functionalist perspective, the role of religion has often been seen in a positive light, providing guidance on acceptable standards of behaviour and a moral framework for society. In contrast, from a Marxist perspective, religion has been viewed as another way in which ruling elites have sought to justify their power and privilege – a promise of heaven for the obedient as a distraction from earthly suffering or, as Marx put it, 'the opium of the people'.

Activities

1 Write a short paragraph explaining the process of socialisation to someone who is not a member of your sociology class.
2 Make a list of positive and negative sanctions that are used to control the behaviour of members of our society. Compare your list with others produced by members of your class. Look for similarities and differences.

Extension

Research the story of Kaspar Hauser (1812–33). What are your conclusions? Was he simply trying to trick people into helping him?

Check your knowledge

1 What do sociologists mean when they use the term 'primary socialisation'?
2 What do sociologists mean when they use the term 'secondary socialisation'?
3 What do sociologists mean when they use the term 'social control'?

Summary

● Human babies have to learn how to behave through the process of primary and secondary socialisation.
● This process equips the growing child with the basics of language and an understanding of how to behave in human society.
● Another example of a social process is social control.

KEY TERMS

Absolute poverty this exists when an individual cannot pay for the basic essentials of life, e.g. food, clothing and shelter

Crime rate a measure of the level of criminal activity in society based on crimes recorded by the police

Media amplification media reporting that exaggerates the significance of an event

Median is a measure of central tendency. If there are an odd number of recorded values, the median is the middle value. If there is an even number, it is the average of the two middle values

Moral panic heightened public concern created by media coverage of an event

Relative poverty this exists when an individual lacks the resources to participate in activities that are widely available to the majority of people in the society in which they live

Social issues

When large groups of people debate and search for solutions to common concerns, those concerns become social issues. Sociologists have always been engaged by social issues; they have proposed both explanations for the problems faced by society and joined the search for possible solutions. They ask fundamental questions that seek to define the issue, measure extent and identify causes.

Poverty as a social issue

In defining poverty, sociologists begin by drawing a distinction between absolute and relative poverty. To experience absolute poverty is to face the prospect of death because you are denied the basic necessities of life. Relative poverty is the idea that you are poor if you lack the resources and opportunities that are enjoyed by the majority of people in your society. When measuring the extent of poverty, official definitions rely upon statistical measures of household income, for example, households whose income falls below 60 per cent of the median. However, this approach does not reveal anything about the experiences of families to enjoy an acceptable standard of living if their income is above the 60 per cent measure. According to the Joseph Rowntree Foundation (JRF), 14.3 million people were living in poverty in 2018, more than one in five of the UK population (22 per cent). As to the causes of poverty, it was traditionally linked to long-term benefits but in-work poverty has been steadily rising and according to JRF stands at 4 million workers in 2018. The Marxist perspective sees poverty as an inevitable feature of capitalist economies with inbuilt social inequalities.

Crime as a social issue

Fear of crime is a persistent social issue. Even when official statistics show a falling trend in the crime rate, this rarely satisfies public concerns. For example, sociological research has shown that the elderly, who when surveyed say that they feel most at risk of street crime, are actually the least likely to become victims of such crimes. Before rushing to the assumption that this 'proves' that a fear of crime is irrational, we should remember that the elderly are less likely to place themselves in danger; they tend not to go out at night or be in situations where they might become the victims of such crimes. On the other hand, young men are far more likely to be in high-risk situations and, consequently, far more likely to be victims. Yet, when asked by researchers, they are far less likely to say that they are afraid of street crime.

Our perception of crime is affected by a number of factors, including what happens in our local community, our own experiences and the way in which various forms of mass media sensationalise particular crimes. Sociologists understand that widespread media coverage of particular crimes (media amplification) can create a moral panic which, in turn, leads the authorities to take action, for example a police 'crackdown' on crime in a particular geographical area or more resources to tackle a certain type of crime. Sociologists ask questions about the true extent of crime and the real nature of our risk of becoming the victim of particular types of crime. For example, in 2015, some reports concentrated on a 14 per cent increase in the number of murders and killings in England and Wales. This amounted to a total of 574 murders and killings, 71 more than the previous year. To put that in context, 4.3 million criminal offences were recorded by the police in the same period.

Activities

1 Visit the website of the Child Poverty Action Group (CPAG) (www.cpag.org. uk/) and do some research. Create a poster or PowerPoint presentation to illustrate some of the key points that you discover, both about the work of the CPAG and the extent of child poverty in Britain today.
2 Design a simple survey to ask the members of your sociology class about the social issues that they think are important. Compare your results and create a list of the top five issues identified by your class.

Extension

Research the life and work of the sociologist Stanley Cohen (1942–2013).

Check your knowledge

1 What makes something a social issue?
2 What do sociologists mean when they use the term 'relative poverty'?
3 What do sociologists mean when they use the term 'media amplification'?

Summary

- When large groups of people debate and search for solutions to common concerns, those concerns become social issues.
- Sociologists have always been engaged by social issues; they have both proposed explanations for the problems faced by society and joined the search for possible solutions.

Key learning

You will be able to:

- explain the difference between biological sex and gender
- describe cultural assumptions about gender roles
- outline feminist perspectives.

KEY TERMS

Homosexuality sexual behaviour between members of the same sex

Identical twins two identical babies of the same sex, born at the same time, from the same fertilised egg

Pre-industrial tribal culture a term used to describe cultures that existed before industrialisation or cultures isolated from the modern world, e.g. the Trobriand Islanders studied by anthropologists in the early twentieth century

Socially organised labour human activity intended to satisfy the economic needs of society

STEM science, technology, engineering and mathematics

Activity

Write a paragraph to explain the difference between sex and gender from a sociologist's point of view.

Link

For more information see feminism and patriarchy on pages 251–253.

Sex and gender

▲ During the 1960s and 1970s many women's equality protests were held

Biological sex and gender

Sex describes a biological difference between men and women – differences that determine their appearance and their biological function. Men father children, women give birth to children. However, to a sociologist, gender is something different; it refers to the way in which society classifies masculine and feminine behaviour. Sex and gender were traditionally viewed in terms of a binary position, but as the discussion below on sexuality shows, attitudes and values change over time. Today, society is open not only to ideas of homosexuality but also non-binary and transgender identities, which are recognised as protected characteristics by the Equality Act (2010). Despite this, many people who are non-binary and transgender still experience discrimination and stigma.

Culture and gender roles

Blue for a boy and pink for a girl, toy guns and toy soldiers for boys, toy prams and dolls for girls – these are just some of the ways in which our own society has drawn lines between men and women, exposing them to different socialisation experiences and traditionally assigning them different roles and character traits, such as the assumption that girls are caring while boys are assertive. In the past girls were advised to become hairdressers, nurses and personal assistants while boys were encouraged into factory jobs, politics and management. Such attitudes have fortunately changed with the breaking down of gender stereotypes. Now girls are encouraged in the education system to have broader aspirations and increasing numbers are entering politics and breaking through the 'glass ceiling' in the workplace. Similarly, television programmes like Casualty portray caring roles like nursing as appropriate and successful for males. Programmes also exist to actively recruit women into particular fields such as STEM-related professions.

While all societies generally make distinctions between men and women, different cultures make different assumptions about what it is to be a man and what it is to be a woman. Anthropological evidence can be used to illustrate these differences. Pre-industrial tribal cultures often adopted roles for men and women that challenge commonly held ideas in the modern industrialised world, for example, about who should care for children (in some tribal cultures men rather than women) or who should grow the food (in some tribal cultures women rather than men). It is clear from the huge varieties of the human condition that many of the assumptions that we make about what it is to be a man or a woman, about how to dress and how to behave, are more a product of culture than they are of nature.

However, it would be misleading to claim that male and female differences are entirely the result of socialisation. Research into identical twins has raised some interesting issues. For example, in one unusual case in Canada a baby boy (one of a pair of identical twins) experienced a serious accident soon after birth. The severity of the child's injury led to a decision to reconstruct their genitals as if they were female rather than male. The child was then raised as a girl, experiencing normal interactions with other girls. However, when the child became older and aware of their circumstances, the individual concerned rejected their status as a female and asserted that they were 'really' a male. The issue of what part biology has to play in forming male and female identity remains controversial.

Religion has played an important part in shaping sexual attitudes. In cultures where rigid codes of behaviour exist, the distance between publicly approved behaviour and private behaviour can be considerable. In Western Europe and the USA, rigid codes of sexual behaviour gave way to a more permissive society in the 1960s, although do not assume that even today all members of society adopt a liberal attitude towards sexual behaviour. For example, some groups and individuals remain strongly opposed to sex before marriage on moral and religious grounds, while intolerance towards those whose sexual identity does not conform to conventional norms still remains a feature of present-day society. Homosexuality exists in all cultures, but in some it is still illegal. The term 'homosexuality' was first used in the 1860s and social attitudes in Britain towards sexual orientation have changed dramatically, becoming far more tolerant since homosexuality was decriminalised in 1967.

Feminist perspectives

Feminists question the way in which biological differences have been used to justify social differences in the treatment of men and women. Male hormones have been blamed for men's aggressive behaviour and to support the assumption that men are somehow naturally more assertive and socially and sexually dominant. Female hormones supposedly make women gentle and maternal, unsuited for leadership and requiring the protection of men. Some radical feminists have gone so far as to reject all ideas about the link between gender differences and biology. They argue that references to biological differences distract from the importance of making social and political changes to improve the status of women and achieve genuine equality with men.

Feminist sociologists argue that in the past many male sociologists either accepted that women had a 'natural' role as wives and mothers, or, alternatively, simply ignored the issue of gender differences. Feminists like Judith Butler deserve credit for challenging the patriarchal nature of sociology in the past and for seeing the social construction of gender roles as a form of socially organised labour.

Activity

Collect pictures of men and women used in advertising. How far do these images continue to portray traditional ideas about masculinity and femininity? Make a poster or a PowerPoint presentation to summarise your conclusions.

Extension

Research the life and work of the anthropologist Margaret Mead (1901–78). Research the status of women in other cultures, for example Saudi Arabia.

Check your knowledge

1 What do sociologists mean when they say that gender is a social construct?

2 What do sociologists mean when they say that boys and girls have different socialisation experiences?

3 When was the term 'homosexuality' first used?

Summary

- Sex describes a biological difference between men and women, while, to a sociologist, gender refers to the way in which society classifies masculine and feminine behaviour.

- While all societies generally make distinctions between men and women, different cultures make different assumptions about what it is to be a man and what it is to be a woman.

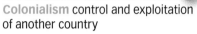

You will be able to:

- explain what 'race' is
- explain what ethnicity is
- describe how sociologists explain 'racial' prejudice and discrimination.

KEY TERMS

Colonialism control and exploitation of another country

Displacement to shift blame to another

Ethnic groups people within a particular society who share a distinct identity based on a common culture and history

Ethnocentrism judging other cultures relative to your own and where the other cultures will present as inferior

Group closure establishing and maintaining boundaries between cultures

Group solidarity common interests that bind people together

Holocaust the race murder (genocide) of the Jewish people and various other groups during the Second World War

Minority ethnic group a social group with a different ethnic identity from the majority population

Prejudice to be hostile towards another individual or social group based on previously formed opinions, frequently refers to racial prejudice

Resource allocation the control of economic resources

Scapegoat an individual, or their community, who is blamed unfairly for a negative event

Race and ethnicity

What is race?

The term 'race' is often confused with 'ethnicity' (see Key terms on page 26); it is in fact different and based upon eighteenth- and nineteenth-century ideas that modern science no longer accepts. Present-day geneticists avoid using the term 'race' as inherited physical characteristics are widely distributed in human populations. This makes any attempt at biological classification based on skin colour, type of hair, the shape of eyes and face, and so on effectively meaningless. However, that does not mean that the term has fallen out of use. It continues to reflect conflicts within society and to be at the root of feelings of prejudice and acts of discrimination.

Theories of race inspired the creation of laws in the USA, South Africa and Germany that were designed to keep the races apart, in the misguided and dangerous belief that racial 'purity' was something that actually existed and needed to be preserved from the polluting effects of sexual relationships between people who were classified as racially different. For example, the Nuremburg Laws in Nazi Germany (1935), which introduced the idea of 'race' into the German legal system, were part of a process that ended eventually in the Holocaust. The idea of 'race' has become associated with beliefs about the superiority and inferiority of certain ethnic groups, nations and continents. It is important to continue to look at 'race', however socially constructed and false the term is, because it has a legacy that continues to be experienced today.

What is ethnicity?

The term 'ethnicity', as used by modern sociologists, has a far more recent history (although the origins of the word itself are much older – dating back to Ancient Greece). To a sociologist, ethnicity is a complicated idea but, in general terms, an ethnic group refers to people who share a common identity based on cultural differences such as language, history and traditions rather than superficial physical characteristics.

The idea of a minority ethnic group is often used in sociology. Members of such groups commonly experience disadvantages (for example, in relation to education or employment) when compared to the majority population. They also tend to experience prejudice and discrimination and, as a consequence, develop strong feelings of group solidarity.

How do sociologists explain 'racial' prejudice and discrimination?

Prejudice refers to the opinions and attitudes of one group in society towards another. Those who hold prejudiced views generally base their ideas on stereotypes and are unlikely to change those ideas even when confronted with new information. Discrimination refers to actions based on prejudice, for example refusing to employ people because of the colour of their skin or denying them voting rights. Displacement and scapegoating are behaviours often associated with prejudice and discrimination. Psychological displacement occurs when feelings of hostility are unjustifiably directed towards something or someone. For example, the Nazis used the Jewish population of Germany as scapegoats, holding them to be responsible for Germany's economic and social problems. In the process, they created a climate of hatred that led first to the social exclusion of Jews and eventually to the horror of the death camps as a 'final solution' to the 'Jewish question'. The origins of racial prejudice are often buried deep in history, linking, for example, to the Atlantic slave trade and to colonial beliefs about the 'superiority' of the 'white races' (an idea used to justify the European exploitation and unfair treatment of people from Africa and Asia).

Sociologists use a number of ideas to explain the existence of 'racial' prejudice and discrimination. Ethnocentrism describes a suspicion of outsiders often combined with the tendency to judge other cultures and to see them as inferior in some way. Group closure is the process of establishing and maintaining boundaries between cultures. Taken to extremes, this can lead to outsiders being seen as aliens, morally inferior and potentially dangerous. Resource allocation refers to the way in which powerful ethnic groups maintain inequalities in the distribution of wealth by denying opportunities to members of less powerful groups.

Activities

1 Write a short paragraph to explain the difference between race and ethnicity from a sociologist's point of view.
2 Find out how the British census (total count) of population defines ethnic groups. What potential problems can you see with the definitions that have been used? You might find this website helpful: www.ons.gov.uk/.

Extension

Research the reporting of immigration as an issue in the mass media. Prepare a brief presentation to share with the other members of your group.

Check your knowledge

1 What do sociologists mean when they use the term 'racial prejudice'?
2 What do sociologists mean when they use the term 'racial discrimination'?
3 What do sociologists mean when they use the term 'scapegoating'?

Summary

● The term 'race' is often confused with ethnicity; it is in fact different and based upon scientific assumptions made in the eighteenth and nineteenth centuries that modern science no longer accepts.
● To a sociologist, ethnicity emphasises the importance of cultural differences, for example language, history and traditions as opposed to superficial physical characteristics.

Making an argument

Extended response answers

At GCSE level, it is important to be able to do three things:

1 To demonstrate that you know something about sociological ideas, evidence and research methods.
2 To apply what you know about sociology. (A simple way of putting this would be that you must answer the question.)
3 To analyse and evaluate sociological ideas, evidence and research methods in order to construct an argument, make judgements and draw conclusions.

When you attempt an extended (12-mark) question, you are expected to do all three things. These questions are called 'mini-essays' because you only have a limited amount of time. All mini-essay questions begin with the same 'stem': 'Discuss how far sociologists agree ...'. You are being asked to consider a minimum of two different sociological perspectives on the issue raised by the question.

Think of your 'mini-essay' in three parts: an introductory paragraph in which you focus on the question and begin your argument; a second paragraph in which you develop your answer (consider an alternative sociological perspective on the issue and other factors/possible explanations); and a final paragraph in which you reach a conclusion.

In the following example, the student has been asked to consider how far sociologists would agree that improving access to high-quality education would be the most effective way to increase upward social mobility:

Some sociologists, such as functionalists like Davis and Moore, say that society is meritocratic, and so people will be able to travel up the social ladder through working hard and achieving good qualifications ...

The student then continues to explain and evaluate the functionalist perspective.

However, many sociologists say that society is not strictly meritocratic. Marxist sociologists believe that society is biased towards the rich and there is limited social mobility ...

The student then goes on to explain and evaluate the Marxist perspective.

Overall, it appears that a good education can help many people to climb up the social ladder, although many sociologists would point out that other factors ...

The student then goes on to develop their conclusions and to suggest other relevant factors affecting social mobility.

Not all of the questions will require an extended response; some test only your knowledge of sociology or limit the scope of your answer.

Some points to remember

- It is worth thinking about your conclusion *first*. Know exactly where you are going with an answer and try not to contradict yourself.
- Support your argument with sociological evidence, for example relevant research studies or statistical data.
- Presentation is important.
- Leave a line between each paragraph in an extended answer.
- Candidates often ask how much they should write. The only answer is: 'As much as you can in the time available.'
- You should allow a few moments to check through your answers and pick up on the obvious mistakes.

Useful phrases to include in your mini-essay

- Some sociologists would agree …
- Some sociologists would disagree …
- However, …
- Sociological research evidence would seem to support …
- Sociological research evidence would seem not to support …
- In conclusion, …

Phrases to avoid in your mini-essay

- It is obvious …
- Everybody knows …
- Common sense tells us …
- Research clearly proves beyond any doubt …
- Research clearly disproves beyond any doubt …

The importance of practice and revision

- You cannot expect to succeed unless you practise.
- Work to improve your skills – try some practice questions and then try them again.
- What can you do to improve your original answer? Try 'peer marking' the answers of your fellow students, making only *positive* suggestions for improvement.

Summary

- Think of your 'mini-essay' in three parts:

  1 An introductory paragraph in which you focus on the question and begin your argument.

  2 A second paragraph in which you develop your answer (consider an alternative perspective on the issue).

  3 A final paragraph in which you reach a conclusion.

Sociology research methods

Key learning

You will be able to:
- outline the important decisions a researcher needs to make
- explain what appropriate aims are
- explain what relevant hypotheses are.

KEY TERMS

Bias people's (often unconscious) values and preferences that shape their understanding and actions. Researchers' biases will affect how they conduct research and interpret their findings

Control theory the idea that people do not commit deviant acts because various factors control their impulse to break social norms

Hypothesis an idea that can be tested by research

Interpretivism an approach to research that aims to understand motives and meanings behind behaviour. It is particularly associated with collection of qualitative data

Positivism an approach to research that is based on the scientific method and is particularly associated with collection of quantitative data

Response rate the number of people who complete a survey divided by the number who made up the total sample

Extension

Some sociologists (positivists) try to remove bias and stay as neutral as possible. Other sociologists (interpretivists) believe you can never get rid of bias so while you should try to avoid bias it is important to recognise it and the impact it has on research.

Research design

Important decisions

Every researcher has to make a series of decisions about how best to approach their chosen subject. Every decision they make will have consequences and the researcher will almost certainly have to make compromises to account for not only the practical problems but also the consequences of their findings, for example the costs involved and the amount of time available to complete the project. Ultimately, a 'good' research project

is one that is 'fit for purpose', avoids harm and reveals something important and valid about that aspect of the social world.

Martyn Denscombe (*The Good Research Guide*, 2001) suggests six key decisions that a researcher has to make:

1 Does it really matter whether the research takes place? In other words, is it worth doing? Will it add something of value to our knowledge of the social world?
2 Can it be done? Is there enough time to complete the work? Are the resources available and can you gain access to the people, events or documents that you wish to study?
3 Are the right things included? Will the research cover all the issues? Will it be possible to make generalisations based on the research outcomes? Will there be an adequate response rate?
4 Will the research produce true and valid findings? Will there be enough detailed and accurate data based on truthful responses?

5 Will the research provide a fair and balanced picture? How will the researcher avoid bias, perhaps by acknowledging where this might derive from? Do they have an open mind about their area of investigation?

6 What about the rights and feelings of those affected by the research? How will the researcher deal with the various ethical issues involved?

We will return to some of these decisions later, but to start at the beginning of the process we need to understand how to formulate appropriate aims and relevant hypotheses.

What are appropriate aims?

Pat Carlen (1939–) explains her aims:

'[My research] is based on the oral histories of thirty-nine women's criminal careers ... the bulk of the book is an ethnographic analysis of their law-breaking and the official response to it. The [analysis] was informed by "control theory" ... [this theory] asks "Why do people conform?" [and it] replies that people are more likely to conform when they perceive that they have a vested interest in so doing, when they have more to lose than gain by law breaking.' (*Women, Crime and Poverty*, 1988)

After reading this extract, can you identify the purpose of Carlen's study and the research method she intended to employ? Including a clear statement of aims tells the reader what a particular sociologist wants to achieve. It also allows the reader to judge the researcher's success in meeting the objectives they have set for their research. Carlen explored what was in the 1980s a neglected area of sociology (women and crime) and she did so using a qualitative methodology – life history research – that other feminist sociologists have subsequently further explored and developed.

All sociological research should aim to increase our knowledge of the social world, improve our understanding of the relationships that exist within that world and develop explanations as to why things happen.

What are relevant hypotheses?

All present-day sociologists have the benefit of drawing upon previous research, testable theories and explanations. Relevant hypotheses are predictions based on prior knowledge; an idea that can be tested and either confirmed or rejected on the basis of subsequent research.

Fiona Devine (*Affluent Workers Revisited*, 1992) tested the idea of 'privatised instrumentalism' suggested by the earlier work of other sociologists. Privatised instrumentalism was the idea that for well-off workers social relationships had become centred on the home with work only as a means to an end. According to this theory, these so-called affluent workers only joined together with their workmates out of self-interest, for example to improve their wages, and not because they held the communal values associated with the traditional working class. In her research, Devine did not find evidence to support the theory. The workers she interviewed still held collective working-class values, they did not accept capitalism without reservations and they continued to resent inherited wealth and class-based inequalities despite their own rising living standards.

Activities

1 Write a short paragraph to explain what sociologists mean when they say that a research project has valid outcomes.

2 Write a short paragraph to explain what sociologists mean when they say a researcher should try to avoid bias in their work.

Extension

Design a research project to explain differences in educational achievement. Establish a clear aim for your project and devise relevant hypotheses based on previous research.

Check your knowledge

1 From memory, write a summary of the six key decisions a researcher has to make before they begin their project. (Check your answer against the list provided.)

2 What is control theory?

3 Why would a low response rate be a problem?

Summary

● The researcher has to make a series of decisions about how best to approach their chosen subject matter. It is not necessarily about choosing between positivism or interpretivism, but what the researcher wants to achieve from their research.

● The 'good' research project is one that is 'fit for purpose'; it reveals something valid and hopefully important about an aspect of the social world.

Pilot studies and the scientific method

▲ A scientist undertaking laboratory research

The importance of planning

Pilot studies are simply a rehearsal for the main event – an opportunity for the researcher to try out their chosen methods and iron out all those troublesome problems with their tools and techniques. For example, any questions that produce irrelevant responses can be eliminated and the **observation schedule** can be revised in the light of experience to account for the types of behaviour that the researcher has failed to anticipate. You can try this out for yourself by designing an observation schedule to use in a classroom situation to monitor the interactions that take place between a group of students and their teacher.

The scientific method

Pilot studies reflect a pragmatic approach used by positivist researchers. Such scientific research depends on choosing the appropriate research tools and techniques. The aim is to make accurate observations and measurements; if the methods are suitable for the purpose, those observations and measurements will stand up to scrutiny by other scientists. This process is called 'peer reviewing'. The scientist publishes not only the results of their research, but also a detailed account of their method. Other scientists can then repeat the research and, if the methods are sound, the results should be the same, indicating a high level of reliability. Unless, of course, they cannot repeat the result, in which case something was either wrong with the method or false conclusions have been drawn on the basis of the available evidence. In general terms, this sort of approach has served physicists, biologists and chemists rather well. It does not guarantee that incorrect research never finds its way into the public domain, but it does mean that, by and large, errors will be revealed and false claims exposed.

Alternative approaches

The positivist approach to scientific research does have its limitations, however, when it comes to the investigation of human society. For some sociologists, this scientific approach has always represented something of an ideal to which they aspire. Early sociologists (such as Comte and Durkheim) believed that by adopting a similar approach to the natural sciences they would be able to reveal 'laws' that governed human behaviour. However, modern sociologists have tended to move away from its assumptions. They no longer spend their time looking for universal laws governing human behaviour or developing 'grand theories' (see page 16) that explain everything about society.

For the interpretivist sociologist, some of the techniques that are available to the natural sciences are completely unsuitable for their purposes. In the laboratory, scientists are able to conduct experiments under controlled conditions. While in the past some social scientists have attempted such an approach, for the majority of present-day sociologists the ethical issues raised by such experiments are simply too serious an obstacle. People have rights and researchers have responsibilities; creating controlled conditions that may make perfect sense from a scientific point of view may well infringe not only on people's rights, they might even break the law if they result in any harm to participants. Many sociologists have now recognised that they impact the environment they are researching and people respond to them based on their ethnicity, gender, religious background, sexuality and even accent! Essentially, it is near impossible to not influence the research process.

If you approach society from an interpretivist perspective, you are trying to understand how the individual makes sense of the social world. For example, interactionism does not readily conform to the conventional scientific approach. If you use unstructured interviews as a research method to talk to people about their experiences and feelings, you are exploring a reality that they create through their interactions with others. The world becomes a complicated web of different meanings with no simple cause and effect explanations of human behaviour. It is a very different thing to a laboratory experiment. Humans are aware of their situation. Informed consent must be obtained so respondents know that they are the focus of the researcher's attention and they may well alter their behaviour as a consequence. Interpretivist sociologists, such as Beverley Skeggs and Ann Phoenix, understand the importance of acknowledging the researcher's role and background in the research process.

Link

For information on the experiments and work of Milgram and Zimbardo, see pages 44–45.

Activity

Is sociology a science? Write a short paragraph to defend the idea that sociology can be described as a science. Key ideas to use: **evidence-based** and **objective**.

Link

For more information on interactionism, see pages 20–21.

Extension

Do some research and find out why scientists sometimes publish misleading or inaccurate research. Use this website as a starting point: www.badscience.net/.

Summary

- Pilot studies are an opportunity for the researcher to try out their chosen methods and iron out problems with their tools and techniques.
- The classical approach to scientific research does have its limitations when it comes to the investigation of human society.

Check your knowledge

1 What is a pilot study?
2 What is a scientific method?

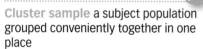

Key learning

You will be able to:
- explain why sociologists use sample surveys
- understand what a sampling frame is
- explain how sociologists select a sample.

KEY TERMS

Cluster sample a subject population grouped conveniently together in one place

Quota sample subjects are selected because they represent groups in the total population (e.g. age, gender) often used in market research

Random sample a group selected for research at random from a particular sampling frame. To be truly random everyone in the group must stand an equal chance of selection

Sampling frame a complete list from which the researcher selects their sample, e.g. all the students in a school

Snowball sample each member of a group of respondents is asked by a researcher to recommend someone who is known to them and who is in a similar situation

Stratified sample a sample selected to represent groups within the total population (similar to a quota sample)

Systematic sample the systematic selection of names from a list, e.g. every tenth name

Sampling

Sample surveys

Sociologists are often faced with very large populations that they wish to study. It can be impractical to collect data from everyone so they use a sample selected from the total population. (In this sense, the term 'population' describes the group who are being studied, for example the pupil population of a school or the employees of a company.) The basic principle behind any sample is that it should be representative of the population under investigation, for example government data gathered by the Office for National Statistics or the use of survey data in the ten-year census of population.

Sampling frames

A sampling frame is simply a list of everyone in the population being studied; it must be an accurate and up-to-date list. Examples of potential sampling frames include school registers, lists of residents or lists of company employees.

However, in reality, a suitable list may not exist or pre-existing lists may well be out of date or contain inaccurate information. School registers and the like have to be kept up to date by law, but other lists may not be as scrupulously maintained. An incomplete or inaccurate list can lead to errors in the sample, for example an imbalance in favour of one particular social group, which may distort the results of the research.

Selecting a sample: probability sampling (this is based on a known population)

- **Random samples:** to be truly random, everyone in the population being studied must stand an equal chance of being selected. 'Names drawn from a hat' is the usual shorthand used to describe this approach. Random sampling can work well with a reasonably large population, but there is always the danger that such a sample may not be representative, for example it may be accidentally biased with certain groups over- or under-represented.
- **Systematic samples:** this is a variation of random sampling (sometimes described as 'quasi-random sampling') and involves choosing, say, every tenth name from a list of the total population. Systematic samples carry with them the same potential problem as random samples, and some researchers argue that they actually increase the risk of producing a result that is not representative.
- **Stratified samples:** this technique involves making a selection in *proportion* to the composition of the total population. For example, if you have a school population with five year groups and an even number of boys and girls, you would select equal numbers of male and female students from each year group. These students can then be selected on a random basis but, although it probably would be representative, the *process* is not truly random because

it predetermines the different strata (age and gender) within the population. It would also be accurate to describe the study of the student population of a single school as a cluster sample, because the school represents a convenient grouping together of young people for the purposes of research.

- Multi-stage samples: this technique involves making a series of selections. The first stage is your original sample, drawn from the students in our imaginary school. The following stages involve the selection of various groups drawn from your original sample, for example sub-groups of students selected from your original sample on the basis of academic achievement or ethnicity.

Selecting a sample: non-probability sampling (this is based on an unknown population)

Sometimes a sociologist may not know the size of the population they wish to study. For example, they may wish to study students who have a negative attitude towards education. They might reasonably assume that this group would be mainly located among students who are the least academically successful, but this assumption might be misleading or at least incomplete. Alternatively, they may wish to study groups who are difficult to identify and locate such as the homeless. Under such circumstances, the researcher might resort to a technique designed to *reveal* the size of the population that they wish to study.

- Snowball samples: like a snowball gathering more snow, this technique involves a relatively small group who form the core of the sample. Each member of this original core group can then be asked to suggest further names, and so on, until a reasonably sized sample has been built up.
- Quota samples: often used in market research, these are a relatively crude version of stratified samples (based on target age and gender groups, for example). This technique can produce a biased sample and unreliable results as the selection may be based on 'friendly faces in a crowd' who are willing to answer questions.
- Voluntary samples: these suffer from a similar problem, as they tend to reflect the often strongly held opinions of a self-selected group who have chosen to sign up for a particular survey.

Some researchers reject the need for a representative sample and argue that their particular research project requires them to select individual respondents, perhaps the best-informed members of a particular group or those who for various reasons are actually 'untypical' (as opposed to a representative cross-section). For example, Fiona Devine studied a group of 'affluent' workers who were not intended to represent a cross-section of the working class (*Affluent Workers Revisited*, 1992).

Activities

1 Collect the names of all the students in your class or group (if you have a particularly small class your teacher may be able to recommend a more suitable list of names). Use each of the following techniques to select a sample from this 'sampling frame': random, systematic and stratified. Compare the samples produced by each technique.

2 Write a short paragraph to explain the advantages and disadvantages of three sampling techniques described above.

Extension

Research the sampling methods used in the 'Great British Class Survey'. You may find this website a useful starting point: http://blog.ukdataservice.ac.uk/the-great-british-class-survey-now-available-from-the-uk-data-service/.

Check your knowledge

1 Why do sociologists use sample surveys?
2 What is a probability sample?
3 What is a non-probability sample?

Summary

- Sociologists are often faced with very large populations that they wish to study. It would usually be impractical to collect data from everyone and so they use a representative sample selected from the total 'population'.

KEY TERMS

Genocide defined by the UN as 'acts committed with intent to destroy, in whole or in part, a national, ethnical, racial or religious group'

Personality test a questionnaire that is supposed to reveal an individual's personality

Social psychology an area of psychology concerned with human interactions

Experiments

Many of you will be used to the idea of experiments from your science classes in school. Experiments can also be used in the social sciences, but are rarely used in sociology. Social psychology has a long tradition of experimental research. For sociologists, data gathered from such experiments may well be of interest but the techniques involve important ethical problems. In summary, experiments have three key features:

1 They involve *controlling the variables* in the experimental situation; factors that might affect the outcome of the experiment need to be identified, introduced and then excluded.
2 The aim of experimental research is to identify the factors that *cause* certain things to happen.
3 Experiments involve detailed observation, measurement and recording.

Experiments used in social research

The Milgram experiment (1963)

The American psychologist Stanley Milgram (1933–84) was interested in the tension between an individual's willingness to obey authority and their understanding that what they had been told to do was wrong. He was aware that after the Second World War (1939–45) those Nazis accused of genocide attempted to justify their actions by saying that they were 'only obeying orders'. Milgram set up an experimental situation at Yale University. He placed advertisements inviting volunteers to take part in a study about 'learning'. Participants drew lots to decide who was to be the 'teacher' and who the 'learner'. What the genuine volunteers did not know was that the ballot was rigged. The learner was actually a member of the research team whose identity had been concealed.

The learner was then hooked up to an 'electric shock generator' while the teacher was taken to another room and apparently given remote control of the machine. A series of switches were clearly marked on a scale from 'slight shock' to 'danger: severe shock'. In reality, the machine was a fake, but the volunteers did not know this. In the experiment, the learner was asked a series of questions to which they deliberately gave wrong answers. Every time they did so the teacher was told to administer a shock. If the teacher refused, they were repeatedly told, by a white-coated authority figure (in reality an actor), that they must comply. Sixty-five per cent of the volunteer teachers did what they were told and continued to operate switches to the highest level 'danger: severe shock'. Milgram concluded on the basis of his research that ordinary people were conditioned by their upbringing to obey authority and that most would do so without question.

The Stanford Prison experiment (1973)

The psychologist Philip Zimbardo (1933–) was interested in the often brutal actions of prison guards; he wanted to know if their violent acts were caused by their personalities (in other words, they were individuals who were inclined to violence) or whether it was the circumstances of prison life. Zimbardo converted a cellar in the University of Stanford into a prison-like environment and then advertised for students who would like to spend a couple of weeks pretending to be either prisoners or guards. He used interviews and personality tests to screen out applicants with any psychological problems or history of drug use. Participants were randomly given either the role of a 'guard' or a 'prisoner'. Volunteer prisoners were then 'arrested' and taken to the mock prison.

Within a few hours, some of the guards began to treat the prisoners badly, insulting them and ordering them about. While the prisoners also began to exhibit behaviours found in real prisons, some began to try to ingratiate themselves with the guards by telling tales on other prisoners. Some became obsessed with obeying every rule no matter how trivial. When a group of prisoners barricaded themselves in a 'cell' and refused to obey instructions, the guards used a fire hose to restore order and put the ringleader into solitary confinement. Over a period of only a few days, the behaviour of the guards became more intimidating and some of the prisoners began to show signs of real emotional distress. The experiment was supposed to last two weeks but was brought to an end after only six days. Zimbardo concluded that the prison environment was the principal cause of the guards' behaviour, none of whom had shown any tendency towards violent behaviour before the experiment began.

Ethical problems

While the results may well be of interest to sociologists, experiments are not generally used in sociological research because of the ethical problems they create:

- Both the Milgram and Stanford experiments had the potential to cause harm to participants: emotional rather than physical in the case of the Milgram experiment; both emotional and physical in the Stanford case.
- The Milgram experiment involved deceit. There was no possibility of obtaining informed consent from the volunteers. If they had been made aware of the actual purpose of the experiment, it would have invalidated the results.

Extension

1 Research the life and work of Jane Elliott (1933–) who conducted the 'Blue eyes–Brown eyes' experiment with her class of primary school children.

2 Research the work of Robert Rosenthal and Lenore Jacobson *Pygmalion in the Classroom: Teacher Expectation and Pupils' Intellectual Development*, (1968).

Check your knowledge

1 What is a variable?

2 What was the link between events in Nazi-occupied Europe and the Milgram experiment?

3 What is an ethical problem? (Refer to page 74 if you struggle with this question.)

Summary

- Experiments can be used in the social sciences; psychology has a long tradition of experimental research.
- For sociologists, data gathered from social experiments may well be of interest but the techniques involve important ethical problems.

Activities

1 a Write a short paragraph explaining the reasons why sociologists are unlikely to use experiments in their research.

  b With the other members of your group, discuss the ethical problems created by experiments.

2 Find out more about what happened in both experiments used as examples on this website: www.simplypsychology.org/.

Surveys

What are surveys?

For sociologists, a **survey** is like a photograph because it provides a 'snapshot' in time – what people thought or how they might have behaved at the moment the survey was completed. Usually, surveys take the form of a questionnaire or structured interview; they are part of the empirical and quantitative tradition in social research with an emphasis on things that can be recorded, measured and expressed in numbers.

Surveys are not a distinct research method and should not really be described as such. They are a research **strategy** and can employ a variety of methods including the most commonly used listed below:

- Postal and online questionnaires: researchers generally send these out in large numbers and expect quite low returns. A response rate below 50 per cent for postal questionnaires would not be unusual and there is no guarantee that response rates to online questionnaires will be much higher (some researchers have apparently experienced lower online response rates). Both approaches depend on people voluntarily giving up their time to complete the survey and their willingness to do so will depend on a number of factors – access to the internet, how well designed the questions are and whether they see the subject matter as important to them. This problem explains the use of incentives (such as cash prizes) used by customer surveys.

- Telephone surveys: these pre-date the use of online surveys, but are similar in that they are relatively low cost and capable of reaching impressive numbers of people. They are certainly cheaper and quicker than face-to-face interviews, but some researchers have suggested that people may be less truthful in their responses, although other researchers dispute this. It has also been suggested that telephone surveys are less likely to be representative because the young and the employed will be difficult to contact or less willing to devote the necessary time. Again, other researchers dispute this and certainly technological change (for example, mobile phones and computer-generated calling systems) has made it easier both to contact people and to obtain a truly random sample.

Advantages of surveys

1 Surveys can generate large amounts of quantitative data that can be used to identify patterns and trends. They use a standardised set of questions and are mainly concerned with gathering factual information about the 'real world' and are often seen to be reliable and treated as significant, even though in reality the validity of some large-scale surveys may be less certain. For example, opinion polls conducted before elections have sometimes produced misleading or contradictory indicators of voting intentions.

2 Surveys are likely to provide a representative picture of society or a particular aspect of social behaviour. It is not really about the number of people involved, but rather the fact that surveys usually include all the possible variables, for example age, gender, socio-economic class and ethnicity. They are often claimed to be an accurate and reliable basis upon which generalisations about society can be made.

3 It is not correct to say that surveys are 'cheap'. Large-scale surveys are often very expensive to commission and frequently require the resources only available to governments, national newspapers and broadcasting organisations rather than sociologists. However, they can be cost effective in comparison to other methods such as the face-to-face unstructured interviews and, of course, not all surveys involve gathering responses from thousands of people.

Disadvantages of surveys

1 Large amounts of data can be difficult and time consuming to interpret. The danger with any large-scale survey is that patterns and trends may not emerge clearly. The careful analysis of data is every bit as important as the collection of data, and the larger the survey the greater the demands placed on the researcher. Alternatively, a low response rate can undermine the representativeness of survey findings by making patterns and trends appear stronger than they actually are.

2 Surveys are only a useful strategy if the researcher does not require the depth of detail that qualitative methods can reveal.

3 There are two ways of looking at survey data. One view assumes that most people are generally honest and will give reasonably truthful responses to the questions that they are asked. The other view questions this assumption. It is not just that people simply lie to researchers, although some may do so for a variety of reasons, including a need to be accepted. It is also about the way in which people react to the experience of being questioned. Beneath the confident public face that people present to the world, they may be less certain of their opinions or intentions and more likely to change their minds or behaviour than the 'snapshot' taken by the survey might suggest.

Extension

Design an online survey about a topic that you (and your teacher) believe would be suitable for use in your school or college. Discuss with your teacher whether it is possible to trial the best example produced by a member of your class (possibly by using a commonly available database of student email addresses). You might like to look at the British Social Attitudes Survey before designing your own.

Activities

1 Write a short paragraph to explain why sociologists describe surveys as a research strategy.

2 Divide the class into two groups: one group should make the case for using online surveys; the other group should make the case against. Hold a class debate and identify the strongest arguments for and against the use of this approach.

Check your knowledge

1 Would it be correct to describe surveys as quick and cheap?

2 From memory, list some of the advantages and disadvantages of surveys. (Check your answer against the lists provided.)

Summary

● A social survey is designed to provide researchers with a 'snapshot' in time – what people thought or how they might have behaved at the moment the survey was completed.

● Surveys are generally concerned with things that can be recorded, measured and expressed in numbers.

KEY TERMS

Closed questions a questionnaire that only allows the respondent to choose from a predetermined set of answers

Open questions a questionnaire or unstructured interview that allows the respondent space to answer as they wish

▲ Completing a questionnaire

Link

For more information on informed consent and confidentiality, see Ethical problems on pages 74–75.

Questionnaires

A questionnaire is simply a written list of predetermined questions that a sociologist wishes to put to a group of respondents. A questionnaire can be sent in the post, posted online or handed directly to participants although, as we shall see when we consider interviews as a research method, delivering a questionnaire in such a way is essentially a 'structured' interview.

The appropriate use of questionnaires

There are a number of questions that need to be considered when deciding whether a questionnaire is an appropriate research tool:

● Does the research project involve large numbers of respondents?
● Are the respondents to be found in a variety of locations, possibly some distance apart from one another?
● Are questionnaires the method most likely to produce honest and informative answers or is there a need for a face-to-face meeting between the researcher and the respondent?
● Does the research project need to produce quantifiable data (data that can be expressed in numbers) from identical questions?
● Will the respondents be able to read and answer the questions asked?

Questionnaires are very useful to researchers who wish to gather factual information or gauge attitudes and opinions on a specific issue. They are much less useful to the researcher who seeks a qualitative in-depth understanding of an aspect of society or a particular form of social behaviour.

Questionnaire design

As with all forms of sociological research, planning and careful preparation are vital.

● The researcher should identify their key issues and be confident that a questionnaire is the appropriate research tool for the job.
● Details should be included that clearly tell the respondent the purpose of the research. Respondents should be aware that completion is voluntary, they must give consent, can withdraw if they no longer want to participate and can have their data anonymised.
● Clear instructions should be given about how to complete the questionnaire, preferably with examples.
● The wording of questions should be clear and easy for respondents to understand.
● None of the questions should be offensive to potential respondents.
● The length of the questionnaire should be kept as short as possible. (The longer and more complex the questionnaire, the less likely it is to be completed.)
● A questionnaire should be trialled before use in the field and any problems resolved before final use.

There are two basic question types:

1 **Open questions** invite an extended response. (This type of question can produce valuable data, but analysing such responses can be time consuming and difficult.)
2 **Closed questions** only allow responses in a restricted number of categories, the most basic of which are 'Yes' or 'No' answers. A more sophisticated approach employs a number of coded responses. These are straightforward to input into a computer database and the outcomes can then be analysed. However, such an approach restricts respondents to a limited number of options and provides data that is relatively superficial.

Advantages and disadvantages

Advantages:
- Questionnaires are generally more cost effective to administer. However, it would be incorrect to describe their use in large-scale research projects as 'cheap' – the more complex the questionnaire, the larger the sample size and the higher the response rate, the higher the 'costs' in time and resources.
- Questionnaires can overcome some of the problems associated with gaining access to respondents; dealing with a document or responding to an online request is very different to finding time to spend with an interviewer.
- Questionnaires generally provide data that is easily quantifiable (expressed in numbers) and they avoid some of the potential problems created by the interaction between an interviewer and interviewee.
- Questionnaires meet the test of 'reliability' and the numerical data they produce can be used to make comparisons between variables and identify patterns and trends.

Disadvantages:
- Questionnaires place limitations on responses. 'Yes' or 'No' answers or coded responses (such as options 1–5) restrict the quality of the data to a relatively superficial level of response.
- Pre-coded questions can also be biased, reflecting ideas and topics the researcher thinks are important. A consequence of this could be that the data produced is forced into a framework provided by the researcher rather than providing an accurate picture of social reality.
- Questionnaires provide little or no opportunity for the researcher to check the truthfulness of responses, whereas interviewers can at least attempt to gauge whether a respondent is telling the truth and then pick up on any points that seem unlikely or inconsistent with previous answers.
- Low response rates can distort the results and make it impossible to draw any general conclusions from the data.

Link

For more information on interviews as a research method, see pages 50–51.

Activities

1 Design a short set of *closed* questions that explore the attitude of students towards an environmental issue, for example climate change or the impact of diesel cars on air quality.

2 Design a similar set of *open* questions on the same issue. Compare the responses you get from different groups of your fellow students to each question type.

Extension

Research the questions used in the 'Great British Class Survey' and compare them with the questions you have designed. You may find this website a useful starting point: http://blog.ukdataservice.ac.uk/the-great-british-class-survey-now-available-from-the-uk-data-service/.

Check your knowledge

1 From memory, make a list of the advantages and disadvantages of questionnaires. (Check your answer against the lists provided.)

2 What is the difference between an open and closed question?

Summary

- A questionnaire is simply a written list of predetermined questions that a sociologist wishes to put to a group of respondents.
- Questionnaires are very useful to researchers who wish to gather factual information or gauge attitudes and opinions on a specific issue.

KEY TERMS

Focus group a small group of people who are asked to consider a particular issue and discuss it in depth with an interviewer

Interviewer bias this occurs when interviewers influence the answers given by a respondent

Semi-structured interview this combines some of the features of structured and unstructured interviews

Transcript a written version of the interview

▲ Interviewing

Interviews

The simplest definition of an interview is 'a conversation with purpose'. As with all forms of sociological research, there should be informed consent; nothing that is said is 'in confidence' and the interviewee must be aware of this. Interviews will need to be recorded and transcribed for later analysis, with the usual guarantees regarding confidentiality and anonymity. The purpose or 'agenda' of the interview is set by the interviewer; they decide upon the topic to be discussed and they control the process, only pursuing those issues that they wish to explore and setting aside anything they do not. It would be a mistake to regard interviews as a 'soft option' for researchers; the successful interview requires careful planning and preparation.

Different types of interview

There are two basic types of interview:

- Structured interviews involve keeping a tight control over the questions, with the interviewer delivering what is in effect a face-to-face questionnaire. Because the questions are so tightly controlled, it is possible to analyse the outcomes in much the same way as a questionnaire – responses can be more easily categorised and expressed in numerical terms, for example, '50 per cent of respondents said XXX in answer to this question'. Structured interviews have many of the disadvantages of questionnaires: they are relatively inflexible and do not really allow for the collection of in-depth qualitative data.
- Unstructured interviews, on the other hand, are specifically intended to reveal qualitative data, to explore the respondent's thoughts, feelings and beliefs. The interviewer sets the general theme of the interview and may well begin with questions that are designed to provoke a thoughtful response, for example: 'What is your opinion of …?' In unstructured interviews, questions are generally intended to be open-ended and the researcher can be flexible in their response, picking up and following a line of enquiry that they may not have anticipated in advance. Unstructured interviews can provide the sociologist with a real insight into particular forms of social behaviour, but they can also be difficult and time consuming to analyse. Some sociologists favour a semi-structured interview approach, which combines elements of both interview types. In this format, some questions are tightly focused allowing answers to be easily compared, while other questions are more open-ended allowing for variable responses.

The most common form of interview is the 'one to one', however, some researchers use group interviews. One popular type (originally designed for use in market research) is known as a focus group. Focus groups are relatively small groups of people, usually selected to represent a cross-section of society, brought together to discuss specific issues. The argument for such an approach is that it can reveal shared attitudes and beliefs representative of the wider population. The interactions between the individual members of the group can produce revealing and informative discussions. One disadvantage of group interviews is that certain strong-minded individuals can dominate the group, expressing forthright opinions that 'drown out' other voices. Another disadvantage is that the group dynamic can limit freedom of expression; individuals may keep quiet on certain issues in order to 'fit in' with majority opinions. In a group setting, it also becomes more difficult for the researcher to maintain confidentiality.

Interviewer bias

Any interaction between two or more people can be affected by a number of variables. The type of questions asked, the appearance of the interviewer and their gender, age and ethnicity can all provoke a reaction from the respondent. This is known as interviewer bias (also known as the interviewer effect). The problem is that respondents may adapt their answers to the questions asked and this is why interviewers often think about who will interview participants if the topic is potentially sensitive; for example, in discussing experiences of Islamophobia, a Muslim researcher might think they are better placed to interview Muslim participants. If careful thought is not put into the interview situation or the topic is not sensitively approached, participants may not be open and honest in their responses and they may try to please the interviewer by saying what they think the interviewer wishes to hear, raising doubts about the validity of the data. In the final analysis, there are only so many things that can be done by the researcher to try to compensate for this problem. Possible strategies include dressing appropriately for the circumstances (either formal or informal) and remaining passive and neutral in reaction to any statements made. However, some feminist sociologists have questioned the need for such neutrality on the part of the interviewer, arguing instead for the need to show emotions in order to establish a sympathetic relationship with their informants.

Advantages and disadvantages

Advantages:
- Qualitative data can be gathered in depth from unstructured interviews, providing insight into various types of social behaviour.
- Unstructured interviews are flexible, allowing the interviewer to pursue an unanticipated line of enquiry.
- Interviews can produce data that is high in validity (an accurate reflection of social reality).

Disadvantages:
- Structured interviews do not allow for the collection of in-depth qualitative data.
- Unstructured interviews are time consuming and complicated to analyse.
- Unstructured interviews can produce data that is low in reliability, as data from different interviews can be inconsistent.
- Interviewer bias can raise questions about the accuracy and truthfulness of responses.

Activities

1 With the support of your teacher, arrange to record a series of short interviews in class on a topic that will be of interest to the members of your group. Experiment with structured and unstructured approaches and discuss the advantages and disadvantages of each.

2 Arrange a group discussion on a similar topic and monitor the contributions made by each member of the group. Identify those with the strongest opinions, those who attempt to 'fit in' with the majority and those who do not contribute much to the discussion.

Extension

Using this textbook, find some examples of sociological research using interviews. Have the sociologists used extracts from their transcripts? Do you see any advantages and disadvantages in using extracts from interview transcripts in the published research?

Check your knowledge

1 What is a structured interview?
2 What is an unstructured interview?
3 From memory, make a list of the advantages and disadvantages of interviews. (Check your answer against the lists provided.)

Summary

- The simplest definition of an interview is 'a conversation with purpose'.
- There are two basic types of interview:
  1 Structured interviews involve keeping a very tight control over the questions.
  2 Unstructured interviews use open-ended questions that are specifically intended to reveal qualitative data.

KEY TERMS

Non-participant observation the researcher watches and observes without taking part in the activities of the group

Observer effect group members alter their behaviour because they are being observed

Participant observation the researcher takes an active part in the activities of the group while observing it

Observation

Observation is watching with a purpose. As a research method, it does not have to depend on what people *say* about their actions and experiences; the sociologist is able to see and record what happens in front of them. However, if you ask two people to observe the same event, there will always be slight differences in the way in which they perceive what is happening. Sometimes there may be important differences. This is a problem that the police and lawyers recognise when dealing with 'eye witness' testimony. People do not usually remember everything that happens. They either selectively recall events or they simply fail to notice certain things. There are various explanations for why this may be so: the emotional or physical state of the observer (for example, they may be distracted or bored); and whether or not some things are familiar events (we tend to remember the unusual and unfamiliar). There is also the question of how the observer chooses to interpret what they see and this can be influenced by a variety of factors, including prejudice or even a need to find evidence in support of a hypothesis. (Grounded theory is an approach that can help to avoid this particular complication.)

Different types of observation

There are two basic types of observation: non-participant (sometimes called systematic); and participant.

● **Non-participant observation** involves the researcher drawing up a detailed observation schedule and recording what they see. As the sociologist is not part of the group, they can stand to one side, making a record of what happens in front of them on a form divided into various categories. (This type of observation is 'overt', meaning open and not hidden.) A typical schedule will be designed to include different types of event and the timing of such events. For example: Who asks questions in class? What sort of questions do they ask? How does the teacher respond to different types of question? It should also enable the observer to record at least some details about the context – the circumstances in which the observation takes place, for example observations of a mixed-gender, top-set Year 9 science class. The purpose of an observation schedule is to eliminate the differences that can occur in what people see and remember (if permission is obtained, events can also be filmed or recorded). The schedule is intended to enable the observer to build up objective data based on systematic observations of a representative sample of people and events, for example different teachers and various groups of students in a school.

● **Participant observation** involves the sociologist 'embedding' themselves in a particular social situation. It can be overt but more commonly uses a 'covert' (meaning hidden) approach in order to avoid the possibility that people will alter their behaviour when they know that they are being observed. Covert participant observation can help to reveal types of social behaviour that are generally hidden from view, for example when the behaviour is restricted to groups such as families or religious sects or when antisocial or even criminal acts are involved. However, under these circumstances accurate recording during the observation can be difficult if not impossible. Yet, participant observation does not have to be covert. It can mean simply becoming accepted by the group you wish to observe.

Advantages and disadvantages

Advantages:
- Direct observation of actions or events.
- Non-participant observation involves objective systematic recording.
- Non-participant observation can be high in reliability.
- Participant observation can produce detailed, contextualised qualitative data that is high in validity.
- Although most participant observation is covert, sometimes overt observation can produce excellent data if undertaken appropriately.

Disadvantages:
- Observation provides data on behaviour, but it tells the observer little or nothing about the intentions of the participants.
- Non-participant observation can oversimplify actions or events (this is generally much less of a problem with participant observation) and provide very little information about the context in which events occur.
- Non-participant observation can alter the behaviour of the group that the researcher wishes to study (known as the observer effect). A researcher who stands to one side recording events is unlikely to become simply part of the background.
- Covert participant observation raises a number of ethical issues, since the participants being observed are not aware of the status of the observer and have not given their permission. The covert researcher must defend their actions by proving that no harm was caused and that the identities of those involved have been concealed.

Activities

1   Pair up with another member of your class. Observe the same event (it could be another classroom or simply the behaviour of a group of students queuing for their lunch). Compare your observations. Look for differences in the recording of events that you both witnessed.
2   On the basis of your experiences and subsequent discussion, work with your partner to design an appropriate observation schedule. (If you have the opportunity, you can both repeat the observation using a common schedule to record events and then compare notes again.)

Extension

Prepare arguments for and against the use of covert participant observation. Read about some examples of sociological research using this method before writing up your arguments, for example James Patrick, *A Glasgow Gang Observed* (1973) and William F. Whyte, *Street Corner Society* (1943).

Link

For more information on a covert approach, see Ethical problems on pages 74–75.

Extension

An example of participant observation is Claire Alexander's study of young black men in *The Art of Being Black* (1996).

Check your knowledge

1   What do sociologists mean when they talk about 'covert' observation?
2   From memory, list the advantages and disadvantages of observation as a research method. (Check your answer against the lists provided.)

Summary

- Observation is watching with a purpose.
- As a research method, observation does not have to depend on what people *say* about their actions and experiences; the sociologist is able to see and record what happens in front of them.

KEY TERMS

Extended family parents, their children and other more distant relatives, e.g. grandparents, aunts and uncles

Kinship relationships of blood and marriage

Nuclear family a family group consisting of parents and their children

▲ Is it really possible to understand a different culture?

Ethnography

Ethnography literally means the study of the culture and structure of a group of people in a society. It generally involves the production of highly detailed accounts of how people in a social setting lead their lives, based upon systematic and long-term observation and/ or interviews with informants. Ethnography is the *observation and description* of a group of people and their way of life. As such, it has its origins in the work of social anthropologists who tried to describe and understand the behaviour of disappearing tribal cultures. In the nineteenth and early twentieth centuries, anthropologists often worked in parts of the world that were being transformed by the colonial ambitions of Europe and the USA, for example Margaret Mead, who worked in Samoa in the 1920s. Her book *Coming of Age in Samoa* (1928) explores issues such as adolescence, gender and social norms and draws comparison between the lives of young Samoans and their US contemporaries in ways that adopted a specific Western view of adolescence and therefore these communities were portrayed as primitive.

Ethnography uses the approach developed by anthropologists to study our own society and it has the following key elements:

- The sociologist using an ethnographic approach will need to spend an extended period of time working in the field recording detailed observations and conducting interviews with people in their natural environment.
- All aspects of domestic life can be included in ethnographic research, for example courtship, marriage and bringing up children.
- Sociologists who use an ethnographic approach want to understand how the people that they are studying understand the world – what they think as well as what they do.
- Sociologists who use an ethnographic approach want to understand everything in its proper context (they look for the background to events). They should also be aware about how the writing up of their research impacts on our knowledge and understanding of different cultures and communities.
- The final product of sociological research using an ethnographic approach will be more than a description; it will involve the researcher reflecting on their experience.

Ethnography as a research method

One of the important points to understand about sociology is the relationships that exist between ideas. To the student encountering sociology for the first time this can be confusing, but, in simple terms, you should understand that the labels we can apply to the work of a particular sociologist are not exclusive. For example, Claire Alexander's *The Asian Gang: Ethnicity, Identity, Masculinity* (2000) covers multiple labels. *Street Corner Society* (1943) by William Foote Whyte is a participant observation case study, but it is also an ethnographic study because it has all of the key elements listed above.

Research in action

In *Street Corner Society* (1943), William Foote Whyte (1914–2000) carried out a study of Italian-Americans living in a slum area of 1930s Boston, which Whyte called 'Cornerville'. He lived with an Italian-American family while completing his research and describes the purpose of his project as an attempt to understand 'Cornerville' from an insider's point of view. Whyte believed that outside observers would see only chaos in what he believed to be a 'highly organised and integrated social system'. His 'corner boys' were groups of young men who centred their activities on street corners, barber shops and pool rooms, and were described as 'the bottom level of society'. Whyte contrasts the lives of these young men with those of the racketeers (organised crime) and politicians, described in his study as the 'big shots', and explores the relationship between the two groups.

In *Family and Kinship in East London* (1957), Michael Young (1915–2002) and Peter Willmott (1923–2000) studied families in Bethnal Green and then contrasted their findings with the lives of people from the East End of London who had moved to a new estate that they called 'Greenleigh' (in reality, Debden in Essex). They directly compared their detailed observations of working-class families to the work of anthropologists attempting to understand family life in tribal societies. They concluded that in Bethnal Green the extended working-class family with its intimate network of relationships based on kinship retained some of the features of 'primitive' family life. However, once the East End families moved to Essex, Young and Willmott observed that they lost many of these close family connections. In the process, these more isolated nuclear families became more like 'typical' modern British families.

Advantages and disadvantages

Advantages:
- Ethnography is based on the direct observation of social behaviour.
- It is a type of qualitative research providing detailed in-depth data.
- It provides a valid, well-rounded picture of the social behaviour that has been observed, exploring the background context and explaining people's ideas.
- It allows for comparisons between different cultures, comparing different ways of life.

Disadvantages:
- Ethnography can provide rich descriptions but weak analysis.
- It can fail the test of reliability; observed behaviour can be misinterpreted or the research can be contradicted by the work of other sociologists.
- There are ethical problems, particularly with regard to the privacy of informants who can reveal intimate details of their lives.
- The observer effect. With ethnographic research, it is often difficult to judge how far the observer has influenced the behaviour of research subjects.
- Ethnographic research tends to be relatively expensive and time consuming.

Summary
- Ethnography can be defined as the observation and description of a people and their way of life.
- It uses some of the methods developed by anthropologists to study our own society.

Activities
1 Write a short paragraph to explain how a sociologist might carry out ethnographic research into a school or college.
2 Read some extracts from *Family and Kinship in East London*. (You may be able to find some useful extracts online.)

Extension
1 Research the life and work of Margaret Mead (1901–78). Find out why some of her work is now regarded as controversial.
2 Find some critical reviews of the studies mentioned in this section by Whyte and Young and Willmott. Discuss your findings with the other members of your group.

Check your knowledge
1 What is ethnography?
2 From memory, list the key elements of ethnographic research. (Check your answer against the list provided.)
3 With what did Young and Willmott compare their research?

▲ Case studies involve looking at groups in detail

Case studies

The term 'case study' comes from medical research. When doctors first come across a disease, they study and record its progress in a group of patients, including how well those patients respond to certain treatments. On the basis of these case histories, other doctors are then able to forecast how the disease is likely to develop in their patients. They will also know what treatments have proved to be effective. In sociology, the term 'case study' is used to describe in-depth investigations of a particular aspect of society, for example a delinquent gang, a school, hospital or prison. Case studies normally reflect qualitative research methods and are conducted using observations and sometimes interviews. The case study usually represents a 'typical' example from a particular time and place. It is not good practice to generalise from case studies, as they may not be typical of the behaviour of similar groups or structures in society. The argument for the use of 'atypical' or unusual examples is that they cast a light on a particular form of social behaviour, for example a religious group with beliefs that are widely rejected by mainstream society. Life histories are a type of case study focusing on the life experiences of one or more individuals; this approach has been used by a number of feminist sociologists.

When is it appropriate to use a case study?

Faced with the choice of using a particular sociological research method, it is important that the researcher chooses the method best suited to the project in hand. Case studies are unlike some of the other research methods we have looked at because they can include a wide range of research techniques, such as observations, questionnaires and interviews. When the following conditions apply, the use of a case study is appropriate:

- When focusing on one (or a limited number) of examples promises to reveal important sociological insights.
- When there is a need for an in-depth investigation. Case studies are all about the details that could never be revealed using mass studies like the Crime Survey for England and Wales.
- When it is necessary to focus on the social relationships within an organisation and on the processes that impact on those relationships, for example between teachers and students and the impact of setting and streaming on achievement.
- When they can be used to explore 'real world' situations that exist independently of the research project. Case studies do not require artificially constructed 'social laboratories'.
- When it is appropriate to use a 'mixed methods' approach, gathering data from multiple sources.
- When a sociologist is interested in building theories (ideas that explain society or forms of social behaviour).

Whatever the subject of the case study, sociologists generally provide a *justification* for the selection that they have made. Possible justifications include typicality (or the opposite if an unusual or extreme case is selected) and the unique nature of an opportunity, for example employment in a particular school, hospital or prison.

When using case studies, sociologists will also usually make *comparisons* with other examples in order to reveal similarities and differences. Possible grounds for comparison might include geographical location (for example, with a similar urban or rural setting) and historical developments (for example, changing forms of school organisation).

Advantages and disadvantages

Advantages:
- Case studies are able to deal with complicated social situations; the researcher can tailor their approach in response to challenging social relationships and complex social processes.
- The use of mixed methods allows for the triangulation of data to support or challenge what is discovered.
- The sociologist is concerned with an in-depth study of real world situations, increasing the likely validity of their findings.
- Case studies lend themselves to the development of grounded theory.

Disadvantages:
- It may not be possible to generalise on the basis of a single case study and researchers who do this may find their results are challenged by other sociologists.
- Case studies can be low in reliability. (A case study is comparable to an unstructured interview in that the circumstances can be unique and other case studies may reveal contradictory data.)
- The researcher may be faced with a number of ethical issues, particularly if they have invested considerable amounts of time and in the process have become accepted participant observers. (Some case studies have involved years of research.)
- The observer effect (a situation where people change their behaviour because they know they are being observed) may distort the data.
- It can be difficult to arrange the necessary access required by the case study approach. For example, an organisation like a school, hospital or prison can be reluctant to allow in a researcher who may gain access to sensitive information.

Activities

1 Write a short paragraph to explain what sociologists mean when they use the term 'case study'.
2 Write a letter to an imaginary school, hospital or prison asking to use them as a case study in your research. Explain what your project is about, the methods you wish to use, the ethical issues you have considered and the steps you intend to take in order to avoid any ethical problems.

Extension

Do some research and find out what you can about *Learning to Labour* (1977) by Paul Willis. (There are some useful online summaries.) Do you think this book can be described as a case study? What evidence can you find to support your conclusions?

Write a report about your findings and compare your conclusions with other members of your group.

Check your knowledge

1 What is the connection between case studies and medical research?
2 From memory, list the advantages and disadvantages of case studies. (Check your answer against the lists provided.)

Summary

- The term 'case study' comes from medical research. In sociology, the term is used to describe in-depth investigations of a particular group or social structure.
- A case study usually represents a 'typical' example.

Longitudinal studies

▲ Longitudinal studies involve looking at a cohort of people over time

A longitudinal study gathers together a group of people who will be studied by sociologists at various intervals over an extended period of time. It means researching a cohort of people over a period of time rather than a snapshot of a particular moment. It could be done using questionnaires, interviews or observation. The idea is to track changes in the lives of the individuals involved, for example changes over time in their economic circumstances or changing social attitudes; the approach can also be used to track changes in organisations or social institutions. A cohort study uses a group of people who were born in the same year (an age cohort).

Examples of longitudinal studies

Beginning in 1968, the American Panel Study of Income Dynamics (PSID) involves 5,000 families and some 18,000 individual participants. The study gathers data on a range of issues including employment, income, health, marriage and child development. Similar longitudinal studies also exist in Germany and Australia.

In Britain in 1964, the director Paul Almond made the first of a series of films based on a group of children who were then seven years of age; the first film was called *Seven Up!* The 14 children involved were selected on the basis of their parents' socio-economic class (little or no consideration was given to other variables). Most of the participants are male with only four females in the group. The participants have been interviewed and filmed at various points in their lives. Although well known and of considerable sociological interest, the series is the work of documentary filmmakers as opposed to sociologists. The films have proved to be a popular success. (The series recently revisited participants, who are now aged well into their sixties.) Participants, have been questioned in detail about their beliefs and attitudes, family life, social class and state of mind. One point of interest is that the study (which is limited in scope) provides little evidence of social mobility. Most of the group who came from working-class families have remained in this socio-economic class.

The UK Household Longitudinal Study is a survey of 40,000 British households. Participants are visited annually to collect information using face-to-face interviews. The aim of the study is to provide data about participants' health, work, education, income, family and social life, together with information about the impact of government policies on the lives of those involved. The study includes four samples: a representative sample of households; a minority ethnic group sample of approximately 1,000 individuals; participants of the earlier British Household Survey providing data that dates back to 1991; and an experimental 'innovation panel' set up to allow the researchers to experiment with different survey methods. The 2018 report of the study (Understanding Society Insights 2018, Economic and Social Research Council) provides data on a range of issues including housing, revealing, for example, that men were more likely to become homeowners after separation than women:

- Separated men and women were most likely to move to private renting. Separated women were also likely to move to social renting whereas men moved to homeownership.
- Separated women with children were most likely to move to social or private renting whereas those without children were most likely to move to private renting, followed by living with relatives or friends.

Advantages and disadvantages

Advantages:
- Longitudinal studies can be used to track lifetime changes in employment and social mobility.
- They enable researchers to look in detail at the relationship between socio-economic class and educational achievement.
- Researchers are able to look in detail at the influence of childhood on adult behaviour.
- They provide an opportunity to research why some individuals remain in poverty while others are able to escape it.
- They can be used to monitor changing social attitudes over time.

Disadvantages:
- Longitudinal studies are time consuming and expensive, for example researchers need to keep track as individuals move house or locate to a different part of the country.
- Participants can drop out for a number of reasons, including ill health and death, or they may simply choose to leave the study (this is known as the **attrition rate**).
- A high rate of attrition can affect the composition of the sample, making it less representative of the wider population.
- If the sample is not representative, it may be impossible to generalise about the wider society on the basis of the research.
- Because they know they are being observed, participants can change their pattern of behaviour.

Extension

Watch extracts from the *Seven Up!* television series. (Extracts can be found online and a DVD is available.) You might also find it useful to visit: https://cls.ucl.ac.uk/cls-studies/1970-british-cohort-study/

Check your knowledge

1 What is a longitudinal study?
2 From memory, list the advantages and disadvantages of longitudinal studies. (Check your answer against the lists provided.)

Summary

- A longitudinal, or panel, study gathers together a group of people who will be studied by sociologists at various intervals over an extended period of time.
- The idea is to track changes in the lives of the individuals involved.

Activities

1 Explore the website for the UK Household Longitudinal Study: www.understandingsociety.ac.uk/. (The site includes free downloadable material including podcasts on various topics.)
2 Download the latest version of 'Insights' from the website. Choose one research topic that you consider to be of sociological interest and summarise the key findings in the form of a poster or PowerPoint presentation.

KEY TERMS

Case study a detailed examination of a single example providing qualitative in-depth data

Interview a research method where questions are asked using either a formal approach (a structured interview) or an informal approach (an unstructured interview)

Observation a research method involving either covert (hidden) or overt (open) observations of a social group

Official statistics government statistics, e.g. the crime rate

Opinion poll a sample survey of public opinion

Qualitative data information presented in a variety of forms that is rich in descriptive detail

Quantitative data information presented in a numerical form

Questionnaire a research method that uses a predetermined list of questions

Reliability data is reliable if research can be repeated and consistently produces similar results

Structured interview an interview using a predetermined list of tightly controlled questions

Subjective judgements that are based on personal opinions

Unstructured interview an informal conversation that allows the respondent to talk freely about the general theme agreed for the interview

Validity data is valid if it gives an accurate picture of the social world

Quality and quantity

Qualitative research

Qualitative researchers collect information from their immediate experience of society – what they can see happening before them and what people tell them about their lives. They may also use documentary sources, letters and diaries, but the principle remains the same. They are concerned with recording directly lived experiences of the social world.

Qualitative researchers tend to use the following methods:

- **Observation**: usually involving an extended period of contact with a particular group of people. This research method is particularly useful when trying to understand an aspect of everyday life, for example **case studies** of the experience of school or work.
- **Interviews**: for the qualitative researcher, these are usually **unstructured interviews** (conversations with a purpose), for example to understand an individual's understanding of their experiences at school or in the workplace.
- Documentary sources: these may include diaries and letters which can be used to add detail and to clarify questions that might arise from observation or interviews. They can also be used as a primary source of information.
- Recordings: visual and sound recordings can be used to provide the researcher with a detailed record of their observations and interviews. They can also be used as a primary source of information.

The use of a qualitative approach has the advantage that it can provide strong descriptions and a deeper understanding of lived experiences, for example of a criminal subculture. However, qualitative research can also be criticised for failing the test of **reliability**. In science, data is reliable if an experiment can be repeated and produce the same results. For sociologists working in the field, this can become difficult to achieve. Different sociologists may observe similar situations and interview people from similar backgrounds and yet reach different conclusions. The representativeness and **validity** (or truth) of **qualitative data** can also be questioned. For example, to what extent are the stories that people tell 'typical' experiences and how much can we rely upon the interpretation placed on these stories by a particular sociologist?

Quantitative research

Quantitative researchers collect information in the form of numbers; they use statistics that measure an enormous variety of social phenomena – everything from school attendance to suicide rates can be reduced to numbers. This allows strong statements to be made, such as 75 per cent of respondents agreed or disagreed. Such statements tend to be treated as facts and, therefore, of greater value than qualitative observations.

Quantitative researchers tend to use the following methods:

- **Questionnaires**: these are often distributed to very large numbers of people. The higher the response rate, the greater the reliability that can be claimed for the results. Large numbers tend to be seen as convincing evidence.
- **Structured interviews**: these are essentially questionnaires that are delivered face to face following a strict pre-designed format that allows responses to the same questions to be compared and expressed as numbers.
- Statistical data gathered by governments (official statistics): this can include census data or crime statistics.
- Content analysis: this can include using predetermined categories to count how often something appears in the mass media.

The use of a quantitative approach has the advantage that it is often seen as an objective measure, free from the problems created by 'anecdotal' evidence (the stories that people tell researchers) and the interpretations of sociologists engaged in small-scale qualitative research. However, in reality, quantitative research has its own problems of reliability and validity. Statistical measures can be based on **subjective** decisions by the researchers involved (for example, what should be counted). Impressive numbers sometimes tend to give uncertain estimates the appearance of being hard facts. For example, **opinion polls** are reported in the mass media as significant news items. They are often treated as reliable indicators of public opinion, even though experience tells us that they can be misleading and inaccurate.

Is there a right approach?

While **quantitative data** is sometimes treated as if it represents a 'gold standard', in reality the division between quantitative and qualitative research is not as great as it first might appear. Sociologists are not faced by a simple choice between one method and another; they will often combine both (mixed methods), for example using unstructured interviews and observations combined with survey data and **official statistics**. All sociologists attempt to reach accurate evidence-based conclusions about society.

Summary

- Qualitative researchers collect information about what they observe and what people tell them about their lives.
- Quantitative researchers collect information in the form of numbers.
- Sociologists are not faced by a simple choice between one method and another; they will often combine both.

Activities

1 Draw up a chart to show the strengths and weaknesses of qualitative research. Then do the same for quantitative research.

2 Use the internet to research some current opinion polls in the UK. You might find this website a useful starting point: www.ipsos.com/ipsos-mori/en-uk/news-and-polls/overview.

3 Prepare a PowerPoint presentation or poster to show your most interesting findings.

Extension

Keep a daily diary about your experience at school or college for one week. (Make your entries anonymously and do not identify anyone by name in the diary.) Work with other members of your group to compare different diaries at the end of the week:

- Can you reach any conclusions based on the evidence of these documents?
- Can you express your conclusions in numbers?
- Can you use selected quotations from the diaries to support your conclusions?
- Is this qualitative or quantitative research?

Check your knowledge

1 From memory, list the research methods commonly used by qualitative researchers. (Check your answer against the list provided.)

2 From memory, list the research methods used by quantitative researchers. (Check your answer against the list provided.)

3 What do sociologists mean when they talk about research using mixed methods?

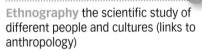
You will be able to:
- explain what primary sources are
- describe the different types of primary data
- explain mixed methods.

KEY TERMS

Ethnography the scientific study of different people and cultures (links to anthropology)

Life histories qualitative research that provides an overall picture of an informant's or interviewee's life experiences

Longitudinal (panel) study a research project that follows the same group of people over a long period of time, used to study trends over time and the impact of social change

Mixed methods social research that combines a variety of methods, e.g. observation, questionnaires and interviews

Representative a researcher's data/sample is not biased but accurately reflects the wider population being studied

Sample a group selected for study by a researcher from a target population

Triangulation (corroboration) of data the accuracy of data gathered using one method can be compared with data gathered using alternative methods, e.g. questionnaires, interviews and secondary sources

Primary sources

What are primary sources?

Primary sources are types of data collected by the researcher themselves as part of their research project. Secondary sources are types of data that already exist; we will look at examples of this type of data and explore some of the other ideas mentioned in this section later in this chapter. Both types of data can be either qualitative (for example unstructured interviews or life histories) or quantitative (for example various kinds of numerical data). The research methods selected for use in a particular project will determine the type of primary data available to the researcher; some topics will generate large amounts of quantitative data, while others will produce more qualitative data, transcripts and recordings, for example.

Before we look at various types of primary data, there are three important ideas that we need to remember:

1 Reliability: in the natural sciences, data is seen as reliable if other researchers using the same methods get the same results. This is relatively straightforward (although not without its own problems) for the laboratory-based physicist, chemist or biologist. For the sociologist dealing with the behaviour of people in society, it presents a different order of difficulty. In simple terms, quantitative sociological data is regarded as reliable for providing a snapshot of information but less so for answering why that pattern has emerged.

2 Validity: to the sociologist, data is valid if it gives an accurate picture of social reality based on evidence. Quantitative sociological data can be reliable but lack validity because it usually only provides a relatively superficial picture of social behaviour. Qualitative approaches may lack reliability, but generally provide a more valid in-depth picture of social behaviour.

3 Practical concerns: quantitative methods are generally most suited to studies requiring a large-scale representative sample. Qualitative methods are most suited to studies requiring an in-depth approach based on a relatively small group of people. Some studies employ a mixed methods approach, combining quantitative and qualitative methods.

Different types of primary data

- Quantitative methods such as questionnaires generally require a relatively sophisticated approach to sampling, but, in general terms, the intention is to produce a representative picture of social behaviour based on a relatively large sample of the population. Because such approaches usually generate impressive amounts of numerical data that can be checked by other researchers, they are sometimes seen as more 'scientific' and generally more 'reliable'. They can certainly be used to establish relationships between various factors (correlations between variables), possible causes and effects and to identify patterns and trends.
- Qualitative methods include case studies, life histories, interviews, observations, ethnography and longitudinal (panel) studies. Their shared purpose is to reveal an in-depth picture of social reality based (usually but not always) on a relatively small number of people. Such approaches generate data that is sometimes less systematically collected and usually not expressed in numerical terms. It is generally very difficult for other researchers to check the findings of qualitative research and, therefore, qualitative data can be challenged as 'unreliable' in comparison to quantitative data. However, those sociologists who favour qualitative methods respond by emphasising that attempting to provide generalisations is 'dancing to the wrong tune' because different researchers going into the same school could find different results.

When researchers reference the work of other sociologists who have used any of the research methods listed above, that material becomes a form of secondary data.

Mixed methods and triangulation

A mixed (or multi-) methods approach avoids some of the problems associated with research that goes down either an exclusively quantitative or qualitative road. Essentially, different methods can be used to collect data on the same research topic. Questionnaires can be combined with observations and interviews, and then cross-referenced with various forms of secondary documentary evidence. Apart from the practical problem that this approach involves, such as the need for more resources (time and money), the obvious advantage is that it allows the researcher to see a particular issue from a variety of different angles. Not only will there be more data for the researcher to analyse, but also the quality of the data may well be improved. A mixed methods approach allows data to be corroborated. For example, possible explanations of social behaviour based on an analysis of questionnaire data can be compared with observations and interviews that either confirm or disprove those explanations. Sociologists sometimes refer to the process of comparing various forms of data as triangulating data (a term borrowed from map reading where you locate your true position in relation to some known fixed points). However, it is important not to take this comparison too far. While some researchers will no doubt agree that it is possible to locate a provable 'truth' about social reality, other researchers are more cautious, arguing that such an approach ignores the complexity of human interactions and the importance of the perspective from which you view any form of social behaviour.

You will be able to:
- explain what secondary sources are
- describe the different types of secondary data
- understand the need for a critical review.

KEY TERMS

Census a government survey of the population of Britain conducted every ten years

Content analysis the analysis of documents or visual material, e.g. newspapers or television broadcasts

Demography the study of population trends

Secondary sources

What are secondary sources?

Secondary sources are types of data collected by other sociologists or from a variety of alternative sources that can provide useful data relevant to a particular research project. Relevant data can be contemporary or historical, quantitative or qualitative; it all depends on the nature of the investigation. There are advantages and disadvantages to the use of any form of secondary data and the use of such data again raises questions of reliability and validity as previously discussed. However, on balance, any disadvantages are far outweighed by the advantages:

▲ Secondary research might involve looking at historical documents or reports

1 They are usually a cost-effective source of data. For example, the internet now provides researchers with ready access to a huge amount of useful information provided by 'open government' access policies.
2 They provide corroboration for research findings (triangulation).
3 They can provide the researcher with a model of good practice (or alternatively a lesson in the potential problems to be avoided).
4 They can provide a unique perspective on social change, a window into the past that researchers can use to explore changing social behaviour or attitudes.
5 They can provide relatively easy access to data from other cultures.

Different types of secondary data

- Official statistics: numbers collected by the government for a variety of different purposes, such as measuring changes in the population or monitoring the effectiveness of health and educational provision. The collection of government statistics is overseen by the Office for National Statistics (often referred to as the ONS).
- Population data: the first real attempt at a systematic large-scale collection of data in Britain took place in 1801 with the first population census. Prior to that, data available to governments about the size and composition of the population was unreliable and often simply based on estimates that were little better than guesswork. The study of population is called demography and census data now provides sociologists with a wealth of information about, for example, birth and death rates, families and ethnicity.
- Crime: the Crime Survey for England and Wales collects data on people's experience of crime. The survey collects information not only about crimes that have been reported to and recorded by the police, but also those that have not. This provides a basis for estimating the total number of unreported and unrecorded crimes

which the 2018 survey (based on returns from 35,000 households) estimated to be six out of every ten crimes committed.

● Social trends: this reference source brings together a range of social and economic data from a variety of government departments and other organisations. It provides sociologists with a broad view of how British society is changing.

● Historical documents: sociologists who are interested in changes in patterns of marriage and family life, for example, need to access historical source material such as parish records. (The only way that births, marriages and deaths were recorded before the nineteenth century was in local church records.) Raw census data (original returns as opposed to analysis) is kept secure under a 100-year rule; this means that detailed raw data from the early years of the twentieth century is only just becoming available for sociologists to study.

● Life histories: personal accounts such as letters and diaries can also be a useful source of sociological data. For example, Young and Willmott (*The Symmetrical Family*, 1973) asked some of the families they were studying to keep diaries about their day-to-day lives.

● Mass media: newspapers, television and even radio broadcasts have now been archived for many years. Potentially, this is a huge resource for sociologists and content analysis can reveal an enormous amount about changing social behaviour and attitudes. Photographs, novels and cinema films can also be a source of useful data, as they can vividly reflect not only contemporary life, but also some of the issues of their day and even shifting attitudes and values.

Critical review

Perhaps this section should have been headed with a large notice saying 'Proceed with caution'. All forms of secondary data (including the work of other sociologists) need to be reviewed with a critical eye and not simply accepted at face value. For example, some sociologists argue that even the most rigorous of government statistics cannot be regarded as simple 'facts' because what is counted, when it is counted and even how it is counted can be heavily influenced by the priorities or political concerns of the government of the day. Similarly, media sources are the work of journalists, novelists and film-makers, not sociologists. As such, they are not objective observers of society. What they report, write about and film can reflect not only their personal agendas but also the concerns of their editors and employers.

Extension

Watch a copy of the film *Cathy Come Home* (BBC, 1966). It is available on DVD.

● What can you find out about the film's impact at the time and the later work and perspective of its director Ken Loach (1936–)?

● What can you learn from the film about life in the 1960s?

● Do you think the film still has any relevance to a modern audience?

Check your knowledge

1 From memory, list three types of secondary data that a sociologist might use. (Check your answer against the list provided.)

2 How many years must pass before a researcher can use raw census data?

3 What are official statistics?

Activities

1 Visit the websites listed below and summarise in the form of a poster or PowerPoint presentation the type of data available to sociologists from each site:

● https://data.gov.uk/dataset/social_trends

● www.ons.gov.uk/census/2011census

● www.crimesurvey.co.uk/.

2 At the start of this section on page 64 there is a list of advantages of using secondary data. Make a similar list of the disadvantages.

Summary

● Secondary sources are types of data collected by other sociologists or from a variety of alternative sources that can provide useful data relevant to a particular research project.

● Relevant data can be contemporary or historical, quantitative or qualitative.

● All forms of secondary data need to be used with care.

Key learning

You will be able to:
- explain what a sociological 'fact' is
- describe what values are
- explain what sociologists mean by structure and agency.

KEY TERM

Empirical facts knowledge gained through scientific observation

▲ Factual evidence – we know it is raining when we get wet

Facts and values

What is a sociological fact?

In science, facts are said to be observable and measureable; if you go out in the rain, you can see it and you will get wet. In sociology, there is a long tradition of objectivity – the attempt to present a picture of the world as it is and not how the researcher might like it to be: sociological 'facts' as opposed to opinions based on value judgements. Max Weber, for example, argued strongly that the researcher should keep empirical facts (the scientific study of society) apart from 'practical evaluations'. However, Weber did not believe that social scientists should have no values or be indifferent to the events that they observe in the world around them. Rather, Weber's position was that the facts and values must be kept clearly separated and made obvious to the sociologist's audience (readers and students).

What are values?

Values are those things that we hold to be important, for example a belief in social justice and democracy. Everyone has a right to an opinion, but values are not just opinions. What makes something a value as opposed to a simple opinion or preference is the moral judgement at its heart, for example the importance of marriage or human rights. It is a controversial question in sociology as to whether there are any absolutely value-neutral facts when it comes to the study of human behaviour, and if it is ever possible to give a completely unbiased account of the social world. Take, for example, the idea of a culture of poverty. If we agree that such a thing exists, and not all sociologists do, what we are in effect saying is that the poor through their own actions are responsible for their own poverty and the future poverty of their children. Is this a 'fact' or a value judgement?

TIP

Try to see both sides of an argument, but do not be afraid to make a judgement based on the available evidence.

Structure and agency

The idea of a social structure is central to the development of sociology. The 'fact' that society exists would seem to qualify as value-neutral (free from any value judgements), but there are different ways of looking at even this most fundamental idea. One interpretation is that society exists independently of its members as a system that determines how people are able to behave within it (the structuralist perspective). Another view suggests that society is actually a collection of individuals who possess free will but, through their actions, establish relationships with one another building a society in the process (human agency as opposed to structure). Functionalists saw society from a structuralist perspective as a system; from their perspective, the institutions of society were created to meet the needs of society, to feed and clothe its members and to educate its children. They believed that the system was capable of adapting to changing needs but individual roles would always be based on rules and expectations enforced by sanctions. Human agency was needed only in so far as it satisfied the requirements of the system. Interactionism, on the other hand, does not see society simply as a system that organises and controls human behaviour. From the interactionist perspective, people create meanings as a consequence of their day-to-day interactions; they see people voluntarily creating society one day at a time as they make choices and take decisions, for example whether to observe social norms or ignore them.

In sociology, there is no agreement as to how people are motivated to act in the world. From one perspective, people are organised by social pressures and constraints that are not of the individual's choosing; while from another, people exercise free will and make choices. For the chemist, biologist and physicist, there are things that can be seen and measured with at least some degree of certainty (although this is not to suggest that these sciences are in any way easier or that scientific understanding is fixed and unchanging). However, for the social scientist studying families, education, crime and social stratification, the observations they make and the conclusions they reach are even more uncertain and open to debate. That is the challenge that faces all sociologists.

Link

For more information, see Research methods on pages 38–77.

Extension

Research the life and work of Howard Becker (1928–).

Activities

1 Make a list of ten 'facts' that you believe to be true about the education system. Do some research and see if you can find some evidence to support your ideas. Compare your ideas with those of the rest of your class. Identify any points of disagreement. How many of your 'facts' reflect your personal values?
2 Make a list of ten things that limit an individual's ability to make choices. Hold a class debate to decide how true it is to say that an individual can exercise free will and make choices in their day-to-day lives.

Check your knowledge

1 What do sociologists mean when they talk about objectivity?
2 What do sociologists mean when they talk about empirical facts?
3 What do sociologists mean when they talk about a structuralist perspective?

Summary

- In sociology, there is a long tradition of objectivity – the attempt to present a picture of the world as it is and not how the researcher might like it to be.
- It is a controversial question in sociology as to whether there are any absolutely value-neutral facts when it comes to the study of human behaviour.

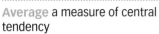

Key learning

You will be able to:
- explain what statistical analysis is
- explain how statistical data is presented
- explain why sociologists look for patterns and trends.

KEY TERMS

Average a measure of central tendency

Interval data data presented on a scale, e.g. calendar years

Mean an arithmetical average

Mode the most frequently occurring value

Nominal data a simple count, e.g. the number of times a particular type of behaviour is observed

Ordinal data counting in categories arranged in rank order

Ratio data data measured on a scale from absolute zero

Raw data numerical data that has not been processed or analysed

Standard deviation the spread of data from the arithmetical mean

Trend the general direction (either increasing or decreasing) as revealed by the data

Interpretation of data (1)

Statistical analysis

Some social scientists think that quantitative data represents a 'gold standard' in social research, but any sort of statistical data needs to be treated with caution. The questions to ask are: What does the data show? Who was responsible for collecting it and why, and when did they do so? For the student studying sociology for the first time, it is not really necessary to have a sophisticated and detailed understanding of statistical techniques. However, it is important to have a basic awareness of different types of statistical data and how such data can be analysed. For example, you should be familiar with the following statistical terms and ideas:

- Official statistics are produced for the government, for example data on crime and social attitudes.
- Non-official statistics are produced for non-governmental organisations such as charities or the mass media.
- **Nominal data** means counting something, for example the number of male or female students in a school or college.
- **Ordinal data** means counting things assigned to various categories in some form of rank order, for example questionnaire responses ranked from disagree to strongly agree.
- **Interval data** uses some sort of scale, for example calendar years.
- **Ratio data** makes similar use of a scale but with the difference that the scale begins with absolute zero, for example the number of children in a family (the family has zero children before the birth of their first child).
- **Raw data** refers to the numbers a sociologist gathers in their research before undertaking any sort of analysis, and would include completed questionnaires among other things. The first step in analysis requires the organisation of raw data into *groups,* such as various types of classroom interactions and the *frequency* of those interactions, for example the number of questions asked by boys as opposed to girls. Collections of related statistical data are known as data sets.

An **average** is a *measure of central tendency* in the data; statisticians use the terms **mean**, median and **mode**. The mean is a simple arithmetical average (add up the total number of test scores and divide by the number of students taking the test and you end up with the arithmetical average or mean score in the test). The median is the mid-point in the data (list all your test scores from the lowest score to the highest, locate the middle value and you have found the median). The mode is the most common value, for example the most frequently achieved test score. **Standard deviation** refers to the spread of data relative to the arithmetic mean. (This is only really useful when dealing with interval and ratio data.)

Presentation

Changing raw data into charts and tables is a step on the way to making sense of the data. However, it is important to remember that it is part of a process and not an end in itself. Charts and tables have a horizontal axis (known as the 'x' axis), which shows the *independent* variables, for example calendar years. The vertical (or 'y' axis) shows the *dependent* variables, for example different types of criminal activity.

- Tables are a useful way of presenting nominal data.
- Bar charts are a good way to show comparisons between categories or the frequency of an event. Bar charts are usually presented vertically and have a gap between the bars. They can also be turned on their side or the bars can be split to show different categories (referred to as a stacked bar chart). Histograms are really a type of bar chart that has no gaps between the bars.
- Scatter plots can be used to show relationships between two variables.
- Line graphs are a useful way of showing trends in the data.
- Pie charts are useful for showing the different proportions of various categories.

Patterns and trends

Sociologists look for patterns and trends in data because they can reveal important truths about society. For example, Peter Townsend in his study of poverty (*Poverty in the United Kingdom*, 1979) created a deprivation index – essentially a list including a number of indicators such as holidays, entertainment and various household amenities. He then gave each household in his study a score on this index. Using these scores, Townsend was then able to identify a threshold for incomes below which the amount of deprivation rapidly increased.

Sociologists look for connections between variables in statistical data: the stronger the apparent connection the more important or significant it becomes. Statistical tests of significance take this one step further by using mathematical techniques to determine how *probable* it is that a relationship exists between variables. Ultimately, the most important question is: What does the data tell us about society? For example, how much crime is there and what standards are being achieved by students taking public examinations?

Check your knowledge

1 What is interval data?
2 What is raw data?
3 What is the alternative statistical term for 'average'?

Summary

- Studying sociology at GCSE level does not require a detailed understanding of sophisticated statistical techniques.
- It is important to have a basic awareness of how quantitative data can be collected and analysed.

Links

- Examples of various types of graphs, charts and tables are shown on pages 70–71.
- For more information on quantitative data, see pages 60–61.

Activities

1 Write a short paragraph to explain the difference between official and non-official statistics. Do some research into how official statistics are collected. You might find this website a useful starting point: https://data.gov.uk/publisher/office-for-national-statistics.

2 Identify some examples of statistical data that would be of interest to a sociologist studying contemporary British society. You might find this website a useful starting point: www.ons.gov.uk/peoplepopulationandcommunity

Extension

Pat Carlen in her study of women and crime (*Women, Crime and Poverty*, 1988) presents a lot of her data in the form of tables. Find some other examples of sociological research presented in the form of graphs, charts or tables.

Interpretation of data (2)

Table

▼ **Table 2.1** Crime statistics (Crime Survey for England and Wales 2019, ONS)

Year	2009	2010	2011	2012	2013	2014	2015	2016	2017	2018
Number of offences (Thousands)	10,432	9,544	9,711	9,593	8,757	7,554	7,177	6,529	6,006	6,244
Number of offences including computer fraud (Thousands)									10,747	10,720

Bar chart

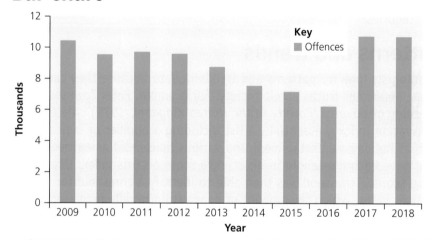

▲ **Figure 2.1** Vertical bar chart showing crime statistics, England and Wales (2009–18)

Line graph

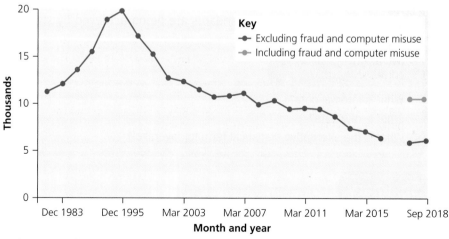

▲ **Figure 2.2** Line graph showing levels of crime, December 1983 to September 2018 (Crime Survey for England and Wales 2019, ONS)

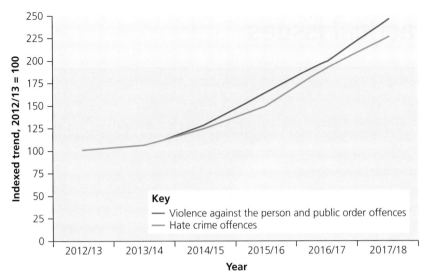

▲ **Figure 2.3** Number of violence against the person and public order and hate crime offences, 2012/13 to 2017/18 (2012/13 = 100) (Home Office Statistical Bulletin 20/18, Hate Crime, England and Wales, 2017/18)

TIP

Always remember to look at statistical data with a critical eye, for example, who collected this data and what does it actually measure?

Activities

1 Can you identify the trends shown in the statistical representations on these pages? Which of the examples best shows trends?

2 Do you notice anything that might be misleading about the presentation or labelling of any of the examples?

3 Draw up a pie chart, a stacked bar chart and a scatter plot based on suitable data. If you are unfamiliar with any of these, your teacher should be able to help. (It might also be worthwhile to spend time becoming familiar with Microsoft Excel.) Remember that pie charts are best suited for showing different proportions based on various categories: a stacked bar chart splits each bar to show different categories (for example, male and female), while a scatter plot shows relationships between two variables. You should find the social trends website a useful source of data: https://data.gov.uk/dataset/social_trends.

Extension

1 What can you discover about the Crime Survey for England and Wales (what, who, when and why)? You should find this website helpful: www.crimesurvey.co.uk.

2 What can you discover about the pattern of divorce? You should find this website helpful: www.ons.gov.uk/peoplepopulationandcommunity/birthsdeathsandmarriages/divorce.

KEY TERMS

Controlled conditions variables that can affect research data are recognised and taken into account

Grounded theory a research method that allows theory to emerge from the data collected

Literature review a critical review of previous work on the topic of your investigation

Plagiarism pretending that the work of another is your own

Practical issues

▲ 'I would rather have questions that can't be answered than answers that can't be questioned', Richard Feynman, physicist

All researchers face practical problems when conducting their research; these are often categorised as time, cost and access. However, this is a little misleading as it would be wrong to assume that practical problems would disappear if there were no time limits, infinite resources and no issues over access, a set of circumstances that in 'real world' terms never exists.

It is perhaps more useful to consider the important decisions that need to be made if a sociologist is to avoid the most common hazards when completing a research project. It is also important to remember that all sociological research is, in a sense, a compromise between what the researchers might like to achieve, given an ideal situation, and what it is actually possible to achieve in the field. For example, can the researcher gain access to a school or prison in order to conduct their research? How will the researcher identify victims of crimes and will those victims be willing to talk about their experiences?

Strategies and solutions

- Purpose: the researcher needs to have a clear idea about what they want to achieve. What is the aim of their research and can they express this purpose simply and clearly? For example, Pat Carlen (*Women, Crime and Poverty*, 1988) captures her purpose as the need 'to understand the relationships between poverty, women's law breaking and women's [imprisonment] rates ... as compared with men.'

- Success: in order to judge the success or failure of a piece of research, it must be judged against its aims.
- Method: are the tools selected suitable for the purpose? For example, while questionnaires might seem to be a relatively cost-effective research tool, are they an appropriate tool to use when investigating a complex area like human relationships?
- Grounded theory: the natural sciences are built around a model of research that begins with testing a theory; you establish a hypothesis built on previous theories. You then establish controlled conditions that allow you to say with at least some degree of certainty that you can prove or disprove your hypothesis. In the social sciences, qualitative research methods such as 'grounded theory' begin from a different starting point. The purpose of the research is to reveal rather than test a particular theory; you observe the behaviour of people in a particular social situation and you suggest, on the basis of your observations, ideas that explain their behaviour. However, such an approach does not free the researcher from the need to establish a clear statement of purpose from the outset.
- Personal interest: the ideal for all scientific research is to establish objective, evidence-based conclusions. However, in the social sciences, the choice of what to research will often reflect a personal interest and previous life experiences. Feminist researchers, for instance, approach the study of society from their own particular perspective. The fact that the vast majority of feminist researchers (though not all) are women can be a real advantage when it comes to working in the field. Without some sense of a shared life experience it is unlikely that feminist researchers would be able to readily access the candid life histories of women, for example in respect of their involvement with crime: 'When I had the children it was my job to go down town every day and pinch them something. Especially when they were starting back at school. It was never clothing for myself, always for the kids' school.' (Carlen, 1988, page 115.) However, it remains the responsibility of the researcher to retain an open mind and support their claims with the evidence they have obtained.
- Background reading: it is necessary for the researcher to be familiar with the work of others in their chosen area of investigation. Researchers refer to this as the literature review; this process helps the researcher to establish what is already known, what research studies have already been conducted and to view this prior knowledge and understanding with a critical eye. Recognising and referring to the work of others is not plagiarism (when someone passes off someone else's work as their own).

Resources

It is still essential for the researcher to cover basic costs, for example photocopying, postage, printing questionnaires and travel. Whatever they hope to achieve, these practical considerations are very real constraints.

Activity

Explain the practical problems you would face in attempting to arrange and carry out a research project in a:

- hospital
- school
- prison.

Extension

Research the methods used by Peter Townsend to investigate poverty (*Poverty in the United Kingdom*, 1979).

Check your knowledge

1 From memory, list three practical problems that a researcher might encounter. (Check your answer against the list provided.)
2 What is plagiarism?
3 What is grounded theory?

Summary

- All researchers face practical problems when conducting their research, such as time, cost and access.
- All research is, in a sense, a compromise between what the researchers might like to achieve, given an ideal situation, and what it is actually possible to achieve in the field.

Key learning

You will be able to:
- explain ethical considerations
- explain informed consent
- explain anonymity and confidentiality.

KEY TERMS

Confidentiality the need for researchers not to publish the personal details of respondents (without their consent)

Data Protection Act the law regarding the storage and use of personal information

Ethical considerations the need for researchers to ensure that their work neither causes harm nor unnecessary offence to participants, e.g. anonymity, confidentiality and informed consent

Generic name in sociological research, a name used to conceal the real identity of a place or organisation, e.g. Cornerville

Key informant a knowledgeable participant in sociological research

Pseudonym in sociological research, a name used to conceal the identity of an individual informant

Ethical issues

Ethical considerations

Ethical considerations are questions of right and wrong. In practical terms, this generally comes down to observing a detailed code of professional ethics designed to guide the researcher through the potential problems they may face and establish a model of good practice. The British Sociological Association publishes such a code that sets out 'to make members aware of the ethical issues that may arise throughout the research process and to encourage them to take responsibility for their own ethical practice'. For example, and in summary, key points include the following:

- The need to ensure the safety of researchers and avoid any harm to participants.
- Avoiding making statements to the media that are based on inadequate evidence.
- Basing relationships on trust and integrity.
- Obtaining consent from individuals involved in the research. (Covert research may be justified under certain circumstances, but such research violates the principle of informed consent.)
- Protecting individuals through confidentiality and anonymity.
- Storing data in a secure manner.

Informed consent

Informed consent is a basic principle of modern scientific research; its origins can be traced back to the idea of universal human rights that emerged after the Second World War. For example, 'The Nuremberg Code' (1946) established the basis for ethical medical research following horrific revelations about Nazi experiments on concentration camp victims and prisoners of war.

Essentially, what this means is that as a general rule anyone who participates in sociological research must be informed of the nature and purpose of that research. They should be able to understand what is expected of them, what they are being asked to do, given an opportunity to withdraw if they no longer wish to participate, and have their information securely stored and anonymised. This restriction can create problems for research involving groups of people who might not be able to give informed consent, for example young children or adults with learning disabilities. However, the British Sociological Association also recognises the existence of other circumstances when it may be impractical to gain such consent and when the researcher may wish to observe covertly (in secret) in order to avoid a situation where 'participants change their behaviour'. Some famous examples of sociological research have been based on such covert observations. For example, in the 1960s, a young Scottish teacher with the help of one of his pupils was able to secretly observe and record violent gang behaviour (James Patrick, *A Glasgow Gang Observed*, 1973).

Anonymity, confidentiality and safety

Anonymity does not exclusively apply to the subjects of research, for example, James Patrick was not the real name of the young teacher who observed the behaviour of Glasgow gangs. He chose to keep his identity a secret, a sensible precaution given that he had secretly observed a group of violent young men. However, for the most part, anonymity is applied to the subject, for example Frances Heidensohn (*Women and Crime*, Macmillan, 1985) concealed the identity of one of her key informants by using the pseudonym 'Rosa'. Similarly, the use of a generic name for an organisation or institution can help to maintain anonymity. For example, the sociologist Stephen Ball used the name 'Beachside Comprehensive' to conceal the identity of the south-coast secondary school that he studied (*Beachside Comprehensive: A Case-Study of Secondary Schooling*, 1981). Some care needs to be taken when using pseudonyms or generic names as some readers will regard this as a challenge and try to solve the riddle of identity. However, it is also important not to distort the data in any way by, for example, changing the gender of informants. The researcher has to maintain a reasonable balance between the need for anonymity and the essential truthfulness of the data.

Sociological research creates a large amount of raw data, interview recordings and transcripts, completed questionnaires and field notes, all of which must be kept securely and not usually revealed to anyone who is not involved in the research project. However, for sociologists, there are limits to this principle of confidentiality. Doctors and priests have a special legal status that allows them to maintain confidentiality under all circumstances, but sociologists have no such legal protection and have a duty to reveal anything that might be used as evidence in a criminal case or that might prevent harm coming to an individual involved in their research. Making your informants aware of the limits of confidentiality is one of the requirements for gaining informed consent.

On a practical level, data needs to be secured and reasonable precautions taken to ensure that it does not become public knowledge. Locked filing cabinets, secure password-protected computers and servers are all reasonable steps that need to be taken. The Data Protection Acts (1998 and 2018) establish legal obligations for researchers to store data securely and ensure that it is only used for the purpose of research.

Researchers also need to be careful to ensure no harm comes to anyone involved in their research; this includes members of the research team (who must not be placed at risk) as well as participants who might suffer emotional or physical harm because of their involvement.

Extension

Research the circumstances that led to the drafting of 'The Nuremberg Code' in 1946. (Be guided by your teacher about access to suitable resources.) Write a paragraph to explain the meaning of 'informed consent' in sociological research.

Activities

1. In a university setting, sociological research has to be submitted for approval to an 'ethics committee'. Run a class simulation of a committee meeting to consider research proposals from members of your group. If you decide to reject a proposal on ethical grounds, you must explain why and then discuss possible solutions. Examples you might consider include research in a:

   - prison
   - hospital
   - school.

2. Devise your own ethical code for researchers. Use the six bullet points based on some of the ideas from the British Sociological Association (see page 74) as your starting point.

Check your knowledge

1. What is informed consent?
2. What do sociologists mean when they talk about a key informant?
3. What is a pseudonym?

Summary

- Ethical considerations are questions of right and wrong. Has the researcher obtained informed consent? Can the researcher ensure the anonymity of informants and the confidentiality of data?

KEY TERM 🔑

Sociological research methods these include questionnaires, interviews and observation

TIP ✅

Base your research on your school or college whenever possible.

Small-scale research projects

Practical experience

GCSE Sociology does not require students to complete coursework. However, the AQA specification encourages teachers to create opportunities for their students to learn from the practical application of research methods:

'Teachers may encourage their students to undertake small-scale research projects in order to develop their understanding of the practical difficulties faced by sociologists working in the field.'

AQA GCSE Sociology Specification (2017)

You are required to know how to use a variety of sociological research methods and to understand how they apply in the specified contexts, such as families, education, crime and deviance and social stratification. Learning from experience will give you a deeper understanding of the advantages and disadvantages of various research methods and prepare you. It can also be an interesting and rewarding experience for all involved.

A checklist for small-scale research projects

- Does the subject of your research clearly relate to the content of the specification?
- Have you found any useful reference material, for example the work of other sociologists?
- Is there enough time to complete the research project and do you have the resources you need (for example the printing cost of questionnaires)?
- Is the research method you have chosen appropriate?
- Do you have access to the people or other sources of information that you need?
- Will you be able to make generalisations on the basis of your research? For example, will it be possible to say that the observations you make of this group of students can then be applied to others in a similar situation?
- Will you be able to say that your research is reliable and valid?
- Is an objective position *relevant* for your study?
- Will you be able to obtain informed consent from your respondents?
- Will your respondents remain anonymous and will you be able to keep your research data confidential?
- Will you and your respondents be safe from any potential harm (emotional or physical)?

Possible research topics

The following list is not intended to be prescriptive (things you should do) or exhaustive (in any way a complete list of all possible topics).

It is intended to make you think about a variety of possible topics for research that you might wish to pursue:

- Investigate the different subject choices made by male and female students.
- Investigate the classroom behaviour of male and female students.
- Investigate attitudes towards masculinity and femininity among students.
- Investigate the division of housework and childcare among married and cohabiting couples.
- Investigate attitudes towards marriage.
- Investigate levels of truancy among school students.
- Investigate attitudes towards alcohol use between students from different socio-economic backgrounds.
- Investigate attitudes towards exercise and diet between students from different socio-economic backgrounds.
- Investigate attitudes in wider society towards immigration following the EU referendum.
- Investigate the crime rate in your local area using secondary sources.
- Investigate the way in which mass media present different images of men and women.
- Investigate attitudes towards the welfare state among students.
- Investigate the way in which mass media report benefit fraud.

Before you begin your project, refer back over the contents of this chapter and make sure you are familiar with key ideas. For example, do you understand why it is important to establish clear aims? Will you be using a pilot study? Do you need a hypothesis?

Writing up and learning from your research

When you write a report on your research try to include the following:

1 Briefly explain your aims: What were you trying to achieve?
2 Explain the research method you chose and justify your choice of research method(s), for example why you used a questionnaire rather than interviews, or why you used both.
3 Did you use a pilot study?
4 Briefly explain how you dealt with any ethical or practical problems.
5 Analyse your results and present them in an appropriate way, for example using graph(s), chart(s), text or a combination of all three.
6 Write a conclusion: What do you think it all means and were you surprised by anything?
7 What have you taken away from the experience? For example, what have you learned about the problems facing sociologists working in the field?

This exercise is all about learning from experience. You should be prepared to read and comment (positively) on the work of others. When you compare notes, the obvious question to ask is: 'If you were going to start this project again, what would you do differently?' If the answer to that final question is 'everything', the student concerned should probably have spent more time working through the checklist above!

Summary

- The AQA Specification encourages teachers to create opportunities for their students to learn from the practical application of sociological research methods.

Sociology research methods

Practice questions

AQA Sociology requires students to demonstrate their understanding of relevant research methods and methodological issues, for example the use of research methods in context. What this means in simple terms is that you will be asked questions about sociological research methods and how they can be applied by sociologists working in each of the four topic areas: Families, Education, Social Stratification, and Crime and Deviance. This includes multiple choice questions based on the 'key terms' relating to research methods to be found in the specification glossary (Appendix A: key terms and concepts).

Question 1 (multiple choice question)

Which of the following terms is used to describe an ethical consideration? [1 mark]

a) Attitude
b) Social class
c) Ethnicity
d) Informed consent

> **TIP**
> Use the glossary to identify key terms that you need to know.

Answer and commentary

Option D (only one option is correct) – sociological research generally requires informed consent from participants, in other words they have agreed to be involved. There are certain circumstances where research can be covert (secret) but this is relatively unusual. Some questions (worth 2 marks) will ask you to evaluate a particular piece of research, e.g. to examine either a strength or weakness of a particular piece of research. An example of this type of question can be found at the end of the chapter on Crime and Deviance referencing the work of the sociologist Pat Carlen.

Question 2 (paragraph answer)

Identify and explain one advantage of using a questionnaire to research parents' attitudes towards education. [4 marks]

Answer and commentary

This question is asking about one advantage of using a questionnaire to research parents' attitudes towards education. Don't be tempted to just describe what a questionnaire is or explain all the disadvantages of questionnaires as a research tool.

Remember that this question is worth 4 marks and you only have to identify one advantage of questionnaires in the context of the question (parents' attitudes towards education). You need to identify an advantage and then develop this into a paragraph.

You could write about:

⇨

- Questionnaires as a relatively cost-effective way of reaching large numbers of parents. It would not be correct to describe questionnaires as 'cheap' but they are certainly not as expensive as large-scale interview-based research projects. Questionnaires are also a 'reliable' research tool (the research can be repeated by other researchers), the data produced can be expressed in numbers that reveal patterns and trends, e.g. are middle-class parents more positive about education than working-class parents?

- Questionnaires can be useful if you are trying to gain access to people who are not usually available during normal working hours. Many school-age children will come from homes where both parents are in full-time employment. Spending some time online or filling in a form is generally easier for working parents than finding time to speak to an interviewer.

- If you are trying to gauge a parent's attitude towards education, questionnaires can overcome some of the problems associated with face-to-face interviews, e.g. some parents might be reluctant to express negative attitudes about their children's education to an interviewer. The parent would probably correctly assume that the researcher has been educationally successful and will have generally positive attitudes about education; the parent might then respond to questions with answers that they think the interviewer wants to hear (this is called the 'interviewer effect' or 'interviewer bias').

Question 3 (mini-essay)

Essay questions will ask you to 'discuss how far sociologists would agree' with a particular statement. You will be given credit by the examiner for demonstrating a relevant understanding of research methods and methodological issues.

Discuss how far sociologists would agree that Britain is a meritocratic society.   [12 marks]

Answer and commentary

In your answer you could choose to include reference to research into education and how open society is with regard to social mobility as part of your answer (see the chapters on Education and Social stratification for other relevant points that you could make in response to this question, e.g. arguments for and against the idea that Britain is a meritocratic society). For example:

'Research conducted by the Social Mobility and Child Poverty Commission found factors like attending private schools and "Oxbridge" were still significant to achieving the top jobs in society. In addition, it found that 65 per cent of people believe "who you know" is more important than "what you know", and three-quarters of people think family background has a significant influence on life chances in Britain today ('Elitist Britain?' Social Mobility and Child Poverty Commission (2014)).'

Diane Reay's work would be crucial for this as she routinely shows that working-class students are routinely suffering the worst educational experiences and opportunities in British schools (see: www.educ.cam.ac.uk/people/staff/reay/bjes-zombie.pdf).

The examiner will expect you to show some evidence that you can analyse and evaluate this research data, e.g. you could raise questions about the size and composition of the survey quoted in the report. You might also cross-reference this research with alternative data, e.g. the relationship between private education and 'top jobs'.

The sociology of families

Functions of the family: functionalist perspective

There are different viewpoints from which sociologists examine society. This is the case when looking at the functions of the family. Different sociologists have different views on the nature and role of the family. These reflect their differing ideas about the nature of wider society. Functionalists, Marxists and feminists explain the functions of the family in different ways.

Here, we look at the functionalist explanation and pages 83–84 look at alternative explanations to functionalist explanations.

Activities

1 Look at the three photographs. What functions are family members performing?
2 In your opinion, can family functions be performed just as effectively by other institutions?
3 What is the role of the family in society?

KEY TERMS

Dysfunctional family a family which does not meet society's needs in socialising children and supporting adults. This may be a family in which conflict, neglect and even abuse are common experiences

Expressive role the family member who provides care and emotional support to other family members

Instrumental role the family provider (usually associated with the traditional role of the adult male)

The functionalist theory of the family

For many years, the sociology of the family was dominated by functionalist theory.

Functionalists always ask about the purpose or function of an institution – what good does the institution do for society and individuals?

Functionalists are interested in identifying the positive functions of a family for society. They view the family as the cornerstone of society because it plays the dominant role among all social institutions in making individuals feel part of wider society, for example through primary socialisation. Functionalists see the nuclear family as beneficial and necessary for the smooth running of society and the personal development of individuals.

Two key functionalists were American sociologists George Murdock and Talcott Parsons.

Murdock (1949) studied 250 societies, from small hunting and gathering societies to modern industrial countries like the USA. In all these societies, he claimed that the nuclear family was universal; some form of it existed in every society.

Murdock argued that all families fulfil four vital functions:

1 Sexual: marital sex creates a powerful emotional bond between a couple, encourages fidelity and therefore commits the individual to family life. This encourages stable relationships which helps maintain stability in society.

2 Reproductive: society requires new members to ensure the continuation of society. This generally occurs within a marital and family context.

3 Educational: culture needs to be transmitted to the next generation, so children need to be effectively socialised into the dominant values, norms, customs and rituals of a society. This is the process of primary socialisation where children learn to talk, learn manners and learn to follow rules, for example.

4 Economic: adult family members provide shelter, food and money for their children. When families buy things to meet the needs of their children, this also helps to maintain the economy.

Link

For more information on functionalism, see pages 16–17.

TIP ✓

Try to memorise the functions of the family identified by both Murdock and Parsons. Practise writing paragraphs to develop these points and give examples. They form the starting point for any answer about functionalism and family functions.

Activity

Do you think the modern family still performs all of these functions? If you think there has been a change to these functions, think about the reasons why these changes have occurred.

KEY TEXT 🔑

Parsons T., 'The social structure of the family' in Anshen R.N. (ed.), *The Family: Its Functions and Destiny*, New York, Harper and Row, 1959.

Parsons (1959) focused on the American family and argued that the family has two important functions that cannot be performed by other institutions:

1 Primary socialisation: Parsons believed that families are vital in passing on the norms and values of society. Families are responsible for teaching children the rules, patterns of behaviour and belief systems that make involvement in social life possible. Reflecting US society at the time, Parsons saw mothers as playing the major role in the process of nurturing and socialising children. He believed men and women were biologically suited to certain roles – women to the expressive role and men to the instrumental role.

2 Stabilisation of adult personality: Parsons argued that the second specialised function of the family is to relieve stresses of modern-day living. This 'warm bath' analogy claims that family life stabilises adult personalities. The family does this by providing a warm, loving home where adults can be themselves and relax. The emotional support and security within the family reduces stress from work and other activities outside the home and this then strengthens social stability.

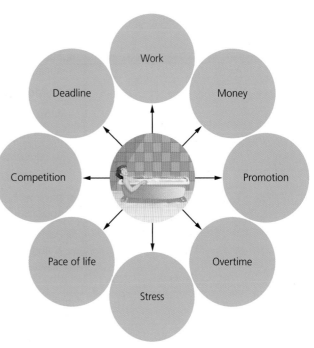

▲ **Figure 3.1** The 'warm bath' theory

Activity

Do you think the modern family still performs these two functions?

Extension

Go back and look at your answers to the activity questions on page 80 – have you included these two functions in your response?

As you will see, the functionalist theory emphasises the integration and harmony between the different parts of society and sees the family as a vital 'organ' in maintaining the 'body' of society. However, this view has been challenged in many ways:

- Functionalists paint a rosy picture of family life and ignore conflict that may occur, in particular the darker side of family life such as violence and child abuse.
- David Cheal (2002) points out that functional relationships can easily slip into dysfunctional relationships and are, therefore, not as harmonious as functionalists believe them to be.
- Functionalists' views on the family are based on white middle-class and American family life and have not considered families that may be different, for example by ignoring how ethnicity, religion and class influence the family structure or that women are not solely responsible for domestic roles.
- Murdock and Parsons' research may no longer be relevant in contemporary society. It might have been relevant in the 1950s, but there has been a steady increase in sexual activity and reproduction outside the family and attitudes towards this have changed in recent years. Also, Parsons' separation of the instrumental and expressive roles is clearly not always the case today where most married and cohabiting couples are both wage earning and share caring tasks.

Check your knowledge

1 Identify and explain the four functions of the family identified by Murdock.
2 Identify and explain the two functions of the family identified by Parsons.

Summary

- Functionalists believe that families are functional for individuals and society.
- Murdock believes that the nuclear family performs four functions:
  1 Sexual
  2 Reproductive
  3 Educational
  4 Economic.
- Parsons believes that the family has two irreducible functions: primary socialisation and stabilisation of adult personality.
- Parsons suggests the 'warm bath' theory – the family provides a warm, loving home where adults and children can relax.

Functions of the family: Marxist and feminist perspectives

As you will know from pages 16–23, there are different viewpoints from which sociologists examine society. Different sociologists emphasise and explain society in different ways; this is also the case when looking at the functions of the family. Functionalist theory is just one theory – others are Marxist and feminist theories of the family, which we will examine here.

Marxist theory on the functions of the family

Marxists look at how the family contributes to the maintenance of society's structure. However, unlike functionalists, Marxists do not regard the nuclear family as a functionally necessary institution for society to work. Marxists see the family within the framework of a capitalist society, which is based on private property, driven by profit and involves conflict between social classes with opposing interests.

Marxists argue that the nuclear family performs several important functions for capitalism:

- Families are seen as 'consumer units' as they buy products for their family, for example family cars, houses, family boxes/bags of food, large televisions, and so on. Capitalism needs consumers to buy its products so the bourgeoisie can make a profit. The family is an important market for consumer goods and families are, therefore, supporting capitalism, and the inequalities of capitalism go unchallenged by a generation fixated on the acquisition of the latest goods.
- Capitalism as a problem remains unchallenged when families effectively become competitive units fighting over resources like school places, housing and childcare. Marxists argue that if resources were communal, the distribution of resources would be allocated according to need rather than the ability to pay.
- Private property is an important asset to the nuclear family and by passing it on, families can build up wealth over generations. Until the 1880s women could not own and control property so historically, men would pass their wealth on to their sons to ensure that it stayed in the family. However, this also meant that the woman became the property of her husband, who controlled her sexuality to ensure he was the father of her children. This reproduced gender inequality as well as the social class system. Women can now inherit property on the same terms as men which has helped reduce gender inequality but families still seek to acquire as much private property as possible over generations.
- The process of primary socialisation in the family reproduces and maintains class inequalities. Marxists claim that the family is one way to maintain and reinforce a set of ideas which in turn maintain capitalist society.
- Families also support capitalism by providing unpaid labour by reproducing, caring for and socialising the next generation of workers, and providing emotional support for workers to help them deal with the exploitation they experience in work.

Link

For more information on feminism and conjugal roles, see pages 22–23 and 96.

TIP ✓

By including different types of feminism in your answer you can show your understanding of different theories.

Check your knowledge

1 Identify and explain two key points of the Marxist approach to the family.

2 Identify and explain one criticism of the Marxist approach to the family.

3 Identify and explain two key points of the feminist approach to the family.

4 Identify and explain one criticism of the feminist approach to the family.

Extension

Describe, compare and contrast functionalist, feminist and Marxist sociological perspectives on conjugal role relationships. A useful approach here would be to draw a table with three columns for the content appropriate for each of the perspectives.

Summary

● Functionalists focus on the positive aspects of the family.

● Marxists focus on inequalities in society and the family.

● Feminists focus on the inequalities that exist between men and women in society and the family.

Criticisms of the Marxist theory

The idea that men marry and have children to pass on property ignores other reasons for getting married or forming families. Also, inheritance tax and other ways of redistributing wealth from families mean that family is not necessarily a safe way to hold on to private property.

The idea that families exist to pass on ruling class ideas ignores the other things that go on in families. People today are more likely to marry for love and affection rather than a social obligation.

Marxism could be seen as being over-negative, playing down the benefits that families hold for their individual members, such as the emotional aspects of relationships and personal fulfilment for both parents and children.

The importance of family cannot be understood by class and inheritance of wealth alone. Classical Marxism ignores factors like gender relations and cultural factors like religion, which also play an important role in social reproduction beyond the economy.

Feminist theories on the functions of the family

Feminism is not a unified perspective and different kinds of feminists take very different views on the extent of patriarchy (male dominance) in the family, as well as having different views on solutions to the oppression of women.

▼ **Table 3.1** Comparing feminist perspectives

Marxist feminist	The nuclear family functions to benefit both capitalism and the patriarchal interests of men. For example, it benefits the wealthy as children are reared and socialised to become the workforce of the future at little or no expense to the bourgeoisie. The family is also seen to benefit men as women traditionally were viewed as responsible for housework and caring for their children. Confining women to the home empowered men as they were the providers. Now the norm is for mothers to work, but taking time out of the labour market to have children often means that women lose out on promotion at the very age when their male partners are experiencing rapid career advancement.
Radical feminist	The nuclear family is a patriarchal institution which mainly functions to benefit men because gender role socialisation serves to empower men. This results in boys and girls behaving in stereotypical ways, for example the sexual division of labour.
Liberal feminist	They recognise inequality between men and women but actively campaign for changes in the law to ensure equality is recognised.

Criticism of feminist theories

Radical feminists and some Marxist feminists assume that all male/female relationships involve male exploitation of women. This is not always the case and modern relationships are becoming equal with shared roles.

Feminist activism has achieved significant social change, such as the expansion and success of women in the workplace. However, it has been less able to tackle other forms of sexism and has sometimes been considered a 'woman's issue' rather than something both men and women suffer from. For example, in recent years more attention has been paid to the mental health struggles faced by men and boys because gender roles do not allow men to express emotions as freely as women.

Family forms

Postmodernists talk about families rather than **family** since in contemporary society there are a range of family types. There has also been a significant increase in the number of people living outside the family, such as in singlehood (lone person households) and child-free couples.

Sociologists define a family as: a group of two or more people linked by birth, marriage, adoption or **cohabitation** based on a long-term relationship.

Activity

Think about the above definition. Describe the type of families you and your friends live in.

Some questions to think about

1 Do you need adults of both sexes in a family?
2 Do you need to have children to be called a family?
3 Is your pet dog a member of the family?

There are many different types of family structure in modern Britain, including:

- **Nuclear family** – a family group consisting of parents and their children.
- **Extended family** – parents, their children and other more distant relatives, e.g. grandparents, aunts and uncles.
- **The reconstituted (or blended) family** – when two adults with children from previous relationships remarry (or cohabit) to form a new family.
- **Lone parent family** – a family with only a mother or father as a consequence of death, divorce or individual choice.
- **Same sex family** – families headed by a couple of the same sex.
- **Beanpole family** – a family whose living members come from many generations, but with few members in each generation.

Key learning

You will be able to:
- identify, describe and explain various family forms (nuclear, extended, reconstituted, lone parent, same sex).

KEY TERMS

Beanpole family a family whose living members come from many generations, but with few members in each generation

Cohabitation partners who live together without getting married

Extended family parents, their children and other more distant relatives, e.g. grandparents, aunts and uncles

Family a group of two or more people linked by birth, marriage, adoption or cohabitation based on a long-term relationship

Family diversity the many different types of family structure that exist in contemporary society

Lone parent family a family with only a mother or father as a consequence of death, divorce or individual choice

Nuclear family a family group consisting of parents and their children

Postmodernism theory that sees society as having distinctly different characteristics to the era of modernity which it replaced, with more diverse and less stable family structures and a blurring of family roles

Reconstituted (or blended) family when two adults with children from previous relationships remarry (or cohabit) to form a new family

Same sex family families headed by a couple of the same sex

TIP

It is important that you know these different types of families.

What is a household?

The term 'household' is used to describe a group of people who live together in the same dwelling, for example a group of people living together and sharing a kitchen and a bathroom. For you, your family and household might be the same thing, but they may be different.

> ## Activity
>
> Are the following families or households?
>
> - A group of students at university sharing a house.
> - A father living with his two children.
> - Parents and children living in the same house as the mother's parents.
> - A lodger renting a room in a 'family home'.
> - A father, mother and their dependent children.
> - A couple providing foster care.
> - Two parents and their children living apart together (e.g. one parent lives overseas, or a child is at boarding school).

> ## Activity
>
> Draw a timeline to show how an individual's family structure could change over their life course.

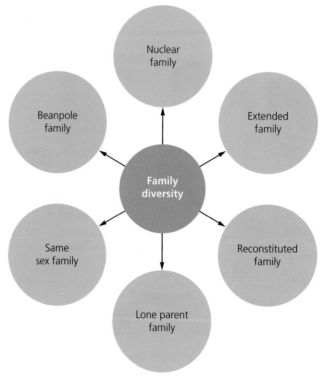

▲ **Figure 3.2** Family types in Britain today

> **TIP** ✓
>
> Make sure you are able to identify and explain the different types of families in modern Britain.

Different family forms

If we look at the variety of families that exist in Britain today, we find that there are many different types of families. This is known as family diversity and is shaped by factors like separation and partnering, changing values and cultural diversity associated with factors like immigration.

Over the last 60 years, many different types of families and households have emerged. Families differ in many ways. For example, they vary according to whether the partners are married, in a civil partnership or cohabiting. They also differ in terms of whether the couple is same-sex, opposite-sex or includes a transgender or non-binary partner.

Family diversity is also experienced by individuals over their life course (during the course of their own lifetime). For example, a baby could be born into a lone parent family and later may become part of a reconstituted family. As a young adult, they could live with friends in a shared house before living on their own in a single-person household. After this, they could live with their partner before having children and forming a nuclear family.

Extension

Ask as many people as you can who they live with. Think about the different types of family discussed and illustrated on these pages in order to decide what questions you will ask them. However, remember that individuals can be sensitive about their own families so may not want to share. If this is the case then you could categorise families on a TV programme.

Summarise your findings and draw a conclusion about the diversity of families in modern Britain.

Check your knowledge

1 Explain the difference between a family and a household.
2 Explain what is meant by a nuclear family.
3 Explain what is meant by an extended family.

Summary

- Families and households are different.
- There are many different types of families in Britain today – this is known as family diversity.
- Family types in Britain today include: nuclear, extended, lone parent, same sex, reconstituted and beanpole families.

You will be able to:
- understand how family forms differ in the UK and within a global context
- explain and evaluate the work of the Rapoports on family diversity.

Family diversity

As you will have seen from pages 85–86, there are many different types of families in Britain today.

Statistics from the Office for National Statistics (ONS) indicate that there are many different family types in the UK.

Activities

1 Look at the statistics in Table 3.2 below and summarise what they show.
2 Identify:
- the different types of families in the UK
- how families have changed over time.

▼ **Table 3.2** Statistics from the Office for National Statistics on different family types in the UK (ONS, 2018)

Family type	1996			2017		
	With dependent children (thousands)	Without dependent children (thousands)	Total families (thousands)	With dependent children (thousands)	Without dependent children (thousands)	Total families (thousands)
Married couple family	5,223	7,418	12,641	4,944	7,890	12,834
Opposite sex married couple family	5,223	7,418	12,641	4,938	7,862	12,800
Same sex married couple	n/a	n/a	n/a	6	28	34
Civil partner couple family	n/a	n/a	n/a	8	47	55
Cohabiting couple family	540	934	1,474	1,251	2,040	3,291
Opposite sex cohabiting couple family	539	920	1,459	1,246	1,943	3,190
Same sex cohabiting couple family	n/a	15	16	4	97	101
Lone parent family	1,631	814	2,445	1,781	1,037	2,817
All families	7,444	9,811	17,254	7,983	11,014	18,997

TIP ✓
Using some statistics shows a good understanding of the topic you are explaining.

KEY TEXT 🔑
Rapoport R. and Rapoport R.N., 'British families in transition' in Rapoport R. *et al.* (eds), *Families in Britain*, London, Routledge and Kegan Paul, 1982.

Statistics show us that the nuclear family is still the most common type of family in the UK. However, families are changing and, as the statistics suggest, there are different types of families in the UK today.

In 1982, Robert Rapoport (1927–96) and Rhona Rapoport (1927–2011) were among the first sociologists to identify these changes that were taking place in UK families. They argued that the nuclear family was increasingly accompanied by a range of other family types and households that were growing in popularity.

Functionalists like Parsons tended to view the nuclear family as 'better' at functioning than any other types. However, the Rapoports were much more optimistic about the increasing prevalence of diversity in family forms and though they were writing almost 40 years ago, pre-empted the postmodernist position that people should have more freedom and choice about the type of family they live in. To their credit, they argued that there is not a 'right' type of family and all families should be accepted.

Robert and Rhona Rapoport identified five types of family diversity.

1 Organisational diversity

There are huge organisational differences between families and within families. The decline of marriage and the increase in divorce has led to a huge increase in different types of families, for example lone parent families and reconstituted families. There is also diversity within families due to different patterns of work inside and outside the home, for example dual-career families, stay at home parents, and the extent to which the division of labour (domestic tasks such as cooking, cleaning, childcare) is shared – or in the case of lone parent families, shouldered primarily by the one parent.

2 Cultural diversity

Cultural differences account for much family diversity. When families migrate to Britain, from areas like Africa, Asia, the Caribbean and even parts of Europe, their culture, ethnicity and religious beliefs can become factors that add to the diversity of British families.

Globally, the family can be quite diverse in terms of family and household composition with different families practising different cultural styles of marriage, such as:

● monogamy
● polygamy
● polygyny
● polyandry.

The Rapoports have also considered how differences in religious beliefs affect family development. For example, they discussed the Catholic Church's strong support of marriage and belief that divorce, contraception and abortion are incompatible with its beliefs. For practising Catholics this has significant influence on family structure in terms of family size, low divorce rate and even reinforcing a traditional division of labour. However, like many other major religions, the influence of the Catholic Church has declined in recent years in Western countries. For example, today there is almost no difference between the birth control practices of Catholics and non-Catholics in the UK.

The Rapoports also suggest that South Asian families in Britain have a distinctive family form, based around patriarchal structures (male dominated), which give seniority to the eldest male. While culturally some South Asian families are often characterised by a commitment to marriage (frequently arranged) and tight-knit families with a strong sense of family loyalty, it is important to avoid over-simple generalisations about minority ethnic families. For example, Richard Berthoud (2000) argued two decades ago that white, Caribbean and South Asian families are all moving in the same direction: declining rates of marriage, growth in cohabitation and a rising divorce rate.

3 Social class diversity

The Rapoports discussed variations in family structures, attitudes and conjugal roles between different social classes (upper, middle and working). They suggested that there is greater instability in lower-class

KEY TERMS

Arranged marriage a matchmaking practice instigated through relatives or friends

Divorce the formal (legal) ending of a marriage

Empty nest family a stage in the life cycle of a family when children have reached adulthood and have left the parental home

Life chances the opportunities each individual has to improve their quality of life

Marriage a cultural phenomenon that gives legal status to a union between two partners and any children they may produce

Monogamy the practice of being married to one person at a time

Polyandry the practice of a woman having several husbands (rare but found in the Himalayas)

Polygamy the practice of being married to more than one wife or husband at the same time

Polygyny the practice of a man having several wives

Activity

One of the criticisms of the Rapoports' work is that they do not give sufficient awareness to cultural differences associated with family life. Do some research into BAME (Black Asian and minority ethnic) families living in the UK today. You might find the following websites a useful starting point: www.ethnicity-facts-figures.service.gov.uk/uk-population-by-ethnicity/demographics/families-and-households/latest and www.runnymedetrust.org/projects-and-publications/appg/david-lammy-on-fatherhood.html

background families. However, the effect of social class on families is a complex area and care must be taken to avoid simplifications and stereotypes.

For example, while there is clearly a world of difference between the family life of an upper-class aristocratic family and what Charles Murray (1984) would call an 'underclass' (see page 239) family living on a run-down housing estate, the old class distinctions of the past have become somewhat blurred in postmodern society. Social class and family life clearly still have an impact on **life chances** such as educational attainment, but there is often as much variation within as there is between social classes when looking at factors like the division of labour or the socialisation of children.

4 Life cycle diversity

Families move through different stages and have different priorities at those different stages. Differences occur when a couple has a baby, when the children reach their teens and, finally, when they leave home (leaving their parents with an **empty nest**). At each of these stages, families may organise themselves differently in terms of work and domestic labour.

For example, when children are very young, traditionally the mother is likely to stay at home and look after the children and take responsibility for the majority of the housework. However, currently it is estimated by the ONS (2018) that around one in seven fathers are the main child-carers and 'millennial' dads are generally more open to the idea of being hands-on with regard to childcare and housework.

5 Cohort diversity

Cohort diversity is about how family structure is different depending on events in the world, for example the impact of war creating more single women (as after the First World War) or lone parent families. The Great Depression in the USA impacted upon fertility rates as well as characterising the economic situation of a generation. Families over time have also had different attitudes towards family life, for example divorce, cohabitation and marriage.

The Rapoports concluded that a fundamental change is taking place in British family life.

Robert Chester (1985), however, criticises the Rapoports' research, claiming that the conventional family was defined by clear gender roles for men and women and that the major change since the 1950s has been the rise of 'neo-conventional families' where wage earning and homemaking are no longer tied to gender roles.

Link

For more information on joint conjugal roles, see page 96.

TIP ✓

This study by Rapoport and Rapoport is important as it provides evidence for family diversity in Britain.

Link

For more information on Robert Chester, see page 92.

Extension

Research more about Robert Chester. Why does he argue that family life has remained unchanged since the 1950s?

Check your knowledge

1 Using an example, briefly explain what is meant by family diversity.

2 Identify and briefly explain the five different types of family diversity identified by Rapoport and Rapoport. Give an example for each family type.

Summary

- There are many different types of families in the UK today – this is known as family diversity.
- Statistics show that many different types of families exist.
- Rapoport and Rapoport identified five types of family diversity and have concluded that there has been a change to family structure.
- Chester does not believe that family structure has fundamentally changed.

Is the nuclear family still important in modern Britain?

Despite the many different types of families that exist today, the stereotypical image of the nuclear family still stands out as being a common choice. In its traditional form, it consists of a mother and father together with their dependent children. The traditional image of the nuclear family implied the male breadwinner of father going out to work and the female homemaker of mother staying at home to do housework and care for the children. However, as the feminist Fawcett Society state: 'the model of the stay-at-home wife and the breadwinner dad belongs to the 1950s'.

For functionalists, the nuclear family is still seen as the ideal, typical family type in society (but others like feminists and postmodernists celebrate family diversity).

> ### Research in action
>
> In a newspaper article in 1968, Edmund Leach (1910–89) recognised the power of this image of the traditional family. Leach called this image the 'cereal packet image of the family' because it was a socially constructed model loaded with assumptions of how families ought to be.
>
> In 1982, Ann Oakley (1944–) described the cereal packet image of the family as one in which 'conventional families are nuclear families composed of legally married couples, voluntarily choosing the parenthood of one or more (but not too many) children'.

As noted in the Research in action box, images of the nuclear family are widely seen throughout the advertising industry. Adverts frequently use the 'cereal packet' family as a stereotypical image to best describe family life in Britain today, although to their credit, advertisers are increasingly using a diversity of family types. This is partly due to campaigns like the 'Get over it' campaign by LGBTQ charity Stonewall.

Using Ann Oakley's definitions, we can recognise that a cereal packet family has to meet the following criteria:

- It needs to be a nuclear family living with one or two of their biological dependent children.
- The couple is seen to be married (excludes lone parent).
- The couple is heterosexual (therefore, no same-sex couples).
- Dad is the breadwinner and Mum stays at home to look after the housework/children. She might also have a part-time job in order to bring extra money into the home.

Oakley concluded that 'there are signs that official stereotypes are felt to be increasingly archaic and that certain groups in the community may be moving towards a more open appraisal of other ways of living – both in and without families'.

In 2017 there were 19.0 million families in the UK. With 12.9 million families, the married or civil partner couple family remains the most common, with the cohabiting couple family growing the fastest. This suggests that despite recent changes in family structures, the nuclear family still remains the most common family structure.

KEY TEXT

Oakley A., 'Conventional families' in Rapaport R. *et al.* (eds), *Families in Britain*, London, Routledge and Kegan Paul, 1982.

Extension

Look up McCain's 'This is family' advert. Think about how it challenged ideas of what a 'normal' family looks like.

Link

Look at Table 3.2 on page 88 to see the different types of family in the UK today.

Activities

1 Watch advertisements during prime time television and make a note of:
   - the products being advertised
   - the roles performed by the mother, father and children.
2 Write a conclusion about whether the adverts show the stereotypical image of the traditional nuclear family.

Some sociologists, particularly the functionalists, see the nuclear family as being the perfect fit in a modern industrial society (see page 81).

The media and the nuclear family

Edmund Leach (1967), with his cereal packet family concept, highlighted how the media in general, and television in particular, present a stereotypical image of the family that is based around the roles of mothers, fathers and children in the traditional nuclear family. However, soap operas are increasingly using lone parent, reconstituted and same-sex families in their story lines.

The family life cycle

When looking at the traditional family, it is important to be aware of the family life cycle. This means the types of families and households an individual is likely to experience in their life. Each of us will have a different life cycle, but, as Robert Chester argues, most of us will spend some time during our lives in a traditional nuclear family.

Research in action

Chester (1985) argues that for most people the nuclear family remains the most typical family type. Most people will live in a nuclear family at some point in their lives. He argues that lone parent families, for example, normally come from nuclear families, and many lone parents will remarry and become nuclear families again. Although many people might live alone, most will marry eventually, or, if they are elderly, will be widows who have already been married.

Check your knowledge

1 Outline three reasons why the nuclear family is still seen as important in modern Britain.
2 Outline and explain three ways in which changes in society may have weakened the traditional nuclear family unit.

Extension

Using information from this section and from pages 88–90 on family diversity, do you think the nuclear family is still important in society today? Add your thoughts to each column in a table similar to the one below.

Yes, the nuclear family is still important	No, the nuclear family is not important

Summary

- The nuclear family is still a dominant structure in society today.
- Chester notes that most people live in a nuclear family at some point in their lives.
- The most common family type in 2018 was the married or civil partner couple family, with dependent children.
- Functionalists see the nuclear family as being the perfect fit in a modern industrial society.
- The cereal packet family was shown in media advertising as the 'ideal family' but alternatives are now increasingly common.

Alternatives to the family

Not living in a family

Not everyone lives within a family. Some people:

- live on their own, as a couple or with friends
- move away from home when they are sent to boarding school or move into higher education
- live on their own or with other single people in sheltered or residential accommodation (primarily older people).

About one in three households today contains only one person, compared to one in 20 in 1901. Under half of these households are over pensionable age, compared to two-thirds in 1971. There is a growth in the number of younger people living alone.

There are nearly twice as many men as women living alone in the 25–44 age group, but there are twice as many women as men aged 65 and over.

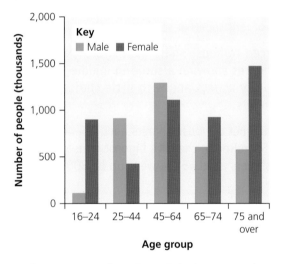

▲ **Figure 3.3** Number of people in the UK (aged 16 and over) living alone by age group (ONS, 2011)

Forms of communal living

Communes

A very small proportion of the UK population live in **communes**. These involve shared ownership of property, shared skills with other members and shared responsibility for people living in the community.

Kibbutz

Kibbutz were first established in 1910 in what became the newly created state of Israel in 1948. They aimed to provide communal living for individuals who wanted to be part of that sort of lifestyle.

The original kibbutz offered a radical alternative to family life. To free up men and women for the economic work of the kibbutz, children were reared and educated communally. In some kibbutz children from the

Key learning

You will be able to:
- identify and explain how family forms differ in the UK and within a global context.

KEY TERMS

Commune a group of people living together and sharing possessions and responsibilities

Infanticide the intentional killing of infants

Kibbutz a collective community in Israel that was traditionally based on agriculture

Patrilineal inheriting or determining descent through the male line

Activities

1 Make a list of the reasons why younger people today are more likely to live alone than in previous years.

2 Look at the graph in Figure 3.3. What trends can you identify in the age distribution of people living alone? Use the above explanations to explain this pattern.

TIP

Use some statistics as evidence in your answers.

age of six months lived in communal 'children's houses' where they ate, studied and slept in mixed dormitories up to 18 years of age. They were looked after by a rotation of staff and would visit their parents for a set time each afternoon until early evening. Adults, when not working in agriculture, a kibbutz industry or enjoying family time, undertook duties on rotation, such as working in the kibbutz canteen or laundry.

Ideologically, kibbutz members wanted to eradicate the traditional nuclear family in favour of the group. Private intimacies between parents and children were discouraged in case they diverted members' energy from the kibbutz project. By the 1990s most had abandoned the communal children's houses and returned to the nuclear family.

Today there are 274 kibbutz groups across Israel.

House share

Shared households are becoming much more common, particularly among young people as a transitional period between youth and adult roles. The cost of housing today often prevents people from buying or renting homes on their own so many engage in shared living. Some people buy a house and then invite a friend or advertise for a lodger to share it with them. People may also buy a house together or rent together so they can share bills.

The number of individuals forced to house share well into their forties has risen dramatically, with figures showing a surge in middle-aged renters priced out of the property market and with little choice but to live with friends or even strangers.

Between 2009 and 2014, the number of house sharers aged 35–44 rose by 186 per cent, according to SpareRoom, the UK's biggest house share website, while the number of sharers aged 45–54 went up by 300 per cent.

Residential homes

Elderly people who struggle to look after themselves may live in residential homes where they have their own room but may also share in the community life of the home.

Families in a global context

There are many different types of families in Britain today and this is also true if we look at families across the world.

Families throughout the world are structured in different ways.

According to Talcott Parsons (1902–79), the contemporary family form is the nuclear family composed of a breadwinner husband, a homemaker wife and their children. Parsons sees this particular family form emerging as a result of modernisation and industrialisation and replacing the extended family.

This functionalist model of the family sees the nuclear family as the ideal family type around the world. This view was especially advanced by William Goode (1963), who believed that, as countries develop, extended families would be replaced by the functional nuclear family. This led Goode to believe that the nuclear family was essential for modern industrial society.

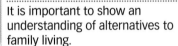

Activity

Do some research on the kibbutz and its way of life. Make a list of the advantages and disadvantages of living in a community like a kibbutz. Why do you think most kibbutz have returned to nuclear family living?

TIP ✓

It is important to show an understanding of alternatives to family living.

However, is this really the case throughout the world?

In the traditional Chinese family, very different roles and rights were assigned to men and women as respectable women were never to be seen in public. This meant men had a lot more power and could participate in public life respectably but women could not. However, the modern family is rapidly changing, with the United Nations Development Programme's Human Development Report (2010) giving China a gender equality ranking similar to the USA.

In the past, the cultural ideal was for three generations (parents of the husband, husband and wife and, usually, one child) under one roof. The role of extended kin, although still important especially in rural China, has lost ground to nuclear families though, particularly in urban areas.

Famously China introduced a one child per family rule in the late 1970s. Because boys were culturally valued within the patrilineal descent system, this resulted in high levels of female infanticide. It is estimated that at least 30 million girls are 'missing' in China, either aborted before or killed after birth. The one child policy was officially phased out in 2016 and in modern China girls and boys are usually treated equally.

When considering families in South Asia, and descendants who have migrated to the UK, the importance of the extended family is significant. However, it is important not to over-generalise family life in a way that ignores differentiation. Such differences not only occur between Sikh, Muslim and Hindu families, but also include the impact of factors such as social class location and individual family aspirations and values. For example, over 30 years ago Westwood and Bhachu (1988) stressed that Asian families are as diverse as white families. They also note that changes that have affected families in general have also affected Asian households, such as a move towards younger generations placing an increasing value on the nuclear family.

Studies of the Caribbean, such as Sheila Stuart (1996), have highlighted how the two most common family systems are, firstly, the importance of either marriage or cohabitation and, secondly, households headed by persons of either sex. However, it is important to emphasise that these characteristics varied across islands and from community to community. Caribbean migrants to the UK brought the tradition of a tightly structured extended family similar to the South Asians, but often the supportive network of relationships goes beyond immediate kin into the broader community.

Activity

Find out more about family structures in different societies. Make a note of the key aspects of family structure and family life within the culture you have investigated.

Summary

- There are many alternatives to living in a family and there are many different reasons why people may not live in a family.
- Communes, house shares, co-housing and residential homes are common alternatives to the family in Britain.
- Families throughout the world are structured in different ways.

Check your knowledge

Identify and explain two alternatives to living in a family.

Key learning

You will be able to:

- identify, describe and explain joint and segregated conjugal roles
- describe and explain the domestic division of labour in both traditional and contemporary families
- recognise how conjugal role relationships impact on decision making, money management and leisure activities.

KEY TERMS

Conjugal relationships the relationship between marital or cohabiting partners

Conjugal roles the roles typically associated with male and female partners

Domestic division of labour household tasks divided between family members

Double shift (dual burden) working women who continue to perform the bulk of domestic labour are said to work a 'double shift' of paid employment followed by an unequal share of household work

Dual career families a family in which both parents have careers

Joint conjugal roles male and female partners share household tasks

Money management the power relationship surrounding how finances are spent within the family

Segregated conjugal roles male and female partners perform different and clearly defined activities

Triple shift the three types of work that create a burden for women: paid work, domestic work and emotional work

Link

Refer back to the work of Ann Oakley on page 91.

Conjugal role relationships

Traditional roles within the family

Domestic labour refers to the roles associated with housework and childcare. A leading exponent of the functionalist perspective, Talcott Parsons, argued that the instrumental role of men as the main breadwinner and the expressive role of women as the homemaker were both natural and normal. While such ideas are now viewed as outdated, it is worth considering that within the UK some minority ethnic groups still adhere closely to traditional roles.

Conjugal roles mean roles divided between cohabiting or marital partners.

In 1957, Elizabeth Bott (1924–2016) argued that there are two types of conjugal roles: segregated and joint. Segregated conjugal roles are where the conjugal couple have separate roles. There is no blurring of tasks with a clear breadwinner and homemaker.

Joint conjugal roles are where the couple share housework and childcare, a relationship that has become more common since the 1970s.

▼ **Table 3.3** Differences between segregated and joint conjugal roles

Segregated conjugal roles	Joint conjugal roles
Partners in a married or cohabiting relationship have clearly separate roles.	Partners in a married or cohabiting relationship have interchangeable and flexible roles.
The breadwinner takes responsibility for bringing in money and often makes the major decisions. Men traditionally (but not always) did the heavier and more technical jobs around the home, such as repairing household equipment and doing DIY. The homemaker has responsibility for housework, shopping, cooking and childcare. They are unlikely to have full-time paid employment.	Both partners are likely to be in paid employment (dual workers). Household tasks and childcare are more likely to be shared between the male and female partners.
Partners are likely to have different friends and different leisure activities.	Partners have the same friends and have similar leisure interests. They also both make family decisions.

The greater equality in marriage or cohabiting relationships is often thought to be shown by women taking on more 'traditional men's work' (especially working outside the home) and men taking on more 'traditional women's work' (housework, shopping and childcare) with shared leisure and decision making. In their research on families who had moved from Bethnal Green to 'Greenleigh', Young and Willmott (1957) talked of 'changing roles' as women became important breadwinners and men were judged to be participating more with domestic labour. Such was the apparent 'jointness' between the marital couples that Young and Willmott described their relationship both in the home and in their leisure time as 'companionate'.

However, feminists in particular challenge the view that conjugal roles are becoming joint with a more equal domestic division of labour. Arlie Hochschild (1989) coined the phrase 'second shift' to highlight the fact that women working longer hours outside the home are still responsible for the bulk of the housework. Research also shows that where men do take on more domestic work, they tend to take on the 'masculine' jobs such as DIY and non-routine jobs that do not need doing every day. Knudsen and Wærness (2007) examined 34 countries and found that there were no modern countries in the world where men do more housework or as much housework as women. Where women are in paid work and doing most of the housework it is referred to as the dual burden (Oakley). In effect, they have two jobs, one outside the house and one inside the house.

The triple shift, identified in 1995 by Jean Duncombe and Dennis Marsden, takes this one step further and adds emotional work to women's responsibilities, where women take primary responsibility for the emotional needs of the family. There is, in addition, the possibility that elderly parents may need to be looked after as well. Increased life expectancy means that people are living longer and the practical burdens of caring for elderly relatives generally fall on the woman in the family, even though they already carry most of the burden of housework and caring in their own homes. Older women in particular are taking on more caring responsibilities, with a quarter of women aged between 50 and 64 regularly caring for an ill, frail or disabled relative, as do 17 per cent of men in this age group.

Research has found that the narrower the gap in financial resources between the couple, the more egalitarian the division of household labour becomes. However, with dual-career, dual-earner, cohabiting and same-sex couples, the dynamics of conjugal relationships is complex, making generalisations difficult.

▲ Men were traditionally seen as the breadwinner while women were viewed as the homemaker, but this is changing

Activity

Ask your parents and grandparents about their experiences of how jobs were divided in the home.

Decision making and money management

In terms of domestic roles, sociologists are interested in decision making. Evidence shows that the person with most resources (money, education, status) exercises most 'authority' in making important decisions. This historically has been the male, but with increasing numbers of dual career families, women's economic status should enhance their participation in decision making. Rank (1980) found women with income, education and occupational prestige had more power in their marriages than women with low resources. The growth of same-sex families removes the gender relationship in decision making. In terms of money management Jan Pahl found that an increasingly large proportion of couples now pool their money, either in a common kitty or in a joint bank account. Nevertheless, inevitably a relationship exists between a person's financial contribution to the household and their power within it.

Leisure

The changing roles perspective, advocated by Young and Willmott, implies a jointness not only in roles but leisure time as well. The prevailing view is of a conjugal companionship centred around shared leisure activities, such as watching television, going to the cinema and dining out. Many leisure facilities are geared to family leisure, such as restaurants, leisure centres and theme parks. However, research by Crawford *et al.* (2004) found that men's leisure preferences often dominated what couples did, proving to be both a cause and a consequence of female partners' dissatisfaction.

Research in action

Edgell (1980)

Stephen Edgell (1942–) interviewed middle-class couples and found that men had decision-making control over things both husband and wife saw as important, while women had control over what they considered to be minor decisions. He linked this to the fact that men often brought higher earnings into a household.

Edgell found women:

- had sole responsibility for decisions in unimportant areas like home decoration, children's clothes and spending on the household, for example food
- were less likely to make decisions felt to be important in the family.

Pahl (2005, 2008)

Jan Pahl was interested in who makes the decisions within opposite sex families, including decisions about how to spend money, where to go on holiday, where to live, how the children should be raised. She found that:

- the method of money management in couples reflects who earns the most
- individuals had some independence in financial matters, for example, own bank account.

This was more likely among younger couples, those without children and those where the woman worked full time. In these cases, nearly a half of men and women maintained some financial independence. Only one-third of women who worked part time had financial independence. Very few women had financial independence if they did not work.

Burns, Burgoyne and Clarke (2008)

Burns, Burgoyne and Clarke looked at decision making for same-sex couples and found greater diversity than in opposite-sex couples.

TIP

Conjugal roles will vary considerably between individual couples and social groups. Try not to generalise too much in your answers.

Activity

The term 'new man' has been introduced to describe a man who is now taking on more traditional female roles within the family. Do you think 'the new man' exists?

Extension

Do you think roles within families are more equal? Use the information in this chapter to complete a table like the one below.

Yes, roles are more equal	No, roles are not more equal
Men are doing more work in the home	Dual burden

Check your knowledge

1 Explain what is meant by the 'dual burden'.
2 Explain what is meant by the 'triple shift'.
3 Explain what is meant by 'the new man'.

Summary

- Traditionally, men went out to work and women stayed at home – this is known as segregated conjugal roles.
- In the modern family, more men help in the home and women go out to work – this is known as joint conjugal roles.
- Feminists believe women still do more in the home. They refer to this as the dual burden and the triple shift.

Conjugal roles: functionalist and Marxist views

As you will know from previous chapters, there are different viewpoints from which sociologists examine society. Different sociologists emphasise and explain different aspects of society. This is also the case when looking at the jobs performed within the family. Different sociologists have different views on who does or should do the household tasks. These reflect their differing ideas about the nature of wider society. Functionalists, Marxists and feminists explain conjugal roles in different ways.

Here, we look at the functionalist and Marxist explanations and pages 101–102 look at feminist explanations.

Functionalist views on conjugal roles

Functionalists believe that everything in society has a function. Writing in the 1940s and 1950s, they argued that it is 'natural' for women to be housewives and men breadwinners. The functionalist view is that both of these jobs are important and it makes sense for women to be the housewives and the carers because of their assumed nurturing characteristics. Functionalists, such as Parsons, argue that the woman should take on the expressive role of looking after the house and children, while the man should take on the instrumental role (breadwinner).

They argue that each partner has an important role to play, which makes the family more stable and is the most effective way of keeping society running smoothly.

An important part of primary socialisation according to functionalists is 'gender role socialisation'. They believe that if primary socialisation is done correctly, then boys learn to adopt the 'instrumental role' – they go on to go out to work and earn money. Girls learn to adopt the 'expressive role' – doing all the caring, housework and bringing up the children.

Evaluation of functionalism

- By looking at the roles that men and women are expected to perform (men – instrumental, women – expressive) in a positive way, functionalists ignore conflict in the family. For example, the feminist Fran Ansley colourfully described the role of women as 'takers of shit'.
- Parsons' view of the instrumental and expressive roles of men and women is very old fashioned. It may have held some truth in the 1950s but, today, with the majority of women in paid work, and the blurring of gender roles, it is more likely that both partners take on both expressive and instrumental roles.
- Functionalists assumed that gender is analogous to sex: that women and men behave the way they do because of their biology. However, there is no biological reason for the male breadwinner and female homemaker roles.

Key learning

You will be able to:
- describe, compare and contrast a variety of sociological perspectives on conjugal role relationships
- describe the key ideas of Zaretsky on families.

Link

Refer back to pages 80–84 on the functions of families.

Activity

Referring to pages 80–82, make a list of the key ideas of the functionalist approach.

TIP

It is really important to be able to evaluate sociological perspectives.

Link

For more information on changes in family structure over time, see pages 105–107.

TIP

If you are referring to Ansley's quotation in an exam, you must put it in quote marks.

- Functionalists tend to ignore the way women suffer from the sexual division of labour in the family. Even today, women still end up being the primary child carers in 90 per cent of families, and suffer the burden of unpaid extra work that this responsibility carries compared to their male partners.
- There is little recognition of family diversity. By assuming that everyone lives in a nuclear family, this ignores families such as those with only one parent, who by implication undertakes all roles.

Marxist views on conjugal roles

The Marxist position on conjugal roles is similar to the feminist perspective in the sense that they share the view that women are exploited and oppressed by domestic work. Marxists interpret the fact that men and women have different roles as evidence of the power of capitalism to control family life. Women and men have unequal roles because that structure supports capitalism.

They see women performing the 'reproduction of labour' on a daily basis as they feed and refresh the workforce ready for work the next day. The unpaid domestic labour women undertake keeps wages low, because if workers had to buy in domestic and childcare services, their wages would need to be considerably higher.

Writing from a Marxist perspective, Eli Zaretsky (1976) does not believe that the family is able to provide for the psychological and social needs of the individual. He argues that the family supports capitalism by providing unpaid labour, reproducing the labour force and being a unit of consumption. Zaretsky also claims that the family cushions the pressures of capitalism, allowing individuals to express their frustrations with capitalism in a non-threatening way. The family offers a haven from the harsh realities of living in a capitalist society. This benefits capitalism as it helps to reduce the stress caused by the exploitation experienced by workers in the workplace. In his view, only socialism will end the artificial separation of family and public life, and make possible personal fulfilment.

Evaluation of Marxism

- The Marxist view ignores family diversity in a capitalist society, and that many women now work full time.
- Feminists argue that the Marxist approach focuses on social class and ignores the inequalities between men and women, which is the real source of female oppression.
- Marxism ignores the benefits of a nuclear family, for example both parents supporting the children.
- Marxists see women's exploitation as a consequence of capitalism, ignoring other possible causes.

KEY TEXT

Zaretsky E., *Capitalism, the Family and Personal Life*, London, Pluto Press, 1976.

TIP

It is important to know the key points for each of these perspectives.

Extension

Make a list of the similarities and differences that exist between functionalist and Marxist theories.

Check your knowledge

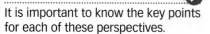

1 What is meant by the instrumental role and the expressive role?
2 Explain one criticism of the functionalist view on conjugal roles.
3 Explain one key point of the Marxist view on conjugal roles.
4 Explain one criticism of the Marxist view on conjugal roles.

Summary

- There are several different perspectives on conjugal roles within the family.
- Functionalists believe each partner has an important role to play, which makes the family more stable and is the most effective way of keeping society running smoothly.
- Marxists believe that women doing unpaid work in the home is supporting capitalist society.

Conjugal roles: feminist view

Feminist views on conjugal roles

On pages 99–100, you learned about functionalist and Marxist explanations of conjugal roles. It is very difficult to measure the extent to which roles are shared within the family. Consequently, there is a lot of debate about this topic and we will now look at feminist views on conjugal roles.

Research in 2012 by the Institute for Public Policy Research found that just one in ten married men does an equal amount of cleaning and washing. They also found that almost half of women still did 13 hours or more housework per week.

A study by the European Social Survey (2013) found that consistently across Europe, including the UK, women continue to be responsible for most of the housework and experience the double burden of paid and domestic work.

Figures from the Office for National Statistics reveal that in 2018 there were just 223,000 stay-at-home dads looking after babies and toddlers, but this figure is up ten-fold compared to ten years earlier. This compares to the 1.91 million stay-at-home mothers recorded in 2017. Nonetheless, this figure is falling, just 9.2 per cent of working-age women today are stay-at-home mothers or housewives, compared to 15.9 per cent when records began in 1993.

Radical feminists focus on patriarchy as the means of oppression within the home. In 1992 Christine Delphy (1941–) and Diana Leonard (1941–2010) argued that it is men rather than capitalism who benefit the most from exploiting women and the family is central in maintaining this structure:

▲ Just like their mothers, daughters tend to do more domestic tasks than sons

Link

For more information on conjugal roles and domestic division of labour, see pages 96–97.

KEY TEXT 🔑

Delphy C. and Leonard D., *Familiar Exploitation*, Cambridge, Polity Press, 1992.

Activity

Copy the table below and summarise the key points on conjugal roles.

Feminists	Marxists	Functionalists

- The family is structured in such a way that men dominate the family.
- Men generally make the important decisions in the family.
- When women have paid employment outside the home, they still have to undertake household tasks – this is known as the 'the dual burden.'

Women often fulfil the emotional role of looking after children, elderly parents and their partner as well as the dual burden – Duncombe and Marsden (1995) refer to this as the triple shift.

Domestic labour

Delphy and Leonard recognise that men do some housework, but the extent of this is rather limited. Women also make the largest contribution to family life, while men contribute the least but gain the most. Writing from a feminist perspective, Delphy and Leonard emphasise that it is men, rather than capitalists as such, who are the prime beneficiaries of the exploitation of women's labour.

Supporting their husbands

Women still carry out the bulk of housework and caring roles within the family as well as supporting men in their leisure and work activities. They do this directly by helping with administration work, if they're self-employed, or indirectly by offering emotional support and guidance if there are any problems at work.

Evaluation of feminism

- Functionalists would argue that feminists put too much emphasis on the negative side of family life because it ignores the possibility that women enjoy running the home, raising children and being married.
- Feminists play down Young and Willmott's ideas on the symmetrical family, and challenge the assumed shift towards greater equalities in family life with more sharing of conjugal roles.

Check your knowledge

1 Outline three reasons for the continuing inequality between men and women in contemporary families.
2 Using one example, briefly explain how family life may disadvantage women's careers.

Summary

- There is still a debate concerning whether conjugal roles are joint or segregated.
- Feminists explain how females are exploited within the family.
- Oakley, Delphy and Leonard, as well as other feminists, believe that women are exploited in the home.

Conjugal roles: research

Sociology and research

It is important that you understand how sociological research is conducted. Doing some research for yourself helps you to develop this understanding.

The previous pages have focused on conjugal roles in the family and how these have changed. Lots of research has been done looking at the roles that husbands and wives fulfil in the family.

Research in action

Jonathan Gershuny (2008) conducted research where he asked couples to keep a diary of all the time they spent on domestic and paid work. Gershuny found that:

- women had to reduce the time they spent on unpaid work, such as housework and family care, when they increased their hours of paid work
- as women's paid work activity increased, men were not compensating by taking up an equivalent of unpaid work.

Gershuny concluded that changes in the domestic sphere lag well behind the changing realities of women's employment.

Research by Man-Yee Kan (2001) at Oxford University found that:

- even though women were now working, they still did the majority of housework and childcare
- women in full-time employment were responsible for 65 per cent of the household chores
- the more a woman earned, the less housework she did. Every £10,000 increase in the woman's annual salary reduced her weekly housework time by nearly two hours
- if both partners had university degrees, there was more equality than less qualified couples.

Key learning

You will be able to:

- apply your knowledge and understanding of sociological research methods to issues relating to the family.

KEY TERM

Target population the whole group that is being researched

Link

For more information, see research chapter on pages 38–79.

Activities

1 Read through these pieces of research. Do they show joint conjugal roles or segregated conjugal roles? Use the evidence/statistics presented to explain why you have come to this conclusion.

2 Think about all the jobs done in the family (including daily jobs, decision making, children, and so on).

 a Write all these jobs on separate pieces of card.

 b Who do you think does these jobs? Distribute them between males and females or both.

 c Why have you distributed them in this way?

Now it's your turn to do some sociological research.

Strongly agree ☐

Agree ☑

Disagree ☐

Strongly disagree ☐

▲ **Figure 3.4** Questionnaire design is important

Research

You are to investigate the distribution of household tasks among people that you know by using a questionnaire.

1 Clearly outline what it is you are trying to investigate – what is the aim of the research?

2 Think about the strengths of using a questionnaire for this research.

3 How are you going to design your questionnaire – is it going to be multiple choice questions, closed questions or open questions? What are the benefits of using different questions?

4 What are you going to include on your questionnaire? Make sure it is relevant and includes the information you need.

5 Who is your **target population**? Think about this carefully – you need to ensure you get the information that you want.

6 How are you going to select your sample? What are the advantages of this sampling technique?

7 How many are going to be in your sample? Explain why.

8 How are you going to distribute the questionnaire? What are the advantages of this method?

9 What are the ethical issues you need to consider?

10 Conduct a pilot study. Why is this important for your study?

11 Amend your questionnaire or your sample, if necessary.

12 Distribute the questionnaire.

Results and conclusions

● Summarise the results – what do they show about conjugal roles?
● Write some key points about what you have found.
● Write a conclusion about what the results show.
● Write a paragraph about whether or not your findings support the Research in action on page 103.
● What difficulties did you have with completing this research?
● How would you do your investigation differently if you did it again?

TIP ✓

Conduct as much research as you can. This will give you a greater understanding of the issues involved in conducting sociological research.

Summary

● There is a lot of sociological evidence (including your own) to show how jobs are distributed within the household.
● Gershuny and Man-Yee Kan have shown that women still do more housework than men. Does your research show the same pattern?

Changing relationships within families

The family has changed considerably over time in terms of:

- size
- function
- roles within the family.

Pre-industrial families, 1600–1800

Pre-industrial families were characterised by the dominance of a family-based economy where all family members worked at productive tasks differentiated by sex and age. They worked as a productive unit producing things needed for the family's survival. The family also performed many functions such as health care, education and welfare.

Parsons (1955) argued that pre-industrial societies were largely based on extended family networks. Land and other resources were commonly owned by a range of relatives extending beyond the nuclear family. The extended family was responsible for the production of food, shelter and clothing and would trade with other family groups for the things they could not produce themselves. However, Peter Laslett (see Research in action) challenges Parsons' work, arguing the typical pre-industrial family in Britain was nuclear. Either way, home and workplace were the same thing – very few people left home to go to work.

At this time there was almost no social mobility, so roles passed from generation to generation and were determined by birth.

Industrialised families

Parsons argued that the Industrial Revolution brought about large changes to the family which became more geographically mobile as they needed to move towards towns for work. Parsons believed the nuclear family facilitated this by making it easier for family members to move away from their wider families to find work. As industrialisation progressed into the nineteenth century, women and children became increasingly excluded from employment by legislation. This served to empower men since the family became dependent upon them being the breadwinner. Since men earned the wages and decided how to spend them, this empowered them regarding household decisions. Women remained in the home, becoming primarily responsible for the socialisation of children and the emotional care and support of family members. A dramatic change occurred as children became seen as vulnerable and in need of protection and, as they were not able to work, children became dependent on adults. Towards the end of the century, as mass education was introduced, children became a concern of the state. The state gradually took over some of the functions of the

KEY TERM

Patriarchal family a male-dominated family group

Research in action

In 1965, Peter Laslett (1915–2001) studied the parish records of 100 villages in sixteenth- to nineteenth-century England. He argued that the average family was relatively small and that most households during this time contained an average of 4.75 people. He concluded that the nuclear family existed widely in pre-industrial England. Only 10 per cent of households contained family members beyond the nuclear family.

family, including education, health and welfare. This enabled the family to become more home-centred and specialise in child-centred functions such as socialisation.

Contemporary families

The family today is characterised by family diversity, with many different types of families. Contemporary families in Britain are more self-sufficient and can become more isolated from other family members. Roles have changed within the family and there is likely to be more sharing of roles by family members within the home. During the twentieth and early twenty-first centuries, families have become more child centred. The amount of time parents spend with children has more than doubled since the 1960s. Parents listen to their children and involve them in family decisions. The family has become a unit of consumption with leisure activities often centred on collective enjoyment, such as having take-aways, dining out or visiting theme parks.

The relationships between children and parents

The idea of childhood as a distinctive phase of life between infancy and adulthood is a relatively modern development. According to Philippe Aries (1914–84) childhood is a social construction, developed in Western societies in the sixteenth and seventeenth centuries. Prior to this, children were seen as miniature versions of adults – 'little adults' – and were expected to take on adult roles and responsibilities as soon as they were able. Children did not lead separate lives but mixed with adults. Until the mid-nineteenth century, child labour was common until restrictions were gradually implemented to protect children. The development of mass education from 1870 resulted in children becoming dependent on adults. This led to the emergence of a phase of 'childhood' where children lacked independence and were supported by adults. This period of dependency is getting even longer today, as young people need to stay in education or training until aged 18.

The relationships between children and parents has changed over time. Parents and older children (teenage children) lead increasingly separate lives. Elizabeth Silva (1996) argues that the role of parents is diminishing and being replaced by the influence of peers, teachers, the internet and computer games. With increased technology, parents can find it more difficult to regulate the behaviour of their children. Children and young people have far more access to unsuitable and harmful materials and this is raising concerns about the 'loss of childhood'. Recently, a lot of media attention has been given to the suicide of a student whose family blamed her death on the fact that she was reading distressing material about depression and suicide on social media.

The functionalist perspective (sometimes known as the 'march of progress' theory) portrays childhood as improving as a result of greater child-centredness within families. Functionalists claim that changes in attitudes have resulted in happier, safer and more valued children. Compared to the industrial family where the family was a unit of production, children have become objects of consumption, fun and pleasure for adults as they invest time and resources upon them. In addition, laws have been created to protect the child from exploitation and neglect within the family.

Feminists traditionally saw childhood as a time when girls became socialised within the family to accept women's secondary position in society. They argued that girls learned their future roles from observing the oppression of women generally and specifically the exploitation of their mothers within the patriarchal family. However, with the slow but positive changes to the role of women in terms of their status within the family, employment and society generally, daughters are increasingly being brought up to be equal to men.

Marxists see childhood as an era where family, and other socialising agencies, socialise children to submit to the capitalist system rather than being encouraged to question it. They also point to the problems that many children suffer from as connected to the capitalist society, such as experiencing poverty, neglect or abuse. Since the system is driven by profit, inevitably children become the casualties of low wages, alienated workers and frustrated parents with debt problems.

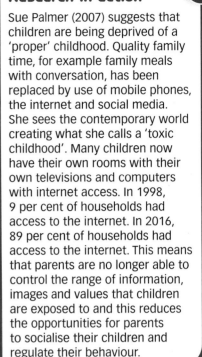

Research in action

Sue Palmer (2007) suggests that children are being deprived of a 'proper' childhood. Quality family time, for example family meals with conversation, has been replaced by use of mobile phones, the internet and social media. She sees the contemporary world creating what she calls a 'toxic childhood'. Many children now have their own rooms with their own televisions and computers with internet access. In 1998, 9 per cent of households had access to the internet. In 2016, 89 per cent of households had access to the internet. This means that parents are no longer able to control the range of information, images and values that children are exposed to and this reduces the opportunities for parents to socialise their children and regulate their behaviour.

TIP

Try to use some evidence in your answers to support what you are saying. We know that young people are spending more time using technology, so provide evidence to support this.

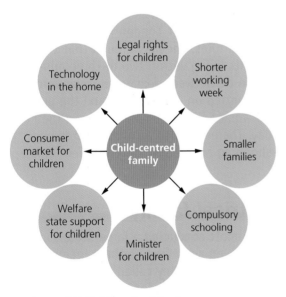

▲ **Figure 3.5** Child-centred family

Check your knowledge

Identify the key characteristics of the following types of families:
- pre-industrial
- industrial
- modern.

Summary

- Family structure, size of the family and roles of parents and children within the family have changed over time as a result of many factors.

Key learning

You will be able to:

- explain the theory of the symmetrical family and the principle of stratified diffusion developed from the functionalist perspective of Young and Willmott
- describe the key ideas of Young and Willmott.

KEY TERM

Symmetrical family a family where both domestic and economic responsibilities are equally shared between male and female partners

KEY TEXT

Young M. and Willmott P., *The Symmetrical Family*, Harmondsworth, Penguin, 1973.

Link

For more information on changes in family structure over time, see pages 105–107.

The symmetrical family

Michael Young (1915–2002) and Peter Willmott (1923–2000) conducted studies to investigate the domestic division of labour within families in London from the 1950s to the 1970s. Using a combination of historical research and social surveys, they traced the development of the family from pre-industrial England to the 1970s. From their research, they have suggested that the family has gone through four stages.

Stage 1: the pre-industrial family

The family is a unit of production with the husband, wife and unmarried children working as a team, generally working in agriculture. This type of family gradually disappeared as a result of the Industrial Revolution.

Stage 2: the early industrial family

This began with the Industrial Revolution (1740–1850). As family members became employed in mills, mines and factories, they operated as a unit of production. In the absence of a welfare state, the wider family often attempted to supported each other.

This type of family began to decline in the early twentieth century, but it is still found in some low-income, long-established working-class areas. Research by Young and Willmott in east London in the mid-1950s found clear-cut segregated conjugal roles. They also found that two out of three married people had parents living within two or three miles of their home. There was also a close tie between female relatives centred on the home and male relatives centred on employment and the pub. Over 50 per cent of the married women in the sample had seen their mothers during the previous day. There was also a constant exchange of services such as washing, shopping and babysitting between female relatives.

Stage 3: the symmetrical family

In the early 1970s, Young and Willmott conducted a large-scale social survey of families who had been moved away from Bethnal Green in the east end of London to new housing estates they called 'Greenleigh'.

They found that, compared to the segregated roles of stage 2, life was largely home-centred with leisure time being spent in the home (for example, watching television). Husband and wife had joint roles, increasingly sharing their chores around the house. A symmetrical family is a nuclear family where there are similar roles for both men and women in terms of housework, decision making and economic work.

Reasons for the rise in the symmetrical family

Improved living standards
Improved living standards at home such as television, central heating and computers have encouraged husbands to become more home- and child-centred – there is less need to go out for entertainment.

Increasing geographical mobility

Due to increased geographical mobility, families no longer live near each other so there is less support from other family members. Both husband and wife, therefore, have to complete the household tasks without the help from other family members.

Reduction in the number of children in the family

Due to more effective contraception, women have fewer children today and are more active in the labour market. With more opportunities for women in the labour market, men are finding that there are jobs to be done in the house and take on some of the more traditionally female jobs.

Commercialisation of housework

This refers to the range of consumer goods and services to help with reducing the burden of housework compared to previous generations, for example freezers, washing machines and online shopping. This means that housework is quicker and less skilled.

Improved status of women

As more women are in paid employment today, men may be more accepting of women as equals and not simply as housewives and mothers. Attitudes towards women have changed, which allows them to take on more jobs within society.

Young and Willmott found that the shift towards a home-centred symmetrical family was more pronounced in the working class. However, feminists like Oakley remained sceptical of its existence.

Stage 4: the principle of stratified diffusion

Young and Willmott claim that the principle of stratified diffusion accounts for much of the change in family life; that over time, whatever the top of the stratification system does, the bottom will eventually do, too. Upper and middle-class lifestyles, patterns of consumption, attitudes and expectations often become the dominant mode of expression, including within some working-class communities.

Applying this principle of stratified diffusion in 1973, Young and Willmott examined the family life of managing directors who were work-centred, whose leisure activities were less home-centred and who were less likely to involve their wives. The family was less likely to be symmetrical and roles were more likely to be segregated.

Young and Willmott controversially predicted that the asymmetrical family represents the next major development, as changes in technology and the reduction in routine work may result in the stage 4 family becoming more common throughout the stratification system.

TIP

Try to remember some of these explanations for the increase in the symmetrical family as they will form the foundation of an answer on changing conjugal roles and how roles within the family have changed.

Activity

Do you think the family today is symmetrical? Give a reason for your answer.

Extension

Using information on these pages and your own knowledge, complete a table with the following two headings to show both sides of this debate:

The family is symmetrical today	The family is not symmetrical today

Check your knowledge

1 Outline three reasons for the growth in the symmetrical family.

2 Explain what is meant by the 'principle of stratified diffusion'.

Summary

- Young and Willmott identified four different stages of the family.
- As the family developed, the structure changed with differences in the roles of men and women within the family.
- Young and Willmott claim that the principle of stratified diffusion accounts for much of the change in family life.

KEY TERMS

Dispersed extended family where kin are geographically separated but still maintain frequent contact

Local extended family where kin live in close proximity

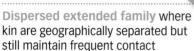

Activity

Think about how these three pieces of legislation influence family structure.

Extension

At the time of writing, in England and Wales for divorce proceedings to begin immediately, one partner needs to be found at fault (for example have committed adultery or behaved unreasonably).
The government is considering changing the law so this is not necessary. Think about what impact no-fault divorce might have on divorce rates. Then look up the effect of the law changing in Scotland where there is already no-fault divorce.

TIP

Make sure you are able to explain the reasons why there is family diversity in Britain today.

Link

For more information, see Reasons for divorce on pages 115–117 and Consequences of divorce on pages 118–119.

Reasons for changing relationships within families

Reasons for family diversity

There are many reasons why there is family diversity in the UK and these are discussed below.

1 Legal changes

There are several legal changes that have influenced family structure:

● Divorce Reform Act 1969
● Equal Pay Act 1970
● Marriage (Same Sex Couples) Act 2013.

The Divorce Reform Act 1969 made it easier for couples to escape an unhappy marriage on the grounds they had lived apart for two years and their marriage had 'irretrievably broken down'. As a result, the divorce rate rose significantly, more than doubling between 1969 and 1972. Today, approximately 42 per cent of marriages end in divorce, which has contributed to an increase in the number of lone parent families, reconstituted families and single-person households.

The Equal Pay Act 1970 stated that women and men doing the same job would get the same pay. This contributed to changes in the organisation of family life, including encouraging women to work outside the home and giving them more independence.

The Marriage (Same Sex Couples) Act 2013 allowed same-sex couples to get married in England and Wales. These marriages are now seen as the same as marriages between a man and a woman under the law of England and Wales. Between 2014 and 2015, 15,098 same-sex couples had legally married.

2 Change in social values and attitudes

The twentieth century brought big changes in priorities of people and their expectations of relationships. People tended to marry later and did not consider creating a family as the most important thing in their life. Today, more and more people choose to live alone, which now has less stigma attached to it than before. Previously, living alone gave negative status to women as it signified failure in finding a partner, but now views have changed and the number of women and men living alone has increased. It is also more acceptable to cohabit today and more people choose to cohabit as an alternative to or prior to marriage. There is also less social stigma attached to same-sex couple relationships.

3 Changing gender roles

An increasing number of women work and no longer need to depend on men for their financial security. Women are now much more likely to focus on their career and continue working once they have a family. For example, women now make up 47 per cent of the workforce. This goes some way to explaining the increase in single-person households. The increased earning power of women also explains the growth of the number of women who have never married and choose to have babies on their own. Although this only accounts for a relatively small number of lone parent households, the numbers are increasing.

4 Benefits for lone parents

The UK government provides benefits to lone parents to support them, which can make the decision to divorce and raise children in a lone parent household more of a reality. Previously, women would stay with their husband because men were commonly the breadwinner of the family and the women had no means of supporting themselves without the financial support from their husbands.

5 Employment opportunities

There are far more employment opportunities for women today, although of the 15.1 million women working in 2017 only 8.8 million women were working full-time with 6.3 million working part-time. Women are cohabiting and marrying later and with their greater educational success this enables them to focus on their careers instead of marrying. Women who cohabit or marry have more control over their fertility by using contraception, and can plan when and how many children to have in order to develop a career for themselves.

▲ There has been a significant growth of financially independent women in their twenties and thirties

6 Longer life expectancy

Life expectancy has increased significantly in the UK.

Date	Males	Females
1900	47	50
2016	79.5	83.1

◄ **Table 3.4** UK life expectancy (ONS)

An increase in life expectancy means that when couples marry today they are likely to spend a considerable amount of their life with one person. Over time, couples' interests and attitudes may change and, if couples divorce, there are still many years left to form a new relationship.

7 Decline in religion

Secularisation refers to the declining influence of religious beliefs and institutions.

William Goode (1917–2003) argued that secularisation has resulted in marriage becoming less of a sacred, spiritual union and more of a personal and practical commitment. Fewer couples get married in a religious ceremony today and marriage is less likely to be seen as a spiritual union between husband and wife. Religious ceremonies accounted for just 26 per cent of marriages between opposite-sex couples (and 0.7 per cent of marriages between same-sex couples) in 2015, compared to more than half in the 1980s. As a result of secularisation, cohabitation and divorce is less likely to be seen as morally wrong in today's society.

Activity

Why do you think life expectancy is increasing? Make a list of as many reasons as you can think of.

Link

For more information on the Rapoports' research, see Family diversity on pages 88–90.

TIP ✓

You should aim to be able to explain why all these factors have led to an increase in family diversity.

8 Extended kin

Writers such as Fiona Devine in *Affluent Workers Revisited* (1992) noted how over time extended kin often moved closer to relatives and can engage in providing services such as childcare or babysitting. This would appear more common among the working class and is sometimes referred to as the 'local extended family'. Peter Willmott coined the phrase 'dispersed extended family' to refer to the situation where relatives are geographically separated but still maintain frequent contact by telephone, email and technology like Skype.

9 Mixed-race families

An important and positive feature stemming from immigration and a multicultural society is the growth of mixed-race relationships, the fastest growing ethnic group in the UK which numbered 1.25 million in the 2011 census. Britain has one of the highest levels of interracial relationships in the Western world. Children that result from such relationships gain a dual heritage, adding to family diversity in the UK.

▲ Today, mixed race families are far more common

Activities

1 Summarise how the following factors affect family diversity. Use this table for revision.

Legal changes	
Change in social values and attitudes	
Changing gender roles	
Benefits for lone parents	
Employment opportunities	
Longer life expectancy	
Decline in religion	
Extended kin	
Mixed-race families	

2 Do you think any of these factors have had a greater influence on family diversity than other factors? If so, which ones? Discuss your reasons with other students.

Some questions to think about

1 Think about the people you know and the type of family they live in. Does this show family diversity?

2 Why do the people you know live in different types of families?

Check your knowledge

1 Outline three reasons for family diversity in Britain today.

2 Outline and explain two changes in society that have contributed to the increase in lone parent families.

Summary

- There are many different types of families in Britain today – this is known as family diversity.
- There are many different explanations as to why family diversity exists today.
- There have been many changes in the twentieth and twenty-first centuries that have led to changes in family structure.

Criticisms of families

The family is at the centre of all societies, but while functionalists have likened its comfort and support to a 'warm bath', others highlight that such views simply encourage over-high expectations resulting in an unrealistic idealisation of family life. Other criticisms of modern families are that the segregation of extended kin can lead to loneliness and isolation, felt particularly by divorced and elderly family members. The problems many women experience from the power imbalance, resulting in their secondary status and role overload within the family, has previously been covered in the discussion on conjugal role relationships. Later on, (on page 118) the problems associated with marital breakdown, separation and divorce are discussed.

Dysfunctional families

There has been a lot of recent media coverage of 'broken', 'troubled' or 'problem' families. The state devotes a lot of resources to such families through Family Intervention Programmes (FIPs). So-called 'troubled' families are often associated with factors such as anti-social behaviour, youth crime, drug or substance misuse, cycles of deprivation and worklessness. Social workers may also be concerned about the 'dark side' of family life, expressed through actions like domestic violence, neglect of children or abuse. Sometimes, if their welfare is thought to be under threat, children are removed from very dysfunctional families and placed in care by social services.

Loneliness and isolation

Loneliness and isolation can apply to a wide variety of individuals, especially those divorced and widowed. Elderly extended kin in particular can feel increasingly cut off with limited contact with wider kinship networks. In their example of families moving to Greenleigh, Young and Willmott describe how the decline in the extended family and growth of the 'privatised' nuclear family impacted most negatively on the elderly left behind in Bethnal Green. Loneliness can be measured using the UCLA loneliness scale which considers lack of companionship, feeling left out and feeling isolated. Isolation can be measured through monthly contact (including face-to-face, telephone or written/email contact) with children and other immediate family and friends, and participation in clubs, religious organisations or other organisations.

Functionalist perspective

Functionalists remain positive about family life and play down any criticisms, seeing the family as supportive and emotionally fulfilling. However, Vogel and Bell (1960) did recognise how the family could be dysfunctional to its members while being functional to society. They outline the role children play in being 'emotional scapegoats' as parents offload their daily stresses onto them. In this way they perform the role of a 'punchbag', which is clearly not good for them, but means it is the family that absorbs conflict, enabling society to continue unquestioned.

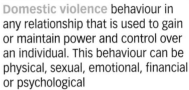

Key learning

You will be able to:

- identify, describe and explain different criticisms of families
- describe, compare and contrast a variety of sociological perspectives on these issues (functionalist, feminist and Marxist).

KEY TERMS

Domestic violence behaviour in any relationship that is used to gain or maintain power and control over an individual. This behaviour can be physical, sexual, emotional, financial or psychological

Power the capacity or ability to direct or influence the behaviour of others

KEY TEXT

Zaretsky E., *Capitalism, the Family and Personal Life*, London, Pluto Press, 1976.

KEY TEXT

Delphy C. and Leonard D., *Familiar Exploitation*, Cambridge, Polity Press, 1992.

TIP ✓

Make sure you are able to identify and outline criticisms of families.

Links

- For more information on conjugal role relationships, see pages 96–98.
- For more information on divorce, see pages 115–117.

Activity

In three columns outline the views of functionalism, Marxism and feminism on criticisms of the family. Identify similarities and differences between them.

Check your knowledge

1 In what ways can the family be criticised?
2 What is meant by the term 'dysfunctional family'?
3 What is meant by the term 'dark side' of the family?

Marxist perspective

Eli Zaretsky (1976) is critical of the modern family, arguing that it is unable to provide for the psychological and social needs of the individual. Instead, the family exists to primarily support capitalism by providing unpaid labour, reproducing a labour force and being a unit of consumption. Zaretsky also claims that the family cushions the pressures of capitalism. Individuals take out their frustrations with capitalism on fellow family members through conflict and fighting, removing any threat to the capitalist system itself. In fact, families promote capitalist profits by promoting a 'keeping up with the Joneses' rivalry between neighbours, ensuring families are always spending money (sometimes incurring debt) in a competition of one-upmanship.

Feminist perspective

Feminists argue that the positive view of family life hides the true amount of unhappiness and frustration experienced by many women in families. Women are increasingly dissatisfied with the patriarchal nature of families, which systematically undermines their status while maintaining an unfair division of labour. Feminists hold up the high divorce rate and the prevalence of illnesses like depression as evidence of women's lack of fulfilment with family life. Delphy and Leonard (1992) believe that the family has a central role in maintaining patriarchy; the family is an economic system involving a particular set of labour relations in which men benefit from, and exploit, the work of women. When women have paid employment outside the home, they experience role expansion since they still have to carry out the bulk of household tasks which are not equally shared with their male partners.

Research in action

The Office of National Statistics estimated in the year ending March 2018 that 2.0 million adults aged 16–59 years had experienced domestic abuse. Women were around twice as likely to have experienced domestic abuse than men (7.9 per cent compared with 4.2 per cent). This equates to an estimated 1.3 million female victims and 695,000 male victims.

Summary

- Ignoring criticisms of the family can lead to an unrealistic idealisation of family life.
- The elderly and divorced can particularly suffer from loneliness and isolation.
- Women can suffer from role overload because of the unequal division of labour.
- Some families suffer from problems and may be subject to social services intervention.
- Functionalists play down criticisms but recognise that children may be used as emotional scapegoats.
- Marxists see the family as serving capitalism over the interests of its members.
- Feminists see the family as patriarchal, serving the interests of men over women.

Divorce

Divorce statistics

Latest statistics (published by the Office for National Statistics in March 2018) estimate that 42 per cent of marriages in England and Wales end in divorce. Around half of these divorces are expected to occur in the first ten years of marriage. It is also estimated that:

- In 2017 there were 101,669 divorces of opposite-sex couples in England and Wales, a decrease of 4.9 per cent compared with 2016.
- In 2017 there were 8.4 divorces of opposite-sex couples per 1,000 married men and women aged 16 years and over (divorce rates), representing the lowest divorce rates since 1973.
- In 2017 there were 338 divorces of same-sex couples, more than three times the number in 2016.
- In 2017 three-quarters (74 per cent) of same-sex couples divorcing were female.
- In 2017 unreasonable behaviour was the most common reason for opposite-sex and same-sex couples divorcing.
- In 2017 the average (median) duration of marriage at the time of divorce was 12.2 years for opposite-sex couples.

Table 3.5 shows that the number of divorces has been falling in recent years since peaking in 1993.

Reasons for the rise in divorce

Divorce laws have changed, which have allowed both husbands and wives to divorce their partner. Long term, the divorce rate has risen dramatically. In 1911, there were just 859 petitions for divorce in England and Wales, but in 1993 there were 165,018 divorces.

The divorce law has undoubtedly affected the divorce rate.

▼ **Table 3.6** Changes in divorce law

Law before 1857	Divorce was only available through Acts of Parliament.
Matrimonial Causes Act 1857	Divorce was possible to obtain if adultery could be established and the grounds were widened to include cruelty and desertion (but for women the adultery of the husband was not considered a sufficient ground in itself for divorce, there needed to be evidence of additional grounds).
Legal Aid and Advice Act 1949	Legal aid was introduced in 1949 helping to fund divorce for women.
Divorce Reform Act 1969	Main grounds for divorce became 'irretrievable breakdown' of the marriage rather than one partner being blamed for the breakdown in the relationship.
Divorce Law 1984	Reduced the time before a divorce petition could take place from three years to one.
Family Law Act 1996	No longer necessary to prove irretrievable breakdown; partners simply had to state that it had broken down. However, this no-fault provision was later deemed unworkable and repealed. A period of reflection was introduced before divorce could be finalised, and greater use of mediation encouraged.
Proposed legislation 2019	Plans for legislation for no-fault divorce were announced in April 2019 to end the 'blame game' in marital breakdowns.

▼ **Table 3.5** Divorce rate over time (ONS)

Year	Number of divorces since 1946
1946	29,829
1960	23,868
1993	165,018
2000	141,135
2017	101,669

TIP

You can use data on the changes in divorce rates to answer questions that ask you to discuss whether the family is in decline. Try to remember some simple statistics that will give you solid evidence for the points you make.

Link

For more information on family diversity, see pages 88–90.

Link

See pages 96–97 to find out why women may feel frustrated about being responsible for the bulk of housework and childcare.

Value of marriage

Functionalist sociologists, for example Ronald Fletcher (1966), argued that divorce has increased because people attach more value to marriage than in the past. If marriage is so important to individuals, they are more likely to want a divorce if their marriage does not meet their expectations. People are demanding higher standards from their partners. People want emotional and sexual compatibility and equality, as well as companionship, and some are willing to go through a number of partners to achieve these goals.

Changes in the status of women

Women's expectations have changed as a result of the improved educational and career opportunities they have experienced since the 1980s. These opportunities mean that they no longer have to be unhappily married because they are financially dependent upon their husbands.

It may also be that divorce may be the outcome of tensions produced by men not undertaking their fair share of domestic work or men losing the traditional male role of primary breadwinner in some households.

Research in action

Nicky Hart (1976) noted that divorce may be a reaction to the frustration that many working wives may feel if they are responsible for the bulk of housework and childcare.

Change in social attitudes and values

Divorce in some communities is no longer associated with stigma and is generally more socially acceptable today. The view that divorce can be a problem-solving route to greater happiness for the individual is more acceptable.

Divorce is the product of a rapidly changing world in which traditional rules, rituals and traditions of love, romance and relationships no longer apply. According to Norman Dennis (1929–2010), as the nuclear family specialises in fewer functions, the bonds between husband and wife are the main force holding the family together (1975). Therefore, if love goes, there is little to prevent marital breakdown.

Individual competition and a free market economy in society today have placed increased emphasis on individuals. Individuals pursue personal satisfaction and are accustomed to the idea of consumer choice and fulfilment coming from such choice. Marriage is, therefore, treated like other consumer products; if it is not providing satisfaction, it is more likely to be discarded.

Secularisation

Secularisation (the decline in religious beliefs) has loosened the rigid morality which in the past made divorce morally unacceptable to some people.

For example, data from the 2001 census showed that 15 per cent of the population had no religion compared to 25 per cent in the 2011 census. Goode (1971) argues that this has resulted in marriage becoming less of a sacred, spiritual union and more of a personal and practical commitment that can be abandoned if it fails.

▲ Many people now choose to get married somewhere other than a place of worship

Summary

- Divorce rates have increased in recent years.
- There are many reasons why the divorce rates have increased, including:
  - legal changes
  - the value of marriage
  - changes in the status of women
  - the change in social attitudes and values
  - secularisation.

Check your knowledge

Identify and explain two changes in society that have contributed to the increase in divorces in the UK.

Consequences of divorce

While divorce affects all groups of the population, there are some groups where divorce rates are higher than average. The highest rate of divorce is among men and women in their late twenties. Teenage marriages are twice as likely to end in divorce as those of couples overall. There is also a high incidence of divorce in the first five to seven years of marriage, and later when the children are older and have left home.

Some working class groups, particularly semi-skilled and unskilled workers, have a higher rate of divorce than the middle class.

Childless couples and partners from different social classes or religious backgrounds also face a higher risk of divorce, as do couples whose work separates them for long periods.

Consequences for husband and wife

Research in action

Paul Bohannan (1920–2007) describes the consequences for husbands and wives under six headings:

1   Emotional effects of a divorce, for example grief, loneliness.
2   Legal aspects relating to a divorce, for example courts, custody of children.
3   Economic aspects of a divorce, for example less money.
4   Co-parental – sharing parental responsibility.
5   Community – possible change in community of one member of the partnership.
6   Psychological effects of getting divorced, for example stress.

Consequences for the family

The increase in divorce has led to an increase in lone parent families. The percentage of lone parent families has tripled since 1971 and Britain has one of the highest proportions in Europe. However, the number of lone parent families in the UK has been decreasing in recent years from 3.0 million in 2015 to 2.8 million in 2017. Around one in four of all families and dependent children lived in lone parent families in 2017, with nine out of ten of them headed by women.

Divorce has also led to an increase in the number of reconstituted families. Most children stay with their mother if she remarries. Eighty-four per cent of stepfamilies in Britain have a stepfather and a biological mother.

Consequences for children

Divorce leads to children having to spend time with parents separately and can often require adjustments to new sets of relationships in reconstituted families. Keeping in contact with parents they do not live with and grandparents on that same side of the family can be difficult.

Consequences for the extended family

Some grandparents might not see their grandchildren often, or at all, while in other situations they might be required to help out in the home and with childcare. Divorce also risks a loss of contact for aunts, uncles and cousins.

Research in action

Bryan Rodgers and Jan Pryor studied 'Divorce and Separation' (1998). They reviewed 200 studies, attempting to find out whether divorce had a negative effect on children. They found that children of separated families have a higher probability of:

- being in poverty and poor housing
- being poorer when they are adults
- exhibiting behavioural problems
- performing less well in school
- leaving school/home when young
- becoming sexually active, pregnant or a parent at an early age
- depressive symptoms, high levels of smoking and drinking, and drug use during adolescence and adulthood.

Rodgers and Pryor suggested divorce alone did not cause the above problems, but they occurred in association with other factors that affected the outcomes when divorce occurs.

Factors affecting outcomes

- Financial hardship can limit educational achievement.
- Family conflict before, during and after separation can contribute to behavioural problems.
- Parental ability to recover from distress of separation affects children's ability to adjust.
- Multiple changes in family structure increase the probability of poor outcomes.
- Quality contact with the non-resident parent can improve outcomes.

According to Rodgers and Pryor, those children whose parents managed to avoid the above were largely unlikely to have suffered from a divorce.

Whatever the consequences of divorce, divorce and remarriage are certainly influencing the rise in family diversity.

Although divorce has many negative outcomes for parents, children and the wider family, there can also be some positive outcomes.

For example, parents may be able to leave an unhappy marriage and the home environment may improve with fewer arguments.

Links

- See pages 148–152 for more information on financial hardship and educational achievement.
- For more information on family diversity, see pages 88–90.

Activity

Draw a table similar to the one below. Add some more positive outcomes of divorce to the table.

Parents	Children	Wider family
● Can escape an unhappy marriage	● Can escape an unpleasant environment	● Grandparents may see more of the children while helping with childcare

TIP

Make sure you know the positive and negative consequences of divorce for parents, children and the family structure.

Check your knowledge

Identify and explain three consequences of divorce for family members.

Summary

- Divorce has an effect on parents, children, grandparents and other family members.
- Many of the effects of divorce are negative, but there can also be positive consequences of divorce.
- Many studies have been conducted that look at the consequences of divorce for different people.

Key learning

You will be able to:

- describe, compare and contrast a variety of sociological perspectives on divorce (functionalist, feminist and Marxist).

Link

For more information on functionalism, see pages 16–17.

Activities

1 Do you agree with the functionalist view of divorce?

2 How would you evaluate this view?

Link

For more information on Marxism, see pages 18–19.

Activities

1 From what you know of the Marxist perspective, summarise the key points of their approach.

2 Think about the Marxist view of divorce. What might they say about divorce?

TIP ✓

Once you know the key points about each of the sociological perspectives, you need to practise applying them to different parts of the specification. For example, always think about how something can be functional and, therefore, how the functionalists might explain something.

Theories of divorce

The functionalist view of divorce

For many years, the sociology of the family was dominated by the functionalist theory.

Functionalists always ask about the purpose or function of an institution – what good does the institution do for society and individuals?

For functionalists, society is a complex system that promotes stability by guiding individuals with a social structure that provides certain social functions. Anything that disrupts the current social structure or function is seen as dysfunctional.

Functionalists are interested in the positive functions of a family. They view the family as the cornerstone of society because it plays the dominant role among all social institutions in making individuals feel part of the wider society. The family is beneficial and necessary for the smooth running of society and the personal development of individuals.

So, how can functionalists see divorce as functional?

The functionalist perspective would explain divorce by identifying the beneficial results to both the individuals involved and to the society, for example we end up with happier people and fewer dysfunctional families. Divorce, when viewed from the functionalist perspective, contributes to the stability of the society as a whole. As a result of divorce, many lawyers, judges and court officials are employed. The public system of health care employs doctors, nurses and social workers who treat and care for people, including for those suffering the effects of divorce. Without the current rates of divorce, many people would be unemployed and this would weaken the structure of society.

Functionalists, for example Fletcher (1966), would argue that the increase in divorce is not necessarily a threat to marriage as an institution, but is a reflection of the higher values and expectations that people place on marriage. Divorce can create instability in society but many people remarry after a divorce, suggesting that marriage and family life are still important and necessary to maintain a stable society.

The Marxist view of divorce

Eli Zaretsky (1976) points to the demands that the public/private divide places on couples to resolve all their exploitation and stress from their work within the confines of the family. While she portrays the family as a 'safety valve' soaking up the stresses of living in capitalism, ultimately this is a lot to ask and many families break up, resulting in divorce.

Unequal access to resources in society can lead to tension within families and within society. The stress that results may reduce the chances of being able to maintain a stable relationship. This could explain the higher rate of divorces among the working classes.

The Marxist-feminist Nicky Hart (1976) argues that high divorce rates have been brought about by changes in the economy. The economy has demanded female labour outside the home. This has meant a 'double-shift' for women (where women work outside the home as well as having responsibility for the jobs within the house), which has increased their dissatisfaction. Being economically active has also increased women's financial independence so their dependence on marriage has decreased.

The feminist view of divorce

Feminists try to understand why women have had a more marginal position in society throughout history, and fight for women's equality with men. When it comes to divorce, feminists have been strong advocates for reforms in the law which give women equal access to raising divorce proceedings, and have carefully researched the negative and positive outcomes on divorce for both men and women. Feminist research has shown that the family is often a less happy place for women than it is for men and it is often women who initiate divorce. For example, feminists argue that women do not just take on the burden of domestic work; they also fulfil a sexual and emotional role. They support men in their careers (far more than men support women's careers) and undertake far more emotion work to keep them happy. Males have more access to leisure and more freedom. The resulting tension from these factors can cause resentment among women, driving them to seek a change in their social structure.

Feminists are not necessarily against marriage, but they do generally see marriage as favouring men more than women. Feminists argue that before divorce was legal in the UK many women were trapped in violent or empty shell marriages. Divorce now allows women to leave unhappy marriages and start again. The fact that most divorces are initiated by women (seven in ten) shows that women are no longer prepared to put up with poor marriages or rely on the social status of their husbands for their position in society.

In 1968, Kate Millett (1934–) argued that the high divorce rate, and the fact that most divorces are initiated by women, confirms the belief that marriage is a patriarchal institution that serves men and exploits women.

Research in action

A study in the USA in 2015, based on a survey of over 2,000 heterosexual couples, found that women initiated nearly 70 per cent of all divorces. This study by Michael Rosenfeld considered 2,262 adults, aged 19–94, who had opposite sex partners in 2009. By 2015, 371 of these people had broken up or got divorced.

Rosenfeld found that:

● women initiated 69 per cent of all divorces, compared to 31 per cent for men
● women were more likely to initiate divorces because married women reported lower levels of relationship quality than married men
● his results support the feminist assertion that some women experience heterosexual marriage as oppressive or uncomfortable.

A similar picture emerged in England and Wales. In 2018, 70 per cent of all divorces granted to one partner (rather than both) were granted to the wife.

Link

For more information on feminism, see pages 22–23. For more information on conjugal roles, see page 96.

Extension

How are functionalist, feminist and Marxist views similar and different in their explanations of divorce?

Check your knowledge

1 Identify and explain three key aspects of the functionalist view of divorce.
2 Identify and explain three key aspects of the Marxist view of divorce.
3 Identify and explain three key aspects of the feminist view of divorce.

Summary

● Functionalists see divorce as functional for society.
● Marxists see divorce as a struggle over resources, creating tension that results in a change in the marital status.
● Feminists view divorce as a power conflict between a woman and a man.

Key learning

You will be able to:

- apply your knowledge and understanding of sociological research methods to particular issues in family and households.

TIP ✓

Do not discuss methods in general. You might know the strengths and weaknesses of using interviews when collecting data, but you must apply what you know to the specific family context, characteristics of the people or situation involved, and to the particular research topic that the question asks about.

Activities

1 Make a list of all the different research methods that you could use when conducting sociological research.

2 a Are they primary or secondary research methods?

   b Do they produce qualitative or quantitative data?

   c What are the strengths and weaknesses of each method?

Methods in context

Potentially, there is a wide range of issues within the family topic that you could be asked about – it is not possible to anticipate the issue except that it must be contained within the specification. This section is about using your knowledge and skills of research methods in appropriate ways to answer the question as well as you can.

Read Item A below and answer the questions that follow.

Item A

A UK-based study conducted by Braun in 2011 explored the ways in which working-class, inner-city families negotiate and resolve childcare and domestic responsibilities between mothers and fathers and how men balance employment and family demands. This study forms part of a small-scale qualitative UK-based research project on working-class families and their engagement with pre-school childcare in two different localities in inner London: Stoke Newington and Battersea.

Seventy families were interviewed for the study: 36 in Battersea and 34 in Stoke Newington, including interviews with 16 men. Of the 16 men interviewed, 15 were resident fathers and one was a live-out father. They were mostly working full time (ten), although five were not in paid employment and one was working part time. All the families had children under the age of five, but they varied in terms of number of children, family structure, occupational status, education qualifications and ethnic background.

Of the 16 fathers, eight were White British, three had Black African/Caribbean backgrounds and two were mixed race. There were also two respondents from other European backgrounds and one from an Asian background. Three of the fathers (two unemployed and one in part-time work) were doing sole childcare for at least part of every week.

Interviews with parents were semi-structured, with an emphasis on giving the respondents freedom to express their concerns, thoughts and practices around childcare and other aspects of their lives with children. The interviews explored how the respondents practise fathering roles in their particular economic, social and family contexts, contrasting a group of 'active fathers' with those we have termed 'background fathers'.

Initial contact with participants was made through visiting public sector nurseries, Sure Start, as well as playgroups and toy libraries in the two localities.

Interviews mostly took place in respondents' own homes.

1 What is meant by qualitative research?

> *Make sure you clearly explain what qualitative data is and give an example of qualitative data from Item A.*

2 Outline two problems of using qualitative data in sociological research.

> *You need to identify two problems of using qualitative data in this specific piece of research. Do not just identify problems of using qualitative data.*

3 Identify and explain one factor that may influence fathers to look after children on their own.

> *Make sure that you refer to this specific study when answering this question.*

4 Identify and explain one advantage of using unstructured interviews to investigate relationships between family members.

5 Identify and explain one disadvantage of using unstructured interviews to investigate relationships between family members.

> *Questions 4 and 5 are asking you to demonstrate your knowledge of unstructured interviews, but you must explain why unstructured interviews would be a good method to use for this specific investigation and why they might not be a good method. Just saying: 'An advantage of unstructured interviews is that they produce qualitative data' would not be an adequate answer. Think about how you could expand this answer to explain why this is a strength or weakness for investigating relationships between family members.*

6 Explain how you would investigate the distribution of childcare between partners by using a questionnaire.

> *This is giving you the opportunity to show your knowledge of using questionnaires, but make sure you explain how questionnaires could be used for this specific study. How effective is this method for investigating the distribution of childcare between partners?*

7 Identify and explain one ethical issue you need to consider when using semi-structured interviews when investigating the distribution of childcare between partners.

> *Do not just identify an ethical issue. Make sure the ethical issue is relevant to the study. You need to explain why the ethical issue you identify is an issue for this specific study.*

TIP

It is important that you can apply sociological research methods to each topic you are studying. You must use key sociological concepts accurately.

When answering these questions, make sure you focus your answer on the specific item given. Use the item in your answers and use concepts specific to the method.

Summary

- There is a difference between qualitative and quantitative data.
- There are advantages and disadvantages of each research method.
- Ethical considerations need to be taken into account when conducting research.

The sociology of families

Practice questions

Question 1 (multiple choice)

Which term do sociologists use to describe a stage in the life cycle of a family when children have reached adulthood and have left the parental home? [1 mark]

a) Empty nest family

b) Privatised nuclear family

c) Extended family

d) Cohabiting couple

Question 2 (descriptive answer)

Describe one type of family that has increased in Britain over the past 30 years. [3 marks]

Question 3 (short answer question linked to source material)

Item A

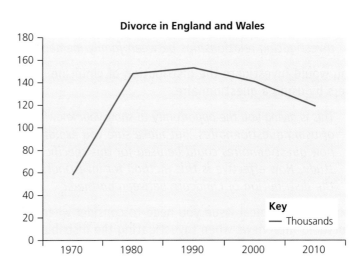

Divorce in England and Wales

From Item A, examine one strength of research using official data on divorce. [2 marks]

Question 4 (paragraph answer linked to the source material)

Identify one reason that the law accepts as grounds for divorce. Identify the trend shown by the data and explain one factor which may account for this trend. [4 marks]

Answer and commentary

It is important to identify a reason that the law accepts as grounds for divorce and also to correctly identify the trend, explaining one factor which might account for this trend other than changes in the law.

Legal grounds for divorce:

- irretrievable breakdown.

You could write about:

- The trend is up (increasing or rising would be accepted). Although the rate of increase has slowed the trend is still clearly upward over the period 1970–2010.
- Changing social attitudes (divorce is more socially acceptable).
- The changing status of women (women are no longer dependent on men for their financial security and are usually granted legal custody of their children following a divorce).
- Secularisation (the declining importance of religion in society).

Question 5 (essay question)

Discuss how far sociologists would agree that families remain an important agency of socialisation. [12 marks]

> **TIP** ✓
> Take a few moments to develop an outline plan of your answer.

Answer and commentary

Remember to think of your 'mini-essay' in three parts: an introductory paragraph in which you focus on the question and begin your argument, a second paragraph in which you develop your answer (consider one or more alternative sociological perspectives on the issue) and a final paragraph in which you reach a conclusion.

You could write about:

- The functionalist perspective on families as an agency of primary socialisation.
- The Marxist perspective on families as a unit of consumption supporting the capitalist system.
- The feminist perspective on families as helping to preserve patriarchy (the dominant position of men in society).
- Alternative agencies of socialisation, e.g. the mass media and the education system.

In each case you will need to evaluate the extent to which a particular perspective represents a valid picture of families in Britain today. Try to reach a clear, logical, evidence-based conclusion and avoid contradictions in your argument.

The sociology of education

Key learning

You will be able to:
- explain the functions of education including fostering social cohesion
- describe the key ideas of Durkheim and Parsons on education

KEY TERMS

Compulsory state education in Britain, state education was first made compulsory in the late-nineteenth century (for children up to the age of ten); this was later extended to include children of secondary school age in the Education Act 1944

Education the process of giving and receiving knowledge, generally associated in contemporary society with schools and universities

Hidden curriculum a set of values, attitudes and principles transmitted to pupils but not as part of the formal curriculum of timetabled subjects

Formal curriculum the timetabled subjects taught in school

Activity

Using your own experience of education, make a list of what you think the purpose of education is. Complete a table with two columns: What does education do for individuals? What does education do for society?

Link

For more information on functionalism, see pages 16–17.

Functions of education (1)

Education performs a very important role in British society. In the UK there are significantly different education systems in the four home countries. However, the content of this textbook will focus primarily on England. It takes children at the age of four or five for 13–14 years and teaches them vast amounts of knowledge and skills.

The period of compulsory state education is an important and influential time in a young person's life, a time that will prepare them for the future. The government sees education as a very important part of British society. Approximately 13 per cent of national spending goes on education – estimated to be £87.2 billion in 2020 (www.ukpublicspending.co.uk).

Different sociologists explain society in different ways. Functionalists, Marxists and feminists explain the functions of education in different ways.

Functionalism and core values

Functionalists focus on what they perceive to be the positive functions performed by the education system. The nineteenth-century classical sociologist Emile Durkheim and the twentieth-century US functionalist Talcott Parsons both saw education as being an essential agency of socialisation, whose function is to transmit core values to the next generation. Schools play a major role in teaching the norms and values of society to each new generation. It is a continuation of primary socialisation that starts in the family. It was Durkheim who suggested that schools are like a society in miniature in which society's values and norms are transmitted to children.

Talcott Parsons developed Durkheim's ideas further. He explains how school acts as a bridge between the home and the wider society.

Creating social cohesion

In order for society to be stable, we all need to know how we should behave and what is expected of us in society. If we all did what we wanted to do, there would be chaos in society. One of the key functions of education is to pass on to the new generation the central core values and culture of a society. We learn the norms and values of society through both the hidden curriculum and the formal curriculum, for example through subjects like citizenship and personal, social and health education (PSHE). This unites or 'glues' people together and builds social solidarity by giving them shared values. This gives us social cohesion or solidarity by making us feel part of something bigger.

Research in action

Durkheim (functionalist) saw the major function of education as the transmission of society's norms and values. He believed that it is a vital task for all societies to weld a mass of individuals into a united whole. Education helps to do this and schools help children to learn that they are part of something bigger, meaning they develop a sense of commitment to the social group. He argued that 'school is a society in miniature', preparing children for life in the wider world and providing an environment where children learn to co-operate with people who are neither friends nor family – preparing them for working with people in later life.

Research in action

Parsons – the school class as a social system

In the 1950s, Parsons developed Durkheim's ideas further. He explained how school is a bridge between the home and wider society. School plays the central role in the process of secondary socialisation, taking over from primary socialisation which takes place in the family (see pages 80–82). Parsons argued that this is necessary because the family and the wider society work in different ways and children need to adapt if they are to cope in the wider world. Schools continue the socialisation process of teaching the norms and values of society.

In the family, children are judged by their parents by what Parson calls particularistic standards – they are judged by rules that only apply to that particular child. Individual children are given tasks based on their different abilities and judged according to their unique characteristics. Parents often adapt rules to suit the unique abilities of the child.

However, in school and in wider society, children and adults are judged according to the same universal standards (for example, they are judged by the same examinations and the same laws). These rules and laws are applied equally to all people irrespective of the unique character of the individual. Nonetheless, in practice individuals may not always be judged in the same way and a feature of education is pupils have different outcomes.

In families, status is fixed at birth – this is ascribed status. However, in society, status is supposed to be based on merit and achieved rather than ascribed. Parsons believed that education makes the transition from family to society possible by getting people used to universal values and achieved status. However, Parsons implies achievement is solely down to effort and ignores structural factors like material deprivation.

KEY TERMS

Social cohesion a sense of belonging to the wider society

Particularistic standards subjective judgements based on individual characteristics – people are seen and judged as individuals

Universal standards attempts to provide objective judgements applied equally to all members of society, regardless of who they are, e.g. a teacher's objective assessment of a child's performance in school, based on test results, as opposed to a parent's subjective view of their child's abilities

KEY TEXT

Durkheim E., *Moral Education*, Glencoe, Free Press, 1925 (republished 1973).

Parsons T., 'The school class as a social system' in Halsey A.H. *et al.*, *Education, Economy and Society*, New York, The Free Press, 1961.

Activities

1 Can you think of other ways school makes you feel part of society? How does it give you a shared sense of identity? Consider what you learn through the hidden curriculum as well as in subjects like citizenship and PSHE.

2 List any skills you have gained at school that you are likely to use in the workplace.

Check your knowledge

Explain in your own words what is meant by:

1 norms
2 values
3 hidden curriculum
4 formal curriculum
5 social cohesion.

Summary

- Functionalists, such as Durkheim and Parsons, argue that education provides important functions.
- Two of these are instilling core values and creating social cohesion.
- Social cohesion and specialist skills are needed to keep society stable and to allow society to function effectively.

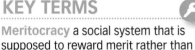
KEY TERMS

Meritocracy a social system that is supposed to reward merit rather than inherited status

Functions of education (2)

Serving the needs of the economy

The term 'division of labour' applies to how the variety and range of work tasks within a society are allocated. Conventionally it is most applicable to the workplace where each person has a specialised role. As a term it was developed first by the economist Adam Smith and subsequently by Karl Marx in his analysis of how the proletariat did all of the work. Durkheim noted that in an advanced industrial economy such as ours, there is a need for a diverse range of skills. Not everyone can be a doctor or a solicitor and factory workers and cleaners play equally important (if less financially rewarded) roles. Consequently, in order for society to function effectively, individuals need to have different skills. He also saw it as having a moral character because it generates feelings of social solidarity. At school, individuals learn the diverse skills necessary for society to function effectively. For example, we may all start off learning the same subjects, but later on we all specialise in different fields when we choose subjects to study at GCSE, BTEC and A level.

Extension

Think about the skills and qualifications that are required for different jobs. Identify and agree among yourselves which jobs you will research and then discuss the skills and qualifications needed for these jobs.

Social mobility

Functionalists such as Durkheim and Parsons think that education allocates people to the most appropriate job for their talents using examinations and qualifications. Access to jobs and greater opportunities depend mainly on educational qualifications and other skills and talents. Therefore, everyone who has the ability and talents and puts in the effort should be able to pursue the jobs they wish.

This ensures that the most talented are allocated to the occupations that are most important for society. According to functionalists, this is fair because there is equality of opportunity – everyone is assumed a chance of success and it is the most able who succeed through their own efforts. This is known as meritocracy.

Education, therefore, offers pupils the opportunity to do well and increase their social position, a process known as social mobility. However, critics regard this view of society as naïve and simplistic, ignoring the unequal chances individuals may experience because of their social class, gender or ethnicity.

Evaluation of functionalism

The functionalist approach emphasises the importance of education as a means of transmitting society's values and promoting a fair and equal society through meritocracy. However, is this always the case?

There may not be a single set of values to transmit. Society consists of different people with different interests, each group having its own set of values. Which set of values does the education system transmit?

Does the education system give pupils a fair and equal chance to achieve? (For example, how do private schools that only the rich can afford equate with meritocracy?)

Does the education system provide young people with the specialist skills required for work? (For example, why is there youth unemployment?)

Do schools actually hinder the learning process because of the formal, structured nature?

Do schools actually promote value consensus? Many classrooms are places of conflict, often with pupils being disruptive and challenging authority.

Check your knowledge

Explain the two functions of education: serving the needs of the economy and promoting social mobility.

Summary

- According to functionalists the two key functions performed by education are:
  - Serving the needs of the economy.
  - Promoting social mobility.
- Functionalists believe education functions are important in order to maintain the stability and effectiveness of society.
- However, critics argue education may not always be functional, as individuals differ and education may not meet the needs of each individual or the needs of a changing society.

Activity

In small groups:

- make a list of the norms and values that are taught by parents during primary socialisation
- make a list of the norms and values that are taught in school during secondary socialisation.

TIP

It is important that you know and can explain these key functions of education. Summarise each function by writing some bullet points for each one.

Extension

1 Ask each member of your class whether they think the education system has been successful in performing the following functions. For each function, answer 'Yes', 'No' or 'Partly'.

- Creating social cohesion.
- Serving the needs of the economy.
- Teaching core values (secondary socialisation).
- Role allocation and meritocracy.

2 What do these answers say about the functions of the education system in Britain today? Write a summary of the findings.

KEY TERM

Correspondence principle the idea that the education system is designed primarily to serve the needs of the capitalist economic system, e.g. by producing an obedient workforce, and mirrors/corresponds to the workplace

KEY TEXT

Bowles S. and Gintis H., *Schooling in Capitalist America*, London, Routledge and Kegan Paul, 1976.

Link

For more information on Marxism, see pages 18–19.

The relationship between education and capitalism

Marxists provide a challenge to the functionalist perspective and suggest that the purpose of education is to serve and maintain capitalism.

Marx argued that there were two basic social classes in capitalist society: a small, wealthy and powerful class of owners of the means of production, which he called the bourgeoisie or capitalists (the owning class); and a much larger, poorer class of non-owners, which he called the proletariat (working class). Marxists see education primarily as a way to reinforce these inequalities in society. Marxists argue that the education system acts as a means of socialising children into their respective class positions, in a way that makes sure that they are unlikely to challenge the system.

Marxist view of education

Marxists challenge the idea that the education system is meritocratic – they argue that this is a myth since many members of the proletariat are schooled to fail. This is because if everyone was successful then who would do the boring, low-paid and low-status jobs that society relies upon? As we see on pages 149–154, the fact that middle-class students tend to be higher achievers deceptively serves to make the system seem fair.

Research in action

Samuel Bowles (1937–) and Herbert Gintis (1940–), writing from a Marxist perspective, argued that the organisation of school mirrors the workplace. They called this the 'correspondence principle' which prepares children to fit easily into their future roles, creating a hardworking, docile, obedient and highly motivated workforce.

Children experience two curriculums in school:

● Formal curriculum: maths, English, science, ICT.
● Hidden curriculum: rules, obedience, routine, dress code, achievement, competition.

According to Bowles and Gintis, the hidden curriculum in particular prepares children for their future role.

Activity

The table below shows a number of similarities between school and work, as identified by Bowles and Gintis. Can you add any more examples to this table?

	School	Work
Respecting authority	Being polite to teachers	Employees expected to respect authority, such as their boss
Being obedient	Sitting quietly, following instructions	Following orders from manager
Dress code	Uniform	Work uniform or dress code
Routine	Arriving at lessons on time. Completing homework by deadlines	Arriving at work on time. Meeting set deadlines
External rewards	Grades in examinations	Pay and promotions
Competition	Encourage competition in sport, for example	Competition for jobs, promotion and so on
Punishment	Detentions for not behaving as expected	Informal/formal warnings, even dismissal
Hierarchy	People with different levels of responsibility, for example head teacher, heads of year	People with different responsibilities, for example managing director, departmental manager

How do these pictures demonstrate the correspondence principle?

Alternative sociological perspectives on the correspondence principle

Many writers have criticised Bowles and Gintis because there is less correspondence between schools and the needs of the economy than they suggest. The critics of Bowles and Gintis believe their research focuses too narrowly on social class and neglects the issues of gender and ethnicity, which are also important factors in educational achievement.

They have been criticised for making the process of schooling too similar to the organisation of work and therefore class inequality. This over-simplistic view fails to recognise the resistance that is a normal part of everyday schooling as illustrated in the work of Paul Willis (see page 148).

They also underestimated working-class resistance to attempts to socially control and exploit them – resistance shown, for example, in workplace strikes.

Summary

● Marxists challenge assumptions made by functionalists that education benefits everyone
● Marxists argue that the education system acts as a means of socialising children into their respective class positions, in a way that makes sure that they are unlikely to challenge the system.
● Bowles and Gintis (1976) argued that the organisation of school mirrors the workplace.
● Bowles and Gintis see the hidden curriculum as vitally important in preparing children for their future worker role.

Key learning

You will be able to:

● describe, compare and contrast a variety of sociological perspectives on the role of education issues (functionalist, feminist and Marxist).

KEY TERM

Genderquake fundamental change to society whereby young females are increasingly striving for a fulfilling career

Links

● Refer to pages 126–129 for the roles and functions of education.
● For more information on inequalities in education, see pages 130–131.
● For more information on functionalism and Marxism, see pages 16–17 and 18–19.
● For more information on the differences in educational achievement between boys and girls, see pages 157–159.

Extension

Referring to pages 126–129, add some more criticisms of the functionalist approach.

TIP

You will be expected to show an understanding of the similarities and differences between the key perspectives on the functions of education.

Extension

Can you add any more similarities and differences to those identified in Table 4.1?

Sociological perspectives on the role of education in society

Education is a major social institution and a major agency of secondary socialisation. This section summarises the different sociological perspectives on the roles and functions of education.

The functionalist perspective

Key aspects of the functionalist perspective:

● There is a link between education and other institutions.
● Education is an important agency of socialisation.
● Education helps to maintain social stability and social cohesion.
● Education prepares young people for adulthood and working life.
● Education passes on the core values of society so that young people know what is expected and how to behave in society.
● Education teaches specialist skills for work.
● Durkheim argued that schools are a 'society in miniature' – a small society that prepares children and young people for wider adult society.
● Parsons explained how schools act as a bridge between home and the wider society.

The Marxist perspective

Key aspects of the Marxist perspective:

● Education prepares young people for capitalist society (correspondence principle).
● Children are socialised into their respective class positions.
● Education is not meritocratic (see page 130).
● The education system acts as a means of social control, encouraging young people to conform and accept their social position in society.
● The hidden curriculum teaches young people the expectations of society and prepares them for their place in society.
● Bowles and Gintis argued that school mirrors the workplace – they referred to this as 'the correspondence principle.'

What are the similarities and differences between functionalist and Marxist views?

▼ **Table 4.1** Comparison of functionalist and Marxist views on education

Similarities	They both look at the big picture by looking at institutions and how they fit into society. They both regard education as playing an important role in shaping attitudes, norms and values of pupils. They see education as preparing pupils for work.
Differences	Functionalists are positive about the role of education. Marxists are critical about the role of education. Functionalists regard education as meeting the demands of an economy in a way that meets everyone's individual needs, as well as the needs of society. Marxists see education as supporting and benefiting capitalism and the ruling classes.

The feminist perspective

Key aspects of the feminist perspectives:

- There are inequalities in the education system between boys and girls.
- There are gendered subject choices of girls and boys.
- Education plays a role in the socialisation of girls and boys.
- Although girls are now outperforming boys at all levels of the education system (except PhD level), feminists still argue that it reinforces the patriarchal views of society, leading to girls moving into lower paid jobs when they leave school.
- This relationship, however, is complex: not all boys are failing and not all girls are achieving.
- Gender achievement is also shaped by factors like social class and ethnicity.

Until the mid-1990s, boys achieved higher grades in school than girls. Feminists believed that girls were overlooked in the education system, with the focus being on boys' achievements. However, although girls, as a group, now outperform boys generally, feminists argue this is in spite of the system, which they still regard as patriarchal and privileges boys at the expense of girls. They strongly disagree with the argument by sociologists like Tony Sewell (2010) who claim there has been a 'feminisation of education' whereby the school has become a female-dominated environment, which has benefited girls and made boys feel less comfortable with their learning environment.

A key focus of their attention is on the subjects that girls and boys choose in school and often the lower paid jobs they get when they leave school. Gendered subject choice occurs when girls choose subjects that are considered 'female' and boys choose subjects that are considered 'male'. This is a complex outcome based on individual preferences as well as the influence of teachers, school environment and parents.

Helen Wilkinson (1994) has used the term 'genderquake' to reflect the increasing aspirations and ambitions of young women towards the labour market that has served to motivate them in education. This finding was echoed by Sue Sharpe (1994) who compared the attitudes of working-class girls in the early 1970s and 1990s. Over the 20-year period of her research she found their priorities had shifted from 'love, marriage, husbands and children' to 'job, career and being able to support themselves'.

Other feminists like Francis and Skelton (2005) have looked at female identities, arguing that girls are adopting more male traits which is empowering them with greater confidence and assertiveness in the classroom.

As noted above, it is important to recognise not all girls are successful in the education system. Louise Archer (2014) has undertaken important research into underachieving working-class girls. She found that establishing a 'glamorous female identity' was their main focus, centred around gaining status from appearance, boyfriends and clothes. Like Willis' study (see page 148), she found that such subcultural attitudes brought about their own underachievement.

TIP

It is important that you know the key points made by the functionalists, Marxists and feminists.

Activity

Using the information on these pages and pages 126–131, draw a table with three columns headed: Functionalists, Marxists, Feminists. Complete the table to show the key points of different sociological perspectives on the roles and functions of education. Make sure you understand everything you write. You can use this table for revision.

Extension

What are the similarities and differences between the three perspectives?

Summary

- These three sociological perspectives all have key points to make about the role and function of education in society.
- Functionalists believe that education is positive and performs very important functions for the stability of society.
- Marxists believe that education prepares young people for working in a capitalist society by creating an obedient and uncritical workforce.
- Feminists believe that women are at a disadvantage in the education system.

KEY TERMS

Comprehensive school a state secondary school that does not select pupils on the basis of ability

National Curriculum subjects that must be taught in all local-authority-maintained schools in England. Non-local-authority schools, such as academies and free schools, do not have to follow the national curriculum but do have to teach a 'broad and balanced curriculum', including English, mathematics, science and religious education

Activity

Find out how many hours of free early education per year a three- or four-year-old is entitled to.

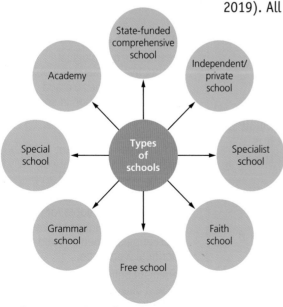

▲ **Figure 4.1** School diversity

Different types of schools

All the different types of schools in Figure 4.1 are funded and managed in different ways. All children in England between the ages of five and 18 are entitled to a free place at a state school. State-funded nursery education is available from the age of three, and may be full time or part time, though this is not compulsory. School attendance becomes compulsory beginning with the term following the child's fifth birthday. However, children can be enrolled in the reception year in September of that school year, thus beginning school at age four or four years and six months. In most parts of the country, children move to secondary school at the age of 11, although some parts of the country still have middle schools where children aged 9–13 are educated.

From 2015, all young people are required to participate in some form of education or training until they reach the age of 18.

▼ **Table 4.2** There are different schools for different ages

School type	Description
Nursery schools	For children aged three and four. They have their own head teacher and staff. Some are state funded, others are private.
Nursery classes	Attached to primary schools and share the same head teacher and staff.
Primary schools	Provide education for children aged 4–11. While at primary school, children start with the Early Years curriculum, followed by Key Stage 1 and Key Stage 2 of the **National Curriculum**.
Secondary schools	Provide education for children aged 11–16 or 18. They take pupils through Key Stages 3 and 4 of the National Curriculum.
Sixth-form colleges	For young people aged 16–19. Pupils study for A levels and other qualifications that can be studied after the age of 16, for example BTEC National Certificates.

The majority of children in England aged between 11 and 16 attend state-funded comprehensive schools; approximately 93 per cent of English school children attend these schools (Department for Education, 2019). All of these are funded through national and local taxation.

The independent/private sector educates around 7 per cent of the total number of school children in England, with the figure rising to more than 18 per cent of pupils over the age of 16. This is funded mostly by parents.

What are state-funded comprehensive schools?

Comprehensive schools aim to educate all pupils, regardless of their background or ability, under one roof. The aim is to ensure that all children have access to the same level and quality of education.

What were specialist schools?

State secondary schools were often specialised, which meant they had an extra emphasis on one or two subjects. These schools received extra funding to support the specialist subjects in an attempt to raise achievement. The programme was ended in 2010 and replaced by academies and free schools.

What are academies?

Academies are independently managed schools set up by sponsors from business, faith or voluntary groups in partnership with the local authority and the government's Department for Education. They have greater control over their finances, the curriculum and teachers' pay and conditions.

What are special schools?

Pupils at a special school have usually been assessed and given a statement of special educational needs (SEN). These may include learning disabilities or physical disabilities. Some special schools are funded by the local education authority and some special schools are independent.

What is a free school?

Free schools are normally brand-new schools set up by teachers, charities, the community, faith groups, universities or groups of parents where there is parental demand. They are funded directly from central government. They also share with academies a greater control over their finances, the curriculum and teachers' pay and conditions.

What is a faith school?

Faith schools are mostly run in the same way as other state schools. Their faith status may be reflected in their religious education curriculum, admissions criteria and staffing policies.

What are grammar schools?

Grammar schools select all or most of their pupils based on academic ability.

What are independent/private schools?

Independent schools set their own curriculum and admissions policies. They are funded by fees paid by parents and investors.

Activity

Find out more about academies and how they differ from schools that are not academies.

Activity

Do you have any faith schools in your local area? Make a list of the advantages and disadvantages of children attending a faith school.

TIP

It is important that you know and can explain the different types of schools that exist in the UK.

Extension

1 To develop your knowledge of different types of schools, copy and complete a table similar to the one below.

2 Investigate different types of schools in your local area and add their name to the table.

3 Draw some conclusions about the different types of schools. Think about the advantages and disadvantages of each of these types of school.

	How are they funded?	Do they have to follow the National Curriculum?	Are they inspected by Ofsted?	Can they have their own admission policies?	Can they set their own term dates?
Academy					
Free school					
Special school					
Grammar school					
Faith school					
Independent school					

Summary

- There are many different types of schools that are funded and managed in different ways.
- Approximately 93 per cent of English school children attend state and state-funded schools, while the independent/private sector educates around 7 per cent of the total number of school children in England, with the figure rising to more than 18 per cent of pupils over the age of 16.

Check your knowledge

Identify three different types of schools and briefly describe each one.

KEY TERMS

Private school a school run by a non-state organisation, where families have to pay for their children to attend

Public school a high-status and expensive private school in Britain

Russell Group the top ranked 18 universities in the UK

State school a school funded by the government

Private vs state school

State or private education?

All children aged 5–18 are entitled to a free place at a state school. Most families take up this place. A few (around 7 per cent) choose to pay for a place at an independent school (also called a private school or, confusingly, for the most elite, public school). Parents pay fees towards the cost of running an independent school. There are around 2,500 independent schools in the UK, which educate around 615,000 children.

The debate about the existence of independent schools and state schools continues. Many people believe parents should have the right to send their children to independent schools, whereas others see them as divisive and providing a privileged education for the rich.

Arguments for independent schools

Class size

There are smaller class sizes, meaning teachers can invest more time in each individual child.

National Curriculum

Independent schools do not have to teach the National Curriculum, which means they can place more emphasis on certain subjects or aspects of a pupil's education; children learn not only basic literacy and maths skills, but also those skills that put them ahead of their state-schooled competitors later in life.

Facilities

They generally have better facilities for pupils because of the funding received from school fees.

Academic culture

It is argued that private schools have an academic culture, in which academic achievement is emphasised, leading to good results.

Admission is normally through entrance examination, so the average ability of pupils tends to be higher than in state schools.

Choice

Parents have the right to choose how to spend their money.

Better level of achievement

▼ Table 4.3 Grade comparisons, 2015–16 (A level and other 16 to 18 results: 2015 to 2016 (revised), www.gov.uk)

	Percentage achieving three A–A* grades or better at A level	Percentage achieving three A–B grades or better at A level
All state-funded schools	11.5	19.9
Independent schools	29.5	43.6

TIP
Knowing points from each side of this debate will be a good way to show evaluation skills in the examination.

Activity
Summarise what the statistics in Table 4.3 show. How do they support the argument for private schools?

Better chance of getting into top universities

In 2018 the Sutton Trust published findings that showed the eight top private schools had as many Oxford and Cambridge acceptances as three-quarters (2,894) of all schools and colleges put together. Only 44 per cent of applicants from comprehensive schools receive and accept an offer from the top 18 'Russell Group' universities compared to 71 per cent from independent schools. Applicants from disadvantaged backgrounds provide fewer examples of the types of work and life experiences that many colleges and universities value, which they use to decide between applicants.

Better job prospects

An independent school education prepares young people for top jobs in society. Although only 7 per cent of the population attend independent schools, many of the top positions in government, the civil service, medicine, law, media and banking are held by privately educated school pupils. This directly challenges the functionalist view that the education system is meritocratic.

▼ **Table 4.4** Percentage of pupils attending private schools and percentage of top job holders who attended private school ('Elitist Britain 2019', The Sutton Trust)

	Percentage
All pupils attending private school	7
Senior judges	65
Civil service permanent secretaries	59
Members of the House of Lords	57
Diplomats	52
Armed forces	49
Newspaper columnists	44

Arguments against independent schools

Inequalities

Private schools increase inequalities in society as a person's position in society is based on the parents' ability to pay. Inequalities continue through to the attendance of top universities and achievement of top jobs.

As outlined above, it is easier for private school pupils to gain entrance to Oxford and Cambridge universities than pupils from state schools.

Socially divisive

Private schools are socially divisive as they split society into two: those who have gone to a private school will often end up in top positions in later life, in comparison to those who go to state schools.

Investment in state education

If everyone had to send their children to a state school, then all (including the rich and powerful) would have a vested interest in making sure that state education was first class.

Link

The Sutton Trust's findings challenge the functionalist view expressed on page 129 that the education system is meritocratic.

Activity

Summarise what the statistics in Table 4.4 show.

Extension

Find out about the top private schools in the UK. Make a list of these and identify some of the key factors about them. For example, do they educate both boys and girls?

Activity

Divide into two groups – each group to choose one side of this debate. Each group should prepare their argument ready for a discussion. Remember, you need to have a persuasive argument so try to use evidence to support it.

Check your knowledge

1 Identify and explain three arguments in favour of independent schools.
2 Identify and explain three arguments against independent schools.

Summary

- State education and private education co-exist in the UK.
- About 7 per cent of pupils are educated in private schools.
- There are arguments for and against private schools.

Key learning

You will be able to:

- describe alternative forms of educational provision, including home schooling and de-schooling.

KEY TERMS

De-schooling the idea that schools should be abolished and replaced with some kind of informal education system

Home schooling when parents take full responsibility for the education of their children rather than allowing them to attend school

TIP ✓

Use Summerhill as an example of alternative schooling in Britain.

Activities

1 Do some more research on Summerhill School, then have a discussion about how this school compares to your own.

   a Think about the advantages and disadvantages of attending a school like Summerhill.

   b Think about the advantages and disadvantages of attending your own school.

2 Write a summary of which school you would prefer to attend and explain why.

Alternative education

What is de-schooling?

De-schooling is associated particularly with the work and ideas of US sociologist Ivan Illich (1926–2002) as well as the educator John Holt (1923–1985). It refers to the belief that schools and other learning institutions are incapable of providing the best possible education for some or most individuals. Some people feel that schools do not allow children to learn at their own pace in their own way. It is thought by some that the teaching methods applied in school are not suitable for every child.

According to this idea, schools stop a child's natural curiosity because the formal environment of the school stops children learning independently. De-schoolers oppose compulsory attendance at school, arguing that parents and children should be free to choose how and where learning takes place. They oppose the way schools structure learning with an emphasis on academic achievement rather than life skills. There is very little flexibility in the school day for children to learn in the way that suits them most.

Today, some educationalists and families are becoming uneasy with this restrictive environment. They are beginning to look for alternative answers to mainstream schooling. An example would be Montessori schools or the many models of 'free' or democratic schools that exist in many countries.

Research in action

The oldest and most famous of democratic schools is Summerhill School, on the east coast of England.

Summerhill is a private school founded in 1921 when discipline was an important part of child-rearing. It is a democratic, self-governing school where the adults and children have equal status. The school's philosophy is to allow freedom for the individual – each child being able to take their own path in life and follow their own interests to develop into the person who they personally feel they are meant to be.

Some key aspects of Summerhill School include the following:

- The right to play.
- An informal atmosphere.
- The use of first names.
- There is not always a clear line between learning inside and outside the classroom. For example, a group of teenagers sitting together and discussing topics of their choice is seen as a valuable learning experience.
- There is a wide choice of subjects up to GCSE level, but pupils do not have to take any.
- A new timetable is created each term when the older children 'sign up' for classes, though there is no compulsion to attend.
- There is free access to art, woodwork and computers.
- There are open areas where pupils not in classes can hang out, amuse themselves, socialise, play games and be creative.
- Adults are not there to create things for the pupils to do. Pupils need to create things for themselves.
- All lessons are optional.
- There is no pressure to conform to adult ideas of growing up, though the community itself has expectations of reasonable conduct from all individuals.

What is home schooling?

Although the vast majority of children attend some type of formal education, some parents decide to home school their children. Figures from the Children's Commissioner (2019) showed almost 60,000 children in England were being home educated at any one time in 2018 (out of a school population of 9.5 million pupils).

It's perfectly legal in the UK to educate a child at home, with the agreement of the head teacher, and parents do not need to be qualified teachers to do so.

Children who are home schooled receive all their education from their parents or carers, sometimes with the help of outside tutors. There are no formal rules about how children are taught or what they are taught.

In some ways, home education is a continuation of the teaching that every pre-school child receives from their parent or carer. However, from the age of five, education is a legal requirement.

Why do people choose home schooling?

- Parents may have philosophical or religious reasons.
- Parents may have been home schooled themselves or raised in situations in which education was not focused on a traditional school environment.
- A child may have special needs.
- A child may be unhappy at school.
- Sometimes parents feel that the methods of teaching in school are not right for their child and that they can provide a better education for them at home.
- Parents sometimes home school because they cannot get a place for their child in a school of their choice.

Activity

Make a list of the advantages and disadvantages of home schooling.

Check your knowledge

1 What is meant by deschooling?
2 What is meant by home schooling?
3 Give three reasons why parents may home school their children.

Summary

- There are alternatives to traditional education.
- Summerhill School is one alternative to traditional education.
- Home schooling is another alternative and approximately 37,000 children are home schooled in the UK.

KEY TERM

Material deprivation refers to the inability of individuals or households to afford the goods and activities that are typical in a society at a given point in time

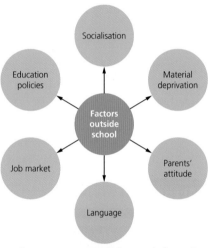

▲ **Figure 4.2** External factors influencing educational success

Educational achievement: external factors beyond school

When sociologists look at educational achievements, they find that there are distinct patterns of educational achievement within different social groups.

Educational success and failure is influenced by many factors. Many of these factors lie outside the school environment and many factors lie within the school itself. These pages look at how factors outside the school influence the success of children, while pages 145–146 look at factors within the school environment. These factors are then discussed in more detail on pages 145–166 when looking specifically at social class, ethnicity and gender. As you read this section, think about how each factor could influence different social groups (social class, ethnicity and gender).

Factors outside school can have a huge influence on children's educational success.

1 Socialisation

Parents and the wider family are important in socialising children and passing on the norms, attitudes and values of society. This takes place in early childhood and the main influence is usually the family (primary socialisation).

It is within the family that children usually learn things, such as how to communicate with others, how to eat, the differences between right and wrong and how to share with others.

There are many differences in socialisation between families and this might have an impact on children in later life, especially in school.

2 Material deprivation

Lack of money can mean cold, overcrowded homes, an inadequate level of nutrition as well as a lack of books and equipment that children need in school. Material deprivation can make it difficult to study at home and may lead to poor school attendance through ill health.

3 Adults' attitudes

The degree of interest and encouragement parents show in their children's education can be a significant element in educational success. In addition, Diane Reay (2006) has researched the impact teachers' expectations have. She found teachers often held stereotypical views on social class and achievement, which could have a negative impact for working-class children, resulting in a self-fulfilling outcome. This often resulted in their underachievement, undermining the notion of meritocracy and limiting their social mobility.

Activities

1 Make a list of how parents' attitudes and behaviour can influence the success of children in school.
2 How do you think the attitudes and behaviour of parents can affect children from different social groups?

4 Language

This is an important factor in educational success among all groups of children. Children from different social classes understand and use language in different ways.

This is also the case with children from different ethnic groups where English may not be their first language. They can be at a disadvantage when they start school because their studies are in a 'foreign' language, but research shows this does not necessarily result in disadvantage when they leave school.

In the case of gender, girls are often more advanced in their language skills than boys and this gives them a head start in school.

5 Job market

There is a competitive jobs market today and this means that not everyone can achieve the desirable jobs. There are more opportunities for women today, meaning they can have higher aspirations and so potentially driving up educational achievement. While this might be assumed to positively influence boys' behaviour in raising the competition, some have argued (for example Mac an Ghaill) that there is a 'crisis of masculinity' with some boys adopting a fatalistic attitude and questioning the need for educational qualifications as the traditional manual jobs they would have done in the past no longer exist. The evidence is that changes to the job market have a differential impact on individuals across social classes, gender and ethnic groups.

6 Education policies

The government changes education policies on a regular basis and this can influence how well pupils do in school. The removal of modular examinations and coursework at A level in recent years may have an influence on certain pupils who excel in these areas. The expansion of higher education (universities) is undoubtedly a factor in encouraging many pupils to continue their education post-18.

All these external factors influence how well pupils do in school. These external factors, combined with in-school factors, have an influence on the educational achievement of different groups of children and young people.

Links

- To learn about the differences that exist in educational achievement between children of different social classes, see pages 149–153.
- For differences that exist in educational achievement between children of different ethnic groups, see pages 162–166.
- For differences that exist in educational achievement between boys and girls, see pages 155–161.

Activity

Using the example above of the influence of the job market on the attitude of boys and girls to school work, explain how the job market could influence the attitudes to school work of different social classes and different ethnic groups.

Check your knowledge

1 Identify and explain two ways in which material deprivation could influence a child's educational achievement.
2 Identify and explain two ways in which parental attitudes could influence a child's educational performance.

Summary

- Children learn a lot through primary socialisation and this influences their achievement in school.
- Many external factors influence educational achievement and these factors interact with in-school factors.

TIP

There are continuing changes in the education system. Make sure you include up-to-date information in your answers.

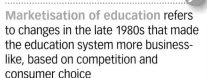

KEY TERMS

Marketisation of education refers to changes in the late 1980s that made the education system more business-like, based on competition and consumer choice

Vocationalism education designed to provide the skills necessary for work

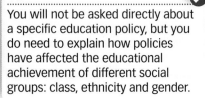

TIP ✓

You will not be asked directly about a specific education policy, but you do need to explain how policies have affected the educational achievement of different social groups: class, ethnicity and gender.

Activities

1 How did education policies before 1979 influence the achievement of different social groups?

2 What effect might these policies have had on different social classes and different ethnic groups? Do you think these policies reduced or increased inequalities?

3 What methods does your school use to compete with other schools in your local area?

The impact of education policies on educational achievement

There have been many significant changes to education through social policies.

Policies throughout the years have intended to widen participation in education and encourage equality between different social groups. However, they have had varying degrees of success.

Education policies before 1979

▼ **Table 4.5** Changes in education policy before 1979

1870 Education Act	Made a commitment to provide education nationally.
1918 Education Act	The age of compulsory education was raised to 14 years.
1944 Butler Act	The age of compulsory education was raised to 15 years. The Act introduced the tripartite system whereby three types of school were introduced to suit different types of students: <ul><li>grammar schools</li><li>secondary modern schools</li><li>secondary technical schools.</li></ul>
1965 Circular 10/65	Comprehensive schools were introduced.

Education policies since 1979

The most influential policy since 1979 was the 1988 Education Reform Act. **Marketisation of education** was one of the key aspects of this Reform Act. Marketisation is the process whereby services, like education, become more like a business based on competition and consumer choice.

This Reform Act introduced by the Conservative government brought in significant changes:

1 The introduction of the National Curriculum – a standard curriculum that all pupils had to follow – made it compulsory for girls and boys to take English, maths and science until they were 16. This also increased the amount of continuous assessment within subjects.

2 League tables encouraged schools to compete for the best results, aiming to drive up standards.

3 Ofsted, the government funded system of inspecting schools, was introduced.

4 Schools were encouraged to 'opt out' of local authority control. This meant that schools could manage their own finances and spend resources where they felt necessary to attract students.

5 Parents no longer had to send their children to their local school, but could choose the school most suitable for their child.

6 There was greater emphasis on **vocational education** for pupils who were less academic, so they would leave education with the skills required by employers.

The Reform Act allowed parents to:

- look at league tables and identify the high-performing schools
- access information about the school that is made available through school brochures, for example
- pay for transport for children to get to the higher performing schools
- visit different schools in order to select the best one.

Link

Refer to the work of Ball on parental choice on page 146.

Education policies since 1997

From 1997 to 2010 the Labour Party was in power. Their focus was to reduce inequality and provide an education system that gave everyone an equal chance of success. Tony Blair (then Prime Minister) famously stated that his priority was 'education, education, education.'

New Labour policies included the following:

1 The introduction of academies – a new type of school partially funded by local businesses to tackle underperforming schools.

2 Free childcare for every pre-school child – meaning women could return to work.

3 Sure Start, introduced in 1999, where pre-school children could receive early intervention and support. This provided support to improve the educational opportunities of children from socio-economically disadvantaged backgrounds.

4 Tuition fees for university were introduced, paid for with student loans. Previously students received a means-tested grant (up to 100 per cent) to study at university and pay for their living costs.

5 Educational maintenance allowance was introduced to encourage students from disadvantaged backgrounds to stay in school after the age of 16.

Research in action

In 2002, Geoff Whitty (1946–) saw conflict between Labour's policies to tackle inequalities and the developments they were making in marketisation. While the government was introducing policies such as Sure Start to tackle inequalities, the tuition fees for higher education were deterring others from going to university.

Activities

1 How did the 1988 Education Reform Act influence the achievement of different social groups?
2 Did all social groups have equal access to the high-performing schools?

Link

Look back to pages 140–141 and think about how external factors may influence access to high-performing schools.

Think about material factors, cultural factors and language and how these might influence access to the best schools.

Education policies since 2010

The coalition government (the Conservatives and Liberal Democrats) 2010–2015 introduced further changes. The Conservative governments (2015 and 2017) have continued these:

1 Educational maintenance allowance (EMA), giving financial support to poorer students to encourage them to stay in education until they were 18, was removed.

2 University tuition fees were increased up to £9,250 per year.

3 A student premium for disadvantaged pupils was introduced to schools to help them provide the additional classroom support and resources needed.

4 Free school meals were extended from 2014 so that every child in the first three years of school was eligible to receive one.

5 The A level system was changed and two-year A level courses were reintroduced.

6 The structure and grading of GCSEs was changed.

7 Academies were promoted in favour of comprehensives and free schools introduced.

The policies introduced by the coalition government have caused considerable controversy. Cuts to funding will have an effect on the equality of achievement and the changes to A levels and GCSEs, for example reducing coursework, are likely to disadvantage certain groups.

Link

For more information about the different types of schools, see pages 134–135.

Activity

Research more about recent government policies. What effect do you think these latest policies will have on the educational achievements of different social groups?

Check your knowledge

1 Identify three aspects of education policies before 1979 and explain how these factors influence the educational achievement of different social groups.
2 Identify three aspects of education policies since 1979 and explain how these factors influence the educational achievement of different social groups.

Summary

- Education policy is constantly changing. Each change has an effect on the achievement of different groups within the education system.

Educational achievement: processes within schools

As you have learned on pages 140–141, there are many factors that affect educational success and failure. As well as the numerous factors that lie outside the school environment, there are many factors within the school environment that influence educational achievement.

1 School ethos

The ethos of a school refers to the character, atmosphere and climate of a school. This might include an emphasis on:

● academic achievement
● the moral, spiritual and religious development of pupils
● equal opportunities with zero tolerance of racism and bullying
● active participation in school life.

2 Hidden curriculum

The school ethos is normally supported by the hidden curriculum. Pupils learn attitudes and values simply by participating in the daily routines of school life. Things underlying the ethos, like punctuality, respect for authority, school rules, uniforms, achievement, queuing, raising their hand in the classroom, and so on, all instil values, attitudes and behaviour among pupils.

Research in action

In 1979, Michael Rutter (1933–) conducted research in 12 schools to investigate whether good schools make a difference to the life chances of all pupils.

Rutter suggested that it is the features of the school's organisation which make this difference. These features included teachers:

● having high expectations of pupils
● setting examples of behaviour
● encouraging pupils to do well
● sharing a common commitment to the aims and values of the school.

3 Labelling and the self-fulfilling prophecy

Once a pupil has been given a label, this can lead to them interpreting their actions in terms of the label with the potential for a self-fulfilling prophecy to result. Some studies have shown that teachers can label pupils based on ethnic, gender and class stereotypes.

4 Streaming and setting

Most secondary schools have a system for allocating pupils to teaching groups. There are three main ways this occurs: setting, streaming and mixed ability.

Key learning

You will be able to:

● explain various processes within schools affecting educational achievement, including: streaming, setting, mixed-ability teaching, labelling and the self-fulfilling prophecy
● describe the key ideas of Ball on teacher expectations
● describe the key ideas of Willis on the creation of counter school cultures
● understand achievement from a functionalist, Marxist, interactionist and feminist perspective.

KEY TERMS

Cultural reproduction the process of obscuring the realities of social class inequality and exploitation of the working class in capitalism

Mixed ability in educational terms this refers to a group of students of all ability levels, taught together in the same class

Setting dividing students into different groups for particular subjects based on their ability in those subjects

Streaming dividing students into different groups (usually referred to as streams or bands) based on a general assessment of their ability rather than their performance in a particular subject

Subculture a group with a distinctive set of values and behaviours who set themselves apart from the wider society

Symbolic violence the term Bourdieu gives to the systematic undermining of working-class characteristics and confidence within schools

Activity

How does the hidden curriculum influence the educational success of different social groups? Think about:

● middle-class and working-class children
● girls and boys
● different ethnic groups.

▼ **Table 4.6** Comparison of systems for allocating pupils

	Advantages	Disadvantages
Streaming: pupils are sorted into classes according to their ability, and they stay in these groups for all their subjects.	Stretches the brightest pupils, while allowing the less able to work at their own level and pace.	Students are likely to be better at some subjects than others.
Setting: pupils are sorted into classes according to their ability, but on a subject-by-subject basis.	It is easier to teach pupils of one ability.	Can lead to low self-esteem for those in the lowest ability classes.
Mixed ability: pupils are sorted into classes that are not based on ability, so the highest and lowest achieving pupils are taught together.	Avoids labelling associated with streaming and setting. Allows for achievement by 'late developers'.	Teachers may lower the level of their teaching to suit the lower-ability pupils.

Activities

1   Can you add any more advantages and disadvantages to Table 4.6?
2   How can streaming, setting and labelling influence the educational success of different social groups? Think about:
   ● middle-class and working-class children
   ● girls and boys
   ● different ethnic groups.

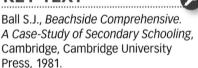

KEY TEXT

Ball S.J., *Beachside Comprehensive. A Case-Study of Secondary Schooling*, Cambridge, Cambridge University Press, 1981.

TIP

All these factors influence how well children do in school. Internal and external factors combine to influence the educational achievement of different groups of children and young people.

Make sure you can explain these factors and how they could influence educational achievement of different social groups.

Link

For more information on the roles and functions of education, see pages 126–131.

Research in action

Ball conducted research at Beachside Comprehensive School, on the south coast of England. His research was based on three years' fieldwork as a participant observer and he examined the internal organisation of the school. At Beachside, first year pupils were placed in one of three bands on the basis of information supplied by their primary school. The first band was supposed to contain the most able pupils and the third band the least able. He compared this group of students with another taught in mixed-ability classes. Ball observed that most pupils were conformist and eager when they first entered the school, but gradually the behaviour of the children began to diverge.

The band 1 child:

'Has academic potential ... will do O levels ... and a good number will stay on in the sixth form ... likes doing projects ... knows what the teacher wants ... is bright, alert and enthusiastic ... can concentrate ... produces neat work ... is interested ... wants to get on ... is grammar school material ... you can have discussions with ... friendly ... rewarding ... has common sense.'

The band 2 child:

'Is not interested in school work ... difficult to control ... rowdy and lazy ... is immature ... loses and forgets books ... cannot take part in discussions ... is moody ... of low standard ... technical inability ... lacks concentration ... is poorly behaved ... not up to much academically.'

The band 3 child:

'Is unfortunate ... is low ability ... maladjusted ... anti-school ... lacks a mature view of education ... mentally retarded ... emotionally unstable and ... a waste of time.'

Beachside Comprehensive, Stephen Ball (1981).

5 Subcultures

Pupil **subcultures** are groups of children who share the same values, norms and behaviour. This gives them a sense of group identity providing them with support and peer group status. However, these values and norms may differ from the dominant culture within the school. These subcultures can be positive school or anti-school subcultures and they can have a positive or negative effect on pupil achievement.

Functionalist perspective

Durkheim likened the processes within schools to a society in miniature. The focus within the classroom on the secondary socialisation of society's norms and values helps turn children into 'social beings' and bring about value-consensus. Talcott Parsons developed Durkheim's ideas, seeing the classroom's promotion of particularistic standards encouraging children to be treated as individuals. Davis and Moore claim that schooling prepares people for their future roles, a process known as role allocation.

However, functionalists generally have been accused of naïvely viewing the education system like a passive machine benefiting everyone by pouring knowledge into the heads of pupils. This is clearly not the case and ignores the reality that the outcome of education varies significantly, not least in terms of an individual's social class, gender or ethnicity.

Marxist perspective

Marxists argue the main purpose of the schooling process is cultural reproduction whereby the realities of social class inequality and exploitation of the working class in capitalism is obscured. Pierre Bourdieu describes how working-class characteristics, such as their subject choices, knowledge, accent and general confidence, are systematically undermined by teachers within schools. In so doing, the working class are daily subjected to a form of what he calls 'symbolic violence'. For an illustration of this look at teachers' comments about band 2 and 3 pupils in Ball's research in action on page 146.

Another French Marxist, Louis Althusser, suggested that the education system conditions young people to accept social inequalities through schools' use of the 'hidden curriculum'. So, by learning to respect authority, accepting the values of the school and being obedient, pupils learn to comply and fit in with the characteristics required by capitalism.

An important recent Marxist contribution to schooling has come from Glenn Rikowski (2001) who sees the marketisation of education since the 1980s as adding to the stress and alienation of not just pupils but equally teachers. Both are now under enormous pressure to achieve in terms of exam results. In addition, he argues, the growth of private enterprise in the British education system, such as private–public partnerships to build and run schools, shows that making profits can be as important as imparting knowledge.

Critics of the Marxist perspective of schooling argue it is over negative and ignores the opportunities education offers to promote upward social mobility.

Interactionist perspective

Interactionists examine the processes that are occurring within schools and classrooms and stress the importance of meanings derived from actions. One key process is institutional and teacher labelling, which can have devastating consequences (both positive and negative) on children's self-esteem, educational ambitions and experience of schooling.

From a study of 60 Chicago teachers Howard Becker (1963) found teachers tended to view middle-class pupils as closest to an 'ideal-type'

KEY TEXT

Willis P., *Learning to Labour*, Farnborough, Saxon House, 1977.

they carried in their heads. Working-class pupils were furthest from this ideal-type and were seen to lack interest and motivation. Becker's work highlights the danger of this labelling becoming self-fulfilling.

Labels are often given to students on the basis of their appearance, their language and their attitudes, without teachers really knowing the potential of the student. (Look again at Ball's Research in action.) Once a pupil has been given a label, it can have devastating consequences on particular students' future academic pathways and their experience of schooling. Teachers label pupils based on their social class background, but also on ethnic and gender stereotypes.

However, critics argue the interactionist perspective is too deterministic. While labels can be dangerous and have devastating consequences, they can also serve to make pupils react by actively challenging or negotiating them.

Research in action

Paul Willis (1950–), writing from a Marxist perspective, focused on the existence of conflict within the education system. He rejected the view that there is a direct relationship between the economy and the way the education system operates. Unlike Bowles and Gintis, Willis believed that education is not a particularly successful agency of socialisation. His work was based on a school in the Midlands situated in a working-class housing estate, where he attempted to understand the experience of schooling from the students' point of view.

He found the existence of a counter culture that was opposed to the values of school. Members of the counter culture did not follow school rules and were not obedient. Their main aim was to avoid attending lessons and they resented the school's attempts to control their time. Willis concluded that their rejection of the school made them suitable candidates for male-dominated, unskilled or semi-skilled manual work.

Willis' research is also in educational achievement and gender, with a different focus.

Feminist perspective

While the performance of girls, as a group, since the 1990s is well documented, feminists argue this has not received the celebration it deserves and is more often portrayed as a 'problem' of failing boys. Schooling, they argue, still perpetuates patriarchal ideology, with the education system serving consciously or subconsciously to prepare too many girls for lower-paid jobs and weaker economic positions in society. The continued gender-pay gap in the workplace is evidence, they argue, of the continued failure of the education system to fully promote the interests of girls, through a range of factors such as encouraging gendered subject choices.

Critics of the feminist perspective argue that while issues in the workplace stubbornly remain, things are slowly improving. In addition, schools and teachers are increasingly valuing girls as an asset, not least in helping to improve exam results, while the steady feminisation of the teaching profession serves to undermine the patriarchal nature of education and offer positive role models. Finally, as Louise Archer (2014) has shown, despite the best efforts of teachers and schools, some underachieving working-class girls, by adopting an anti-school subculture, help bring about their own underachievement.

Summary

- There are many factors within schools that can influence educational achievement of different social groups.
- These factors interact with external factors to influence educational achievement.
- Functionalists, Marxists, interactionists and feminists each provide an insight into the processes that operate within schools.

Social class and educational achievement: evidence

Statistics show that there is a clear link between social class and educational achievement.

The existence of a social-class gap means that middle-class children tend to have higher levels of attainment than working-class children of the same ability. Middle-class children benefit from material prosperity, as well as what Pierre Bourdieu calls cultural capital: the ideas, skills, interests and values passed on to children by their middle-class parents. These include, for example, language skills, attitudes, motivation and support within the home as well as cultural visits to museums, the theatre and sites of historical interest that generally help encourage educational success.

Research in action

According to Emma Perry and Becky Francis (2010), social class remains the strongest predictor of educational achievement in the UK, where the social class gap for educational achievement is one of the most significant in the developed world. There are major differences between the levels of achievement of the working class and middle class and, in general, the higher the social class of the parents, the more successful a child will be in education.

There is no easily available data on the social class of parents of children in school. One way researchers attempt to measure social-class disadvantage is the eligibility of children for free school meals.

Children who live in families with low incomes are eligible for free school meals. Children are eligible for free school meals if parents receive certain benefits, for example families that receive Universal Credit and Child Tax Credit.

Looking at the number of children receiving free school meals allows sociologists to measure the educational achievements of this group of pupils. Statistics show that children who are eligible for free school meals:

- do not reach the expected level at Key Stage 2 – only 53.5 per cent of pupils eligible for free school meals reach the expected level (Department for Education, 2015)
- are disproportionately likely to have been in care and/or have special educational needs
- are more likely to start school unable to read
- do less well in tests such as SATs
- are less likely to get places in the best state schools
- are more likely to be placed in lower streams and sets
- generally attain poorer examination results – for example, around three-quarters of young people from upper middle-class backgrounds get five or more GCSEs 9–4 compared to fewer than one-third from lower working-class backgrounds
- are less likely to go on to further education and higher education (university level).

Key learning

You will be able to:
- identify and describe the patterns of educational attainment of different social classes
- describe the key ideas of Halsey on class-based inequalities.

KEY TERM

Cultural capital the skills and values passed on to their children by middle-class parents, e.g. language skills and the motivation and support required to succeed in the education system

Pupil premium additional funding granted to state-funded schools in England to raise the attainment of disadvantaged pupils

Activity

Summarise what Table 4.7 shows about the educational achievement of pupils eligible for free school meals in comparison to pupils who do not receive free school meals.

TIP

Using some statistics in your answers will provide evidence for what you are writing.

Extension

Do some research on schools in your area and find out what percentage of pupils are entitled to pupil premium in different schools. Compare this to the performance tables of these schools.

KEY TEXT

Halsey A.H., Heath A. and Ridge J.M., *Origins and Destinations*, Oxford, Clarendon Press, 1980. See also the Sutton Trust: www.suttontrust.com/.

Link

For more information on social class, see pages 218–235.

TIP

Use evidence to show you understand the differences in educational achievement between different social classes.

Activities

1 What conclusions can you draw from this study on social class and educational achievement?

2 There are clearly differences between the educational achievements of different social classes. Make a list of the reasons why you think these differences exist.

Extension

Read through this page and write a paragraph, using appropriate statistics as evidence, to show the differences that exist between different social classes.

Check your knowledge

Identify two pieces of evidence to show that there is a relationship between social class and educational achievement.

▼ **Table 4.7** Percentage of pupils eligible for free school meals and all other pupils achieving the main attainment indicators (www.gov.uk)

	Five or more A*–C (including maths and English)		Entering the EBacc		Achieving the EBacc	
	2014	2015	2014	2015	2014	2015
Free school meals	33.5	33.1	21.0	21.2	9.7	9.9
All other pupils	60.5	60.9	41.7	41.5	26.6	26.6
Gap	*27.0*	*27.8*	*20.7*	*20.3*	*16.9*	*16.7*

Schools also receive **pupil premium**, which is additional funding for state-funded schools in England to raise the attainment of disadvantaged pupils of all abilities and to close the gap between them and their peers. Pupil premium funding is available to schools for each child registered as eligible for free school meals at any point in the last six years.

Research has shown that there is a relationship between social class and educational achievement.

Research in action

A study by Halsey, Heath and Ridge found clear class inequalities in education. They used a sample of 8,000 males born between 1913 and 1952, and divided them into three main groups based on their father's occupation.

1 The service class (professionals, administrators and managers).

2 The intermediate class (clerical or sales workers, the self-employed and lower grade technicians and foremen).

3 The working class (manual workers in industry and agriculture).

The research showed that an individual from the service class, compared to one from the working class, had four times as great a chance of being at school at 16, eight times the chance at 17 and ten times the chance at 18, while the chance of an individual from the service class attending university was 11 times greater than one from the working class.

While they found a correlation between income and educational opportunity (such as not being able to afford school uniform or educational trips), they also found two more significant factors influencing educational success. These were:

● home encouragement and parental attitudes

● the uneven distribution of grammar schools with more being in middle-class areas than working-class areas.

Although this study is 40 or so years old, despite significant social changes to both society and education the social class achievement gap stubbornly remains. Therefore, the findings of this dated study remain relevant today, as illustrated by the findings of contemporary organisations like the Sutton Trust.

Summary

● Statistics show that children from lower social classes achieve lower grades in school than children from middle-class backgrounds.

● There are many factors that interact to affect the educational achievement of different social classes.

● Halsey's research has shown that several factors combine to influence educational achievement, including material factors at home and school as well as parental attitudes and encouragement.

Social class and educational achievement: explanations

On pages 149–150, you learned that educational achievement in schools can be affected by social class.

There are a range of factors that sociologists have identified when explaining the pattern of differences in educational achievement. These can be grouped into two linking categories:

- External factors: factors beyond the school environment.
- Internal factors: factors within the school environment.

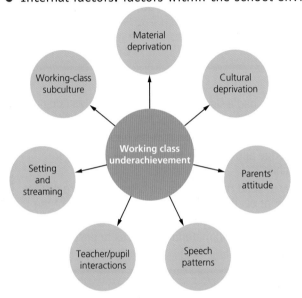

▲ **Figure 4.3** Factors influencing working-class underachievement

How external factors affect educational achievement of different social classes

Material deprivation

Research in action

Kerris Cooper and Kitty Stewart (2013) found that money makes a difference to children's educational achievements. A lack of money can mean:

- cold and overcrowded houses
- inadequate levels of food and nutrition
- a lack of books and computers
- limited internet access
- lost opportunities for school trips, sports equipment.

Although state education is free, there are hidden costs of sending a child to a state school amounting to around £1,517.85 each year per child (2017). These are the costs parents need to pay for things such as:

- school uniform
- PE kit
- school trips
- stationery
- school photographs.

Material deprivation may lead to pupils having to work part time, which may mean they are too tired to study at home or at school.

Key learning

You will be able to:
- explain various factors affecting educational achievement of different social classes
- explain functionalist, Marxist and feminist explanations of social class and educational achievement.

KEY TERM

Cultural deprivation the controversial idea that some groups, for example working-class children, lacked the cultural capital that helps achieve educational success

Activity

Look at the spider diagram in Figure 4.3. Divide these factors into external and internal factors.

Link

For more information on educational achievement and external or internal factors, see pages 140–148.

Activity

Think about the influence of material and cultural deprivation on educational achievement. Which do you think has the greater influence on educational performance? Explain your answer.

Cultural deprivation

This is a very controversial idea that some groups, for example working-class children, lacked the appropriate attitudes, norms and values that are necessary to succeed in education. However, as Nell Keddie (1973) responded, working-class children are culturally different rather than culturally deprived.

Cultural deprivation may include:

- parents' attitudes to, and interest in, education
- parents' level of education, resulting in less support with homework
- a lack of cultural experiences, for example books in the house, reading with parents, visits to museums and going on holiday.

Parents' attitude

KEY TEXT

Ball S.J., Bowe R. and Gewirtz S., 'Market forces and parental choice' in Tomlinson S. (ed.), *Educational Reform and its Consequences*, London, IPPR/Rivers Oram Press, 1994.

Research in action

In 1977, Pierre Bourdieu (1930–2002) suggested that the middle-class cultural capital is as valuable in education as material wealth. Bourdieu believes that middle-class children are at an advantage because they have the right kind of cultural capital – the more cultural capital you have, the more successful you will be in education.

Research by Stephen Ball, Richard Bowe and Sharon Gewirtz investigated the process of choosing a secondary school. They studied 15 schools in neighbouring LEAs (local education authorities) with different population profiles (for example, class and ethnicity). They found that middle-class parents had a significant advantage over working-class parents when selecting a school for their child.

They found that middle-class parents had the:

- knowledge and contacts to find the best school for their child
- money to send their children to better but more distant schools, or even move into the catchment area of the best schools
- cultural capital and material resources to ensure success.

TIP

It is important to know key studies which influence the educational achievement of different social classes.

Activity

Summarise what Ball, Bowe and Gerwitz's study shows about the influence of culture on educational achievement.

Speech patterns

It has been suggested that because the linguistic skills of middle-class children correspond more closely to the language of textbooks and teachers, this gives them an advantage in education, for example in entrance exams.

According to Basil Bernstein (1924–2000), there are two speech codes (1971):

Extension

How do you think speech patterns affect the educational achievement of children from different social classes? Make a list of the different ways speech can influence educational success and then write a detailed paragraph using the points from your list.

▼ **Table 4.8** Speech codes identified by Bernstein

Elaborated code	Restricted code
Used by middle classes	Used by working classes
Complex sentences	Simple sentences
Greater vocabulary	Limited vocabulary
Correct grammar	Grammar mistakes

However, Bernstein's work could be viewed as rather generalised. For example, not all children with restricted speech codes necessarily under attain.

How internal factors affect educational achievement of different social classes

Teacher/pupil interactions

There are a number of processes in schools that have been linked to the gap between working-class and middle-class achievement.

Teachers are inevitably involved in making judgements and classifying pupils. Labels are often given to pupils on the basis of their appearance, language and attitude. In 1971, Howard Becker (1928–) interviewed 60 Chicago high-school teachers and found that they judged their pupils on the basis of their appearance and conduct. Becker argued that the middle-class pupils were more likely to be seen as 'ideal students'.

Setting and streaming

Labelling can lead to pupils being placed in different ability groupings within school. For example, Gillborn and Youdell (2000) found that working-class pupils and some minority ethnic group members *on the borderline* between two sets are less likely to be given the benefit of the doubt and allocated to lower sets than other children performing work of the same standard.

Subculture

Some pupils rebel against school and form anti-school subcultures that can affect the work they do and their achievements. As has been noted earlier (see Willis' research on page 148), subcultures can be associated with social class, but can also be linked to gender and ethnicity.

Functionalist perspective

Functionalists are optimistic about the role of education for society. They believe it promotes a meritocracy and allows talented pupils, regardless of social class, gender or ethnicity, to advance individually. The functionalists Davis and Moore claim that education prepares people for their future roles, a process known as role allocation. Therefore, functionalists believe that education responds to the needs of the economy and provides the right amount of workers for the particular skills that the economy demands.

The functionalist perspective on education has been criticised for its naïve assumption that the education system is organised in a way that benefits everyone. Critics argue that this is simply not the case, pointing out how the top jobs in society are still primarily occupied by sons of rich white families.

Marxist perspective

Marxists challenge functionalist consensus theory, arguing that the education system is not meritocratic. Instead they argue meritocracy is little more than a myth to ensure that the system seems fair. Marxists see the education system as serving to reproduce the inequalities that prevail in capitalism. They point to the role of private schools and

Activity

Draw a flow diagram to show how a label given to a pupil can affect their educational achievement.

Oxbridge in providing the bulk of incumbents in the elite positions in society. Middle-class students are encouraged to aspire to managerial and professional positions, while working-class students are prepared largely for mundane repetitive work. Therefore, as a major socialisation agency, education serves to ensure that children learn their respective class position.

Critics of the Marxist perspective argue it is over negative and fails to appreciate the opportunities education can offer to all, regardless of their background. For example, the recent expansion of higher education (universities) has helped open up society and opportunities.

Feminist perspective

The feminist perspective is primarily focused on gender relations and the patriarchal nature of the education system. However, despite the general improvement of girls in terms of their achievement over boys, the exam performance in terms of passes and grades of working-class girls remains a concern.

Feminists have been criticised for failing to consider the issue of class differences sufficiently when considering gender issues in education. There are now many concerns about boys, especially in terms of underperforming working-class boys.

Check your knowledge

1 Identify and explain how two internal factors can affect the educational achievement of children from different social classes.
2 Identify and explain how two external factors can affect the achievement of children from different social classes.

Summary

● There are many factors that influence the achievement of different social classes.
● External factors, including family and home life, and internal school factors all play a part in educational success.
● Functionalists, Marxists and feminists all offer explanations for social class educational achievement.

Gender and educational achievement: evidence

How does gender affect achievement?

Statistics show that there is a clear link between gender and educational achievement.

Historically, boys significantly outperformed girls at all levels of education, although girls had begun to improve in the 1980s. During the 1990s, girls overtook boys in most areas and subsequently at all levels in the education system (except PhD). However, it is important not to generalise, as not all boys are underachieving, and neither are all girls doing well.

The social class differences discussed earlier are generally more important than gender in explaining differences in achievement.

> **Research in action**
>
> According to Perry and Francis (2010), girls who are entitled to free school meals continue to do less well in education than both boys and girls not entitled to free school meals. Also, middle-class boys, even if they are outperformed by middle-class girls, are likely to achieve more than working-class girls.

In 2018 at GCSE girls came out on top across all subjects except maths. In addition, at A level boys continued the trend begun in 2017 to receive more A and A* grades than girls.

Statistics show that girls:

- do better than boys at every stage in National Curriculum tests in English and science
- do better than boys in language and literacy
- are more successful than boys in most GCSE subjects, outperforming boys in every major subject except maths
- are more likely than boys to get three or more A level passes and achieve higher average point scores than males
- are more likely to get top First-class and Upper Second-class university degrees.

Subject choice

The pattern of AS and A level choices of subjects tends to follow gender stereotypes.

Boys prefer to take more practical subjects, such as maths, physics, computing, ICT or business studies, and are more likely than girls to choose two or more science/maths subjects.

Girls prefer to take subjects involving languages or the humanities, such as English, psychology, sociology, art and design, and are more likely than boys to choose at least one modern foreign language, although uptake of modern foreign languages is relatively low for both males and females.

Key learning

You will be able to:
- identify and describe the patterns of educational achievement of boys and girls.

TIP ✓

When studying gender and education, it is important that you address the patterns of educational achievement of both boys and girls. Although the educational achievements of both boys and girls have improved in recent years, there is still a big difference between them. It is therefore important to consider both.

▼ **Table 4.9** Comparison of percentage passes by gender at GCSE (www.gov.uk, 2018)

	Girls	Boys	Gap
Grade 9	5.2	3.8	1.4
Grade 7 or above	24.6	18.5	6.1

Activity

What do the statistics in Table 4.9 show about the achievement of boys and girls?

Table 4.10 shows striking differences in the percentages of boys and girls taking certain subjects at A level. For example, only 8.5 per cent of those taking a computing examination were girls. In addition, boys were approximately three times more likely than girls to take physics. On the other hand, girls were approximately three times more likely than boys to take English, psychology, sociology and art and design.

▼ **Table 4.10** Percentage of boys and girls taking the most popular subjects at A level (www.gov.uk, 2015)

Subject	Boys	Girls
Computing	91.5	8.5
Physics	79	21
Sociology	23	77
Psychology	24	76
English	28	72
Maths	72	28
Art and design	24	76
Drama	31	69
French	31	69
Religious studies	31	69

Activity

Summarise what the statistics in Table 4.10 show about the subjects chosen by boys and girls at A level.

TIP

Using statistics in your answers is a good way to show sociological understanding.

Activity

There are clear differences between the educational achievements of boys and girls and in the subject choices they make at A level.

Make two lists:

- The reasons why you think there are differences in the achievements of boys and girls.
- The reasons why boys and girls choose different subjects at A level.

Check your knowledge

1 Identify and explain two differences between the educational achievement of boys and girls.
2 Identify and explain two differences in the subject choices of girls and boys at A level.

Summary

- There are clear differences in the educational achievements of boys and girls at all levels of the education system.
- There are differences in the subjects chosen by boys and girls at GCSE, A level and vocational qualifications

Gender and educational achievement: explanations

On pages 155–156, you learned that there is a clear link between gender and educational achievement.

There are a range of factors that sociologists have identified when explaining the pattern of differences in educational achievement. These can be grouped into two linking categories:

- External factors – factors beyond the school environment.
- Internal factors – factors within the school environment.

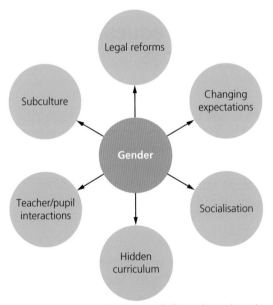

▲ **Figure 4.4** Gender factors influencing educational achievement

How external factors affect educational achievement of girls and boys

Legal reforms

Changes in the law, such as the Equal Pay Act 1970 and the Sex Discrimination Act 1975, have encouraged women to become more involved in the labour market. Greater career opportunities have inspired girls to work hard in school to achieve top positions that, in earlier years, were less open to them.

Changes in education policies have played a major role in contributing to gender differences, in particular the Education Reform Act 1988. The Act introduced the National Curriculum, which made maths and science compulsory to the age of 16 for all girls and boys.

Changing expectations

The women's movement and feminism have achieved considerable success in improving the expectations and self-esteem of women. Women can now look beyond being a housewife and mother as their main role in life.

Activity

Refer back to the research by Willis on page 148. Make some key points about what the study states about the achievement of boys and girls.

▲ Although girls are generally outperforming boys in schools, subject stereotypes persist and fewer girls than boys study STEM subjects

Activity

In what way does the ratio of male and female teachers influence the educational achievement of boys and girls?

Socialisation

Parents tend to buy girls different toys such as dolls, which encourage their language skills. This puts girls at an advantage because school is essentially a language experience and most subjects require good levels of comprehension and writing skills. Given the increased opportunities in schools, girls have the skills to achieve.

Research in action

McRobbie (1991) argues that the bedroom culture of girls (girls spend time in their bedrooms chatting with their friends) can create their own subcultures. They chat and read, which allows them to develop communication skills that are valued within school.

How internal factors affect educational achievement of girls and boys

Hidden curriculum

In the past, the hidden curriculum served to undermine girls by reinforcing the message that they were second best. Boys tended to be more dominant in the classroom and teachers tended to expect them to do better than girls. However, although since the 1980s girls as a group have outperformed boys, there is still progress to be made, particularly with working-class female attainment, and encouragement of females into STEM subjects.

Teacher/pupil interactions

With broadening opportunities for girls, more is expected of them today. Teachers have different expectations of girls. Some sociologists have suggested that there has been a 'feminisation of education', which means that schools have become a female-dominated environment that benefits girls but makes boys feel less comfortable.

The Department for Education's school workforce statistics 2016–17 show that less than one in three teachers are male (30.5 per cent) compared to 69.5 per cent female. At primary school level, the proportion of female teachers is currently 82.4 per cent and rising.

Tony Sewell (2010) argued that girls are generally more willing to conform to the school rules, whereas boys are not. Boys are expected to be livelier than girls and girls are expected to be more studious than boys. Teachers often respond to these stereotypes.

Subculture

The male peer group often devalues schoolwork, and boys may achieve peer group status by disruptive classroom behaviour. They may lose classroom time because they are sent out of the room. According to the Institute for Public Policy Research, boys are three times more likely than girls to be excluded from school, either permanently or for fixed terms, with the most common reason for these exclusions being persistent disruptive behaviour (2017). School work is often seen by boys as 'girly' and some develop a laddish anti-school subculture where it is not 'cool' to work hard.

Functionalist perspective

The functionalist perspective would point to the opportunities education offers to anyone with the inclination to work hard. Thus, the meritocratic principles of the education system would be seen to benefit anyone, regardless of their gender.

However, functionalists have been criticised for ignoring gender issues generally and promoting patriarchal attitudes through their support for traditional gender roles with regard to the family and employment.

Marxist perspective

The Marxist perspective sees education's role as primarily in reproducing capitalism. Some, like the Marxist sociologist Paul Willis, have embraced class and gender. In his research on his young working class 'lads' he demonstrated how masculinity was an important characteristic of their anti-school subculture. Although not strictly a Marxist, Máirtin Mac an Ghaill sees the 'crisis of masculinity' as particularly applicable to young working-class men who are both low achievers in school and likely to be less successful in employment.

A general criticism of the Marxist's perspective is that it focuses too much on social class, at the expense of considering gender issues, but this is not always fair.

Feminist perspective

Feminists stress how schools can still promote patriarchal values. They point to a gendered curriculum that fails to engage working-class girls and, through the gendered subject choices, often leads women into unfulfilling and low paid employment. Feminists have long accused the teaching profession of negative labelling of girls and insufficient encouragement, but with good female exam performance generally, teachers are in a position to bring about a self-fulfilling prophecy if they label female students positively.

A criticism of the feminist perspective is that it underestimates the change in the position of females both in education and employment. The insufficient encouragement of female pupils may be changing with the feminisation of the teaching profession. Increasing numbers of female teachers and head teachers now also act as role models for female pupils. There has also been a concerted effort to attract girls into STEM subjects.

Extension

Look back to pages 149–154 on social class and educational achievement. Can you see any links between social class and gender? Do further research to identify whether there is a relationship between the two factors.

Link

For more information on Willis, see page 148.

TIP

The study by Willis is useful to know about as it can be used as evidence in answers on gender and educational achievement, social class and educational achievement, as well as evidence for research conducted in sociology.

Check your knowledge

1 Identify and explain three factors that might explain why girls outperform boys in their GCSEs.
2 Identify and explain three factors that might explain why boys underperform compared with girls in their GCSEs.

Summary

- Statistics show that there is a difference in the achievement of boys and girls in school.
- There are many factors that interact to affect the achievement of boys and girls.
- Research by Sharpe has shown a change in girls' priorities.
- Research by McRobbie has shown a change in career opportunities for women which has influenced the performance of girls in school.
- Willis has shown that some boys prepare themselves for their future jobs by developing an anti-school subculture.
- Functionalists, Marxists and feminists all offer explanations for gender educational achievement.

You will be able to:
- apply your knowledge and understanding of sociological research methods to gender and subject choice.

Gender and subject choice

It is important that you understand how sociological research is conducted and doing some research for yourself helps you to develop this understanding.

Pages 155–159 have focused on education and gender. Lots of research has been done looking at gender and educational achievement.

▲ There is now far more encouragement to get girls into STEM subjects and careers

Research in action

Christine Skelton *et al.* (2007) point out that young males still typically study technical and science-oriented subjects, while young women typically pursue caring, or arts and social science subjects. Skelton suggests that the science subjects are often seen as more difficult and of a higher status than the 'softer' subjects chosen by girls.

Patricia Murphy and Jannette Elwood (1998) show how early socialisation can lead to different subject choices in school. Boys read hobby books and information texts,

while girls are more likely to read stories about people. This contributes to explanations about the disparities between boys and girls studying 'hard sciences'.

Naima Browne and Carol Ross (1991) argue children's beliefs are shaped by their early experiences and the expectations of adults. Often, girls and boys are encouraged to play with toys that are gender specific, for example boys with cars and girls with dolls.

Activity

Summarise what researchers say about the reasons why there are differences in the subject choices of girls and boys in school. Use the evidence presented to explain why you have come to this conclusion.

Now it's your turn to do some sociological research.

Research

You are to investigate the choices made by girls and boys in school by conducting either an interview or a questionnaire. Refer back to Chapter 2 research methods to help you.

1 Clearly outline what it is you are trying to investigate – what is the aim of the research?
2 Think about both research methods. What are the strengths and weaknesses of each method?
3 Decide which method would be the best to use for your investigation and give reasons why you have chosen this method.
4 Think about the questions you will include – will you use open or closed questions? Explain why you have chosen the questions you have.

5 How are you going to conduct your research – are you going to give out questionnaires or email them to students, for example?

6 Who is your target population? Think about this carefully – you need to ensure you get the information that you want. You could use sixth-form students, GCSE students or possibly both.

7 How are you going to select your sample? What are the advantages of this sampling technique? Remember, you need both males and females in your sample.

8 How many are going to be in your sample? Explain why.

9 Are there any ethical issues you need to consider? How would you overcome these ethical issues?

10 Think about conducting a pilot study. Why is this important for your study?

11 Amend your questions or your sample, if necessary.

Results and conclusions

- Summarise the results – what do they show about the subject choices of girls and boys?
- Write some key points about what you have found.
- Write a conclusion about what the results show.
- Write a paragraph about whether or not your findings support the Research in action above.
- What difficulties did you have with completing this research?
- Do your results give an accurate picture of the gender division in subject choice?
- How would you do your investigation differently if you did it again?

TIP

Conduct as much research as you can. This will give you a greater understanding of the issues involved in conducting sociological research.

Summary

- There is a lot of sociological evidence (including your own) to show the difference in subject choice between girls and boys.

- Skelton *et al.*, Murphy and Elwood, and Browne and Ross have shown that differences in subject choice still exist.

- Does your research show the same pattern?

Key learning

You will be able to:
- identify and explain the patterns of achievement of different ethnic groups.

Ethnicity and educational achievement: evidence

Education and ethnicity

It is easy to assume that because Britain is a multicultural society there are equal chances for all ethnic groups in education. However, when we look at the performance of different ethnic groups there are clear patterns in relation to those who are likely to achieve in education.

Many minority ethnic groups do extremely well, whereas other groups underachieve. This is not based on their merit or effort, but on the factors we will discuss on pages 164–167.

On average, Chinese, Asian and Mixed ethnic group pupils score higher than the national average for Attainment 8 (which measures how children perform in eight GCSE-level qualifications) and get better A level results than all other ethnic groups, including the White British ethnic majority.

The lowest achieving groups are Black and Mixed Caribbean, Black African and Black other students who generally have lower levels of achievement, especially among boys. The worst performing ethnic group of all are Gypsies/Travellers. Additionally, the lowest performing major ethnic group are white working-class boys.

Black Caribbean children are overrepresented in special schools for those with learning difficulties and are three times more likely to be permanently excluded from school than White British students of the same sex.

However, the picture surrounding ethnic attainment is changing. In 1992, White British pupils were more than twice as likely as Bangladeshis to achieve five or more GCSEs at grades A*–C, but in 2017 Bangladeshis were four percentage points above White British students in Attainment 8.

Activities

1 Summarise what the graph in Figure 4.5 on page 163 shows about the achievements of different ethnic groups.
2 Why do you think these differences exist? Using your knowledge of gender and social class differences in educational achievement, make a list of the reasons why these differences exist between different ethnic groups and then discuss your ideas with other students. Are some factors more important than others?

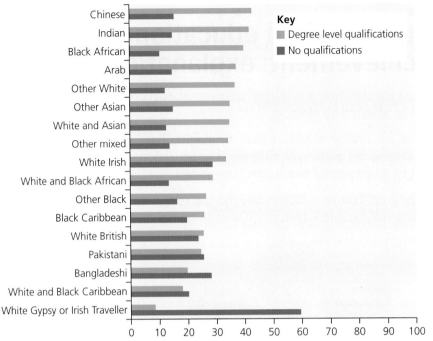

▲ **Figure 4.5** Percentage of people aged 16 and over with degree level qualifications and no qualifications (2011 Census, ONS)

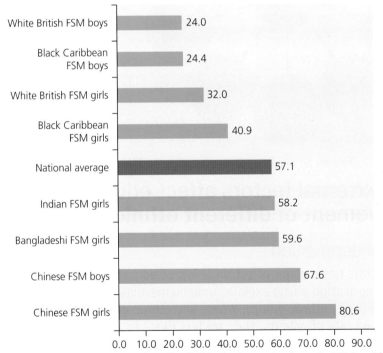

▲ **Figure 4.6** Percentage of pupils eligible for free school meals (FSM) achieving five or more A*–C grades at GCSE, including English and maths, by ethnic group and gender (Department for Education, 2015)

Key learning

You will be able to:

● explain various factors affecting educational achievement of different ethnic groups

● explain functionalist, Marxist and feminist explanations of ethnicity and educational achievement.

KEY TERMS 🔑

Ethnocentric curriculum subjects taught within schools or universities that uncritically assume the superiority of certain customs and behaviours

Institutional racism organisational procedures, practices and attitudes which either intentionally or unintentionally discriminate against a minority ethnic group

Activities

1 Look at the spider diagram in Figure 4.7. Divide these factors into external and internal factors.

2 How might labelling and subcultures affect the educational achievement of different ethnic groups?

TIP ✓

You must acknowledge that both internal and external factors contribute towards difference in educational achievement of different ethnic groups. It is important to explain this link.

Link

For more information on educational achievement and external or internal factors, see pages 140–147.

Ethnicity and educational achievement: explanations

On pages 162–163, you learned that educational achievement in schools can be affected by ethnicity.

There are a range of factors that sociologists have identified when explaining the pattern of differences in educational achievement. These can be grouped into two linking categories:

● External factors – factors beyond the school environment.
● Internal factors – factors within the school environment.

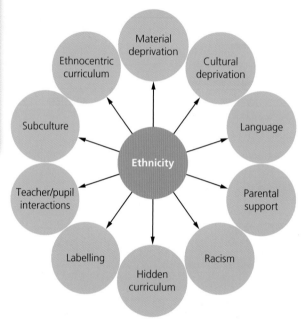

▲ Figure 4.7 Ethnicity factors influencing educational achievement

How external factors affect educational achievement of different ethnic groups

Material deprivation

As social class has a major effect on levels of educational achievement, material deprivation partly explains underachievement by members of some minority ethnic groups. Where any ethnic group has a higher than average rate of poverty, they are less likely to be able to afford equipment needed for school such as computers and classroom equipment. They may also struggle to pay for the correct uniform or school trips.

This also means that some minority ethnic groups face problems like poor quality housing and overcrowding, which may affect achievement levels at school.

All the explanations discussed on pages 149–154 relating to social class differences in educational achievement may also be relevant in explaining the differences between ethnic groups.

While social class remains a major influence on educational achievement, social class factors do not completely override the influence of ethnic inequality. Pupils from the same social class background but from different ethnic groups still show clear inequalities in achievement. For example, White British students from middle-class homes may perform better than minority ethnic students from the same class background.

Cultural deprivation

It has been suggested that different ethnic groups place different levels of importance on education. However, such ideas are rooted in stereotypes and dangerous generalisations. Asian and Chinese families are seen to value education and encourage children to work hard. When other ethnic groups show a lower commitment to education, this can affect the success of children within the education system. However, just as there is a huge variation in white families' attitudes to education, it naturally follows there will be variation in all ethnic groups.

Language

For many children, English is not their first language. This places them at an immediate disadvantage because all their lessons in school will be in English.

Many parents of minority ethnic students may not speak English and, therefore, may be unable to help and support their children with homework. Children in school may have difficulty in understanding instructions, which might put them at a disadvantage even though they are as academically able as English speaking students. However, evidence shows that by the age of 16 English as a second language has ceased to have any negative effect.

If parents have limited or no English, this could impact negatively on a child. For example, it may be more difficult for them to follow the process of applying for school places, by not reading prospectuses or realising when open days occur.

Parental support

All the factors above, material deprivation, cultural deprivation and the lack of English, can have a cumulative effect making it more difficult for parents to support their children in school.

How internal factors affect educational achievement of different social groups

Racism

The intentional or unintentional discrimination that occurs in education may take many forms, for example not recruiting some ethnic groups as teachers or to senior management. Some sociologists refer to schools as **institutionally racist**. This is where the policies, the curriculum and attitudes unintentionally stereotype and discriminate against minority ethnic groups.

TIP

It is very important not to generalise about the outcomes of some ethnic minorities. Also, be aware that there are differences in the educational performance within ethnic groups. Gender and social class differences can result in a wide array of differences within some ethnic groups.

Link

To read about the work of Tony Sewell and achievement of black boys, see Methods in context on pages 168–169.

School curriculum

The school curriculum could be seen as an ethnocentric curriculum – a curriculum that favours British knowledge and traditions over alternative cultures. Languages taught in the National Curriculum are mainly European and history tends to focus on British or European history. Examples like assemblies and school holidays may also fit with the culture of one particular group rather than another.

Hidden curriculum

This also tends to be centred on the mainstream, white, middle-class culture better than other ethnicities, for example the values underpinning success and who the teachers view as 'worthy' of educational investment.

Teacher/pupil stereotyping

Despite the existence of equal opportunity policies in schools, teacher stereotyping has devastating consequences for particular groups of students.

Subcultures

Boys of the same ethnic background may form groups within schools for support, and these groups may become distinctive subcultures. The influence of these groups could affect their educational achievement.

> **Research in action**
>
> Research by Cecile Wright (1992) in inner-city primary schools found some teachers hold ethnic-based stereotypes with more positive expectations of Asian students, particularly Asian girls, generally seeing them as relatively quiet, well behaved and highly motivated. In contrast, Black Caribbean pupils, particularly boys, were often seen by teachers as having low academic potential and were often expected to be, and labelled as, disruptive troublemakers.

These stereotypes can lead to the labelling of pupils. This, in turn, could affect how they are taught, what they achieve and may ultimately lead to the self-fulfilling prophecy.

Functionalist perspective

The functionalist perspective, through its support of the meritocratic argument, explains achievement very much in individual terms and characteristics. However, by doing so, it ignores the significant structural factors that have been discussed throughout this book such as material deprivation families might experience and the poor quality of local schools.

Marxist perspective

Marxists would see variations in ethnic achievement as shaped primarily by their social class. Therefore, education performance is less to do with ethnicity and more to do with factors associated with

Activity

What other aspects of the formal curriculum and the hidden curriculum might favour British culture more than other ethnicities? How might these influence the educational achievement of different ethnic groups?

class inequality, such as material deprivation. However, this fails to explain why some ethnic groups do better than others, despite being in the same social class.

Feminist perspective

While the focus of research has been on underperforming black boys, some feminists like Mary Fuller (1984) have examined the meanings and behaviours black girls can bring to education. She researched Black African-Caribbean girls in a London comprehensive who reacted to negative stereotypes from teachers by forming anti-school subcultures. In school they displayed an 'attitude' which Fuller described as 'practised resistance with accommodation'. They did not try to gain approval from their teachers, who they often saw as racist, but recognised the importance of impressing the markers of their exams. So, they worked hard at their school work at home while appearing to reject the school rules. This suggests that students have a variety of responses to labelling and also that negative labelling by teachers does not always lead to failure or underachievement of students.

Extension

Social class, gender and ethnicity all have an effect on educational achievement. Think about how these three factors are linked.

● Which external factors and internal factors have the greatest effect on educational achievement?

● Do some factors affect all social groups or are some factors more important in affecting the educational achievement of some groups than others?

Check your knowledge

1 Identify and explain two external factors that might explain why some ethnic groups outperform others in school.

2 Identify and explain two internal factors that might explain why some ethnic groups outperform others in school.

Summary

● Statistics show that there is a difference in the achievement of different ethnic groups.
● There are many factors that interact to affect the achievements in school.
● Many of the reasons to explain why lower social classes underperform are relevant when explaining the achievements of ethnic groups.
● Functionalists, Marxists, interactionists and feminists all offer explanations of ethnicity and educational achievement.

Key learning

You will be able to:

● apply your knowledge and understanding of sociological research methods to educational issues.

KEY TERMS

Primary data information gathered at first hand by a researcher

Secondary data data from pre-existing research, e.g. previously published research papers exploring the same social phenomena

Link

For more information on families in a global context, see pages 93–95.

Methods in context

Activities

1 Make a list of all the different ethical issues you would need to consider when conducting sociological research.

2 When you have made this list, explain what each ethical issue is and explain why it is important to consider it when conducting research.

TIP

Do not discuss methods in general. You might know the strengths and weaknesses of using questionnaires when collecting data, but you must apply what you know to the specific context on education, characteristics of the people or situation involved, and to the particular research topic that the question asks about.

Read Item A below and answer the questions that follow.

Item A

Starting in 2006, Sewell conducted research titled 'Generating Genius Programme – how to raise black boys' achievement'.

His experiment involved placing 25 black boys of academic promise, all from failing schools, into the unfamiliar world of the academic environment of top universities. Starting at the age of 12–13, he planned to get them interested in science and engineering. The boys spent three weeks or more of their summer holidays working alongside scientists at some of Britain's top universities, such as Imperial College, London.

Sewell claims that these boys achieved amazing GCSE results and from the first group of students at least three achieved places at Oxford and Cambridge.

Sewell argued that the Generating Genius Programme worked because it established the right ethos and high expectations – which effectively combated the disadvantages that his students faced. Sewell argues there has been a feminisation of education which makes it harder for some boys to adapt to the demands of school. In addition, it makes black boys vulnerable to negative influences of peer pressure and street culture.

He sees street culture, in the form of wanting to be a 'street hood', as a primary explanation of why so many Black-Caribbean pupils' achievement declines while at secondary school. This culture of masculinity provides what Sewell refers to as a 'comfort zone' and peer status while undermining the value of schooling and education qualifications.

1 From Item A, what research method was used by Sewell?

Make sure you read the item carefully so you can identify the research method used.

2 Examine one strength and one limitation of using this research method.

> *You need to identify one strength and one limitation of using this research method for this investigation. Do not just identify an advantage and limitation of the research method. Your answer must link to the investigation. For example, why is this research method good/not so good for investigating the educational achievement of black boys?*

3 Identify and explain one factor that may influence the underperformance of black boys.

> *Make sure you refer to this study when answering this question.*

4 Identify and explain one ethical issue of this research.

> *Do not just identify an ethical issue, make sure the ethical issue is relevant to the study. You need to explain why the ethical issue you identify is an issue for this specific study.*

5 Explain how you would investigate the achievement of boys and girls in school by using a different primary research method than the one used by Sewell.

6 Identify one secondary source you might use and explain why it would help with your research.

> *For questions 5 and 6 you can select any primary research method and any secondary research that is relevant to this study on investigating the achievement of boys and girls in schools. You must explain why the method you have identified is specifically used for this piece of research.*

> **TIP**
> ....
> Remember to use as many technical terms as possible in answer to research methods questions.

> **TIP**
> ....
> It is important that you can apply sociological research methods to each topic you are studying.
>
> When answering these questions, make sure you focus your answer on the specific item given. Use the item in your answers and use concepts specific to the method.

Summary

- All research methods used in sociological research have strengths and weaknesses.
- Ethical considerations need to be taken into account when conducting research.

The sociology of education

Practice questions

Question 1 (multiple choice)

Which of the following terms is used to describe a school that does not charge students a fee?   [1 mark]

a) Public school

b) Comprehensive school

c) Independent school

d) Private school

Question 2 (descriptive answer)

Describe one way that schools encourage social mobility.   [3 marks]

Answer and commentary

This question is asking about one way that schools encourage social mobility so you must describe one way that schools can encourage it. Do not be tempted to just explain what social mobility is.

Remember that you only have to identify one way that schools encourage social mobility. You need to identify a reason and then develop this into a paragraph.

You could write about:

- the way in which schools provide the opportunity to achieve recognised qualifications which give students access to higher education and employment opportunities
- the way in which schools can raise the aspirations of pupils regardless of their home background
- the way in which schools can improve students' life chances by giving them access to experiences and opportunities that their families may be unable to provide.

Question 3 (short answer question linked to source material)

Item A

Next Steps, previously known as the Longitudinal Study of Young People in England, follows the lives of around 16,000 people born in 1989–90. The study began in 2004, when the cohort members were aged 13–14, and has collected information about their education and employment, economic circumstances, family life, physical and emotional health and well-being, social participation and attitudes. The Next Steps data has also been linked to National Pupil Database records, which include the cohort members' individual scores at Key Stages 2, 3 and 4. In 2014 a report from the House of Commons Education Committee made use of this data when investigating concerns into the underachievement of white working-class students.

From Item A, examine one strength of the research.   [2 marks]

Answer and commentary

It is important to identify a potential strength of the research and to suggest why this element should be seen as a potential strength.

You could write about:

- Longitudinal studies measure change over time, for example the impact of educational achievement on future life chances or levels of social mobility.
- The study involves a very large number of participants (approximately 16,000) making it more likely to be representative.
- The survey data is constantly updated using annual interviews with participants, making it more likely to show patterns/developments over time.
- The survey measures a wide variety of variables including economic circumstances and physical and emotional health and well-being, making it more likely to be representative.

Question 4 (paragraph answer linked to the source material)

Identify and explain one factor which might account for the underachievement of white working-class students referred to as a concern in Item A.   [4 marks]

Question 5 (essay question)

Discuss how far sociologists would agree that school-based factors are the main cause of differences in the educational achievement of different social groups.   [12 marks]

Answer and commentary

Remember to think of your 'mini-essay' in three parts: an introductory paragraph in which you focus on the question and begin your argument, a second paragraph in which you develop your answer (consider one or more alternative sociological perspectives on the issue) and a final paragraph in which you reach a conclusion.

You could write about:

- School-based factors such as setting, streaming and teacher expectations.
- The importance of alternative factors such as ethnicity or gender.
- The functionalist perspective on differences in educational achievement, for example the idea that the education system is primarily designed to identify and reward the most ambitious and the most able (in these terms 'underachievement' represents a failure by the system to appropriately support, recognise or reward working-class students).
- The Marxist perspective on differences in educational achievement, which focuses on class-based inequalities and the ability of privileged groups in society to purchase the best available education for their children.
- The feminist perspective on differences in educational achievement, for example the idea of a 'gendered curriculum' that fails to engage working-class girls and/or directs them into low paid employment.
- You will need to evaluate the extent to which a particular sociological perspective represents a valid picture of contemporary British society. Try to reach a clear, logical, evidence-based conclusion and avoid contradictions in your argument.

TIP

Take a few moments to develop an outline plan of your answer.

Answer and commentary

It is important to identify a relevant factor accounting for the underachievement of white working-class students and to provide a detailed and well-developed explanation of your chosen factor.

You could write about:

- The home background of working-class students, where material and cultural resources may be poorer compared to middle-class homes.
- Lack of social and cultural capital, e.g. working-class parents may have high expectations of their children but are unable to provide them with the same opportunities and level of support enjoyed by children from middle-class homes.
- Restricted language codes, e.g. working-class families who are unfamiliar with the language of teachers and textbooks.
- School-based factors, e.g. curriculum content that fails to engage working-class students and low teacher expectations.
- Peer group pressure, e.g. anti-school subcultures found among some working-class students.

5

The sociology of crime and deviance

Key learning

You will be able to:

- identify, describe and explain the differences between crime and deviance
- explain the social construction of concepts of crime and deviance.

Link

To read more about crime at different times, in different places and in different cultures, see pages 179–180.

What is the difference between crime and deviance?

A crime is any form of action that results in breaking a written, formal rule in society, for example a bank robbery or murder. A crime is an act that breaks the law. If a person commits a crime and is detected, they could be arrested, charged and prosecuted. If found guilty, they will receive a sentence such as a community order, fine or imprisonment.

Deviance is behaviour that does not conform to the dominant norms of a specific society. If a person behaves in a way that is seen as deviant and this is discovered, it could lead to negative sanctions, such as being told off, ignored, ridiculed or cast out of their community. Acts of deviancy could include not wearing your tie in school or picking your nose in public. Some, but not all, deviant acts are also illegal.

An act can be deviant and criminal – killing someone is both criminal and deviant and deserves punishment.

An act can be deviant but not criminal – breaking social but not legal rules, for example drinking alcohol when pregnant.

An act can be criminal but not necessarily viewed as deviant by everyone – such as tax evasion.

Activity

Look at the photos. Which images show a criminal act and which show a deviant act? Explain why.

Definitions of crime and deviance change over time and from place to place. Whether an action is seen as criminal or deviant can depend on the time, place, social situation and culture in which it occurs:

- Time: when the act takes place can influence whether it is criminal or deviant. For example, many people would consider drinking alcohol in the morning compared with nine o'clock in the evening deviant;

smoking in public places in the UK is illegal but may be deviant in someone's house. Suicide was considered a crime until 1961, but it is now not considered a crime in the UK.

- Place: where the act happens, for example being naked on a nudist beach is expected but being naked at a cricket match would get you arrested.

- Social situation: the context in which the act takes place, for example chanting and flag waving at a funeral compared with the same behaviour at a football match.

- Culture: different cultures have different expectations, for example using cannabis in some Arab states is legal while drinking alcohol is a serious crime.

Activities

1 Copy and complete the table below to show some examples of crime and deviance.

Examples of crime	Examples of deviance

2 Think of other examples of how time, place, social situation and culture may determine whether an act is criminal or deviant.

▲ In the USA in the 1920s during the period of Prohibition, the possession, sale and consumption of alcohol was a criminal offence. Any alcohol found by the authorities was poured down the drain

Extension

1 Think of some acts that would be seen as criminal at all times and in all places.

2 Think of some acts that would be seen as deviant at all times and in all places.

Activity

Would you consider the following to be criminal, deviant or both?
- Leaving a coffee shop without paying for your drink.
- Driving at 33 miles per hour in a 30 mile an hour speed limit area.
- Walking across a pedestrian crossing when the red figure is displayed.
- Burping after a meal.
- Playing your music loudly on the beach.
- Walking through the town centre with a group of mates singing.
- Wearing hoodies.

TIP

Make sure you can explain the differences between crime and deviance and that you can use appropriate examples to explain the difference between them.

Summary

- Crime is breaking the law.
- Deviance is not conforming to the dominant norms of society.
- What is seen as crime and deviance is influenced by time, place, social situation and culture.

Check your knowledge

1 Using examples, explain what is meant by crime.

2 Using examples, explain what is meant by deviance.

KEY TERMS

Chivalry factor the idea that a male-dominated police force and criminal justice system treats women offenders more leniently because of their gender

Dark figure of crime the unknown amount of criminal activity that is not reported to or recorded by the police

Official crime statistics government statistics on crime based on official sources, e.g. police records

Recorded crime crime that is reported to and recorded by the police

Reported crime crime that is reported to the police – not all reported crime is recorded

Self-report study a survey that asks respondents to identify crimes they have committed, but for which they have not been caught

Victim survey a survey that asks respondents about their experience of crime, regardless of whether or not those crimes have been reported

Link

For more information on secondary sources of quantitative data, see pages 64–65.

Data on crime: official statistics

There are different ways of building up a picture of crime:

- official crime statistics
- victim surveys
- self-report studies.

These pages look at official crime statistics and pages 177–178 look at victim surveys and self-report studies.

Official crime statistics

Police crime statistics have been collected since 1857 and are now published quarterly by the government. The statistics are useful in showing patterns and trends in offending. They are a secondary source of quantitative data.

Official statistics show the following trends in recorded crime:

- From 1902 to the early 1950s, there was a gradual rise in recorded crime.
- From the early 1950s to the early 1980s, there was a steeper rise.
- From the early 1980s to the mid-1990s, there was a rapid increase.
- From the mid-1990s to 2015, there was a gradual annual decline.

Why do sociologists use official statistics?

- They provide a cheap and easily available resource.
- They can show change and trends over time.
- They can compare crime between different areas and social groups.
- They contain a large amount of information (for example, the Crime Survey for England and Wales).
- The data can be combined with the results of victim surveys and self-report studies to estimate the rate of crime.

Do official statistics tell the whole story?

Although statistics are a good way of measuring crime rates, they need to be treated with caution. There are many reasons why not all crime is included in official crime statistics.

Activities

1. Visit www.ons.gov.uk (for Scotland: www.scotland.gov.uk; for Northern Ireland: www.nisra.gov.uk) and find the latest crime statistics. Explore the kind of things covered by the crime statistics and identify the three most common and three least common crimes recorded by the police.

2. Investigate the crime rates in your local area. What are the three most common crimes recorded? How does this compare with national crime statistics?

Detection

Not all crime is detected. If a crime is observed and identified as a crime, the police may be informed. However, if crime has not been detected by the police, it cannot be included in official statistics. Many crimes, therefore, go undetected and are not included in official crime statistics. For example, some crimes like drug use and smuggling are unknown to the police, so remain undetected.

Reporting

Many crimes are not reported to the police. There are many reasons why crimes are not reported to the police.

- The victim may fear the consequences from the criminal if they report the crime.
- The victim may neither trust the police nor believe they will do anything.
- The crime is thought to be too petty.
- The crime is considered too private.
- It may be too sensitive or traumatic, for example rape.

Crime in the workplace may not be reported because a company may prefer to dismiss the person rather than involve the police.

People are now more willing to report some crimes to the police, for example the number of rapes in England and Wales recorded by police increased five-fold between 2011 and 2018. In 2018, police recorded 57,600 reports of rape, compared with 10,160 in 2011–12, according to crimes recorded by police. Women are significantly more likely than men to report rape. However, the CSEW shows that around five in six of all victims (83 per cent) still do not report sexual assault to the police.

Recording

Not all **reported crimes** have to be recorded by the police. Only about 40 per cent of the offences reported to the police are actually recorded by them.

Some crimes are not recorded because the:

- reported crime is seen as too trivial
- reported crime was not actually a crime
- victim may decide not to proceed with the complaint
- police may decide there is not enough evidence of the offence being committed.

Official statistics, therefore, do not give an accurate picture of crime. Sociologists argue that official statistics ignore the **dark figure of crime**. A very small proportion of actual crime is ever reported and recorded in official statistics.

This pattern of crime shrinkage can be represented by an iceberg. The often large proportion of crime that is not reported or recorded is hidden below the surface of the water and is known as the dark figure of crime.

Activity

What sort of crimes are people most likely and least likely to report to the police? Explain why.

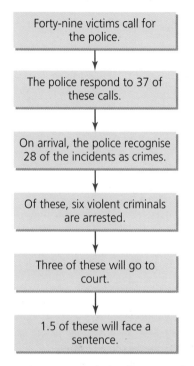

▲ **Figure 5.1** Estimated outcome for every 100 violent crimes

TIP

It is important that you can explain the reasons why crime is not always reported and recorded.

Link

To read more about the dark figure of crime, see pages 179–180 (the social construction of crime) and 177–178 (data on crime).

Sociological perspectives on crime statistics

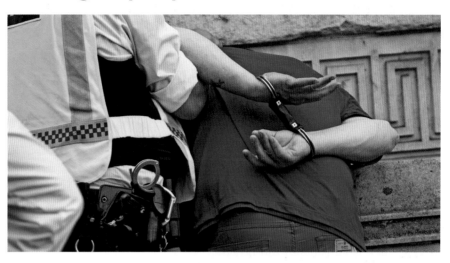

Functionalism

Functionalists tend to take official statistics on crime and deviance at face value, seeing them as an accurate reflection on acts of crime, crime rates and the culprits. Unlike most sociologists, they play down accusations that crime statistics are socially constructed.

Marxism

Marxists criticise official statistics for their concentration on working-class offences. Consequently, they argue that official statistics fail to reflect the considerable amount of white-collar and corporate crimes. This concentration by the police on working-class crime, they argue, stems from ideological pressures to conceal the crimes of the powerful.

Interactionism

Interactionists criticise official statistics because of the way they are constructed, which ignores the labelling process whereby some people are more prone to be viewed as deviant and criminal than others. They argue that because the police operate to stereotypes, they target mainly deprived urban areas and working-class offenders. This generates a picture of crime that reinforces the image of a typical criminal as working class, male, disproportionately black and under the age of 25.

Feminism

Feminists are critical of official statistics for underrepresenting the huge 'dark figure' of unreported and under-recorded crimes where women are victims, especially of personal attack. Crimes such as rape and domestic violence are seriously underrepresented in crime statistics. When it comes to offending, it seems that women are under-estimated in official statistics due to the fact that they are much more likely to be cautioned than charged. Agents of control are said to be influenced by a 'chivalry factor' resulting in women being less likely to appear in official statistics.

Check your knowledge

1 Explain why official statistics may not be an accurate reflection of the amount of crime committed.
2 Explain what is meant by the dark figure of crime.

Summary

- Official statistics are one way that crime can be measured.
- They are available and are an up-to-date way of measuring crime, but there are also many issues involved in using official statistics.
- Not all crimes are detected, reported or recorded.
- Official statistics ignore the dark figure of crime.

Data on crime: victim surveys and self-report studies

As seen on pages 174–175, official crime statistics are one way of measuring crime rates. Other ways include:

- victim surveys (note the CSEW (below) is both a victim survey and an official statistic)
- self-report studies.

Victim surveys

Victim surveys can be large-scale surveys (like the CSEW) or small scale of a local population (such as the Islington crime survey), where people are interviewed and asked what crimes have been committed against them in a given time period.

The Crime Survey for England and Wales (CSEW) is a large-scale victim survey, formerly called the British Crime Survey (BCS). It has been conducted by the government since 1981 and includes a very large sample (now around 50,000 people). It measures the amount of crime in England and Wales by asking people about crimes they have experienced in the last year. The CSEW includes crimes that are not necessarily reported to the police, so it is an alternative to police records. The findings of the CSEW (2018) indicate crime levels about twice that found in police-recorded crime and suggest that only four in ten crimes are actually reported to the police, showing that police-recorded crime may be the tip of the iceberg in the case of some crimes.

What are the advantages and disadvantages of victim surveys?

Although victim surveys like the CSEW include crimes not reported to the police and therefore highlight the dark figure of crime, they also have a number of drawbacks.

▼ **Table 5.1** Advantages and disadvantages of victim surveys

Advantages of victim surveys	Disadvantages of victim surveys
May uncover some of the hidden figures of crime.	They tend not to survey all crime, for example theft against businesses and victimless crime.
Give a more accurate figure of crime than official statistics.	People may still not admit to being a victim of some crimes, for example rape.
Include crime not reported to the police.	Victims' memories of crime may be inaccurate.
The CSEW now includes a specific victim survey on domestic violence.	People may not be aware that they are victims of crime.

Self-report studies

Self-report studies ask people to reveal crimes they have committed and, if so, how often they have done so.

They include lists of criminal and deviant acts (for example, stealing from a shop) and people are asked to tick the activities that they have committed within a given time period. Responses are always given anonymously, so

Links

- For more information on factors affecting criminal and deviant behaviour see pages 194–205.
- For more information on research methods, see pages 38–79.

▶ **Table 5.2** Advantages and disadvantages of self-report studies

TIP ✓
It is important that you can explain the advantages and disadvantages of the different methods of measuring crime.

Check your knowledge

Briefly explain what victim surveys and self-report studies are. Give two advantages and two disadvantages for both victim surveys and self-report studies.

Summary

- Official crime statistics include both police-recorded crime and the CSEW.
- Official statistics are figures collected by the Home Office.
- Victim surveys and self-report studies give an insight into the dark figure of unreported and unrecorded crime.
- Victim surveys ask respondents about their experience of crime.
- Self-report studies are surveys that ask respondents to identify crimes they have committed.
- Each of these different methods has advantages and disadvantages.

that people can feel free to admit to crime. Self-report studies provide another useful alternative to official crime statistics and they also suggest that criminal activity is more common than official statistics indicate.

The following is an example of a self-report study.

Have you committed any of these acts in the last two years?

- I have ridden a bicycle without lights after dark.
- I have, aged under 16, driven a car or motorbike.
- I have played truant from school.
- I have dropped litter in the street.
- I have stolen something from a shop.
- I have carried a weapon.
- I have had a fight in a public place.

What are the advantages and disadvantages of self-report studies?

Advantages of self-report studies	Disadvantages of self-report studies
May uncover some of the hidden figures of crime.	People may lie or exaggerate.
It is possible to find out about hidden offenders' ages, gender, ethnicity, social class and even their location.	Most self-report studies are carried out on young people and students because they are easy to study. There are no such surveys on professional criminals or drug traffickers, for example.
It is also the most useful way to find out about victimless crimes, such as illegal drug use.	The majority of the crimes uncovered tend to be trivial because people do not want to admit to committing serious crimes.

This information is useful not only for explaining how to measure crime, but it is also very important when discussing who commits crimes. If the official statistics are not giving us an accurate picture of overall crime rates, it is unlikely they will give us an accurate picture of who commits crimes.

Activity

Read through pages 174–178 on measuring crime and write a paragraph for each of the following:

a Explain what official statistics are.

b Explain one advantage and one disadvantage of official statistics.

c Explain what victim surveys are.

d Explain one advantage and one disadvantage of victim surveys.

e Explain what self-report studies are.

f Explain one advantage and one disadvantage of self-report studies.

g Write a conclusion summarising the different methods of measuring crime.

Extension

Look at the different ways of measuring crime. How valid, reliable and representative are these measurements of crime?

Complete a table similar to the one below. Explain why they may or may not be valid, reliable and representative.

	Valid	Reliable	Representative
Official statistics			
Victim surveys			
Self-report studies			

Social construction of crime

As we saw at the beginning of this chapter, crime and deviance only become seen as crime and deviance when a label is attached to certain forms of behaviour. Whether or not something is considered to be a crime will depend on many different factors such as:

- time
- place
- social situation
- culture.

What is considered criminal and deviant behaviour changes depending on the situation and it is, therefore, socially constructed. No act is in itself criminal or deviant – deviance largely depends upon the reaction of others and crime depends upon what behaviour legislators deem unlawful.

Activity

Referring back to pages 172–173, add some more examples to a copy of the table below.

Crime and deviance is defined by:	Example
Time	Suicide was a crime until the early 1960s.
Place	A knife fight outside a nightclub in London resulting in a person dying and a knife fight with an enemy soldier during a war.
Social situation	A man dressed as a woman at a fancy-dress party and a man dressed as a woman for work.
Culture	Alcohol consumption in Britain and Saudi Arabia.

▲ Killing is deviant and criminal when it is murder or manslaughter but can be justified and even honoured in war

Another example of the social construction of crime and deviance is homosexuality. Practising homosexuality between men was a crime in Britain until 1967 when the Sexual Offences Act was passed, which decriminalised private homosexual acts between men aged over 21.

In 1994, the Criminal Justice and Public Order Act lowered the age of consent for gay men from 21 to 18, and in 2001 it was further lowered to 16.

In 2004, the Civil Partnership Act was passed and came into effect in December 2005, followed by the Marriage (Same Sex Couples) Act 2013.

Key learning

You will be able to:
- explain the social construction of the concepts of crime and deviance.

KEY TERM

Social construct patterns of behaviour based on the norms and expectations of a society

Link

For more information, see What is the difference between crime and deviance? on pages 172–173.

Extension

Do some research to find out where homosexuality is still seen as criminal behaviour. Explain how this demonstrates the social construction of crime.

Activity

Using homosexuality as an example, show how this is an example of crime and deviance as a social construction in a copy of the table below.

Crime and deviance is defined by:	Homosexuality
Time	
Place	
Social situation	
Culture	

TIP ✓

Using examples in your answers will show good knowledge of sociology.

Links

- For more information on the work of Becker and the sociological factors affecting criminal behaviour, see pages 181–184.
- For more information on data on crime, see pages 174–178.

How to define deviance

Deviance is even more difficult to define than a crime; it is really difficult to decide what members of any society or group regard as deviant behaviour. What is defined as deviant will depend on the social expectations about what constitutes 'normal' behaviour and, therefore, whether or not something is defined as deviant will depend on how others react to it.

For example, swearing in front of your peer group is unlikely to be seen as deviant, but swearing at your teacher in school is much more likely to be seen as deviant and have serious consequences, for example detention/exclusion.

Becker (1963) suggests that an act only becomes deviant when others perceive and define it as such, and whether or not a deviant label is applied depends on the reaction of society. This is known as labelling theory.

Activity

Consider the situations below where swearing loudly would or would not be considered deviant. What does this say about labels given to the same act?

- on the bus
- at home alone
- in class
- in the supermarket
- at a football match
- in a place of worship
- in the street.

Check your knowledge

Using examples, what is meant by the social construction of crime and deviance?

Summary

There is no doubt that crime and deviance is socially constructed.

What is defined as a criminal or deviant act depends on:

- what the act is
- who is defining the act
- where the act takes place
- when the act takes place
- why the act has occurred.

Sociological explanations for crime and deviance

Activity

From what you know about sociological explanations for behaviour, which could you use to explain criminal and deviant behaviour?

There are many different sociological explanations for crime and deviance.

Socialisation

There are accepted norms and values in society and most people know and follow these. We are taught norms and values of society through the primary and secondary socialisation process. However, some young people are inadequately socialised within the family or they have learned criminal norms and values in their subcultures and may have criminal role models. This is an explanation particularly favoured by functionalists and especially the New Right.

Activity

Primary and secondary agents of socialisation are responsible for socialising children. Referring back to pages 28–29, how do you think these agents may influence the deviant and criminal behaviour of young people? Record your thoughts in a copy of the table below.

Primary socialisation	Secondary socialisation

Peer group and subcultures

Some sociologists, such as functionalists like Albert Cohen (1955), explain deviance and criminal behaviour in terms of the influence of peer groups and the formation of subcultures. Being part of a group gives individuals a sense of belonging. Individuals within the group are likely to follow the norms and values of the majority, particularly if they want to be accepted by the group.

Many of these groups are likely to develop their own norms and values, which may differ from the norms and values of society. These groups then become known as subcultures. Following the norms and values of the subculture may lead individuals into criminal behaviour.

Structural explanations

Structures are things that impact upon people from outside. With regard to crime, structures that might be associated with criminal activity include factors such as poverty and relative deprivation,

Key learning

You will be able to:

- identify, describe and explain various sociological explanations of crime and deviance including anomie, labelling, structural theories, subculture theories and interactionist theory
- describe the key ideas of Merton on the causes of crime
- describe the key ideas of Becker on the causes of crime.

KEY TERMS

Anomie the breakdown of norms governing accepted social behaviour

Deviant career a process that develops over time as the individual progresses through various stages of deviant behaviour, accepting and adopting external social labels, for example the young person who is labelled as a 'troublemaker' and who then goes on in later life to exhibit gradually more serious forms of criminal behaviour

Status frustration a sense of frustration arising in individuals or groups because they are denied status in society

Activity

Give an example of how anomie might be relevant in society today.

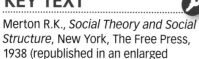

KEY TEXT

Merton R.K., *Social Theory and Social Structure*, New York, The Free Press, 1938 (republished in an enlarged edition in 1968).

unemployment and what Robert Merton would see as blocked opportunities to getting on legitimately in society (see Research in action on page 182). Merton argued that crime is a result of the tension and strain arising from people trying but failing to attain the goals that society has set for them. When people are unable to achieve their goals by these socially accepted means, they may look for other routes – some of which may be criminal. For example, many people have the goal of financial success and if structures, such as poverty, prevent this from being possible, they may turn to crime to achieve it.

▲ Structural explanations for crime include poverty and deprivation

Research in action

Robert King Merton (1910–2003), a functionalist, suggests that social order is based on agreement around social goals and approved ways of achieving them (1968). Most people share goals, for example financial success and having their own home, and most conform to the approved ways of achieving them, like working hard in paid employment. However, Merton argues that not all individuals have the same opportunities to achieve these goals by approved means because of such barriers as unemployment, racism and lack of educational success. Individuals face a sense of stress when there is a mismatch between their goals and the means of achieving those goals (anomie). People may look for other routes to achieve their goals – some of which may be criminal.

Merton believed that American society was unbalanced because greater importance was attached to success than to the ways in which that success was achieved.

Merton described five possible ways in which individuals could respond to success goals in American society:

1 Conformity: this describes individuals who work towards achieving success by conventionally accepted means, for example by gaining educational qualifications which in turn give them access to secure, well-paid employment. Other conventional routes to success include talent, hard work and ambition.

2 Innovation: this describes individuals who are unable to succeed using conventionally accepted routes and turn

to deviant means, usually crime. Merton believed that this route was most likely to be taken by individuals who came from the lower levels of society and who are denied the usual routes to success because they are, for example, less likely to gain the necessary educational qualifications.

3 Ritualism: this describes middle-class individuals who are deviant because they abandon conventional success goals. They are unable to innovate because they have been strongly socialised to conform, but they have little opportunity for advancement and remain stuck in low paid, low status 'respectable' jobs where they may exhibit an enthusiasm for rules and petty bureaucracy.

4 Retreatism: this describes individuals from any social class position who are deviant because they abandon both success goals and any means of achieving them. They 'drop out' of society; this response can be applied to explain the behaviour of social outcasts of all kinds including vagrants and drug addicts.

5 Rebellion: this describes those individuals who reject success goals and the usual means of achieving them, but then replace those that they have rejected with different goals and means. They are deviant because they wish to create a new society. In Merton's view, they are typically members of a 'rising' social class who may well attempt to organise a revolution.

Status frustration

The functionalist Albert Cohen (1918–2014), writing in 1955, offered a subcultural alternative to Merton's strain theory in order to explain non-material crimes associated with juvenile delinquency such as vandalism, graffiti and antisocial behaviour generally. He argued that the working classes (young boys in particular) hold the same success goals as the wider society but, as a consequence of educational underachievement and limited employment opportunities, cannot reach their goal. Cohen called this status frustration and describes how their reaction was subcultural in the sense that they sought status as rule-breakers instead. They formed a 'delinquent subculture' with different values to the rest of society. Risk-taking behaviour such as stealing cars and vandalism do not help achieve material goals but can help achieve status within the peer group.

Labelling (interactionist approach)

Labelling theory is particularly associated with Howard Becker (1928–). A label is a tag that is often attached to an individual or group. Labelling a person as criminal can have serious consequences for a person's identity. It is a form of power abuse since it does not have the informed consent of the individual. If the negative label of criminal is successfully applied, it tends to stick and people see this person as this label ('master status'). After constant reinforcement, the individual may come to believe the label and takes on the role ('deviant career'). The label then becomes a self-fulfilling prophecy. See the Research in action on page 184.

KEY TEXT

Becker H.S., *Outsiders*, New York, The Free Press, 1963.

▲ Even when doing no harm, groups of young men are likely to be labelled as 'troublemakers'

Research in action

Labelling can also lead to criminal or deviant behaviour. A label is a tag that is often attached to an individual or group. Becker (an interactionist) argues that society creates rules and anyone who acts outside of these rules is a deviant. Becker believes everyone acts in ways that are deviant. However, he is particularly interested in why some acts become determined as deviant while others do not. He suggests that an act only becomes deviant when others perceive and define it as deviant and whether or not a deviant label is applied to the act. Interactionists would point out how in one context an act is considered deviant, yet in another it is normal.

Agencies of social control, for example the police, use considerable discretion and selective judgement in deciding whether and how to deal with illegal or deviant behaviour. The police do not have the resources to identify and prosecute all crime. Becker suggests that they use pre-existing conceptions and stereotyping of what they believe is a criminal type and criminal area and these can influence their responses to deviant behaviour when they come across it.

Interactionists say this labelling can lead to groups being targeted by the police. For example, certain groups such as black youths may be stereotyped and labelled by the police as 'troublemakers' and the focus of the police will therefore be on this group of youths rather than other groups in society. As the police will be focusing on this group, individuals of this group are more likely to be singled out by the police, stopped and searched, arrested and charged with a criminal offence. This is reinforced in Home Office statistics which show that black people were nine and a half times as likely to be stopped and searched as white people in 2017/18. The previous year they were just over eight times as likely, and in 2014/15 they were just over four times as likely. Labelling someone as deviant can become a self-fulfilling prophecy and they begin to act in a deviant way. This can lead to a deviant career where they continue to behave in a deviant way. However, this is by no means always the case.

Cicourel's 1976 study of police and juvenile officers in California found police were more likely to arrest people who fitted the picture of having poor school performance, low-income backgrounds and minority ethnic membership, while middle-class individuals who were arrested tended to be counselled, cautioned and released by police officers, despite often committing more serious crimes.

TIP

Remember that a criminal and/or deviant act is only seen that way if it is labelled as criminal or deviant.

Activity

John has been arrested for supplying illegal drugs. This is not his first conviction and he is sentenced to prison. John now has a criminal label attached to him.

Draw a flow diagram of how John develops a deviant/criminal career as a result of the criminal label given to him.

Relative deprivation

In the 1980s new thinking on crime developed from previous Marxist ideas which highlighted relative deprivation as a cause of crime (along with subculture and marginalisation). Growing up in a poor environment and lacking certain resources that the majority of others have, for example the latest mobile phone, could lead to criminal activity. This idea has a lot in common with Merton's strain theory. As contemporary society has become more materialistic, there is increasing pressure to buy expensive items such as trainers and designer clothes. If these cannot be bought legitimately, people may be tempted to turn to crime to acquire them.

Activity

In the following table add evidence and evaluation points to each of the explanations for crime.

Explanation	Evidence	Evaluation
Biological		
Psychological		
Sociological: socialisation		
Sociological: peer group/subculture		
Sociological: status frustration		
Sociological: labelling		
Sociological: relative deprivation		

Check your knowledge

1 Identify and explain two sociological factors that could explain criminal behaviour.

2 Explain the difference between structural and subcultural explanations of crime.

3 Explain how the process of labelling can lead to criminal behaviour.

Summary

- Sociologists offer different explanations for criminal behaviour, including anomie, labelling, structural theories and subcultural theories.
- Merton's *structural* explanation of crime centres on the strain between wanting society's goals but not having the means to achieve them.
- Becker's labelling theory ignores structures but focuses on the *process* whereby the activities of some, rather than others, is defined as criminal or deviant.

Theories of crime: functionalists

Functionalist explanations of crime and deviance formed some of the earliest theories of crime.

Functionalism is a consensus structuralist theory:

- Structuralist: the source of crime and deviance is located in the structure of society. Each society has structures that constrain behaviour; blocked opportunities may encourage people to commit crime (Merton).
- Consensus: in order for society to function effectively, there needs to be a general agreement of the rules of society. Shared common values (the collective conscience) form the basis of appropriate behaviour. Functionalists therefore see laws as reflecting the consensus will of the people.

How do functionalists explain crime?

The functionalist perspective owes much to the work of Durkheim, who believed that deviant behaviour, in small amounts, is necessary for society to function. He argued that deviance is inevitable as not everyone can be fully integrated into the norms and values of society.

Durkheim argued that each society has a set of shared values that guide our actions. It provides a framework, with boundaries, which distinguishes between actions that are acceptable and those that are not. Durkheim argued that crime can perform a function within society.

According to Durkheim, 'crime is an integral part of all healthy societies'. He argued we need rule-breakers, people ahead of their time, to take society forward. So, for example, without the Suffragettes committing acts of deviance and crime (condemned by many at the time) women would not have gained the vote.

Functions of crime

Re-affirming the boundaries of society

Every time a person breaks a law and is taken to court, the resulting court action and the publicity surrounding the crime reminds members of society what happens if boundaries are crossed.

Changing values

Every so often, when a person is taken to court and charged with a crime, such as attacking a burglar, a degree of sympathy can sometimes occur for the person prosecuted. The resulting public outcry signals a change in values and, in time, this can lead to a change in the law to reflect the changing values.

Key learning

You will be able to:

- describe the functionalist perspective on the social construction of crime and deviance.

KEY TERM

Collective conscience the shared beliefs and values that bind communities together and regulate individual behaviour

TIP

Make sure you can define and use the key concepts of the functionalist perspective.

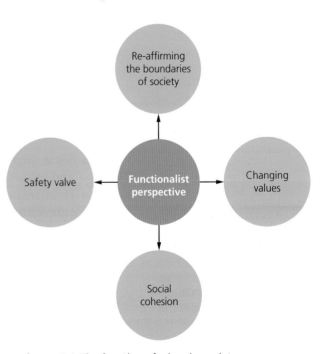

▲ **Figure 5.2** The function of crime in society

Activity

Do some research to find a case where changing values have led to a change in law.

Activity

Carry out some research on the murder of Ann Maguire. How does the response to her death support the idea of social cohesion?

Links

- For more information, see Sociological explanations for crime and deviance on pages 181–184.
- Read about the work of Merton and factors affecting criminal behaviour on page 182.
- Read about the work of Cohen and factors affecting criminal behaviour on page 183.

Check your knowledge

Explain the four functions of crime described by functionalists.

Summary

- Functionalists, such as Durkheim, believe that a small amount of crime in society is positive as it can drive positive change, re-affirm the boundaries of society, change values, bring about social cohesion and act as a safety valve.
- Merton believed that the strain brought about by trying to achieve the goals set by society led to deviant and criminal behaviour.
- Cohen believed that some young people reject the norms and values of society in favour of the norms and values of a delinquent subculture.

Social cohesion

A third function of crime, according to Durkheim, is to strengthen social cohesion. He pointed out that when particularly horrific crimes have been committed, the entire community draws together in shared outrage, and the sense of belonging to a community is thereby strengthened.

Safety valve

Deviant acts may be functional as a form of pressure release – releasing stresses in society. Deviance can allow individuals to express themselves in ways that may not be criminal. For example, a demonstration might be an outlet for expression of discontent avoiding wider and more serious challenges to society.

Strain theory

As we saw on pages 181–182, in the 1930s Merton tried to locate deviance within a functionalist framework. For Merton, crime and deviance were evidence of a poor fit or a strain between the socially accepted goals of society and the socially approved means of obtaining those desired goals. The resulting strain led to deviance and Merton referred to this as anomie. For Merton crime came down to blocked opportunities: not being able to achieve legitimately the shared goals of society. However, he can't explain why those with successful means to achieve society's goals can still undertake crime, such as the white-collar crime of the middle class and above. In addition, he also cannot explain why so many people who are denied access to society's goals are actually quite conformist.

Subculture theory

Albert Cohen (1955) accepted much of what Merton had to say on the structural origins of crime and deviance. However, Cohen noted that Merton could not explain non-material crime such as juvenile delinquency, like vandalism and graffiti, as these have nothing to do with goals and means.

- Some youths make a decision to completely reject mainstream norms and values. This is because of the status frustration they feel.
- Mainstream norms and values are replaced with alternative deviant subcultural norms and values. For Cohen, a high value is often placed on delinquent acts, for example, joy riding, arson and vandalism.
- The deviant subculture provides an alternative means of gaining status and striking back at an unequal social system that has branded them as 'failures'.

Criticisms of the functionalist approach

- Interactionists argue that functionalists ignore how crime and deviance is learned and transmitted by the proximity of deviant people around (a process known as differential association).
- Some sociologists have criticised functionalist subcultural theory arguing that, instead of adopting a counter culture, young people actively embrace mainstream values so much they turn to crime to acquire consumer goods.
- Postmodernists claim that functionalists miss the obvious point about crime and deviance that it is frequently enjoyable as 'edgework' (see page 205). Thus, there is not necessarily a rational reason behind crime.

Theories of crime: Marxists, interactionists and feminists

How do Marxists explain crime?

The Marxist approach is a conflict theory as opposed to the consensus theory of functionalism. Marxists see people's behaviour as influenced by the structure of society (like functionalists), but Marxists regard this structure as based on conflict between the different groups in society (the bourgeoisie and the proletariat, see pages 12–13) with social inequality as the driving force behind crime. Capitalist society is unequal, which could explain criminal behaviour.

The basis of laws

Laws are made by the powerful and will essentially benefit the ruling class (the bourgeoisie), and reflect their interests. Criminal law, therefore, operates to protect the rich and powerful.

Law creation

The ruling class imposes their values (values that are beneficial to themselves) upon the rest of the population. They do this through agencies of secondary socialisation, such as the education system and the media.

Law enforcement

Because Marxists see that laws are created to reflect the interests of the ruling class, this inevitably results, they argue, in the rich and powerful being treated more leniently as the criminal justice system is focused on working-class crime. For example, white collar crime is significant in terms of its value but receives very little attention in terms of resources and police time.

Individual motivation

Marxist theory provides an explanation for the increasing emphasis on economic self-interest, greed and personal gain. Capitalist society is based on competition and consumerism, for example, wanting the latest mobile phone. Those living in poverty are not able to compete in today's consumer world and may be driven to crime by relative deprivation.

Criticisms of the Marxist approach

It could be argued that Marxists over-emphasise class inequality in relation to crime and ignore other inequalities such as ethnicity and gender. They see people as being forced into crime by circumstances beyond their control. This is not always the case – not all people in poverty commit crimes.

How do interactionists explain crime?

Interactionist theories of crime and deviance are commonly referred to as labelling theory. Labelling theory tries to explain why only some people and some acts are defined as deviant or criminal, while others, carrying out similar acts, are not.

Key learning

You will be able to:

● describe Marxist, feminist and interactionist perspectives on the social construction of crime and deviance.

KEY TERM

White collar crime criminal activities typically of a financial nature such as fraud, embezzlement, forgery, etc.

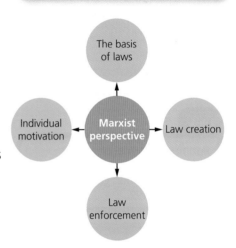

▲ **Figure 5.3** Marxist explanations of crime

Activity

Referring to the chapters on crime and social class, gender, ethnicity and age, summarise how these different groups are treated differently by the criminal justice system.

Links

● For more information on deprivation, see pages 237–238.
● Read about the work of Becker and the labelling theory and factors affecting criminal behaviour on pages 183–184.

Link

For more information on the accuracy of crime statistics, see pages 174–178.

Activity

It is Saturday night in any town in England. The police want to patrol the town to ensure that any deviant or criminal acts are dealt with.

a Where do the police focus their attention, the bingo hall or the nightclub?

b Explain why you have given the answer you have.

c How could this example be used to explain labelling theory?

Link

For more information, see Factors affecting criminal and deviant behaviour: gender on pages 196–199.

Check your knowledge

1 Identify and explain two key features of the interactionist approach to crime.

2 Identify and explain two key features of the feminist approach to crime.

Summary

- There are many different sociological theories of crime and deviance.
- Marxist theory is a conflict theory and believes that crime occurs as a response to inequalities in society.
- Interactionists believe that crime and deviance are only seen as criminal and deviant acts when someone is labelled as committing an act.
- Feminist theory focuses on female offending and experiences of women in the criminal justice system.

The labelling theory suggests that most people commit deviant and criminal acts but only some are caught and labelled for it. It is for this reason that interactionists focus on what is defined as crime and deviance and how people react to it, rather than looking at the causes of the initial act.

Home Office statistics show that in 2017–18, there were three stop and searches for every 1,000 white people, compared with 29 stop and searches for every 1,000 black people. While there is no evidence to suggest black men are inherently more criminal than any other ethnic group, stop and search allows police officers to act on stereotypical assumptions centred on racial profiling. Interactionists would highlight the obvious danger here that those targeted and labelled will internalise that label and proceed to engage in more criminal behaviour as a result.

Criticisms of the interactionist approach

- It tends to remove the blame for deviance away from the deviant and on to those who define them as deviant.
- It assumes the act is not deviant until it is labelled as deviant.
- It does not explain how some people choose deviant and criminal behaviour.

How do feminists explain crime?

Feminists view society as patriarchal. The sociology of crime and deviance tends to focus mainly on men. Female offending has not been studied until recently but, in recent years, there has been more of a focus on women who commit crime. Although it is true that approximately 80 per cent of offenders are men, there is the other 20 per cent who are women who are simply ignored in many sociological theories.

The feminist perspective has made a number of contributions to the study of crime and deviance:

- A new focus on female offending and experiences of women in the criminal justice system.
- A new focus on women as victims of crime.
- The application of existing theories and the development of new theories to explain female crime.

Activities

1 Look at the different theories of crime and deviance, and summarise the key points for each theory.

2 How might the different perspectives explain crime and deviance?

3 Using information on pages 185–188, complete a copy of the table below.

	Crime and deviance
Functionalists	
Marxists	
Feminists	
Interactionists	

Informal social control

Societies need to have rules in order for them to work successfully. Without rules and social control, societies would be in chaos (anomie). Social control refers to the methods that are used to control individual and group behaviour, which leads to conformity of rules of a particular society.

There are two forms of social control:

1 Informal social control: this is based on the approval and disapproval of people around us, for example family, friends and peer group. If they disapprove of our behaviour, they will tell us and criticise our behaviour. We may also be excluded from the group in certain cases (negative sanctions). However, if they approve of our behaviour, we will be accepted into the group or praised for our behaviour (positive rewards).

2 Formal social control: this is where our behaviour is controlled through organisations that exist within the criminal justice system to enforce order, for example the police, the judiciary and prisons.

These pages look at informal social control and pages 192–193 look at formal social control.

All societies need rules to ensure social order. Rules in general are a set of explicit or understood regulations governing conduct within a particular environment, for example you can, you cannot, you must, and so on.

Each society has written and unwritten rules:

- Written rules are clearly stated and are enforced in society; they can also be laws that we abide by, for example stopping at a red light.
- Unwritten rules are usually rules of social behaviour that are known by most people but are neither official nor written down, for example not talking with your mouth full or holding the door open for someone.

It is important that individuals know written rules and unwritten rules in society and these are passed on to us through the socialisation process.

Agencies of social control need to ensure that we follow the rules of society, specifically the written rules.

Informal social control

The main way through which social control is produced is through the ongoing, lifelong process of socialisation that each person experiences. Through this process we are taught the norms, rules and behaviour expected within society.

Informal social control is enforced by rewards (positive) and sanctions (negative). Reward often takes the form of praise or compliments, but also takes other common forms, like high marks on school work, promotions at work and social popularity. Sanctions used to enforce informal social control can take the form of teasing, poor marks in school or the ending of a relationship.

Positive rewards are generally used to encourage desirable behaviours and negative sanctions are generally used to discourage undesirable behaviours. For example, within schools rewards and sanctions are used to influence behaviour. Informally, they teach social control through the hidden curriculum, which reflects society's values and prepares students for their place in society (see page 130).

Key learning

You will be able to:
- describe and explain informal methods of social control including unwritten rules and sanctions
- describe, compare and contrast a variety of sociological perspectives on informal social control
- describe the key ideas of Heidensohn on female conformity.

KEY TERMS

Agencies of social control institutions that influence the process of social control, e.g. families, schools or the police

Judiciary the system of courts that interprets and applies the law in a country

TIP
Linking different areas of the specification in your answers will show good sociological understanding.

Figure 5.4 shows the informal agencies of social control. These are institutions that ensure that we behave in appropriate ways.

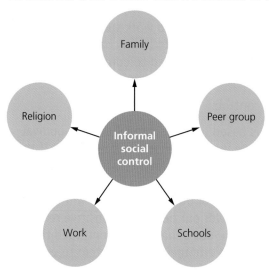

▲ **Figure 5.4** Informal agencies of social control

Research in action

David Farrington (1944–) and Donald West (1924–) studied 411 working-class males born in 1953 until their late thirties (1990). The study found that there was a correlation between family traits and offending. Offenders were more likely to come from homes where the father had criminal convictions. They also found that offenders were more likely to come from poorer and lone parent families. This research, therefore, suggests that the failure within the family to provide adequate socialisation and informal social control can lead to crime.

Functionalism

Functionalists would emphasise the positive role that agencies of socialisation play in promoting informal social control by shaping behaviour, especially of children. As children grow up they learn to fit into society by learning consensus norms and values. The family, as the agent of primary socialisation, is responsible in many ways for the behaviour of children. This socialisation is supported by secondary agencies such as education, peer groups and the media.

Marxism

Marxists also highlight the importance of socialisation in promoting informal social control, but view it more negatively as helping to maintain capitalism. They would see socialisation as serving to promote false consciousness, whereby the proletariat becomes blind to the exploitative nature and fundamental unfairness of capitalism by actually supporting it.

Interactionism

Interactionists would see socialisation as resulting in meaningful behaviour by individuals. Since society and its members all benefit from the stability that informal social control brings, it follows that people will see shared norms and values positively.

Feminism

Feminists see the mechanisms of informal social control as there to promote patriarchy in society. Socialisation serves to therefore reinforce norms and values that promote the interests of men at the expense of women.

KEY TEXT

Heidensohn F, *Women and Crime*, London, Macmillan, 1985.

Research in action

Frances Heidensohn (1942–) in 1985 argued from a feminist perspective that the striking feature of women's behaviour is conformity; they commit fewer crimes than men. She argues that this is because patriarchal society imposes greater control over women and reduces their opportunities to offend, therefore making it more difficult for women to offend. Control in the home revolves around women's domestic role, with its constant round of housework and childcare that imposes restrictions on their time and movement and confines them to the house for long periods, reducing opportunities to offend. Often, women who try to reject their domestic role find their partners impose it by force, such as through domestic violence. Men, as the main or sole breadwinners, also have financial power over their wives. Daughters are more closely controlled than sons. They have more limits on when they may leave the home and they are expected to contribute more to domestic tasks. In public, women are controlled by the threat of male sexual violence and by the idea that inappropriate behaviour may bring loss of reputation and shame upon the family.

Activity

How do the formal curriculum and the hidden curriculum act as a means of social control? Add your thoughts to the table below.

Formal curriculum, e.g. within the classroom	Hidden curriculum, e.g. school rules, routine, dress code

Summary

- Agents of social control are important in teaching us the norms and values of society.
- The family, peer groups, schools, work and religion are all important informal agents of social control.
- Functionalists, Marxists, interactionists and feminists all see socialisation as important in instilling informal social control.

Check your knowledge

Identify two informal agencies of social control and briefly explain how they can control behaviour.

KEY TERMS

Formal social control where our behaviour is controlled through organisations that exist to enforce order, e.g. the police, judiciary, prisons

Probation system Her Majesty's Prison and Probation Service (HMPPS) which supervises high-risk offenders released into the community, or community rehabilitation companies (CRCs) which monitor low and medium-risk offenders given community service rather than custodial sentences

Terrorism the unlawful use of violence and intimidation, especially against civilians

Youth crime crimes committed by individuals who are too young to be sent to an adult prison; in Britain, children aged ten and above can be held responsible for their actions

▲ **Figure 5.5** Formal agencies of social control

Formal social control

As you have learned from page 189, there are two forms of social control. Here, we look at formal social control.

Formal social control

Rules of behaviour that are written down, in societies such as our own, apply equally to everyone. It is the job of agencies of formal social control to enforce the law. In our society, the main agency of formal social control is the criminal justice system.

Formal rules and social controls exist to tell everyone within a society or social group what is and is not acceptable in terms of behaviour.

Figure 5.5 shows the formal agencies of social control. These are institutions that influence the way we behave.

It is the role of the criminal justice system to deliver justice for all, by convicting and punishing the guilty and helping them to stop offending, while protecting the innocent.

The criminal justice system works in partnership with the police, courts, the Home Office, the Ministry of Justice and other agencies throughout the criminal justice system.

The government

The government is responsible for making the laws of society and, in doing so, determines what is considered acceptable and unacceptable behaviour.

The police

There are 43 police forces across England and Wales, along with the British Transport Police and the separate police forces of Scotland and Northern Ireland, which are responsible for the investigation of crime, collection of evidence and arrest and detention of suspected offenders. The role of the police is to act as 'gatekeepers' to the criminal justice system.

In many cases, a simple police presence is enough to create formal social control. In others, police might intervene in a situation that involves unlawful or dangerous behaviour in order to stop it and ensure that social control is maintained.

The courts

There are various courts in England and Wales:

- Crown Courts deal with the most serious offences where people face a judge and a jury.
- Magistrate courts deal with less serious criminal offences.
- Youth courts deal with youth crime, with defendants aged between 10 and 17 years.

It is up to formal bodies like the courts to give sanctions when someone fails to comply with the laws. Formal punishments include: fines; community service; probation; prison; discharge; referral orders; youth rehabilitation orders; ASBOs.

The Home Office

The Home Office is a ministerial department of the government, responsible for immigration, security and law and order. The first duty of the government is to keep citizens safe and the country secure. The Home Office has been at the frontline of this since 1782.

The Home Office is responsible for the police, fire and rescue services, visas and immigration, drug policy, counter-terrorism and the security service (MI5).

The Ministry of Justice

The Ministry of Justice has responsibility for courts, prisons and the probation system, including criminal and family justice as well as democracy, rights and the constitution.

The Serious Fraud Office

The Serious Fraud Office prosecutes serious or complex fraud and corruption. It is part of the UK criminal justice system covering England, Wales and Northern Ireland and investigates a small number of large, financial crime cases.

Sociological views on the criminal justice system

Functionalists believe the criminal justice system reflects the dominant ideas about what is considered to be right and wrong within society. They argue that laws exist to reflect the consensus will of the people.

Marxists argue that the criminal justice system reflects the values of the ruling class who dominate the criminal justice system. Marxists argue that laws tend to reflect the interests of the rich and powerful. Marxists point out that the resources of the criminal justice system are focused on crimes committed by the working class, while the white collar crimes of the rich go largely undetected.

Interactionists argue that laws tend to reflect the interests of those in a position to exercise power in society, such as newspaper editors, chief constables, senior clergy and politicians. They have a collective name for these powerful people: 'moral entrepreneurs'. Such people have the ability to set agendas and campaign for new legislation to deal with 'moral panics' associated with 'folk devils'. The Home Office was accused of stirring up racial tension in 2013 with vans appearing across London calling on illegal immigrants to 'Go home'.

Feminists see laws existing to protect men at the expense of women. For example, it was not until 1991 that husbands could be convicted for the rape of their wives. They also point to the lack of support the criminal justice system offers to female victims of crime. For example, rape victims are often subjected in court to a character assassination in an attempt to make them appear responsible for being attacked.

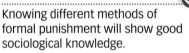

Activities

1 How do the police control crime in your area? Do you see the police on the streets? Do they come into school? What part do they play in your local community?
2 Find out more about the different sanctions that can be given to people who break the law.
3 Find out more about the Ministry of Justice. Who is the current Minister of Justice and what are their responsibilities?

TIP ✓
Knowing different methods of formal punishment will show good sociological knowledge.

Extension
Find out more about the different responsibilities of the Home Office.

Link
For more information, see Factors affecting criminal and deviant behaviour: social class on pages 194–195 and Social construction of crime on pages 179–180.

Check your knowledge
Identify two formal agencies of social control and briefly explain how they can control behaviour.

Summary

- The criminal justice system is very important in maintaining formal social control.
- Functionalists, Marxists, interactionists and feminists differ in their views of why laws exist and the mechanisms of formal social control.

Factors affecting criminal and deviant behaviour: social class

There is a clear link between a person's social class and the likelihood that they will be convicted of a crime. In the UK, crime statistics do not refer to the social class of convicted people. However, research has shown that the working classes are disproportionately more likely to be convicted and sent to prison than middle- and upper-class people. As Marxists highlight, there is a considerable amount of white collar and corporate crime that rarely results in detection, prosecution and conviction. For example, research from the University of Portsmouth (2012) estimates only 1.5 per cent of frauds are ever reported and only 0.4 per cent ever receive a criminal sanction. If punishment does occur, it is often considered lenient compared to working-class crime.

Sociological explanations for differences between social classes

Inaccurate statistics

As you have seen, statistics on crime are not necessarily accurate. Some studies have identified a link between crime and individuals who either have no job or are in lower paid jobs. However, it may be that they commit crimes that are more identifiable and are more likely to be targeted by the police, so are more likely to be arrested and prosecuted than middle-class and upper-class individuals.

Socialisation

Children develop the norms and values of their parents. The Cambridge Study in Delinquent Development (1995) found a correlation between criminal children and poor parental child-rearing behaviour, including harsh and inconsistent discipline. New Right sociologists, like Charles Murray, controversially argue children from one-parent families are inadequately socialised – but this is not supported by evidence.

Functionalist explanations

Merton's strain theory can explain the connection between working class members and crime. Anomie occurs when there is a mismatch between goals and the means to achieve the goals. If they are faced with blocked opportunities and do not have the means to afford the goals of goods and activities that are typical in society, this may lead some individuals to turn to crime to obtain the things that others have. The Cambridge Study in Delinquent Development (1995) found a correlation between criminal children and family poverty and poor housing. Albert Cohen saw 'status frustration' as particularly applicable to working-class boys and Walter Miller saw the deviant subcultural values of 'focal concerns' as applying to the lower working class.

Marxist explanations

Marxists feel that crime statistics over represent working-class crime at the expense of white collar crime, which is often invisible and more associated with the middle and upper classes. Their argument is that the police and courts focus their attention on working-class crime while misdemeanours of the ruling class largely go unpunished or are treated more softly. When the working class do commit crime, they acknowledge wider structural factors like poverty, material deprivation and unemployment as also having an influence.

Interactionist explanations

Interactionists would highlight the role of labelling in constructing crime as associated with lower classes. Labelling theory asks why some people and their behaviours, but not others, become defined as deviant and criminal. Poorer groups in society are more likely to be the victims and perpetrators of crime and it is likely that the police and courts label those at the bottom of the social scale more readily. The working class is more likely to commit the kinds of crimes that are more visible, such as antisocial behaviour, vandalism and theft, while the middle class is more likely to commit crimes such as fraud and embezzlement, which are very much hidden from the public.

Once identified and labelled as a criminal, people are more likely to be seen as criminals. If someone reflects stereotypical criminal characteristics, they are more likely to be labelled as deviant or criminal, running the risk of a miscarriage of justice.

White collar crime

Although official statistics show that most criminal activity appears to be associated with working-class young people, there are other types of crime that probably cost society more than the value of burglaries and bank robberies put together. White collar crime is committed predominantly by middle- and upperclass individuals, often in the course of their work.

The term 'white collar crime' was introduced by Edwin Sutherland (1883–1950) in the 1940s. This crime takes several forms:

- Occupational crime: crime carried out by individuals in work, for example theft and fraud.
- Professional crime: crime carried out as a lifetime career, for example drug running.
- Corporate crime: crime carried out by directors, for example in order to increase profits within their organisation.
- Computer crime: crime carried out by using a computer, for example the illegal transfer of funds.

The value of white collar crime is staggering. For example, the University of Portsmouth's Centre for Counter Fraud Studies (2016) estimated the cost of fraud in the UK could be as high as £193 billion per year compared to the estimated cost of burglaries of £2.2 billion by the Association of British Insurers (ABI) in 2015.

KEY TEXT

Farrington, D.P., 'The development of offending and antisocial behaviour from childhood: key findings from the Cambridge Study in Delinquent Development', *Journal of Child Psychology and Psychiatry*, vol. 36, pp. 929–964, 1995.

TIP

Make sure you can explain how white collar crime and punishment differs from other forms of crime and punishment.

Extension

Find out more about some famous white collar crimes, for example, Guinness and Enron.

Check your knowledge

1 Identify and explain three reasons why working-class individuals may be more likely to be associated with crime than higher social class individuals.

2 Using an example, briefly explain white collar crime.

Summary

- There is a clear link between a person's social class and the likelihood that they will be convicted of a crime.
- There are many reasons why this pattern exists, including socialisation, material deprivation, education, labelling.
- Functionalists, Marxists, interactionists and feminists differ in their explanations of social class and crime.
- White collar crime appears to be committed by middle classes and above and includes fraud, counterfeiting and embezzlement

KEY TERMS

Bedroom culture the subcultures created by girls, which allow them to develop communication skills within their own homes

Chivalry thesis the idea that a male-dominated police force and criminal justice system treats women offenders more leniently because of their gender

Glass ceiling (in relation to women in employment) an informal barrier that prevents women from achieving senior positions in their chosen career

Factors affecting criminal and deviant behaviour: gender

Statistics show that men commit more crime than women. For example:

- In March 2019, the total number of people in prison and young offenders institutes in England and Wales was 82,643. Of these, 78,806 were men and 3,837 were women (ONS, 2019).
- About 90 per cent of people found guilty of burglary, robbery, drug offences and criminal damage are male.
- Men are about 60 times more likely to be found guilty for sex offences.
- Men are 14 times more likely to be found guilty for robbery.
- Men are 13 times more likely to be found guilty for possession of weapons.
- Men are seven times more likely to be found guilty for criminal damage.
- Men are four times more likely to be found guilty for theft.

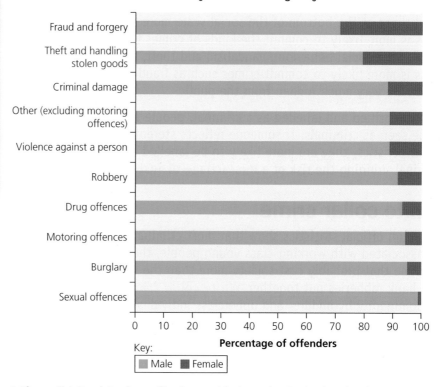

▲ **Figure 5.6** Graph to show offenders and their gender, England and Wales, 2011–12) (ONS)

Sociological explanations for differences between genders

Inaccurate statistics

As you have seen, statistics on crime are not necessarily accurate. Statistics show that males commit more crime than females, but this might obscure some female crime. Females tend to commit less visible crimes that are less likely to be detected and, therefore, less likely to be reported and recorded, for example shoplifting. Another factor is the chivalry thesis which argues that within a male-dominated police force and criminal justice system women offenders are treated more leniently because of their gender.

Feminist explanations

Feminists have examined gender differences in crime as associated with socialisation, differing opportunities to commit crime and the social control of women.

Gender socialisation encourages men and women to adopt traditionally gender-based characteristics. For example, males are seen as more aggressive and rough. Women are often perceived as less risk taking; hence their lower involvement in crime.

Females have fewer opportunities to commit crime than males simply because men and women inhabit, to some extent, different worlds. During teenage years, girls are more likely to spend time with their friends in their bedrooms (bedroom culture). As women are assumed to be the primary carers within the family, this means that they lack the opportunity to commit crime. However, even in work, women may not have the same opportunities to commit work-related crime as they face the glass ceiling – an invisible barrier of gender discrimination that makes it difficult for women to reach the same top levels in their chosen career as similarly qualified men. This restricts their opportunities to engage in white collar crime such as fraud.

Social control theory therefore emphasises the ways in which females are controlled in both private and public spheres and why they tend to be more conformist than men. Women are controlled by a wide range of informal sanctions, reflecting the feminist view that they spend most of their lives being controlled by men. Women also face the threat of losing their reputation if they engage in deviant behaviour and may be condemned for a lack of femininity. This puts greater pressure on women to conform than on men.

Functionalist explanations

Functionalists have often been criticised by feminists for ignoring gender altogether with regard to crime and deviance. For example, both Albert Cohen in his analysis of 'status frustration' and Walter Miller in his analysis of 'focal concerns' only published results of juvenile delinquency associated with males.

Marxist explanations

Marxists also have little to say about gender and crime as they see it as primarily associated with social class. They point to how the prevailing ideology of crime as a working-class problem is constructed, which serves to subtly obscure the extent of white collar crime. Men are primarily associated with crime generally, but with the changing position of women in the labour market, it may be that with greater opportunities to commit white collar crime, we may see an increase in women committing crimes like fraud.

Activity

Based on your own experience, how are boys and girls brought up differently?

Extension

Look up the case of Lavinia Woodward, an Oxford University student who stabbed her boyfriend in 2016. Do you think her sentence might have been influenced by her gender?

Interactionist explanations

Interactionists would see labelling and stereotyping as key factors in the construction of crime as primarily a male activity. In terms of meaning, males can enhance their masculinity by engaging in delinquency, such as fighting or football hooliganism. In contrast, females may be discouraged from delinquency for fear of undermining their femininity.

Research in action

Rebecca Dobash and Russell Dobash (1979) show many violent attacks result from men's dissatisfaction with their wives' domestic duties. Men exercise control through their financial power by denying women funds for leisure, increasing their time in the home. Daughters are also subject to patriarchal control and are less likely to be allowed to stay out late than boys in the family. This gives boys more opportunity to engage in deviant behaviour on the streets.

Activity

As shown on pages 251–253, women have more opportunities in society today and also have more power. Do you think the social control explanation is still a valid explanation of crime rates of males and females?

TIP

The research above was conducted quite a long time ago and things might be very different now. You could use this timeframe as a way of evaluating research. For example, this research may be outdated and may reflect society of the 1970s and 1980s rather than contemporary society.

Chivalry thesis

There is a common belief that the male-dominated police and courts are easier on women. According to this chivalry thesis, women offenders are seen as 'less guilty' as they are more vulnerable and in need of protection, and they are therefore treated more leniently than men. They are often seen as 'sad' rather than 'bad' and in need of 'help' rather than 'punishment'.

Activity

Do you think this is true? In a group of boys and girls, discuss the chivalry thesis. Do boys and girls have different views on this?

Research in action

Pat Carlen (1939–), writing from a feminist perspective, studied a group of mostly working-class women aged between 15 and 46 who had been convicted of one or more crimes. Carlen carried out in-depth unstructured interviews with each of the women, a number of whom were in prison or youth custody at the time. In Carlen's view, working-class women have been controlled through the promise of rewards. They make a class deal which offers respectable working-class women consumer goods in return for their wage. They make a gender deal for the psychological and material rewards offered by male breadwinners in return for their love and domestic labour. When these rewards are not available, then crime becomes a viable alternative. If women had failed to find a legitimate way of earning a decent living, they were left feeling powerless, oppressed and the victims of injustice. Many of the women had experienced problems and humiliations in trying to claim benefits. Some of them had always been in poverty and felt they had nothing to lose by using crime to escape from poverty.

Is this pattern changing?

Although men still commit more crimes than women, this pattern is slowly changing in the UK and internationally. There is a growing increase in the number of crimes committed by women.

The number of arrests for female offenders (juveniles and adults) in 2017–18 decreased by 43 per cent and 32 per cent respectively compared to 2013–14 (Ministry of Justice). Overall, females are substantially underrepresented among those prosecuted. In 2017, females accounted for just 27 per cent of all prosecutions at the magistrates' court and 10 per cent of all defendants tried at the Crown Court (Ministry of Justice, 2018). This pattern tends to be reflected in convictions, remands and sentencing, although the conviction ratio is marginally higher for women. Women are less likely to receive custodial sentences compared with men, receiving fines or conditional discharges instead. When women are given custodial sentences, the trend over the past decade has been for them to receive shorter immediate custodial sentences.

KEY TEXT

Carlen P., *Women, Crime and Poverty*, Milton Keynes, Open University Press, 1988.

Activity

Make a list of the reasons why the female crime rate has risen.

Extension

When looking at gender and crime, two main issues emerge:
- Males commit more crime than females.
- Police are more likely to arrest and charge males rather than females, and males, therefore, are more likely to appear in crime statistics.

Which of these issues do you think is the most accurate? Give reasons for your decision.

Summary

- Statistics show that more males commit crime than females.
- There are many reasons for this difference in crime statistics, including different socialisation, opportunities to commit crime, social control.
- Statistics may not be a true reflection of the crime committed by males and females.
- Functionalists, Marxists, interactionists and feminists differ in their explanations of gender and crime.

Check your knowledge

Identify and explain three reasons why there are differences in the crime rates of males and females.

KEY TERMS

Institutional racism organisational procedures and practices that either intentionally or unintentionally discriminate against a minority ethnic group

Police caution a formal warning given by the police to anyone aged 10 years or over who has admitted that they are guilty of a minor crime

Scapegoat an individual, or their community, who is blamed unfairly for a negative event

Activity

Write a paragraph summarising the statistics in the graphs in Figure 5.7. Explain what these mean.

TIP

It is difficult to untangle ethnicity from class and gender, so remember that all three factors need to be explored together as well as separately.

Factors affecting criminal and deviant behaviour: ethnicity

Statistics suggest that there are higher levels of arrest rates among some ethnic groups, particularly the black (African-Caribbean male) population and Asian males, but as discussed earlier this may be due to stereotyping and racial profiling by the police. Both these groups are over-represented in the prison population. There is a clear link between a person's ethnic group and the likelihood that they will be convicted of a crime.

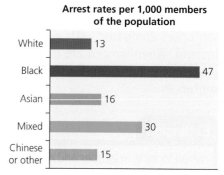

▲ **Figure 5.7a** Stop and search rates per 1,000 members of the population (Ministry of Justice, 2016)

▲ **Figure 5.7b** Arrest rates per 1,000 members of the population (Ministry of Justice, 2016)

According to the Ministry of Justice, in 2019, compared to white people, black people were:

● over twice as likely to receive a police caution
● over three times as likely to be arrested
● more likely, if arrested, to be charged, remanded in custody and face court proceedings than to receive a caution
● more likely, if found guilty, to receive a prison sentence
● five times more likely to be in prison.

Compared to white people, Asian people were more likely to:

● be charged and face court proceedings than to receive a caution
● receive a prison sentence if found guilty.

A report in the *Guardian* newspaper (2018), as part of the *Guardian's* Bias in Britain project, found that the Metropolitan Police tasered black people more than four times as often as white people, and used restraint four times as often. Black people make up 19 per cent of the population of London but were involved in 40 per cent of incidents where the Met used a taser in 2017. Overall, black people accounted for 29 per cent of all London arrests in 2017, which points to racial bias in the approach and treatment of individuals under the law.

Certain ethnic groups are more likely than white groups to be sentenced to immediate custody for offences that can be tried in the Crown Court (indictable offences).

Sociological explanations of differences between ethnic groups

Inaccurate statistics

As you have seen, statistics on crime are not necessarily accurate. Not all crime is reported and not all crime is recorded and, therefore, an accurate picture of all crime is not possible.

Institutional racism

The Macpherson report (1999) on the police investigation of the murder of teenager Stephen Lawrence found that institutional racism in the police force was widespread. Sir William Macpherson (1926–) argued that the culture of the police, who are mainly white, tends to label particular groups as criminal and take some ethnic groups less seriously.

On the eve of the twenty-fifth anniversary of Stephen Lawrence's death (April 2018), black and Asian police officers declared that the Metropolitan police force was still institutionally racist.

The Metropolitan Black Police Association (BPA), the biggest group representing minority officers in the force, believed that the police force had failed to tackle the institutional racism in the criminal justice system despite the training and community initiatives put in place since Stephen Lawrence's death.

Functionalist explanations

Functionalists would explain the link between ethnic minorities and crime through Merton's strain theory and Cohen's subcultural theory of status frustration. Both theories can be seen to be applicable, given that members of some minority ethnic groups statistically underachieve in the education system. As a consequence, strain theory suggests they are faced with blocked opportunities to good jobs and the concept of status frustration implies they form subcultures, where rule breaking becomes their primary source of status.

Marxist explanations

Marxists argue higher levels of crime by some ethnic minorities could be linked to their social class – they are more likely to experience poverty and social exclusion. In addition, they claim that the UK state and its criminal justice system are racist, resulting in a deliberate policy of oppression against black people. Hall *et al.* (1979) claimed that that 'mugging' was constructed by politicians and the media as a young black male problem in order to scapegoat them as muggers and detract attention away from what they saw as a 'crisis of capitalism' occurring at the time. Marxists argue that given ethnic minorities' background of high levels of unemployment and, for those in employment, frequently low-paid and low-status work, they may turn to crime because of relative deprivation resulting in criminal activity in order to gain the things they need/want.

Activities

1 Using what you have learned so far, make a list of why the statistics may not give an accurate picture of the crime rates of different ethnic groups.

2 Perhaps the statistics are a reflection of the labelling of certain ethnic groups by the police rather than the fact that individuals from minority ethnic groups commit more crime.

How true do you think this statement is?

Link

For more information on the social construction of crime, see pages 179–180.

Activities

1 Do some individual research to find out more about Stephen Lawrence. Find out what happened and why the Metropolitan Police were accused of being institutionally racist.

2 Do some research to find out which forces do not have any black or Asian British officers.

Links

- For more information, see Factors affecting criminal and deviant behaviour: social class on pages 194–195.
- For more information on stratification and social class, see pages 222–223.

Interactionist explanations

Racism and racial stereotyping in police culture and practice mean the behaviour of black and South Asian Muslim individuals is more likely to be labelled as criminal. Black and South Asian Muslim individuals, especially young males, fit police stereotypes of 'troublemakers' and are therefore targeted by the police. Historically, since the first significant arrival of African-Caribbean immigrants in the 1950s there have been discussions about the existence of a 'black criminality'. Consequently, police focus more on these groups, which leads to more arrests and more ethnic groups appearing in crime statistics. This is apparent in the stop and search procedures conducted by the police. Figures from the Home Office (2019) show that black people were nine and a half times as likely to be stopped and searched as white people in 2017–18.

Feminist explanations

Feminists explore the complex relationship between ethnicity, gender and crime. Black feminists, in particular, have encouraged an understanding of crime that goes beyond examining gender within a patriarchal society and explore the interrelationship of ethnicity, gender and class in the treatment of ethnic minorities by the police and criminal justice system generally. For example, there is a danger of labelling and stereotyping, illustrated by the fact that black women were more than twice as likely to be arrested as white women.

Media reinforcing views

Any criminal activity is fuelled by selective publication of crime statistics in the media. Through the reporting of criminal activities by certain groups of people, black and Muslim youths become seen as a threat, even if they are not doing anything wrong. This generates a growing mistrust and hostility among black people towards the police. This conflict often leads to more criminal activity.

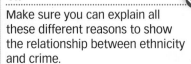

TIP

Make sure you can explain all these different reasons to show the relationship between ethnicity and crime.

Link

For more information, see Debates on crime: the media on pages 212–213.

Extension

When looking at ethnicity and crime, two main issues emerge:
- Some ethnic groups commit more crime.
- Police are more likely to arrest and charge certain ethnic groups which are, therefore, more likely to appear in crime statistics.

Which of these issues do you think is the most accurate? Give reasons for your decision.

Check your knowledge

Identify and explain three reasons why there are differences in the crime rates of different ethnic groups.

Summary

- There is a clear link between a person's ethnic group and the likelihood that they will be arrested, prosecuted, convicted and sentenced.
- There are many reasons why this pattern continues to exist, including labelling, institutional racism, social class factors and the power of the media.
- Functionalists, Marxists, interactionists and feminists differ in their explanations of ethnicity and crime.

Factors affecting criminal and deviant behaviour: age

There is a clear link between a person's age and crime rates. According to the statistics:

- the peak age of offending in England and Wales is 17
- more young people (aged 14–25 – the peak ages for criminal activity) live in urban areas that provide more opportunities for crime: more shops, cars, houses, and so on
- after age 25, there is a steep drop as people take on new roles such as wage earners, parents and spouses
- young people are more influenced by peer pressure (subcultures)
- there is more pressure on young people to have the latest 'must-have' items.

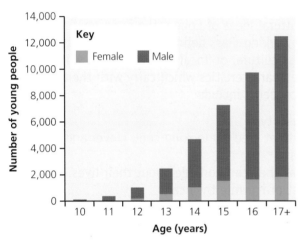

▲ **Figure 5.8** Age and gender of young people convicted of an offence, March 2015 (Youth justice statistics, www.gov.uk)

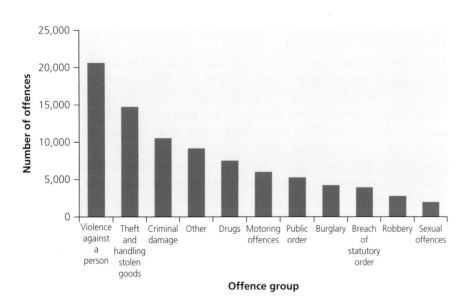

▲ **Figure 5.9** Age and proven offences by young people, March 2015 (www.gov.uk)

Key learning

You will be able to:

- describe the patterns of crime and deviant behaviour of different age groups
- explain the factors affecting criminal and deviant behaviour of different age groups
- describe, compare and contrast a variety of sociological perspectives on factors affecting age and criminal and deviant behaviour.

KEY TERM

Edgework behaviour at the edge of what is normally allowed or accepted; risky or radical behaviour, e.g. stealing and racing a car

Activity

Summarise what the graph shows in Figure 5.8.

TIP

Using data in your answers will show that you can use sociological evidence.

Activity

Summarise what the graph in Figure 5.9 shows about the different offences committed by young people.

KEY TEXT

Cohen A., *Delinquent Boys*, Glencoe, The Free Press, 1955.

Before reading further, can you think of any reasons why young people are more likely to commit crime?

Sociological explanations for differences between age groups

Functionalist explanations

The functionalist Albert Cohen's (1955) concept of 'status frustration' (see page 183) argues that the connection between young working-class people and crime is subcultures. When unable to achieve consensus goals of success (for example achievement in education) Cohen argued a reaction led to 'status frustration' with feelings of failure and inadequacy. Cohen describes how delinquent youths rebound from conventional failure (for example in schooling) by creating their own status centred on challenging authority and as rule-breakers. The influence of their peer group may encourage them to get involved in minor acts of deviance and crime, which they would not engage in on their own.

In contrast to the subcultural ideas of Cohen, the functionalist Walter Miller (1962) sees male working-class delinquent behaviour as a normal part of macho lower-class culture, or 'focal concerns', into which they are socialised. These are characteristics which carry with them the risk of law breaking. These concerns include:

- toughness and masculinity
- smartness – having 'street cred' by looking cool, clever and amusing
- excitement and thrills
- fatalism – a sense that they can do little about their lives, so they need to make the best of it while they can
- trouble – an acceptance that life involves violence and fights.

Miller suggested that these characteristics are shared by many lower working-class males of all ages, but they are likely to become exaggerated in the lives of young people as they seek to achieve peer group status.

Marxist explanations

The Centre for Contemporary Cultural Studies (CCCS) at Birmingham University offered Marxist explanations in the 1970s into the association between youth and crime. They published a range of Marxist-based ethnographic studies of working-class subcultures. For example, Mike Brake (1985) described youth as a 'magical' response to the dull and dreary world that capitalism demands from adults as wage slaves. Because youth is furthest removed from the financial pressures of adulthood, they are in a strong position to resist the controlling mechanisms of capitalism and free to engage in deviant and criminal activities. Eventually, youth resistance and rebellion end as they become trapped by capitalism's economic constraints of rent, mortgages and debt.

Link

Refer to the work of Cohen on page 183.

Activity

How would Cohen's theory of status frustration explain:
- why a substantial amount of crime occurs in gangs
- why so much crime occurs among working-class males?

Link

For more information, see Factors affecting criminal and deviant behaviour: social class on pages 194–195.

Interactionist explanations

The interactionist David Matza (1964) explains juvenile crime in terms of 'drift'. The lack of responsibilities and the search for excitement mean that young people drift into deviant and criminal behaviour. However, when they take on adult responsibilities, such as gaining full-time employment and settling down in long-term relationships, they drift out. Although a postmodernist, Stephen Lyng's (1990) work on edgework can also highlight the meanings young people attach to delinquent behaviour. They are increasingly looking for excitement and thrills in today's society. He highlights the pleasures of thrill seeking and risk taking and the 'buzz' generated by the excitement and adrenalin involved in living on the edge in acts like shoplifting and fighting.

Interactionists would also highlight the role labelling plays in stereotyping young people as typical offenders. The police often see young people as a source of problems in society and this stereotype involves them spending more time observing and checking on young people. As a result, more get caught, become defined as offenders and appear in statistics.

Feminist explanations

Feminists argue we are taught norms and values of society through the primary and secondary socialisation process. As a result of socialisation, girls could be said to be 'lacking' in the elements which are generally associated with delinquency, particularly the elements of toughness and aggressiveness associated with masculinity in our society. We have also come across ideas that girls are constrained by 'bedroom culture' (page 197) and suffer more social control (page 196). However, statistics show an increasing participation of young females in delinquent activities suggesting a growing engagement with risk-taking behaviour and the adoption of more male attitudes such as a 'ladette' culture.

Extension

Is youth crime the problem in society that the media portray it to be?

Summary

- There is a clear link between a person's age and the likelihood that they will be convicted of a crime.
- There are many reasons why this pattern exists, including status frustration, social class, edgework, socialisation and police stereotyping.
- Functionalists, Marxists, interactionists and feminists differ in their explanations of age and crime.

Check your knowledge

Identify and explain three reasons why there are differences in the crime rates of people of different age groups.

Link

For more information, see Formal social control on pages 192–193.

Debates on crime: treatment of young offenders

The debate

Should young people be punished for crimes or should they be treated in a way designed to prevent them recommitting crime in the future?

This is an ongoing debate. Some believe that young people should be punished for their crimes, whereas others believe because of their age they do not have criminal responsibility.

The criminal age of responsibility is ten years

Penal reformers argue there are too many young people coming into contact with the criminal justice system. The age of criminal responsibility in England and Wales is 10 years and courts have a range of different sentences they can give offenders aged 10–17:

- Fine: for offenders under 16, paying the fine is the responsibility of a parent/guardian and it will be their ability to pay that is taken into account when setting the level of the fine.
- Referral order: this requires the offender to attend a youth offender panel and agree a contract which will last between three months and a year. The aim is for the offender to make up for the harm caused and address their offending behaviour.
- Youth rehabilitation order: this is a community sentence, for example curfew, supervision, unpaid work, electronic monitoring, drug treatment, mental health treatment and education.
- Custodial sentences: young offenders can receive youth custody sentences but they will only be imposed in the most serious cases.
- Civil injunctions, Community Protection Notices (CPNs) and Criminal Behaviour Orders (CBOs) have replaced Antisocial Behaviour Orders (ASBOs) in England, Wales and Northern Ireland, but ASBOs are still used in Scotland.

For more serious offences, young people over the age of ten may be sentenced to long periods of detention.

If a young person is convicted of a specified offence and the Crown Court considers that there is a significant risk of serious harm to members of the public from the young person committing further specified offences, then the court may pass a sentence of detention for life or an extended sentence of detention.

Should young people be put in custody?

Arguments for sentencing young people:

- They have committed a crime and must take the punishment for the crime.
- If they are seen as a danger to society, they should be removed from society.
- They need to learn the norms and values of society so they can be effective adult citizens.

Arguments against sentencing young people:

- Too many young people are reoffending. Home Office (2019) figures show the 2017 rate of youth proven reoffending is 39.9 per cent, while the rate among adults is 28.2 per cent. Sentencing does not seem to be effective.
- Large sums of money are spent on youth offender institutes, secure training centres or secure children's homes.
- The average annual cost (2018) per inmate in a Young Offender Institution (YOI) is £76,000, but in a Secure Children's Home (SCH) is £210,000.
- Young offenders need education and training to enable them to return to school or college or find employment, but too many lack basic skills.
- Although the number of young people entering the system and the number of young people in custody have decreased in recent years, there is still a concern that the most prolific adult offenders commit their first crimes at a very early age. Therefore, perhaps they need education rather than a sentence.

▼ **Table 5.3** More children are being locked up in England and Wales than in any other country in Western Europe (Her Majesty's Prison and Probation Service, www.gov.uk)

Under 18s in custody: average for March 2019	
England and Wales	835
Finland	2

- Until 1995, courts could only send a child into custody if they'd committed a serious crime such as rape, murder or grievous bodily harm (GBH). The number of children being sent to prison for such crimes has dropped since then, but thousands more are being locked up for relatively minor crimes.
- Vulnerable young offenders are at risk of serious and long-term problems because the youth justice system is failing to support their needs.
- Figures released by the Ministry of Justice in 2018 revealed that the average number of young people in custody self-harming is 106 per month. Four people under 21 died in prison or YOIs in 2018, while incidents of physical restraint have risen year on year.
- About a quarter of young offenders (approximately 20,000 in England and Wales) have some kind of learning disability. More than 60 per cent have difficulty communicating, while an extremely high proportion have emotional and mental health needs.

TIP

Knowing different methods of formal punishment will show good sociological knowledge.

Extension

Find out more about the different responsibilities of the Home Office.

Find out more about punishments given to young people in other countries. Compare these with the punishments given in Britain.

Link

For more information on the correlation between crime and age, see pages 203–204.

Activity

After reading these pages, have your views on this debate changed? If so, how and why?

Check your knowledge

1 Give two reasons why young people should be put in custody.
2 Give two reasons why young people should not be put in custody.

Activities

1 Look at the points made above and then discuss with other students whether or not you think young people should be sent to prison. Summarise your discussion in a copy of the table below.

Young people should be sent to prison	Young people should not be sent to prison

2 Write a conclusion to summarise your findings.

Summary

- There is an ongoing debate about whether young people should be sent to prison or whether they should be educated so they do not return to criminal activities.

KEY TERM

Prison system the deprivation of liberty is the ultimate punishment in British society; British prisons vary from open institutions for low-level offenders to high security institutions for offenders who are convicted of serious offences and are held to pose a risk to other members of society

Activity

Jon Venables, who was found guilty of murdering James Bulger, was released at the age of 18 from a secure care centre. Following his release, he developed a drug and alcohol problem and began acting antisocially. Visits to his home found that he had downloaded 102 indecent images of children and had also been distributing indecent images. He was jailed for two years.

What are your initial thoughts on this debate? Use the case of Jon Venables as an example.

Activity

There are many arguments for and against the use of prisons as a form of punishment.

Do you think prisons are a good idea? List the advantages and disadvantages for both society and individuals.

Debates on crime: prison system, rehabilitation and punishment

The debate

Should people be punished and sent to prison for their crimes or should they be rehabilitated?

This is an ongoing debate. Some believe that people should be punished for their crimes, whereas others believe that they would benefit more from being rehabilitated.

Prison as a form of punishment

Home Office (2019) figures show that in May 2019 there were 84,345 people in prison in England and Wales. The major purpose of the prison system is to stop people committing more crimes.

Arguments for the use of prisons as a form of punishment:

● Criminals deserve to be shamed and punished. Being deprived of their liberty is an effective way of doing this.
● Prisons act as a deterrent to other offenders.
● Prison is essential to keep people safe from violent offenders.
● Criminals are off the streets while they are in prison and are not a danger to the public.

Arguments against the use of prisons as a form of punishment:

● Prison does not make people take responsibility for their actions or face up to what they have done.
● The proven reoffender rate is 28.2 per cent of adults and 39.9 per cent of young offenders (prison population figures 2019, www.gov.uk). Reconviction rates of non-violent offenders are much higher: four out of five shoplifters and car thieves are reconvicted within two years of leaving jail.
● Criminals experience limited rehabilitation in prison.
● Heavily structured regimes can damage prisoners' abilities to think and act for themselves, with knock-on effects in areas such as employment and housing.
● Prisons can damage relationships with family members.

Research in action

ComRes (a research consultancy) collected figures after surveying 1,000 18–30-year-olds across the UK.

Of those surveyed, 62 per cent said they thought prison conditions in the UK were not tough enough, compared with only 3 per cent who said they were too tough.

Case studies

Justizzentrum Leoben

In response to worldwide alarm over the ineffectiveness of how we manage criminals, a growing number of prisons are embracing a new style of imprisonment. By giving inmates more responsibility, comfort and freedom within the prison walls, governors say they are offering prisoners the chance to change. In Austria's *Justizzentrum Leoben* minimum security prison, convicts live in one-bed cells. Each cell comes with a television and en-suite. Halden prison in Norway has a two-bedroom house where inmates can enjoy overnight visits from family members.

Bastøy Prison

Bastøy Prison, situated on an island off the coast of Norway, is a minimum security prison, home to over 110 inmates, but only 69 staff members. Every type of offender may be accepted and they are free to cycle the island's tracks and fish in the surrounding waters. When interviewed, many of its prisoners expressed eagerness to start families and enter employment upon release.

In 2015, reoffending rates were reported at 16 per cent at Bastøy Prison.

Activities

1 Read the case studies. Discuss your views on these types of prison system with other students. Do you think these are effective systems?

2 Using the information in Table 5.4, summarise what the table shows about reoffending rates.

3 After reading these pages, have your views on this debate changed? If so, how and why?

Alternatives to prison

Only a fraction of those found guilty by the courts are sentenced to prison. The majority of offenders are either fined or sentenced to community penalties. Liberty can also be restricted through the use of electronic tagging.

Some argue that these alternative punishments are better than prison because they do not take prisoners away from their family and home and provide continuity so that prisoners can carry on working or attending college. They say that they also tackle the causes of offending behaviour, instil a sense of responsibility and put an emphasis on paying back to society.

Research has shown that well-resourced and well-managed community punishments can be very effective in reducing reoffending. Community-based sentences give slightly better results: they have been found to reduce reoffending by 6 per cent. Opponents, however, say that offenders see community sentences as a soft option. They claim that these do not act as a deterrent to offenders. The now part-privatised probation service, which is supposed to monitor those given community service, has also come in for criticism by parliament's Public Accounts Committee (2019) for 'failing to reduce reoffending'.

Check your knowledge

1 Give two arguments why prisons should be used as a form of punishment.

2 Give two arguments why prisons should not be used as a form of punishment.

Summary

- There is an ongoing debate about the effectiveness of prisons.
- There are arguments for and against the use of prisons for punishment.
- There are arguments for and against the use of community punishments.

▼ **Table 5.4** Rates of reoffending, 2017 (Ministry of Justice, 2017)

Percentage of reoffending based on length of prison sentence, 2017	
Less than 12 months	64.1%
More than 10 years	28.5%

Activities

1. What are your initial thoughts on this debate?
2. Look at these statistics and summarise what they show.

TIP

It is important that you are able to give both sides of an argument in any discussion.

Debates on crime: violent crime and sentencing

The debate

Should violent criminals be sentenced to life in prison?

This is an ongoing debate. Some believe violent criminals should be sentenced to life in prison, whereas others believe that this is too harsh.

Some people believe that violent criminals should be sentenced to a longer time in prison and should not be released early before the end of their sentence.

Ministry of Justice (2019) statistics show:

- 11 per cent of violent criminals convicted for first-time offences are sent to prison
- 44 per cent of first-time sex offenders have been given prison sentences, while 28 per cent of offenders who committed robberies have been sent to prison
- 59 per cent of those convicted of sex offences received a prison sentence.

Changes in the law

From December 2012, the law was changed:

- Mandatory life sentences are to be given to people convicted of a second very serious sexual or violent offence – the two strikes rule.
- For those dangerous criminals who do not come under the two strikes rule, the government introduced a new sentence for dangerous criminals convicted of serious sexual and violent crimes: they will not automatically be released from prison halfway through their jail term. They will only be released when they have served at least two-thirds of their prison sentence and may be kept inside prison until the end of their term.

Activities

1. There are many arguments for and against whether sentencing should be harsher for violent criminals. What do you think? Add bullet points to a copy of the table below.

Sentences for violent crimes should be harsher	Sentences for violent crimes should not be harsher

2. Using your bullet points, write a summary of this debate.

Violent crimes may be reported to the police and may be recorded as a crime, but not all violent crimes result in the offenders being punished.

Offence	Recorded crime
Violence against the person	1,608,505
Sexual offence	159,740
Robbery	82,566
Theft offence	2,002,253
Criminal damage and arson	571,767
Drug offence	144,741
Possession of weapons offence	44,294
Public order offence	438,286

◄ **Table 5.5** Crime recorded in England and Wales, year ending December 2018 (Home Office, Police recorded crime, December 2017–18)

There appears to be a concern in society over the amount of violent crime, but is this concern justified? Clearly, violent crime does occur in society and people are undoubtedly concerned about it, especially if it is within their own community.

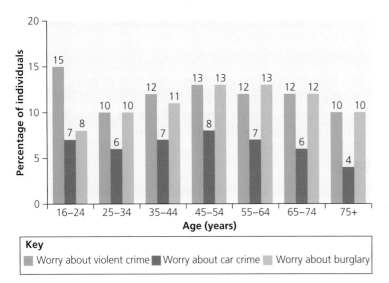

▲ **Figure 5.10** Percentage of individuals with high levels of worry about crime by crime type and age , 2013–14 (Crime Survey for England and Wales, ONS)

The Crime Survey for England and Wales (CSEW) looked at people's perception of crime in the year ending March 2016 in their local area and in the country as a whole. It also examined people's perceived likelihood of becoming victims of crime and their worry about crime.

- 60 per cent thought that crime in the country as a whole had risen over the past few years. However, less felt that crime had risen in their local area with 46 per cent of victims and 29 per cent of non-victims feeling that crime had gone up locally.
- News programmes on TV and radio were most often cited as a source of information that had influenced perceptions of national crime levels (cited by 67 per cent of people). In contrast, word of mouth was most often cited as a source influencing impressions of local crime rates (cited by 54 per cent).
- 11 per cent of non-victim adults were classified as having a high level of worry about violent crime, 10.3 per cent about burglary and 5. 7 per cent about car crime.
- Around 1 in 5 people (19.1 per cent) thought they would be a victim of crime within the next 12 months.
- Those who had been a victim of crime in the last year were more likely than non-victims to: consider both local and national crime rates to have risen over the last few years; have a high level of worry about crime; and to think it likely they would suffer victimisation in the year ahead.

Activities

1 Look at the statistics in Table 5.5. Explain what they show.
2 Compare the amount of recorded crime (in Table 5.5) with the levels of worry about crime (shown in Figure 5.10).
   a How do the recorded levels of crime compare with the worry about crime?
   b Write a summary about what these statistics show about crime.
3 After reading these pages, have your views on this debate changed? If so, how and why?

Link

For more information, see Debates on crime: the media on pages 212–213.

Check your knowledge

1 Give two arguments for giving violent criminals longer sentences.
2 Give two arguments for not giving violent criminals longer sentences.

Summary

- There is an ongoing debate about whether sentences for violent crime should be harsher.
- Not all crime that is reported and recorded results in sentencing as a criminal offence.

KEY TERMS

Deviancy amplification the exaggeration of a particular social issue as a consequence of media coverage, e.g. antisocial behaviour by groups of young people

News value the importance given to a particular event by newspaper editors or television producers

Right of appeal the opportunity to challenge a judicial court's decision

Debates on crime: the media

What do we mean by the media?

The media are one of the secondary agents of socialisation. Through the media we learn a lot about society.

When you watch a television programme, read a magazine, watch a film or use the internet, you are experiencing a form of mass communication. The information and ideas you are presented with are specifically designed to reach large numbers of people. This information can have an influence on our thoughts and behaviour.

The debate

There are two major debates within this topic of media and crime.

1 Are the media biased in their presentation of crime?
2 Do the media create crime in society?

1 Are the media biased in their presentation of crime?

The media have a particularly important role to play in the process of defining what is and is not acceptable behaviour. When individuals do not have direct knowledge or experience of what is happening, they rely on the media to inform them.

Crime seems to be in the news a lot and the media are powerful as they decide what does and does not get reported. The media set the agenda in terms of what is considered to be important. Sociologists are interested in exploring what the media consider newsworthy and the reasons behind the decisions.

People are only able to discuss and form opinions about the crime that they have been informed about. This means that people's perceptions of crime and deviance in society are influenced by what the media choose to include.

Do the media present an accurate picture of crime?

Media coverage of crime and deviance is filtered through what editors and journalists see as 'newsworthy'. This means a story has to be a good story that media audiences want to know about. There are values and assumptions held by editors and journalists that guide them in choosing what is newsworthy and, therefore, what to report.

This means that journalists tend to include and emphasise the elements of a story that make it more newsworthy (news value). In relation to crime, stories are more likely to be reported (have more news value) if:

- children are involved
- violence is involved
- celebrities are involved
- right of appeal occurs
- the event has occurred locally
- the event is easy to understand
- graphic images are involved.

It is certainly the case that crime and deviance make up a large proportion of news coverage. Ditton and Duffy (1983) found that 46 per cent of media reports were about violent or sexual crimes, however, these only made up 3 per cent of all crimes recorded by the police.

This disproportionate coverage of violent crime can lead people to assume that it happens much more regularly than it does and overestimate their likelihood of becoming a victim of violent crime. The latest crime figures from the Office for National Statistics show that you are much more likely to be a victim of a crime like fraud than a violent crime and that the risk of being a victim of any crime has fallen from about four in ten in 1995 to two in ten in 2018.

Sociologists often refer to **deviancy amplification** when attempting to describe the impact of the media on the public perception of crime.

The seaside skirmishes of the mods and rockers in the 1960s are a good example of deviancy amplification, as is gun and knife crime and drug use. This links to moral panics where the reaction enlarges the problem out of all proportion, in relation to its seriousness. Media coverage means the public identify a group as a folk devil, which then poses a threat to societal values.

2 Do the media create crime in society?

There has long been concern that media content has a negative effect on the behaviour of young people, especially children. It is suggested that some individuals may imitate violence and immoral or antisocial behaviour seen in the media. The media are regarded as powerful secondary agents of socialisation and produce a copycat effect (where children copy what they see).

Many studies have shown the link between the media and crime, including increased aggressive behaviour in everyday life. Estimates suggest that by the time they are 18, American children will have seen on television around 16,000 real and fictional murders and 200,000 acts of violence. Such media violence is often blamed for increasing crime and violence in society.

In 2003, Anderson (1952–) claimed that research showed conclusively that media violence increased the likelihood of aggressive and violent behaviour, both immediately and in the long term.

Other researchers, including Ferguson, have challenged the position that video game violence harms children. Ferguson (2009) argues that laboratory results have not translated into real world, meaningful effects. He also claims that much of the research into video game violence has failed to control other variables such as mental health and family life, which may have impacted the results. His work has found that children who are already at risk may be more likely to choose to play violent video games. According to Ferguson, these other risk factors, as opposed to the games, cause aggressive and violent behaviour.

Summary

- Serious and violent crime is reported disproportionately in the media, giving the idea that crime is an area of real concern in society.
- There is an ongoing debate about the influence of the media on behaviour.
- The debate about whether the media leads to violent behaviour is inconclusive. Obtaining clear-cut evidence of a cause and effect relationship is almost impossible.

Activity

Research the work of Stanley Cohen, *Folk Devils and Moral Panics: The creation of the Mods and the Rockers* (1972).

a Explain how this demonstrates deviancy amplification by the media.

b Explain how this could be linked to current issues.

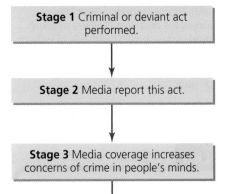

Stage 1 Criminal or deviant act performed.

Stage 2 Media report this act.

Stage 3 Media coverage increases concerns of crime in people's minds.

Stage 4 Public outcry – something must be done. This is referred to as moral panic, where public concern is created by media coverage of an event.

▲ **Figure 5.11** Stages of deviancy amplification

Extension

Do you think violence on television and in computer games influences children to behave more aggressively? Give reasons why you think it does and reasons why you think it does not.

Check your knowledge

1 Give two arguments showing that the media are biased in their presentation of crime.

2 Give two arguments showing that the media create crime in society.

Methods in context

This section is about how you use your knowledge and skills of research methods in appropriate ways.

Read the following item and answer the questions that follow.

Item A

Using unstructured tape interviews, Pat Carlen (1988) conducted a study of 15–46-year-old working-class women who had been convicted of a range of crimes, including theft, fraud, handling stolen goods, burglary, drugs, prostitution, violence and arson.

Of the 39 women interviewed, 20 were in prison or youth custody at the time of the interviews.

Carlen argued that working-class women are generally led to conform through the promise of two types of rewards or 'deals':

● The class deal: women who work will be offered material rewards, with a decent standard of living and leisure opportunities.

● The gender deal: patriarchal ideology promises women material and emotional rewards from family life by conforming to the norms of the conventional domestic gender role.

If these rewards are not available, crime becomes more likely.

The class deal:

● If women had failed to find a legitimate way of earning a decent living, this left them feeling powerless, oppressed and the victims of injustice. Many of them had experienced problems and humiliations in trying to claim benefits.

● As they had gained no rewards from the class deal, they felt they had nothing to lose by using crime to escape from poverty.

The gender deal:

● Many of the women saw few rewards and many disadvantages in family life.

● Some had been abused physically or sexually by their fathers, or subjected to domestic violence by partners.

● Over half had spent time in care, which broke the bonds with family and friends.

● Many women reached the conclusion that 'crime was the only route to a decent standard of living. They had nothing to lose and everything to gain'.

Carlen found that as patriarchal controls and discrimination have lessened, and opportunities in education have become more equal at work, women have begun to adopt male roles in both work and criminal activities.

As a result, women no longer just commit traditional 'female' crimes such as shoplifting and prostitution, they also commit typically 'male' offences such as crimes of violence and white collar crime, for example fraud.

1 From Item A, what research method was used by Carlen?
2 Examine one strength and one limitation of using this research method.

> *You need to identify one strength and one limitation of using the research method for this specific piece of research. Make sure you explain why this is a strength and limitation for this specific piece of research.*

3 Identify and explain one factor that may influence women to commit crimes.

> *Refer to the item and identify one factor that may influence women to commit crime. Once you have identified one factor, make sure you explain why this may influence women to commit crime.*

4 Identify and explain one ethical issue of this research and explain how you would deal with this issue.

> *Do not just identify an ethical issue. Make sure you explain why this is an ethical issue for this specific research.*

5 Explain how you would investigate the criminal activity of males and females by using a different research method to the one used by Carlen.

> *This question is giving you the opportunity to show your knowledge of using different research methods. Make sure you explain how the research method could be used for this specific study. How effective is this method for investigating criminal activity of males and females?*

6 Explain how you would investigate the criminal activity of males and females by using a secondary research method.

> *This question is giving you the opportunity to show your knowledge of secondary research methods. Make sure you explain how the research method could be used for this specific study. How effective is this method for investigating criminal activity of males and females?*

TIP

It is important that you can apply sociological research methods to each topic you are studying. You must use key sociological concepts accurately.

When answering these questions, it is important to focus your answer on the specific item given. Use the item in your answers and use concepts specific to the method.

Summary

- All research methods used in sociological research have strengths and weaknesses.
- Ethical considerations need to be taken into account when conducting research.

Answer and commentary

Option D (only one option is correct) – criminal activity that is neither reported to nor recorded by police is known as the 'dark figure of crime'.

TIP ✓

Use the glossary to identify key terms that you need to know.

The sociology of crime and deviance

Practice questions

Question 1 (multiple choice)

Which term do sociologists use to describe the unknown amount of criminal activity that is not reported to or recorded by the police? [1 mark]

a) White collar crime

b) Unknown crime

c) Unsolved crime

d) Dark figure of crime

Question 2 (descriptive answer)

Describe one way in which sociologists attempt to measure the amount of crime in society. [3 marks]

Answer and commentary

The question requires you to describe one way in which sociologists attempt to measure the amount of crime in society. You should aim to develop an accurate and logical description of a relevant method that is clearly linked to the question. Remember to be concise and keep to the point.

You could write about:

● The use of police recorded crime (you should note that there have been regional and historical differences in the collection of these statistics that raise doubts over their reliability and validity).

● The use of the Crime Survey for England and Wales (the most extensive national survey of crime).

● Victim surveys and self-report studies.

Question 3 (short answer question linked to source material)

Item A

In the 1980s the feminist sociologist Pat Carlen researched the link between women, crime and poverty based on the 'oral (spoken) histories' of 39 women. The women she interviewed gave her an account of their criminal careers. She describes her method as an ethnographic analysis based on 'control theory'; this theory suggests that people are less likely to break the law and more likely to conform when they have more to gain by obeying the law and conforming than they would by turning to crime. Carlen suggests that the 'oral histories' of the women in her study clearly show that they became law breakers because they felt that they had 'nothing to lose' and that a life of crime offered them 'friendship, financial gain and excitement' as opposed to a disappointing conventional marriage, low paid employment or a life spent depending on welfare benefits.

From Item A, examine one weakness of the research. [2 marks]

Answer and commentary

It is important to identify a potential weakness of the research and to suggest why this element could be seen as a potential weakness.

You could write about:

- The relatively small number of women involved in the study (Carlen interviewed 39 women), raising questions over the reliability of the data, e.g. representativeness/ability to make generalisations.
- The validity and reliability of interview data, e.g. the impact of the interviewer effect/interviewer bias.
- As a feminist researcher Carlen's perspective may have influenced her analysis, raising questions about the validity of her conclusions, e.g. the effect of patriarchal (male-dominated) criminal justice and welfare systems. Some questions that reference sociologists who have been named in the specification (like Carlen) will ask you directly what you know about the 'perspective' of that particular sociologist. It is important to show that you know that the sociologist concerned is, for example, a feminist or a Marxist, and so on.

TIP
You should be familiar with the content of the summaries in the specification (Appendix B).

Question 4 (paragraph answer linked to the source material)

Identify and explain one factor which might explain why some sociologists have suggested that female criminals are treated more leniently than men by the police and judges. [4 marks]

Question 5 (essay question)

Discuss how far sociologists would agree that negative labelling leads to criminal and deviant behaviour. [12 marks]

Answer and commentary

It is important to identify a relevant factor which might explain the relatively lenient treatment of some women who commit crimes.

You could write about:

- The chivalry thesis suggests that police officers, magistrates and judges may treat women more leniently than men because they regard women as vulnerable and needing protection.
- The family responsibilities of women with children (or for the care of an elderly relative) might make it more likely that they will be cautioned for less serious offences.
- The nature of many of the crimes committed by women (e.g. shoplifting and other non-violent offences) may make it less likely that they will be sent to prison.

Answer and commentary

Remember to think of your 'mini-essay' in three parts: an introductory paragraph in which you focus on the question and begin your argument, a second paragraph in which you develop your answer (consider one or more alternative sociological perspectives on the issue) and a final paragraph in which you reach a conclusion.

You could write about:

- Interactionist ideas about crime and deviance, e.g. labelling theory (deviancy as a label that defines an individual).
- Functionalist ideas about criminal and deviant behaviour as an inevitable feature of society.
- Marxist ideas about the links between the capitalist system, crime and deviance, e.g. different social groups are policed differently with middle class 'white collar' crimes like fraud seen as less serious than crimes committed by members of the working class such as burglary.
- Feminist ideas about the links between gender, crime and deviance, e.g. the socialisation experiences of girls make it less likely that they will commit crimes.
- In each case you will need to evaluate the extent to which a particular perspective represents a valid picture of crime and deviance in Britain today. Try to reach a clear, logical, evidence-based conclusion and avoid contradictions in your argument.

TIP
Take a few moments to develop an outline plan of your answer.

6 Social stratification

●●●●●●●●●●●●●●●●●●●●●●●●●●●●●●●●●●●●

What is social stratification?

▲ The Sutton Trust (2019) found that while just 7 per cent of the population attend private schools they make up 65 per cent of senior judges, 59 per cent of top civil servants and 57 per cent of Members of the House of Lords

Social stratification

Stratification borrows an idea from geology; when you look at a cliff face you can sometimes see different layers or strata in the rock face. To a sociologist, society is also built up of different 'strata' rising in a hierarchy from the least privileged powerless members of society at the bottom, to the most privileged and powerful elite groups at the top. Sociologists refer to the differences between the various strata of society as social inequality, for example in terms of power, status, wealth and income. Societies can be stratified in terms of social class, and also gender, ethnicity and even age.

Different types of social stratification

Sociologists identify four different systems of stratification that have existed in human societies:

1 Slavery: enslaved people are those who become the property of other members of society; the classic form of slavery existed in the Greek and Roman Empires where they were used to supply all basic forms of labour and domestic service. In this classic form of slavery, it was possible for former slaves to be granted their freedom, sometimes as a reward for long periods of loyal service. In Africa, enslaved people were also used to provide basic labour. Europeans exploited this tradition to establish the Transatlantic Slave Trade; enslaved people in this system were permanently removed from Africa and often treated with extreme brutality. It is a form of slavery that continued in the USA well into the nineteenth century. Under this system, known as chattel slavery, enslaved people were regarded as

Key learning

You will be able to:
- describe and explain the functionalist theory of social stratification.

KEY TERMS

Achieved status social status gained by an individual as a result of educational qualifications and/or success in their career

Aristocracy an elite social group with inherited titles

Ascribed status social standing given to an individual on the basis of inheritance

Chattel slavery where enslaved people were property, bought, sold, traded or inherited

Class a type of social stratification based on economic factors

Closed society when social mobility is limited or absent altogether

Elite a minority group who have power and influence over the other members of society

Estate a type of social stratification based on the ownership of land and feudal duties

Gentry a group of landowners with social standing below the aristocracy

Hierarchy the organisation of society into a rank order of importance

Modern slavery the harbouring of children, women or men through the use of force for the purpose of exploitation

less than human and inferior to the 'white races', one of the historic causes of racism. Modern slavery exists when vulnerable individuals are exploited, for example migrant workers who are trapped in employment in a foreign country that they are not free to leave.

2 Caste: the caste system is a form of ascribed status found in India and is based on Hindu religious belief, in particular the idea of reincarnation. The caste that a child is assigned at birth is linked to the occupation of their parents' ancestors, for example priest, warrior or merchant. People at the lowest levels of society are believed to be suffering a punishment for their behaviour in a previous life. Hindu religious ideas divide human actions into pure and impure; handling the bodies of the dead, for example, is an 'impure' activity. Individuals at the lowest level of society are the 'untouchables'. Traditionally, untouchables were employed in all impure activities; they worked as cleaners and disposed of the bodies of the dead. Despite attempts in modern Indian society to move away from this system and to allow open access to education and employment regardless of birth, caste remains important. In present-day India, it has even been a factor in acts of violence including rape and murder. Because individuals remain in their caste for life, sociologists describe caste as a closed system.

3 Estates: the feudal system in medieval Europe involved the idea of different social groups (or 'estates') and entitlement to the ownership of land; again, these groups were organised in a hierarchy. At the top of this system in the first estate were the members of the aristocracy and the gentry. The ownership of land was granted by the monarchy to powerful aristocrats, who then divided the land they had been given between their followers. Each group owed a debt of service for the land they were granted, a debt that could be paid in the form of a tax or by providing military service. The Christian Church formed a second estate. Powerful members of the Church were also given grants of land and the income from those lands financed the building and upkeep of religious communities (monasteries and convents). A third estate was the commoners, including serfs and the peasant farmers who worked on the land, together with merchants and craftsmen.

4 Class: socio-economic class will be discussed in more detail at a later point in this chapter but, essentially, class is different from enslavement, caste and feudal estates because it is possible for an individual to move between social classes (sociologists call this an open system). Class systems rely at least in part on achieved status, they are principally based on economic differences and do not depend on personal relationships, such as those that existed between owner and enslaved person or between a feudal lord and his followers.

However, these different types of stratification are not necessarily exclusive. For example, enslavement existed alongside social classes in nineteenth-century America, characterised by patriarchal oppression of women.

Check your knowledge

1 What do sociologists mean when they use the term 'elite group'?
2 What do sociologists mean when they use the term 'ascribed status'?
3 What do sociologists mean when they talk about an open system of social stratification?

Activities

1 Design a simple table including the key features of the four systems of social stratification. For example, is the system open or closed? Is status ascribed or achieved?

2 Draw a pyramid diagram to explain the meaning of the term 'hierarchy' using the feudal estates as your example. Would you describe feudalism as a closed system?

Extension

Research examples of modern slavery. You should find this website a useful starting point: www.gov.uk/government/collections/modern-slavery.

Research the history of apartheid in South Africa. Does this system fit any of the four types of stratification described above?

Summary

- Society is built up of different 'strata' rising in a hierarchy from the least privileged powerless members of society, to the most privileged and powerful elite groups at the top.

- Sociologists refer to the differences between the various strata of society as social inequality.

KEY TERMS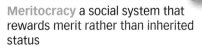

Meritocracy a social system that rewards merit rather than inherited status

Nepotism the practice of favouring relatives or friends, especially by giving them jobs

KEY TEXT

Davis K. and Moore W., 'Some principles of stratification' in Bendix R. and Lipset S.M. (eds), *Class, Status and Power,* second edition, New York, The Free Press, 1966.

The functionalist perspective

Role allocation

The functionalist perspective believes that for society to function effectively roles must be allocated in a manner that ensures they are only undertaken by those with equivalent talent and skills. In order to motivate the most talented to undertake the most demanding roles, performance needs to be linked to the promise of rewards. In 1945, two American sociologists Kingsley Davis (1908–97) and Wilbert Moore (1914–87) argued that the 'mechanism' allowing these things to happen was a system of social stratification that attached unequal rewards and privileges to the different positions in society. By attaching the highest rewards (higher status and income) to those functionally important positions, Davis and Moore argued that people with the necessary talent, drive and ambition would be encouraged to compete for them. They believed that society was a meritocracy and the most talented would and should achieve the highest status and the greatest rewards.

Davis and Moore believe social stratification was a 'universal necessity' for all known human societies. They believed that for any society to survive and operate efficiently it was necessary for the following things to happen:

- All roles in society must be filled.
- Those roles must be filled by those who are best able to perform them.
- Necessary training must take place.
- All roles must be performed conscientiously.

Functionalists believed that such systems were a 'universal' feature of human society (common to all societies) and that they served to match the most able people to the functionally most important positions in society.

Criticisms of Davis and Moore

The publication of the original article created some controversy at the time; in particular, the American sociologist Melvin Tumin (1919–94) raised a number of significant criticisms, some of which are summarised below:

1 Functional importance is not just difficult but far from easy to establish with any certainty. Tumin pointed out that the engineers in charge of a factory depend on their workforce and the workers are 'as important and indispensable' as the engineers.
2 Davis and Moore assume that only a limited number of individuals in society have the necessary talents to fill important positions. Tumin agreed that, while in every society there are a range of different talents, it is by no means the case that talent and ability will be rewarded. Elite groups in society will always attempt to preserve their power and privileges and will, therefore, 'place limits on the search, recruitment and training of functionally important personnel'.
3 Education and training do not necessarily justify extreme lifetime inequalities in the rewards offered to those who complete their

education and training. Davis and Moore argued that those individuals who successfully completed long periods of education and training had made 'sacrifices' that entitled them to a lifetime of higher material rewards. Tumin believed that education itself could be intrinsically rewarding and that, in any event, simply the possession of certain qualifications did not justify a lifetime of far greater material rewards.

4 Tumin did not believe that systems of social stratification ensured that societies survived and operated efficiently. He argued that because inequalities in social rewards could never be made fully acceptable to the less privileged, social stratification systems encouraged 'hostility, suspicion and distrust' among the different groups in society.

Marxist and feminist criticisms

Marxists are very critical of the functionalist perspective, arguing that far from being an open society where talent and merit determine position, society is fundamentally unfair and serves to reproduce existing inequalities through factors like social background, elite education and nepotism. Not only are opportunities fundamentally unfair and unequal but this has dramatically increased over time. For example, in 1946 the sociologist C. Wright Mills published a research paper about the 'middle class in middle sized American cities'. In 'Central City', he analysed the average weekly income of various social groups:

- Senior business people and executives earned $137.
- Higher 'white collar' workers earned $83.
- Wage workers earned $59.

According to Mills' analysis, an executive earned just over twice as much as a 'wage worker'. In 2016, the journalist Thomas Frank looked at the relative incomes of average wage workers and chief executives in Decatur, Illinois (the location of 'Central City') and noted that income inequality had dramatically increased:

- The chief executive of Archer Daniels Midland (the largest company in the city) earned 261 times as much as an average wage worker.
- The chief executive of Caterpillar (another major employer) earned 486 times as much.

To Marxists, this excessive divide in earnings reflects the greed of the capitalist class (bourgeoisie) who reward themselves at the expense of the workers (proletariat).

Feminists, such as Beverley Skeggs (2004) are equally critical of the functionalist support for the idea that society is a meritocracy. They point to the existence of the 'glass ceiling' of sexist prejudice and discrimination that historically has acted as a barrier preventing women reaching the top jobs. Their argument highlights the huge waste of female talent that is constrained through a lack of equality of opportunity.

Extension

Some people believe that complicated systems of welfare payments should be replaced by a 'universal basic income'. Do some research and prepare a report explaining your evidence-based reasons for either supporting or rejecting the proposal to introduce a 'universal basic income'.

Activities

1 Do you agree that social stratification is a 'universal necessity' for society? Look at the arguments made on these pages, do some additional research and then write a paragraph summarising your conclusions.

2 Does it matter that some people earn much more than others as long as everyone can earn a 'living wage'? Research income inequality in the UK and hold a class debate to discuss this question.

Check your knowledge

1 From memory, list the four reasons the functionalists Davis and Moore gave for regarding social stratification as a 'universal necessity'. (Check your answer against the list provided.)

2 Summarise Tumin's criticisms of Davis and Moore.

3 Briefly outline the Marxist and feminist criticisms of functionalist support for a meritocracy.

Summary

- The functionalist perspective promotes the idea that role allocation results in a meritocracy.
- Davis and Moore argued that social stratification was a 'universal necessity' for all known human societies.
- Marxists challenge the idea that society is meritocratic arguing that inequalities are not only unfair but widening over time.
- Feminists point to the existence of the glass ceiling as evidence we do not live in a meritocracy.

KEY TERMS

Economic inequality differences in income and wealth

Subjective class the socio-economic position a person feels they are located in

Trade union an organisation of workers designed to protect their common interests through negotiation and collective action

Urban towns and cities; sociologists often refer to social groups such as the urban working class

White collar workers non-manual workers in offices and the service sector

Link

You might like to look at the 'Great British Class Survey': http://blog.ukdataservice.ac.uk/the-great-british-class-survey-now-available-from-the-uk-data-service/ for comparison.

Extension

Do some research into economic inequalities in Britain today and prepare a report on your findings. You should find this website a useful starting point: www.equalitytrust.org.uk/scale-economic-inequality-uk.

Socio-economic class

Socio-economic class

Socio-economic class is the type of social stratification most commonly found in urban industrial societies, including present-day Europe, North America and the developed world generally. It is based on economic inequality. Classifications of social class are normally based on objective criteria, such as sharing a similar position in society relative to a person's wealth, status and power (or the lack of). The term 'subjective class' refers to the socio-economic position a person thinks they are located in.

The upper class

The upper class is the elite in our society. Estimated to be no more than the top 6 per cent of the population, according to the Great British Class Survey, the upper class includes the owners and directors of major companies, important members of the aristocracy and some senior politicians. They are sometimes referred to as the 'establishment' or the ruling class. Members of this class enjoy access to high levels of income and own a large share of the national wealth. In 2016:

- households in the top 10 per cent of the population enjoyed an income that was calculated to be 24 times greater than that of the poorest 10 per cent
- the richest 10 per cent of the population held 45 per cent of the nation's total wealth (property, savings, and so on), in contrast to the poorest 10 per cent who owned only 8.7 per cent.

Wealth brings with it access to power, not only because these individuals occupy powerful high status positions in society, but also because governments in capitalist societies generally believe that the economic security of the nation depends on the profitability of private industry and protecting the economic interests of wealthier citizens.

The middle class

According to Ipsos Mori (2016) the size of the middle class exceeded that of the working class in 2000. The most commonly found definition of the middle class is people with 'non-manual' occupations. However, this simple definition hides some of the significant changes in British society. In twenty-first-century Britain, the middle class is a diverse group with a significant gap opening up between the lives of those at the lower and upper ends of this socio-economic class. Members of the upper-middle class are more likely to have been privately educated and hold higher professional jobs (such as lawyers, doctors and architects). Lower professionals (such as teachers, social workers and nurses) traditionally have also be drawn from the middle class but recruitment is now more open. Professional and managerial employees enjoy greater economic security and have more access to power than routine white collar workers and manual workers. Non-manual workers continue to enjoy significantly better physical health than manual workers, are educationally more successful and are more likely to own their own homes.

The working class

The definition of the working class has historically been applied to 'manual workers'. Due to the shift towards a post-industrial society, the size of this group relative to the rest of the population has fallen significantly over the last 50 years or so. Some sociologists have argued that it is wrong to see the working class as simply manual workers, for example many workers in the service sector who work in fast-food restaurants or call centres are engaged in tasks that are repetitive, require few skills and are poorly rewarded. Low-income earners are less likely than middle- or high-income earners to be members of trade unions, and have little or no power to influence their pay and conditions due to factors like globalisation. In 2017 the TUC accused 'bad bosses' of using migrant workers from the European Union to undermine existing terms and conditions by substituting British workers with cheap labour.

National statistics socio-economic classification

The Office for National Statistics (ONS) uses the following occupational scale to produce statistics on different types of occupation and the changing socio-economic status of the workforce:

- Higher managerial, administrative and professional occupations, for example high court judge or chief executive.
- Lower managerial, administrative and professional occupations, for example teacher, social worker or software designer.
- Intermediate occupations, for example clerical worker, call centre worker or nursery nurse.
- Small employers and own account workers, for example publican, shop or restaurant owner.
- Lower supervisory and technical occupations, for example motor mechanic, plumber or electrician.
- Semi-routine occupations, for example postal worker, farm worker or security guard.
- Routine occupations, for example van driver, waitress or bar staff.
- Never worked and long-term unemployed.

Criticisms of socio-economic classifications

Functionalists tend to take socio-economic classifications like the one above at face value. However, the system used by the ONS is actually much more complex than this simple scale would suggest. Any attempt to put people into categories based on their occupation is going to create problems. Where, for example, would you put authors or actors on this scale? Marxists criticise such classifications as excluding those who do not work, such as the very rich members of the upper class. Feminists are highly critical of classifications that define the class of households on the head of the household, who is invariably assumed to be male. This, they argue, tends to render women invisible. They consequently call for any classification to be based on individuals rather than households.

Activities

1 Draw up a simple chart based on the ONS scale and then draw lines across to represent the upper, middle and working classes. Compare notes with other members of your teaching group, looking for similarities and differences.

2 Make a list of ten jobs that are not included as examples on the ONS scale. Decide the category in which you would place them. Compare notes with other members of your teaching group, looking for similarities and differences.

Check your knowledge

1 Who are the elite members of British society?

2 What percentage of the British population can be described as middle class?

3 Why do some sociologists believe it is wrong to see the working class as exclusively manual workers?

4 Outline criticisms of socio-economic classifications such as those used by ONS.

Summary

- Socio-economic class is the type of social stratification most commonly found in urban industrial societies.
- It is based on economic inequality; the members of each 'class' share a similar position in society relative to their wealth, status and power (or the lack of).
- Attempts at socio-economic classification has been criticised by both Marxists and feminists.

KEY TERMS

Alienation individuals who feel that they have become separated from the wider society are said to be alienated, e.g. they lack power and control over their lives

Class conflict the conflicting interests of socio-economic classes

Egalitarian the principle of equality for all people

Marxism ideas based on an interpretation of the ideas of Karl Marx

Means of production the resources from which wealth is derived, such as land, factories, etc. Ownership of these defines the ruling class

Petty bourgeoisie owners of small businesses

Polarisation of social classes increasing differences between the lives of different socio-economic classes

KEY TEXT

Marx K. in McLellan D., *Karl Marx: Selected Writings,* Oxford, Oxford University Press, 2000.

Activities

1 Do you think that the idea of social alienation is relevant to life in Britain today? Do some research and hold a class debate.

2 Do you think that the idea of the polarisation of social classes is relevant to life in Britain today? Do some research and record your findings as a poster or PowerPoint presentation.

Marx on class

◀ Marxist portrayal of the fundamental inequalities and injustice of capitalism

Marxism

Karl Marx believed that, in the distant past, an age of primitive communism existed where the **means of production** were simple forms of hunting and gathering. In such 'primitive' communities, everyone worked together to ensure that they all had shelter and enough to eat. However, as societies developed, Marx theorised that a specialised division of labour emerged, for example some people became full-time farmers and produced the food while others built shelters, manufactured goods using increasingly sophisticated tools or became full-time warriors. With this division of labour came the ownership of private property and the emergence of distinct social classes.

As capitalist societies developed in the eighteenth and nineteenth centuries, the means of production became steam power, machinery and the factory system. Marx saw two major classes in this type of society: those who owned the means of production were the capitalist class (or bourgeoisie), while those who worked in the factories or mines became the working class (or proletariat). Because they did not own the means of production, the workers could only survive by selling their labour power. At the heart of this system, Marx understood that there was a basic conflict of interest.

Class conflict

Capitalism as an economic system has the capacity to provide for all, but Marx believed that the capitalist class used their position of power to exploit the labour of their workers and increase profits. The workers created the wealth with their labour, but the economic rewards went mostly to the capitalist class who owned the means of production. It was in the owners' interests to keep wages as low as possible and to spend the bare minimum required to keep their workers housed and healthy enough to work. Meanwhile, the workers' interests would be best served by seizing ownership of the means of production and establishing the fair and equal society of communism.

Polarisation of social classes

Marx believed that capitalists would always attempt to maintain profits by keeping wages as low as possible and by introducing new forms of technology that replaced workers with machines (mechanisation). As time passed, this would create greater and greater differences between the classes and increase class conflict between them. He described this process as the polarisation of social classes. In time, society would consist of a small wealthy elite and large numbers of relatively poor workers. For example, Marx believed that members of the petty bourgeoisie (such as small-scale manufacturers and craftsmen) could not compete with larger industrial concerns and that they would inevitably be driven out of business and forced into the working class.

Alienation

Marx observed that while capitalism could produce an apparently endless supply of material goods, it did not seem to make people happier or more satisfied with their lives. He believed that capitalism created social alienation, for example people were unhappy because they were not in control of their lives and often lived in fear of losing their jobs and homes. Marx said that capitalism treated people as if they were 'commodities' – things that could be bought or disposed of as required.

Crisis of capitalism

Capitalism as an economic system is unstable; periods of prosperity and relatively full employment are followed by economic recessions, with wages falling in value and/or rising unemployment. Ultimately Marx believed that the capitalist system would collapse; this would create the conditions for a political revolution and the establishment of a 'classless' communist society, an egalitarian society which would serve the interests of all its members.

Functionalist and feminist criticisms of Marx

- Marx saw history as governed by 'laws' that determined how society developed. Functionalists suggest that this view greatly underestimates the openness of society and the capacity of talented people to make decisions and change their destinies.
- Marx believed that economic factors shaped human society. Feminists argue that focusing solely on economics makes this theory over-deterministic and ignores other important social factors such as gender.
- Other sociologists have argued that Marxist ideas give little attention to factors like racism that can limit the opportunities of minority ethnic groups.
- Writing in the nineteenth century, Marx believed that the collapse of capitalism was going to happen in the near future; in reality, capitalism has proved to be more resilient than Marx anticipated. Capitalist societies have also proved to be more stable than he anticipated, capable of supporting comprehensive welfare systems and creating rising living standards.

Extension

Using the two resources of http://classonline.org.uk and www.suttontrust.com, research evidence of social class inequalities within the UK.

Check your knowledge

1 What did Marx mean when he used the term 'proletariat'?
2 What did Marx mean when he used the term 'class conflict'?
3 From memory, identify functionalist and feminist criticisms of Marx's ideas. (Check your answer against the list provided.)

Summary

- As societies developed, Marx theorised that a specialised division of labour emerged, with which came the ownership of private property and the emergence of distinct social classes.
- In capitalist societies, Marx saw two major classes: those who owned the means of production and those who worked for them.
- Functionalists believe Marx plays down the ability of talented members of society to get on.
- Feminists argue by focusing solely on class, Marxist analysis ignores gender oppression.

KEY TERMS

Life chances the opportunities that an individual has to share in the cultural and material rewards that a society has to offer, e.g. access to education and employment

Lifestyle the various ways in which social groups choose to use the resources that are available to them, reflecting the attitudes and priorities of the group

Market situation Weber believed that socio-economic classes developed in market economies in which individuals compete for economic gain; those who achieve a similar share of available resources (e.g. access to education, ownership of housing and other forms of property) occupy a similar market situation

KEY TEXT

Weber M., *The Theory of Economic and Social Organizations,* New York, Free Press, 1947 (republished 2012).

Weber on class

▲ Weber recognised differentiation within the proletariat, based on factors like status, qualifications and power

Weber

Max Weber accepted that social class was essentially about economic factors. However, he did not share the Marxist idea that society was broadly divided between the capitalist class and the working class. Weber believed that the deciding factor with regard to class was market situation; some workers were more skilled than others and, therefore, able to command a larger salary and enjoy more job security. Weber thought that to put these skilled workers in the same group as unskilled workers and to describe them as the 'working class' was to over simplify the complexities of socio-economic class. Weber saw not two great class groups but many different grades of occupational class, and he believed that the people within each particular class would enjoy broadly similar life chances. His view of class is better able to explain the importance of the middle class who do not easily fit the Marxist model of society as divided between capitalists and workers. Weber saw a more complex picture involving four broad categories: a property-owning upper class (individuals with economic power); the professional middle class (or 'intelligentsia'); the petty bourgeoisie (lower middle-class owners of small businesses); and the manual working class. Weber did not see any evidence of the 'polarisation' of classes, but he did see evidence of an expanding middle class. He did not believe in an inevitable collapse of capitalism, although he did recognise that those who occupied a common market position might take collective action to improve their situation.

Status

'Status' is the term sociologists use to describe the level of prestige or importance attached to a particular group or individual in society. In Weber's view, different social classes compete with each other for a greater share of status. Because the members of a particular class group share similar values and have a broadly similar lifestyle, they can signal their membership of the class group by the property they own, for example the car they drive, the clothes they wear and the house they live in. Weber theorised that people make judgements about others and confer status upon them largely based on their patterns of consumption (how they spend what they earn) rather than production (how they earn their money). Weber believed that, while class, status and power often overlap with one another, they are not as closely linked as Marxists suggest. This explains why some individuals and groups in society have higher status but less economic worth than others. Members of the aristocracy, for example, may have relatively little wealth when compared to the chief executive of a major corporation.

Party

Weber used the term 'party' to describe not just political parties but also any organised group that sought to exercise power, for example trade unions, pressure groups and professional associations. Weber theorised that these groups compete for power in a similar way that classes compete for a share of status. A 'party', Weber believed, could have an appeal that cut across class differences. For example, they could be based on national identity or membership of certain religious groups, such as Catholics and Protestants in Northern Ireland. However, one key idea that shows an important difference between Weber's view of social stratification and that of Marx is that Weber did not believe that economic wealth automatically brought with it greater power than that which can be exercised by a politician, a trade union leader or a civil servant, for example.

Functionalist, Marxist and feminist criticisms of Weber

- Functionalists would see Weber's analysis as over-structural, ignoring an individual's opportunity to shape their destiny in society through merit and hard work.
- Marxists believe that capitalist society exploits its workers and that Weber's multi-layered view of class based on market situation hides the fundamental distinction between those who own the means of production and those who work for them. Put simply, the wealthiest members of society still tend to be the most powerful, while the poor remain powerless.
- Feminists would argue that there is not enough specific attention given to gender relations. For example, because of prejudice and discrimination in employment, women and men from the same social position do not necessarily occupy the same market situation.

Links

- To learn more about Weber's theory of power in greater detail, see pages 245–246.
- To learn more about Weber's concept of life chances, see pages 228–231.

Extension

Draw up a chart to compare the ideas of Marx and Weber on socio-economic class. Research the work of the sociologist Frank Parkin (1931–2011).

Check your knowledge

1 What did Weber mean by the term 'market situation'?
2 What did Weber mean by the term 'lifestyle'?
3 What did Weber mean by the term 'party'?

Activities

1 Advertisers use the idea that their products can be sold as representing an 'aspirational lifestyle choice'. In other words, if you buy their product you are signalling your ambition to join a higher status social group.

   Do some research and find examples of adverts that fit this description. Record your findings as a poster or PowerPoint presentation.

2 a Work with other members of your class or group to produce a list of 20 occupations (paid employment). Arrange them in order of status (high to low importance).

   b Arrange the same list in order of income (high to low pay).

   c Look for differences between the two lists. Can you explain any differences you find by using the ideas of Max Weber?

Summary

- Weber accepted that social class was essentially about economic factors.
- He did not share the Marxist idea that society was broadly divided between the capitalist class and the working class.
- Weber believed that the deciding factor with regard to class was market situation.

Life chances

'Life chances' is a term associated with Max Weber that refers to the opportunities that an individual has in life. It remains an uncomfortable truth that where we are born, who our parents are and where we go to school can all have a very real impact on our future lives. In Britain in the twenty-first century, it is still possible to say that social class, gender, race and ethnicity, sexuality, age, disability, religion and belief can impact upon our opportunities and future careers.

Social class and life chances

Social class inequalities, although the central concern of Marxists, are played down in the twenty-first century by many sociologists as less significant. Indeed, postmodernists go so far as to claim that 'class is dead'. When so much political and media attention is devoted to racial and gender differences, class inequalities are frequently overlooked. However, figures from the respected Luxembourg Income Study (2019) highlight the marked social class inequality in income within the UK. The poorest 10 per cent of households in the UK have lower incomes than the poorest 10 per cent in France, Germany, Belgium, the Netherlands, Denmark, Sweden, Norway, Finland, Switzerland or Austria. Meanwhile the top 10 per cent in the UK make more than their counterparts in those countries. Income and wealth enable the rich to enjoy better health, have longer life expectancy, send their children to the best private schools and subsequently gain the top jobs in society. The Social Mobility and Child Poverty Commission conducted a study based on 4,000 leaders in politics, business and the media. They found a dramatic over-representation of those educated at independent schools and Oxford and Cambridge, and concluded that Britain is 'deeply elitist'. Even the government's own Social Mobility Commission's 'State of the Nation 2018 to 2019' (2019) reported that 'class privilege remains entrenched as social mobility stagnates'.

▲ Getting to a top university like Oxford or Cambridge is still closely linked to an individual's social class position

Gender and life chances

Although women can expect to live a longer life than men (83 years compared to 79 years), males generally expect to spend a larger proportion of their lives in 'good' general health compared with females. Thanks especially to their success in education, women's employment has broadened and expanded over time into management and the professions. However, feminists point to their continued concentration in work that seems to be a simple extension of their domestic work: cooking, cleaning, childcare or clerical work, which traditionally involves supporting men. According to the Trades Union Congress (TUC, 2019), 28 per cent of women are in low paid work compared to 17.2 per cent of men, and with a current gender pay gap at 17.9 per cent for all employees women are effectively working for free for 65 days a year compared to men. However, Susan Faludi argues that the workplace can also seem threatening to men through fear of redundancy, shrinking pay and a longer hours working culture. All these factors can serve to undermine the secure 'breadwinner' role they once enjoyed as males.

Ethnicity and life chances

Statistics show consistently higher premature death rates for BAME (Black and minority ethnic) men and women than for white men and women. The ONS (2018) found people descended from Pakistan and Bangladesh, living in the UK, have the highest mortality rates. In terms of educational attainment, some ethnic groups like those of Chinese and Indian descent do better than average, while other ethnic groups underachieve compared to the majority white children. However, the worst performing ethnic group is white working-class boys. Historically, most minority ethnic groups have experienced discrimination in the labour market resulting in levels of unemployment approximately twice that of the white population. Government figures, published in 2018, reveal that worklessness impacts particularly on young people from minority ethnic groups, with young black people having the highest rate of unemployment.

Sexuality and life chances

Homosexuality was a criminal offence in the UK until 1967. Since then the UK has become a more tolerant society of sexual difference. However, the then Education and Equalities minister, Nicky Morgan, stated in 2015 that homophobic bullying in British schools is preventing LGBTQ kids from pursuing their passions and is subsequently 'screwing' their future prospects. Fear of homophobia can still prevent people expressing their true sexuality for fear of negative reactions and reprisals from family, friends and employers. Globally there are still anti-homosexuality laws in 79 countries.

Age and life chances

The British Social Attitudes survey (2018) found that experiences of ageism (age discrimination) are more common among younger groups, with under-25s twice as likely to experience it than other age groups.

Research from the English Longitudinal Study of Ageing (2018) reveals high levels of age discrimination faced by older people, a situation that worsens as they age. They found that 33 per cent of elderly people experience age discrimination, with less wealthy older men being at highest risk. Retired older people were 25 per cent more likely to report age discrimination than those who were still employed. There are accusations that the elderly can suffer age discrimination in healthcare, either by being denied treatment available to younger people or by negative attitudes of staff towards them.

Disability and life chances

Discrimination experienced by disabled people is known as disablism. People with disabilities have historically been subject to widespread and systematic discrimination. Since 2010 it has been governmental policy to subject two million people to medical tests in assessment for Work Capability Assessments (WCAs), which unfairly serves to reinforce ideas of people who are disabled as workshy. The principle of integration within mainstream education was enshrined by the Salamanca Statement and Framework for Action on Special Needs Education (1994) which was endorsed by 92 countries including the UK. However, the reality is that there appears to be significant levels of underachievement by disabled children in education. With regard to employment, people with disabilities experience discrimination in hiring practices and have a level of unemployment at around 50 per cent, far higher than people who have no disability.

Religion and belief and life chances

Historically, religious belief was often a source of both direct and indirect discrimination. However, the Equality Act 2010 now protects people from being discriminated against if they hold a particular religion or a particular philosophical belief. It also protects people from being discriminated against for not being religious or holding a particular philosophical belief. The media sometimes highlights case studies where people of religion feel they are being discriminated against in the workplace because of a workplace dress code or uniform policy. For example, Muslim women may feel they are denied employment if a workplace rule forbids the covering of the face. Whether a situation is unlawful will often depend upon an employer's justification. For example, banning a full-length robe or the wearing of jewellery on the grounds of health and safety would probably be lawful.

Functionalist perspective and life chances

Functionalists, as supporters of the meritocracy argument, believe that life chances are a direct reflection of the talent, effort and skills of the individual. A meritocratic society, they argue, allocates people to the division of labour that best reflect their abilities. This process is known as role allocation. Therefore, it follows that the most talented individuals will occupy the most challenging and demanding roles. They should, therefore, be rewarded with both income and status, resulting in high and positive life chances. This inequality in the reward of life chances is positively embraced by functionalists who see it as acting to motivate the rest of society. However, both Marxists and feminists dismiss this view as naïve and simplistic and point to the huge waste of both working class and female talent respectively that are simply not given the opportunity to occupy the top positions in society.

Marxist perspective and life chances

Marxists believe that life chances reflect the unequal distribution of resources in society in the first place. They point to the two-tier education system (state vs private schools) that denies the potential life chances of the working class (and to a lesser extent the middle class), by excluding them from private schools and universities like Oxford and Cambridge which are seen to educate a privileged elite. Such educational establishments are responsible for filling the top jobs in society. For example, despite only educating 7 per cent of the population, private schools account for 71 per cent of senior judges, 62 per cent of senior armed forces officers, 55 per cent of senior civil servants, 53 per cent of senior diplomats and 50 per cent of members of the House of Lords. Although occasionally very bright children from the working class are highly successful (such as Alan Sugar), Marxists argue that they are very much the exception to the rule, but their success is used to instil a sense of false consciousness and hope that anyone can make it to the top. However, as the Social Mobility Commission (2019) states: 'class privilege remains entrenched as social mobility stagnates'.

Feminist perspective and life chances

Feminists argue that life chances in society historically reflect the way it has been constructed to serve the interests of men while at the same time oppressing women. Radical feminists see the family as the key source of women's oppression and consequently undermining their life chances to get on in employment and public life. By being tied to the home, because of their assumed responsibility for domestic work and childcare, renders most mothers in a situation of being excluded from the labour market or confined to part-time employment. However, childless women have not had this burden, but still faced the 'glass ceiling' of prejudice and discrimination that served to exclude them from top jobs. Fortunately, due to legislation (the Equal Pay Act, the Sex Discrimination Act and the Equality Act), achievement in education and changing attitudes, women's life chances have improved recently and are moving towards those of men.

Activity

Consider the factors that shape life chances by making a list of each one and applying it to yourself. How important do you think each factor is in determining your own life chances?

Extension

Complete an internet search into the impact private schools have on society. In drawing up your conclusions, assess the degree of influence that private schools have in populating the top jobs in society.

Check your knowledge

1 What do sociologists mean when they use the term 'life chances'?

2 What do sociologists mean when they talk about the 'glass ceiling'?

3 From memory, list six factors affecting life chances other than education. (Check your answer against the list provided.)

Summary

- Life chances are influenced by social class, gender, race and ethnicity, sexuality, age, disability, religion and belief.
- Differing sociological perspectives hold opposing views on the distribution of life chances.

231

KEY TERMS

Affluence having an abundance of money

Class identity this is the social class with which an individual identifies

Embourgeoisement the adoption of middle-class values and behaviours by prosperous members of the working class

Instrumentalism describes the attitude of some working-class people towards their jobs and any form of collective action, e.g. work as simply a way of earning money and self-interest rather than traditional working-class collective values

New working class home-centred members of the working class with instrumental attitudes (first described in the 1960s)

The affluent worker

Embourgeoisement

In the nineteenth century, Marx predicted that the petty bourgeoisie (the lower-middle class) would become part of the working class due to its inability to compete with capitalist industries. In the twentieth century, sociologists began to argue that the opposite was happening; the middle class was expanding and increasing numbers of the old working class were becoming prosperous members of the middle class. This idea became known as embourgeoisement (becoming middle class).

▲ Vauxhall car workers in Luton formed the basis of the study of 'affluent workers' in the 1960s

The affluent worker in the class structure

In 1969, the sociologist John Goldthorpe (1935–) and a group of colleagues tried to find evidence of embourgeoisement. They chose Luton for their study. At the time, Luton was a newly prosperous area of south-east England with expanding industries, particularly the car industry. Goldthorpe and his fellow researchers selected a sample of 229 manual workers and 59 white collar workers (for comparison with the larger group). Nearly 50 per cent of the manual workers had moved to the south-east of England in search of secure and well-paid employment. Of these, 57 per cent were homeowners (or in the process of buying a home) and all of them were married. In comparison to other manual workers, they were described as having affluence, being well paid and their incomes compared favourably with the white collar group. The researchers found that the 'affluent workers' in their study had an instrumental attitude towards their work; it supported their standard of life but they had little or no interest in the work itself. They were members of trade unions, but they joined as self-interested individuals seeking to improve their wages and working conditions rather than out of any sense of social solidarity with other workers (the researchers described their attitude as instrumental collectivism) – 56 per cent saw money as the basis for class divisions in society. However, although the researchers found little evidence to support the idea that these affluent workers were adopting a more middle-class lifestyle, they did find that their domestic lives were home centred and privatised, for example there was no evidence of traditional working-class community-based activities. In terms of their political beliefs, the researchers found no evidence that the affluent workers were becoming more likely to vote for the Conservative Party (in the 1959 General Election 80 per cent had voted Labour). In their conclusions, the researchers suggested that while the affluent workers were not becoming middle class, they could be described as members of a new working class, with home-centred (privatised) domestic lives and an instrumental attitude towards work and trade union membership.

Privatism and the working class

In the late 1980s, sociologist Devine revisited the idea of privatised instrumentalism (*Affluent Workers Revisited*, 1992). Devine based her research on indepth interviews with 62 Luton residents, all of whom were either workers at the Vauxhall car plant or their wives. Devine agreed that the lifestyle of her sample was not as communal as the traditional working class, nor was it as 'privatised' (or home centred) as the 1969 study had suggested. She also rejected the idea of a new working class; she pointed out that the workers in her study were often critical of capitalism despite their rising living standards and aspirations as consumers. She quoted one of her interviewees as saying:

'I could be out of a job tomorrow. I live in fear of new technology and what's happening in the car industry. I've been with the company 11 years and I've seen them take on people and now they are making people redundant. I've seen the start and I'll see the end. With new technology they have no need for people.'

While Devine found evidence of rising living standards, many of those she interviewed continued to resent the privileges of inherited wealth and held a sense of injustice at the existence of extreme inequalities in society. However, while they still had some of the values of the traditional working class, many of her interviewees had lost faith in the ability of the Labour Party to deliver a more just and equal society.

Working-class attitudes

Only 25 per cent of British people work in routine and manual occupations (traditional working-class jobs), but the 2015 British Social Attitudes survey found that 60 per cent of the population regarded themselves as working class. The survey found that many 'socially conservative' traditional working-class values remain, even among those who have become socially mobile and who would be classified as middle class. Although feelings of class identity may have a great deal to do with family background (working-class parents), researchers suggest that it may also reflect a feeling of being disadvantaged in comparison to the wealthy elite in society.

Activities

1 Write a paragraph to explain what sociologists mean by the term 'affluent worker'.
2 Survey the members of your teaching group: compare the occupation of their parents (to classify their socio-economic class) with the social class that they identify with.

KEY TEXT

Devine F., *Affluent Workers Revisited*, Edinburgh, Edinburgh University Press, 1992.

Extension

Complete an internet search for the 'Great British Class Survey' (BBC, 2011). Write a report about the key findings of the survey and how the original research is being developed.

Are old ideas about class (upper, middle and working) now outdated? Hold a class debate on this question.

Check your knowledge

1 What do sociologists mean when they use the term 'embourgeoisement'?
2 What do sociologists mean when they talk about instrumental attitudes towards work?
3 What do sociologists mean when they talk about a privatised domestic (home) life?

Summary

- In the twentieth century, sociologists began to argue that the middle class was expanding and increasing numbers of the old working class were becoming prosperous members of the middle class.
- This idea became known as embourgeoisement (becoming middle class).

KEY TERMS

Absolute poverty this exists when an individual cannot pay for the basic essentials of life, e.g. food, clothing and shelter

Culture of poverty when poverty is seen as inevitable and becomes a way of life

Poverty line a measure of minimum income required to meet the essential cost of living

Poverty trap poor families in receipt of means-tested welfare benefits become 'trapped' in poverty if their earnings marginally increase, resulting in the loss of benefits and, as a consequence, no improvement in their economic situation

Relative poverty when an individual lacks the resources to participate in activities that are widely available to the majority of people in society

State standard of poverty definition of poverty when households have an income of 'less than 60 per cent of the national median'

Subjective poverty an individual's perception of their level of deprivation

Poverty

What is poverty?

Sociologists use two main definitions of poverty: absolute and relative.

- **Absolute poverty** refers to an individual's inability to satisfy even their basic needs for food, clothing and shelter.
- **Relative poverty** refers to an individual whose standard of life falls well below that of the majority of the population.

Sociologists disagree about which is the best definition to use, but the consensus tends to favour relative poverty in contemporary society. Either way, both definitions are an attempt to measure poverty objectively. **Subjective poverty** is an individual person's perception of deprivation.

Material deprivation

One of the earliest systematic studies of poverty was conducted by Seebohm Rowntree (1871–1954). Rowntree focused on material deprivation through the idea of a 'poverty line', essentially a basic income level below which an individual's income was 'insufficient to obtain the minimum necessities'. In his research, Rowntree used the term 'primary poverty' to refer to what a modern sociologist would describe as absolute poverty, for example insufficient money to pay for basic essentials like housing costs, heating and enough food on the table to avoid going hungry. In the 'affluent society' of the 1950s and 1960s there was a myth that poverty had ended, however this myth was successfully dispelled by Peter Townsend (1979) with his work on relative poverty (see pages 237–238). Today, there are still many families living in material deprivation. For example, the Social Mobility and Child Poverty Commission (2015) stated, 'child poverty is set to rise not fall in the next five years' and the Social Metrics Commission (2018) estimated 4.1 million children – one in four – were living in absolute poverty in 2016–17. Research by Kellogg's (2015) highlighted how school holidays can exacerbate poverty since children entitled to free school meals have to be fed out of the family budget. The Children's Society (2012) estimated holiday time can increase the weekly shopping bill by between

£30 to £40. It was found that a third of parents have skipped a meal so that their children could eat during the school holidays.

Measuring poverty

Measuring poverty has always been controversial; if poverty is defined in absolute terms, the proportion of the population classified as being in poverty will always be smaller than when a relative measure is used. The state standard of poverty suggests that households are living in poverty if they have an income of 'less than 60 per cent of the national median'. In 2019 a report from the Resolution Foundation included the following indicators:

- Government figures show over 4 million children in the UK were living in relative poverty in 2018.
- The number of children living in relative poverty is on course to hit 37 per cent, topping the previous record high of 34 per cent recorded in the 1990s.
- Over the past decade household income has been particularly damaged by welfare cuts, benefit freezes and a lack of pay growth.

Explaining poverty

Sociologists have suggested a number of possible explanations for the causes of poverty; most do not accept that the individual can be blamed for their condition, although some come uncomfortably close to the nineteenth-century idea that poverty was a consequence of 'moral degeneracy'.

Link

See pages 237–238 for more detailed information on relative poverty.

- Dependency theories: this idea suggests that social security benefits discourage the poor from taking responsibility for their own welfare; the poor are stuck in a poverty trap because employment pays less than the benefits they would lose once they entered the workforce or worked longer hours if they already have a job. The government has attempted to redress this problem through a series of measures. The controversial Universal Credit combines both in-work and out-of-work benefits in order to make the transition from benefits to work significantly easier. In addition, increases to the National Living Wage and cuts to income tax (by increasing the threshold before tax is paid) have been designed to encourage employment. Finally, the household benefit cap was introduced in 2013 to restrict welfare, so no household can receive more in benefits than average earnings.
- The culture of poverty: this idea suggests that poverty can be seen as a way of life that is passed from one generation to the next. However, Marxists would argue the main causes of poverty are structural factors such as lack of jobs and affordable housing, low wages and a gig/zero-hours contract economy.
- The cycle of deprivation: this idea suggests that social, environmental and economic factors (situational constraints) lead the poor to behave differently to the wider society. All their energies are consumed with simply trying to survive and their environment offers few, if any, opportunities to improve their situation, for example the local schools are underperforming and fail to attract good teachers. Poor children growing up in this environment are, therefore, unlikely to be able to escape from poverty when they grow into adulthood.

- The economic system: people in poverty used to be associated with those excluded from the labour market (for example the disabled, the chronically sick and the elderly) but currently the largest sector of people living in poverty are those in employment but in receipt of low wages. Official statistics show that 55 per cent of people experiencing poverty live in a working household. In the UK, 20.5 per cent of full-time employees are in low paid jobs, compared to the Organisation for Economic Co-operation and Development (OECD) average of 17.1 per cent.

Functionalist perspective on poverty

Functionalists generally adopt an individualistic view on poverty, seeing it primarily in terms of failings of the individual. Poverty impacts on those lacking talent, qualifications or personal drive who thus fail to thrive in what they believe is a meritocratic society. The poor are therefore equated with characteristics of being lazy or workshy, resulting in blaming the poor for their poverty. Looking at how poverty could be viewed as functional to society, the functionalist Herbert J. Gans identified three functions. Firstly, the poor invariably end up doing the worst jobs that no one else wants to do. Secondly, the existence of the poor creates lots of jobs to deal with them and their problems, such as social workers and welfare workers. Thirdly, poverty is comforting to the non-poor because there are people worse off than them who can be used as scapegoats for society's problems.

Marxist perspective on poverty

For Marxists the origins of poverty lie within the inequalities and unfairness of capitalism. When firms exist to maximise profits, inevitably there will be pressure to pay low wages and dump workers when demand for goods and services declines due to fluctuations in market forces. Consequently, the solution to poverty is to move to a more equal society where resources are distributed more equitably. Poverty is, therefore, a class rather than an individual or group issue, since all workers are under the threat of losing their job and entering the quick spiral downwards into material deprivation.

Feminist perspective on poverty

Feminists talk about the 'feminisation of poverty' which highlights the fact that women are more likely to live in poverty than men. One factor to explain this is that the majority of single parents and single pensioners are women. Another factor is the gender pay gap (currently 17.9 per cent for all employees according to the TUC, 2019) which means women earn less than men do and accumulate lower pensions to live on in old age. Even when women live with men, household income may not be equally shared. For example, Jan Pahl (1989) found that men were more likely to have money for personal spending than their female partners. The contemporary definition of domestic violence embraces the fact that women can be denied sufficient financial resources. Feminists conclude that understanding women's poverty can only be understood in the context of the gender power relations that exist both in the home and in the workplace.

Activity

Design a list of 'basic essentials' that every family should have.
- Compare your list with those produced by other members of your teaching group.
- Look for similarities and differences and discuss the reasons for any differences.

Extension

Research the problem of homelessness in Britain. You should find this website a useful starting point: www.homeless.org.uk/facts-figures. Discuss your findings with the other members of your group.

Check your knowledge

1 Differentiate between the terms 'absolute poverty' and 'relative poverty'.
2 How have governments attempted to alleviate poverty and unemployment?
3 How do functionalists, Marxists and feminists differ in their views on poverty?

Summary

- Sociologists use two main definitions of poverty: absolute and relative.
- There are a range of ways to explain poverty.
- Functionalists, Marxists and feminists differ in their understanding of the nature and causes of poverty.

Relative deprivation

▲ According to the Department of Work and Pensions (2019) there are an estimated 2 million pensioners in relative poverty and 1.6 million in absolute poverty

Relative deprivation

When sociologists use the term 'relative deprivation', they are referring to a measure of the extent of poverty; sociologists who accept a relative definition do so because they believe that people have a right to be able to participate in the lifestyle available to the majority of the population. Even if you can pay for shelter, clothe and feed yourself to a minimum standard, you are still impoverished if you lack the choices and opportunities that most people take for granted, for example you cannot afford to watch satellite or streamed television, adequately heat your home in winter or enjoy a few other 'luxuries'.

Poverty in the United Kingdom (1979)

In the late 1960s, the sociologist Peter Townsend (1928–2009) conducted a major survey of poverty in Britain based on a sample of over 2,000 households and more than 6,000 individuals located in various geographical areas. The results were published in 1979 in a report entitled 'Poverty in the United Kingdom'. Townsend identified three possible ways of defining poverty:

1 The state's standard of poverty on which official statistics were based. This was calculated on the basis of an individual entitlement to claim certain benefits and Townsend believed this to be arbitrarily determined (a subjective decision) by the government of the day. He concluded that 'by the state's standard (the basic welfare benefit scales plus housing costs), 7 per cent of households were found to be in poverty and 24 per cent on the margins of poverty'.
2 The relative income standard of poverty was based on identifying those households whose income fell below the average for similar households. Townsend believed this measure to be arbitrary, potentially misleading (it did not take into account the level of welfare payments available) and inadequate (it did not account for the lifestyles available to those who were relatively materially disadvantaged). He concluded that 'by the relative income standard

You will be able to:
● explain what relative deprivation is
● describe the key ideas of Townsend on relative deprivation.

KEY TERM
Industrial democracy involving employees in the management of an industry

KEY TEXT
Townsend P., *Poverty in the United Kingdom,* Harmondsworth, Penguin, 1979.

Activities

1 Write a paragraph making the case for or against using a relative definition of poverty.

2 How might governments try to reduce 'excessive' income and wealth and should they attempt to do so? Research the issue and then hold a class debate.

Extension

Carry out an internet search for examples of 'industrial democracy' in action and prepare a report on your findings. Discuss your findings with the other members of your group.

Check your knowledge

1 How many households were involved in Townsend's survey?

2 From memory, list three possible ways of defining poverty identified by Townsend. (Check your answer against the list provided.)

3 What percentage of households did Townsend consider to be in poverty?

Summary

- When sociologists use the term 'relative deprivation', they are referring to a measure of the extent of poverty.

- Sociologists who accept a relative definition do so because they believe that people have a right to be able to participate in the lifestyle available to the majority of the population.

(households having an income of less than 50 per cent of the mean for their type), 10.5 per cent of the households were in poverty'.

3 Relative deprivation, Townsend's preferred measure. Townsend argued: 'Individuals can be said to be in poverty when they lack the resources to obtain the types of diet, participate in the activities and have the living conditions and amenities which are customary, or at least widely encouraged or approved, in the societies to which they belong.' Using his preferred measure, Townsend found that '25 per cent of households were in poverty'.

Townsend's research was based on a questionnaire that asked detailed questions about some 60 'indicators' of deprivation. These included variables such as diet, fuel and clothing, housing conditions, working conditions, health, education and social activities. For example, he specified the following indicators of 'work deprivation' and to each indicator he allocated a score:

- Subject to one week's notice or less = 1
- All working time standing or walking about = 1
- Poor (or very poor) working conditions = 1 (or 2)
- Working before eight o'clock in the morning or working at night = 1
- No wages or salary during sickness = 1
- No entitlement to occupational pension = 1
- No entitlement to holiday with pay, or less than two weeks = 1
- Possible maximum = 8

Based on this index, Townsend found that only 16 per cent of non-manual workers scored 3 or more compared with 69 per cent of manual workers. In other words, manual workers were far more likely to be in insecure employment, experience poor working conditions and have few work-related benefits.

Criticisms of Townsend

Some researchers criticised Townsend's work on the basis that much of it measured 'inequalities' in society rather than poverty. These criticisms tended to come from sociologists who did not accept the idea of relative poverty. Other sociologists have criticised specific elements of Townsend's research method. For example, Townsend included the following in his 'summary deprivation index':

- Does not have fresh meat (including meals out) as many as four days a week.
- Has not had a cooked breakfast most days of the week.
- Household does not usually have a Sunday joint.

It can obviously be argued that eating meat or a cooked breakfast is an indicator of personal preference rather than reliable measures of deprivation.

However, in general terms, Townsend's study represents a classic and hugely detailed account of the extent of poverty in Britain at a particular moment in time. In his conclusions, Townsend also made a number of recommendations to policy makers seeking to deal with the causes of poverty. These included putting a stop to 'excessive' income and wealth, the need for universal access to education and the reorganisation of employment practices to include, for example, industrial democracy.

The underclass

Key learning

You will be able to:
- explain who the members of the underclass are
- describe the key ideas of Murray on the underclass including links to New Right theories
- explain the criticisms of Murray.

▲ When Charles Murray wrote about 'the emerging underclass in Britain' he described it as predominantly white working class

In the nineteenth century, Marx identified what he called the lumpenproletariat, including in this group 'misfits, vagrants and thieves'. The term 'underclass' came into popular use in the 1980s and described those individuals who were particularly deprived and were excluded from the relative prosperity of the wider society.

Links to the New Right

In 1984, the American political scientist Charles Murray published *Losing Ground,* a controversial history of American welfare programmes between 1950 and 1980. The book was widely discussed at the time and was believed to have an influence on the thinking of welfare reformers both in the USA and in Britain. It is clearly associated with the ideas of the New Right.

Murray began by stating that he was struck by two things. Firstly, that welfare programmes in the USA were not succeeding and, secondly, why when some people obviously needed help was that help so often ineffective? Murray suggested three 'premises' (principles) upon which to base welfare reform:

1 People respond to incentives and disincentives (rewards and punishment, or the 'carrot and the stick').
2 People are not inherently hard working or moral. In the absence of a good reason not to, people will avoid work and behave badly.
3 People must be held responsible for their actions if society is to function properly.

Murray argued that in the USA over the period 1950–80 various changes in welfare, education and the criminal justice system had changed the balance between rewards and sanctions. It was no longer the case that people needed to have a job, work hard in school, get married if they

KEY TERMS

Eugenics a belief in the possibility of improving the qualities of the human species by selection

Lumpenproletariat the lowest level of the working class in nineteenth-century society

New Right economic and political ideas closely associated with the governments of Margaret Thatcher in Britain and Ronald Reagan in the USA; key features included support for free market economics, a reduced welfare state and a weakening of social democracy and trade unions

Political science a branch of social science concerned with systems of government

Underclass a group of people at the very bottom of the social scale who are dependent on welfare benefits

KEY TEXT

Murray C., *Losing Ground,* New York, Basic Books, 1984.

were going to have a baby or obey the law if they wanted to avoid prison. Murray proposed three laws that governed national welfare programmes:

1 **The law of imperfect selection:** in other words, some people will always be excluded from impersonally managed national programmes even though they should have been included.

2 **The law of unintended rewards:** for example, by supporting people who abuse drugs or fail at school a welfare programme has the unintended consequence of 'rewarding' that behaviour (or at least removing the consequences for an individual of their own actions).

3 **The law of net harm:** Murray believed that in democratic societies most national programmes do 'net harm' when they attempt to deal with the most difficult problems (for example long-term unemployment or drug addiction) because they tend to support rather than end such behaviours.

Murray's suggested solution was radical: he proposed the complete abolition of national welfare programmes and their replacement with locally managed solutions.

When Murray visited Britain in the 1980s, he suggested that Britain was developing an underclass similar to that which already existed in the USA. He identified rising rates of illegitimacy, a rising crime rate and increasing numbers of young people who were unwilling to seek employment as signs of a developing 'underclass'.

Criticisms of Murray

Critics have identified a number of problems with Murray's analysis:

- Many of the so-called 'underclass' have very conventional attitudes. They want stable relationships and they want secure jobs.
- Lone parenthood is not a sign of a growing underclass. In Britain, lone parenthood tends to be short lived. Most mothers eventually marry. The largest group of lone parents claiming welfare payments in Britain has tended to be divorced mothers rather than 'socially irresponsible' unmarried mothers.
- Murray's statistics (upon which he based his arguments about American welfare programmes) are selective. For example, he excluded spending on the elderly, which in 1983 accounted for 86 per cent of national social welfare spending in the USA.
- Murray's solution of locally managed welfare systems assumes that they would be an improvement. In the nineteenth century, such locally managed systems in Britain were often indifferently managed and poorly funded.
- Viewed more sympathetically, the underclass can be seen as victims of social inequality rather than the cause of social problems. Murray's ideas have been associated with eugenics and racism.

Summary

- The term 'underclass' refers to the most disadvantaged individuals at the very bottom of society.
- In 1984, Charles Murray published *Losing Ground*, a controversial history of American welfare programmes. The book was believed to have an influence on the thinking of welfare reformers both in the USA and in Britain.

Globalisation and poverty

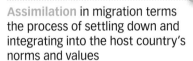

◀ McDonalds is an example of a global brand but often adapts its products to reflect local tastes and customs

Key learning

You will be able to:
- explain what globalisation is
- explain the impact of globalisation on the UK.

Globalisation

Globalisation describes the way in which nation states have become increasingly interdependent; the world economic order allows major corporations to operate across national borders, shifting jobs, investment and production from one country to another in order to maximise profits. The consequence of this has been a growth of 'outsourcing' whereby global firms shift production around the world to where labour costs are cheapest, resulting in job losses in developed countries like the UK. The economies of countries to which jobs and manufacturing have been transferred have undoubtedly benefited and it has helped alleviate poverty there. However, the resulting unemployment in the UK can be devastating to areas, particularly if they relied on a particular industry, for example Redcar in North East England with the closure of the steel works in 2015.

Within Sociology there is a continuing debate about globalisation in terms of who benefits from it and who loses out. Neo-liberals tend to have a positive view of globalisation seeing it as having the potential to create wealth, bringing new opportunities and raising living standards for some, if not all, with wider consumer choices and cheaper prices. On the other hand, conservative nationalists and Marxists tend to have a negative view, especially with regard to job security and the power of transnational corporations (TNCs) to put their profit motive before the interests of people and environmental policies.

Critics of globalisation

Globalisation has a direct impact on the lives of ordinary working people. In both the public and private sectors, a 'job for life' is increasingly rare and many workers today suffer with poor job security, low pay and few work benefits as businesses drive down costs in an attempt to remain globally competitive. Employment in manufacturing industries in developed economies has declined (deindustrialisation) and those workers previously employed in manufacturing have often been unable to find replacement jobs that are as secure and well paid. Even though in 2019 the UK achieved a new record of 32.5 million people in paid employment, a lot of the growth in jobs has been of a temporary and part-time nature, frequently

KEY TERMS 🔑

Assimilation in migration terms the process of settling down and integrating into the host country's norms and values

Asylum seekers people who have left their home country as political refugees in order to seek asylum in another

Deindustrialisation social and economic change resulting from the loss of manufacturing industry

Emigrant a person who leaves one country to live in another

Environmental policies governmental laws, regulations and policies concerning environmental issues

Immigrant a person who enters a country from another

Neo-liberals those who favour capitalism and the free market to allocate resources

Outsourcing practice of firms to relocate manufacturing in countries with cheap labour

Private sector part of the economy that is neither owned nor controlled by the government and that exists to create profits for shareholders

Public sector part of the economy that is owned or controlled by government

Secondary labour market sector of the labour market characterised by low-paid, low-status and insecure employment

Extension

Read *The Road to Wigan Pier* by George Orwell.

Check your knowledge

1 What is the link between globalisation and poverty?
2 Why might the recent growth in employment in the UK not necessarily be a cause for celebration? (Check your answer against the information provided.)
3 Why are migrant workers particularly prone to poverty?

Activities

1 Write a paragraph to explain what sociologists mean by 'deindustrialisation'.
2 Complete some research into the positive and negative impacts of globalisation on the UK economy. Look for some examples of companies that import goods manufactured outside the UK. What can you discover about working conditions in the countries that produce these goods? Then hold a class debate on the question: Who benefits from globalisation?

Summary

- Globalisation describes the way in which nation states have become increasingly interdependent.
- Globalisation allows major corporations to operate across national borders, shifting jobs, investment and production from one country to another in order to maximise profits.
- Globalisation facilitates the movement of migrant workers who some see as undercutting prevailing wage rates.

on a zero-hours contract. Global forces have been a driving factor behind a shift in employment to the secondary labour market. This is characterised by low wages, low status, low skills and insecure employment with little or no prospect of promotion. Therefore, employment figures can disguise the nature and type of work as well as the insecurity and type of contracts people are employed on.

Globalisation has also encouraged the movement of people, especially economic migrant workers. An example is the emigrant 'ten pound poms' whose passage from the UK to Australia was subsidised by the Australian government at just £10 per family between 1945 and 1972 because Australia needed more workers. Attracted by the sunshine and lifestyle, many found assimilation difficult and returned home. Many immigrant workers have come to the UK. This has benefited the economy by filling skills shortages. For example, the NHS could not function without its migrant workers. However, some organisations like the TUC (2017) have accused 'bad bosses' of using migrant workers to undercut wage levels, causing the income of all workers to be suppressed. Others, like Felicity Lawrence (2013) have highlighted how migrant workers can be exploited and impoverished, such as working as casualised agency workers employed by 'gangmasters' in agriculture, service industries like car cleaning or the sex trade. They are often paid hourly rates below the legal minimum wage and can be subjected to illegal deductions from their pay.

Globalisation and the UK

In 2011, the Joseph Rowntree Trust published research into the impact of globalisation on the UK. The report examined a number of case studies:

- In 'Heathrow Village', located near the major West London international airport, researchers investigated an industrial dispute at airline caterer Gate Gourmet. One respondent is quoted in the report as saying: 'They are kicking people out so they can bring in cheap labour ... they want no sick pay, they don't want organised persons [trade union members], they don't want anybody going sick, they don't want to raise pay; they want their good option which is agency, minimum wage.'
- In north-east Lincolnshire, researchers investigated the causes of unofficial strikes in the engineering construction industry at the Lindsey Oil Refinery. They found that employers were using Italian workers employed through a subcontractor at lower rates than UK workers.
- In Newhaven, Sussex, Parker Pen closed its factory with the loss of 180 jobs. The work that had previously been done in Newhaven was reported to be moving to Nantes, in France.

The report's conclusions:

- The costs and benefits of globalisation are unevenly distributed among the UK population.
- People on low incomes were particularly anxious about future job security. The report noted the shift in employment practices, including the increased use of contract and agency work and the use of migrant labour.
- Price increases in food and fuel caused by changes in the global economy particularly affect people on low incomes.

Negative attitudes towards migrants can also include asylum seekers who come to the UK to seek refuge.

The welfare state

At the end of the nineteenth century, the British government came under increasing pressure to take more responsibility for the welfare of its citizens. This pressure came from a variety of sources:

- Organised labour, the trade union movement and the voting power of working-class men. (The right to vote was not extended to women until the early years of the twentieth century.)
- Concerns about the general fitness of the population in comparison to other European nations (particularly Germany). At the end of the nineteenth century, many young men were rejected by the British Army due to their poor physical health.
- Research evidence documenting the extent of poverty. The work of Charles Booth in London and Seebohm Rowntree in York revealed that approximately one-third of the population lived in poverty.

Early reforms were introduced in the early years of the twentieth century by Liberal governments. They were not particularly generous and provided only basic health insurance, unemployment insurance and a small pension (the system essentially provided for the needs of working men, not their families). This limited system was severely tested by the worldwide economic depression of the 1930s. When Britain entered the Second World War (1939–45), there was a clear understanding that promises made to a previous generation who had fought in the First World War ('a home fit for heroes') had not been kept. The 1942 Beveridge Report provided the basis for the modern welfare state. William Beveridge (1879–1963) wanted to abolish what he called the 'five evils' of Want, Disease, Ignorance, Squalor and Idleness (in effect, poverty, poor health, lack of education, slum housing and unemployment). The intention was to provide support for citizens 'from the cradle to the grave' with a system of universal benefits based on need rather than the ability to pay.

The post-war Labour government established the modern welfare state, introducing slum clearance and public housing programmes, the National Health Service (NHS), a reformed education system and economic programmes designed to create full employment, together with more generous support for those who could not find work. For much of the 1950s and 1960s, a consensus existed between Britain's major political parties that the welfare state was a positive benefit to society. Economic growth and virtual full employment supported that point of view. However, in 1979, the increasing cost of welfare brought this consensus to an end with the election of a Conservative government led by Margaret Thatcher. There had been previous reforms limiting the availability of some services, but during the 1980s the underlying principle of a comprehensive welfare system open to all according to their needs was brought into question.

New Right perspectives on welfare

From a right-wing perspective, state welfare provision interferes with the individual's right to choose. The funding of the welfare state depends on taxes paid by all and not just by those who actually

KEY TERMS

Beveridge Report a report on future welfare provision to the wartime coalition government

Centre-left (social democrats) the political beliefs generally associated with the British Liberal Party and past Labour governments

Right-wing the political beliefs of the majority of the British Conservative Party and other right of centre politicians

Welfare state government systems for supporting the health and general well-being of the population. In Britain, this term is often used to describe post-1945 welfare reforms including the introduction of the National Health Service in 1948

THE DAWN OF HOPE.

Mr. LLOYD GEORGE'S National Health Insurance Bill provides for the insurance of the Worker in case of Sickness.

Support the Liberal Government
in their policy of
SOCIAL REFORM.

▲ The 1911 Liberal government introduced the concept of National Insurance but it only applied to (typically male) workers, not their families

use the system. Government spending and, therefore, taxation keeps rising in an attempt to meet increasing demand. Government planners make decisions that are inflexible and based on what they think people need rather than what they actually want. (Market-led solutions, on the other hand, deliver only what people are prepared to pay for.) High taxation makes the economy inefficient and drives out alternative welfare provision by increasing costs. Finally, the welfare state creates a situation where people become dependent on welfare rather than taking responsibility for their own lives. (See the ideas of Charles Murray on page 239.)

Centre-left perspectives on welfare

From a centre-left (social democratic) perspective, market forces are not capable of making the economy work for the benefit of all. Unemployment and poverty are not caused by the welfare state but by a capitalist economy that, without government regulation, would work only for the benefit of the few and not the many. If the wealth created by capitalism is not redistributed through a fair taxation system, some members of society will always be left in poverty, for example those with long-term health problems and the elderly. Welfare provision increases social cohesion. Without the provision of adequate social security and health care, ordinary working people will no longer feel invested in society; they may look for radical alternative solutions to their problems, creating conflict and instability.

Marxist and feminist perspectives on welfare

From a Marxist perspective, the welfare state is seen as a mechanism that capitalism uses to preserve itself, a means of controlling working people and preventing revolution. In other words, the welfare state promotes a sense of false consciousness as the proletariat feels grateful for the minimum acceptable provision for their health and well-being provided by a 'benevolent' state. Marxists also accuse companies from profiting financially from the existence of the welfare state. For example, the organisation Global Justice Now (2017) highlighted how the prostate drug Abiraterone's development was funded by the UK taxpayer, but is subsequently being sold by a pharmaceutical company to the NHS for £98 per patient per day when a generic alternative is available for £4. Feminists (although generally more positive about welfare programmes that benefit women) emphasise that government welfare policies tend to support conventional family structures and, by doing so, reinforce patriarchy and female dependency on men.

Activities

1 Research how health care was provided in Britain before the introduction of the NHS. Prepare a report on your findings.

2 Is the welfare state a positive benefit to our society? Gather evidence for or against and hold a class debate.

Extension

Research how health care is provided in the USA. Write a paragraph comparing health care provision in the USA and Britain.

Check your knowledge

1 From memory, list the reasons why the British government came under pressure to introduce welfare reforms at the end of the nineteenth century. (Check your answer against the list provided.)

2 List the five evils identified by the 1942 Beveridge Report. (Check your answer against the information provided.)

3 What was the consensus view of the welfare state during the 1950s and 1960s?

Summary

- Early welfare reforms were introduced at the start of the twentieth century. They were not particularly generous and provided only basic health insurance, unemployment insurance and a small pension.
- The 1942 Beveridge Report provided the basis for the modern welfare state.

Weber on power

Weber's definition of power

Weber has a particularly straightforward view of power: you either have it or you don't. For example, in an institutional setting like the armed forces, power reflects a hierarchical, top-down characteristic. If someone in a higher rank gives commands, those below must obey. A similar power relationship can be recognised between parents and children, teachers and pupils or employers and employees. However, obedience is not always guaranteed; only where authority is respected is the compliance of others forthcoming.

Formal and informal sources of power

Weber saw formal sources of power as conforming to the hierarchical, top-down structure within organisations where a position is under the control and supervision of a higher one. In a formal hierarchy, the official roles and positions of all members of the system are clearly defined and demarcated from each other.

Weber also saw informal sources of power in everyday interactions between people, expressed through norms and values as well as verbal or non-verbal communication. These interactions are shaped by the social positions of the people involved and power is reflected through the dominance and subordination of their different status position.

Types of authority

Weber believed that it was possible to distinguish three types of authority:

1 rational authority
2 traditional authority
3 charismatic authority

He drew a distinction between these 'legitimate' forms of authority and compulsion (being forced to obey orders), but he believed that only enslaved people obeyed authority on an 'absolutely involuntary' basis.

Rational (legal) authority

This formal type of rule-based authority has been compared to the behaviour found in the military. Officers' authority rests on the power to give orders that should be obeyed without question in recognition both of their status and a rational acknowledgement of their ability to lead. The issuing of military orders and obedience to those orders follows a clearly established code of rules and regulations. Failure to obey a legitimate order can result in the swift application of sanctions; in wartime, soldiers have even been shot by their own side for refusing to obey orders (a set of circumstances that reveals at least an element of compulsion in this model).

Traditional authority

This type of authority based on custom and tradition can be explained by looking at the traditional role of the monarchy and the aristocracy in British society. Monarchy is a hereditary system with nobility based on inheritance. While the power of the aristocracy in Britain is more

KEY TERMS

Bureaucracy when the administration of rules and procedures dominates the practice of organisations

Charismatic authority a type of authority based on the unusual personal gifts of a particular leader

Hereditary peer an inherited aristocratic title, e.g. duke or duchess

Legislation refers to the various laws that govern behaviour in society

Prime minister the head of the British government

Rational authority rules and procedures that are generally believed to be fair and impartial

Traditional authority a form of power based on established customs and inherited status

limited than it was, it still remains a feature of our political system. For example, our 'constitutional monarchy' still has the ability to influence decisions made by elected politicians and to hold them to account. The prime minister is required to regularly 'brief' the monarch; some of the prime minister's power to make certain decisions comes directly from the monarch and legislation is still approved by royal authority.

▲ Hitler is often described as an example of a 'charismatic leader'

Charismatic authority

Weber saw charisma as 'a certain quality of an individual personality by virtue of which he is set apart from ordinary men and treated as endowed with supernatural, superhuman, or at least specifically exceptional powers or qualities'. Examples of such men might include Jesus Christ or Adolf Hitler, both of whom for very different reasons and in very different circumstances were capable of inspiring many of their followers to place complete faith in them. The authority of charismatic leaders is often informal and rests, not on tradition nor a rational (legal) basis, but on their 'exceptional' personal qualities.

Weber believed that the modern state was organised on bureaucratic lines. In his view, its structures were based on rules and regulations that were designed to make sure that the most able individuals were appointed to positions of power and that, once in power, they would make decisions that were in the best interests of the majority. In reality, Weber's models are 'ideal' types of authority. In the real world, politicians and the leaders of large organisations are unlikely to conform precisely to any of his models.

Summary

- Weber recognised that power relations could be identified in the formal hierarchical setting of an organisation as well as the informal interaction between two people.
- Weber believed that it was possible to distinguish three 'legitimate' types of authority: rational, traditional and charismatic.
- Weber's models are 'ideal' types of authority. In the real world, politicians and the leaders of large organisations are unlikely to conform precisely to any of his models.

Activities

1 Can your school or college be described as a bureaucratic organisation? Write a paragraph to explain your conclusions.

2 Read about Steven Lukes' 'three faces of power' on page 247. Can you see any connections between Lukes and Weber or are their ideas completely different? Write a paragraph to explain your conclusions.

Extension

Research some additional examples of Weber's three types of authority from both recent history and contemporary society. Compare notes with other members of your teaching group and see if you agree or disagree with their choices.

Check your knowledge

1 What did Weber mean when he used the terms 'formal' and 'informal' sources of power?

2 What did Weber mean when he used the term 'rational authority'?

3 What did Weber mean when he used the term 'traditional authority'?

4 What did Weber mean when he used the term 'charismatic authority'?

Political power

The idea of political power is on one level very simple: some groups in society have the power to make decisions while others (the majority) have to live with those decisions. However, this simplistic view hides a much more complicated reality, particularly when we consider the nature of decision making in democratic societies and the 'power' of the majority to overturn the established order by voting for radical alternative solutions. The sociologist Steven Lukes (1941–) suggested that power has three dimensions – he described these as the 'faces of power':

1 Who makes the decisions?
2 Who controls the agenda (who decides what can be discussed)?
3 Who has the ability to manipulate the wishes of others?

The sociologist Talcott Parsons (1902–79) argued that political power should not be seen as fixed or constant but variable. For example, in times of war, political decision makers can exercise enormous power over the lives of individual citizens. However, if things go badly, the central political authority of the wartime state can swiftly collapse into chaos.

The idea of the state

All modern societies are nation states, which means that their system of government claims control over a specific geographical area. They have some form of parliament and civil service, a formal code of law and they possess military forces to control and protect their borders. Nation states use nationalistic symbols that create a sense of belonging to a particular community, for example a national flag and anthem. Modern nation states emerged with the growth of capitalism and the decline of feudal systems of government. Their populations are regarded as citizens with common rights and duties rather than subjects of monarchical authority, although this distinction is not always obvious in societies like our own that retain the institution of a monarchy.

Democracy

The idea of democracy has its roots in Ancient Greece and means 'rule by the people'. In Ancient Greece, citizenship was confined to free male citizens of city states, while most of the actual work was done by slaves, and women had no say in the matter.

Modern democracy is based on universal suffrage, where everyone over a certain age has the right to vote in constituencies for a variety of political candidates and parties. The electoral system in Britain is described as a 'first past the post' method of voting where the candidate with the most votes wins and is elected as a member of parliament. Normally the leader of the largest political party becomes the prime minister and is ultimately responsible for the policy and decisions of the government. On the surface, the British system would appear to be very democratic; each constituency votes for the candidate it wants to represent its views in parliament. In reality, things are more complicated as this system tends to favour the

KEY TERMS

Class alignment when people vote out of loyalty for a particular political party

Class dealignment when individuals become less loyal in terms of their support for a particular political party

Constituency a geographical area where voters elect a representative to a legislative body

Democracy a political system that allows individual citizens to elect their representatives to parliament, used more generally to describe the right of citizens to participate in political debate

Dictatorship a political system where power is concentrated in the hands of a single individual or small group

Fascism an extreme right-wing nationalistic ideology centred on dictatorial power

First past the post voting system in which the candidate who receives the most votes wins

Member of parliament person elected to represent the interests and concerns of their constituents

Nation state an independent geographically located state, whose citizens recognise a common nationalistic identity

Oligarchy a small group of people having control of a country

Proportional representation a term that describes various systems that allocate seats in parliament based on a proportion of the votes cast

Referendum a national vote on a single issue

dominant parties (Conservative and Labour). Smaller parties favour an alternative voting system of proportional representation, such as occurs in Germany, but opponents criticise this as the outcome is usually a coalition government where several parties hold power.

How people voted in the UK used to be seen as expressing class alignment. The assumption was that social class was the main influence on voting behaviour: the working class tended to vote Labour and the middle class tended to vote Conservative. This behaviour was not entirely uniform, as Conservative governments could not have been elected without some working-class support and many supporters of the Labour Party (including the majority of its MPs) came from the middle class. The shifting patterns of voting that have been observed since the 1970s are described as class dealignment and reflect changes in the wider society, such as the decline of traditional industries and the increase in home ownership.

The notion of voting according to people's choice results in a pluralistic system, supposedly reflecting what functionalists would describe as the will of the people. However, Marxists argue democracy under capitalism is largely a myth since those individuals and organisations with the most economic power exert most influence through their ability to lobby politicians to legislate in ways that benefit them rather than the interests of ordinary working people, who have little or no impact on government decisions.

Dictatorship

In many countries in the world democracy is replaced by rule by dictatorship. This is an authoritarian form of government where voting is either denied or takes the form of simply endorsing the ruling leader or oligarchy. Under dictatorships, there is usually no, or only very limited, political pluralism. Examples of dictatorships in the past include Mussolini, Franco and Hitler who introduced the political system of fascism into Italy, Spain and Germany respectively in early twentieth-century Europe. Fascism is a right-wing nationalistic ideology centred on dictatorial power that ruthlessly suppressed opposition and persecuted groups that were scapegoated for society's problems, such as Jews. However, dictatorships can reflect left-wing as well as right-wing ideologies and currently exist in many countries globally.

Summary

- The idea of political power is, on one level, very simple: some groups in society have the power to make decisions. However, this hides a much more complicated reality.
- All modern societies are nation states.
- Democracy has its roots in Ancient Greece.
- A political party is an organisation whose purpose is to achieve power by election to government. Britain's electoral system is based on geographical areas.
- People tend to vote for the party that they believe will best look after their interests rather than out of party loyalty.

Power relationships

In sociology, the idea of **power relationships** refers to how one group is able to control or influence the behaviour of another. The Equality Act 2010 recognises nine protected characteristics which it is now illegal to discriminate against, empowering these previously oppressed groups. The following different factors all involve power relationships:

- Social class: Marx believed that the structure of society was determined by the way in which its economy was organised. In capitalist societies, those who own and control the means of production (the capitalist class) use their economic power to exploit the labour of their workers.
- Gender and sexuality: feminists believe that society is dominated by men (patriarchy). Despite the progress that has been made towards gender equality, women still tend to occupy fewer positions of power in society than men, they continue to take the main responsibility for caring and they provide unpaid domestic labour that supports the capitalist economic system. Members of the LGBTQ community face discrimination and hostility from some members of society with the consequence that individuals can be reluctant to reveal their sexual orientation, fearing damage to their careers or reputation. Transgender is now a protected characteristic recognised and protected against discrimination by the Equality Act.
- Ethnicity: members of minority ethnic groups continue to experience prejudice and discrimination from some members of society and are less likely to occupy positions of power. Black people were nine and a half times as likely to be stopped and searched by police as white people in 2017–18 ('Stop and search', www.gov.uk), while only one out of every 20 British judges came from a BAME (Black and minority ethnic) background.
- Age: children and young people are vulnerable to exploitation and abuse by adults. Workers at both extremes of the age range remain vulnerable to exploitation by employers who seek to maximise profits and remain 'competitive' in the market economy. Young adults find that they are unable to obtain secure long-term work and are forced to accept low-paid short-term contracts. Older workers (who can cost employers more in wages and associated benefits) experience age-related discrimination, compulsory redundancy and early retirement.
- Disability: individuals with physical disabilities or chronic health problems can experience prejudice and discrimination, limiting their opportunities to access services or find employment.
- Religion and belief: members of some minority religious communities can experience prejudice and discrimination (often but not always linked to their ethnicity). Examples include members of the Muslim community (Islamophobia), the Jewish community (anti-Semitism) and the experience of Catholics in Northern Ireland.

Key learning

You will be able to:
- identify, describe and explain different factors affecting power relationships
- describe, compare and contrast a variety of sociological perspectives on power relationships (functionalist and Marxist).

KEY TERMS

Gatekeepers (mass media) owners and editors who control the content of the media

Interest (or pressure) groups formally organised groups created to represent the interests of a section of society

Power relationships the ability of one group in society to control or influence another

Functionalist and Marxist perspectives on power and authority

Functionalists see nothing wrong with an unequal distribution of power, since they believe in a meritocracy whereby the most talented people rise up to occupy the roles of leadership. Government power helps maintain order and is representative, viewed as operating in the interests of the people. The most functional government is one democratically elected and reflective of the people's consensus norms and values. Politics is seen as benevolent, representing the will of the masses, resisting rapid social change and regulating any conflict in society.

Marxists see power as located within the upper class (bourgeoisie) and derived from their ownership of the means of production. Through this economic power comes political power through their control over the state. By owning these key assets and the propaganda machine of the mass media the upper class are gatekeepers, in a position to shape ideology (or ideas) in society in a way that justifies and supports their powerful position. Ironically, they even get the working class (proletariat) to support them by developing false class consciousness.

The British Marxist sociologist Ralph Miliband (1924–94) believed that the British state was run not by a single capitalist class but by a number of elite groups. Miliband believed that these elite groups had a shared interest in maintaining the existing social order, defending private property and preserving the capitalist economic system. The American sociologist C. Wright Mills believed that society was run by a series of elites in the form of federal (national) government, major corporations and the military, comprising the power elite of closely connected individuals who came from a similar educational and social background.

Interest groups

Interest groups seek to influence government policy in the best interests of the people they represent (a pluralist view of how democracy works). Generally, they focus on a limited range of issues, for example the interests of a particular industry. Sociologists distinguish between protectional and promotional interest (or pressure) groups. As the name suggests, protectional groups seek to look after the interests of their membership, for example trade unions. Promotional groups have a common cause, for example local groups campaigning against road building or airport expansion. Some sociologists suggest that a more important distinction can be found between those groups that can be described as insider and those that can be considered outsider. Insider groups are usually treated respectfully by government and enjoy relatively easy access to important decision makers, for example groups representing major employers such as the Confederation of British Industry (CBI), while outsider groups are less likely to gain access to key decision makers, for example groups campaigning against government policies.

Patriarchy

Feminist perspectives on power relationships

Feminism developed as a response to the marginalised status of women and the lack of recognition of the importance of the roles undertaken by women. It was felt necessary to have a voice for women to check male domination expressed through the patriarchy that ran through society and all its institutions including the family, education, the world of work, the media and public life such as politics.

Liberal feminism views gender inequality in power relationships as stemming primarily from the unequal structures that reflect male interests and stem from the strength of socialisation and 'sex-role conditioning'. Their solution to gender power inequality is through legislation and educating men.

Marxist feminists see patriarchal power relationships created by capitalism. It serves the dual role of firstly providing cheap female workers while also ensuring household chores are done cheaply. Marxist feminists argue that the solution to gender power inequality is the abolition of capitalism, which would remove both economic exploitation in the workplace and patriarchy in the home.

Radical feminists see the source power relations between men and women as particularly concentrated within the family. They argue that gender power equality can only be achieved by actively challenging and eradicating the prevailing systems of patriarchy.

Walby on patriarchy

The feminist sociologist Sylvia Walby (1953–) defined patriarchy as 'a system of social structures and practices in which men dominate, oppress and exploit women' (*Theorizing Patriarchy*, 1990). She described six patriarchal 'structures' in society:

1 The household: while women had the freedom to dissolve marriages and work outside the home, 'liberation' from marriage (divorce and/or lone parenthood) could mean for many women a move into poverty.
2 Paid work: inequality between men and women in terms of pay, conditions and access to 'top' jobs had declined. However, women continued to be 'segregated' into low-paying occupations and part-time work.
3 The state: women's position at the head of lone parent families remained 'economically perilous', with an inadequate welfare system.
4 Male violence: while violence towards women was officially condemned, the state intervened infrequently and women who sought help from male violence were often humiliated in the process.
5 Sexuality: heterosexual women felt under pressure to marry or cohabit with a man and sexual double standards were 'alive and well'.
6 Cultural institutions: the media continued to show women as either sexually glamorous or wives and mothers, while men were shown in positions of power.

Key learning

You will be able to:

● describe, compare and contrast a variety of sociological perspectives on power relationships (feminist)
● describe the key ideas of Walby on patriarchy.

KEY TERMS

Cultural institutions organisations that promote or preserve a particular culture, e.g. the media and the education system

FTSE the *Financial Times* Stock Exchange Index (top 100, top 250 companies, and so on)

Home secretary senior government minister in charge of the Home Office

Stock exchange a market in company shares (stocks)

KEY TEXT

Walby S., *Theorizing Patriarchy*, Oxford, Blackwell, 1990.

Walby believed that while feminists had achieved considerable success in their fight for equality with men, much remained to be done. (Out of the examples given above, how many could still be said to remain valid and how far are women's careers limited if they choose to have children?) In her view, the nature of patriarchy had changed, creating 'new traps' for women and finding new ways to exploit them. In the nineteenth century, Walby described a 'private' form of patriarchy based on the household, with men directly controlling their wives and daughters. In the modern world, she saw a form of 'public' patriarchy based on structures that were outside the home: 'Women are no longer restricted to the domestic hearth, but have the whole society in which to roam and be exploited.'

Women and political power

Historically, women have held few powerful political positions in British society, but the situation is slowly improving. Britain has now had two female prime ministers and a number of the powerful offices of state, for example home secretary and other senior ministerial positions, have been held by women. In the 2017 general election, 208 women were elected as MPs – 32 per cent of the total (the highest level ever recorded). In 2016, women held 35 per cent of the seats in the Scottish parliament, 42 per cent of the seats in the Welsh National Assembly and 28 per cent of the seats in the Northern Irish Assembly. Forty-one per cent of British Members of the European Parliament were women. In England, 32 per cent of local authority councillors were women. In Scotland, 24 per cent of councillors were women. Women held 26 per cent of council seats in Wales. In Northern Ireland 25 per cent of councillors were women.

◄ Women, although still a minority, account for over a third of MPs, such as Caroline Lucas of the Green Party

Women who choose to enter politics have to overcome a number of obstacles:

- Women with children have to balance the demands of family life with the often antisocial hours worked by politicians.
- Male-dominated political institutions traditionally value 'masculine' qualities of assertiveness and aggression, while undervaluing 'feminine' qualities such as consensus building and a willingness to seek compromise solutions.
- The political agenda has often underplayed the importance of women's issues, such as sexual harassment and gender-based discrimination over pay and conditions.
- Female politicians have experienced abusive and threatening behaviour from members of the public based on their gender, appearance or physical characteristics.

Women and business power

In business, women remain under-represented in senior positions. In 2018, only 8 per cent of executive directors of major British companies (FTSE 100) were women, although this has increased from 5.5 per cent in 2011. In medium-sized companies (FTSE 250), there were just 30 women in full-time executive roles in 2018 (down from 38 in 2017), amounting to just 6.4 per cent of the total. They include six female chief executives and 19 female chief financial officers. In 2011, the government published a report 'Women on Boards', which made a series of (voluntary) recommendations. These included:

- FTSE 100 companies should aim for a minimum of 25 per cent female executive directors.
- Companies quoted on the stock exchange should disclose the number of their female executive directors each year.
- Companies should have a policy on establishing greater gender diversity in their boardroom.
- Company appointment processes (including the advertising of posts) should encourage greater gender diversity.

Activities

1 Write a paragraph to explain the meaning of patriarchy from a feminist perspective.
2 Do some research and hold a class debate to discuss why women in our society still tend to earn less than men.

Summary

- Types of feminists differ in their explanation and solutions to unequal power relationships.
- The sociologist Sylvia Walby defines patriarchy as 'a system of social structures and practices in which men dominate, oppress and exploit women'.
- Women face marked inequalities in political and business power.

Extension

1 Search the internet for the latest 'Woman's Hour' Power List (BBC Radio 4).
2 Research the abuse of female MPs. A useful starting point is www.independent.co.uk/ voices/mps-abuse-online-anna-soubry-female-politicians-rape-threats-research-jo-cox-a8726796.html.

Check your knowledge

1 Summarise different feminist positions on power relationships.
2 What did Walby mean when she used the term 'private patriarchy'?
3 From memory, list the six patriarchal structures in society identified by Walby. (Check your answer with the list provided.)
4 From memory, list the obstacles that women who enter politics have to overcome. (Check your answer with the list provided.)

Key learning

You will be able to:

- apply your knowledge and understanding of sociological research methods to social stratification.

Methods in context

This section is about how you use your knowledge and skills of research methods in appropriate ways.

Read the following item and answer the questions that follow.

Item A

Workers in Britain are working harder and have less say, but are less anxious about losing their job or having their job changed in some way, according to the findings from the latest Skills and Employment Survey.

A recent survey of workers supported by the ESRC and others sheds new light on some of the more important job quality dimensions and how they have changed. The Skills and Employment Survey 2017 (SES 2017) is a nationally representative sample survey of individuals in employment aged 20–65 years old in Britain. A total of 3,306 individuals took part. They were interviewed in their own homes for around one hour. The 2017 survey is the seventh in a series which began in 1986.

The latest results show that the quality of jobs in the UK is worsening in more respects than it is improving. It shows that workers are working harder and have less say, but are less anxious about losing their job or having their job changed in some way. Almost a half (46%) of workers in 2017 strongly agreed that their job requires them to work very hard compared to just a third (32%) of workers in 1992. School teachers in state schools top the list. A remarkable 92% of teachers strongly agreed that their job requires them to work very hard, up from 82% in 2012.

Alan Felstead and Francis Green, 'More work, less say', Economic and Social Research Council, 2019

TIP ✓

Although you might know the strengths and weaknesses of using different research methods to collect data, you must apply what you know to the specific context on stratification.

1 From Item A, what research method was used by the Skills and Employment Survey 2017?

2 Examine one strength and one limitation of using this research method.

> *You need to identify one strength and one limitation of using the research method for this specific piece of research. Make sure you explain why this is a strength and limitation for this specific piece of research.*

3 Identify and explain one factor about how workers feel negatively about their job.

> *Refer to the item and identify one factor that has been expressed about changing attitudes to their work. Once you have identified one factor, make sure you explain why this makes them feel negatively.*

4 Identify and explain one practical issue of this research and explain how you would deal with this issue.

> *Do not just identify a practical issue. Make sure you explain why this is a practical issue for this specific research.*

5 Explain how you would investigate the attitudes to work by using a different research method to the one used by the Skills and Employment Survey 2017.

> *This question is giving you the opportunity to show your knowledge of using different research methods. Make sure you explain how the research method could be used for this specific study. How effective is this method for investigating attitudes to work?*

6 Explain how you would investigate job satisfaction by using a secondary research method.

> *This question is giving you the opportunity to show your knowledge of secondary research methods. Make sure you explain how the research method could be used for this specific study. How effective is this method for investigating job satisfaction?*

TIP

When answering these questions, it is important to focus your answer on the specific item given. Use the item in your answers and use concepts specific to the method.

Summary

- All research methods used in sociological research have strengths and weaknesses.
- Practical considerations need to be taken into account when conducting research.

Social stratification

Practice questions

Question 1 (multiple choice)

Which term was used by Marx to describe the lowest levels of the working class in the nineteenth century? [1 mark]

a) Proletariat
b) Bourgeoisie
c) Underclass
d) Lumpenproletariat

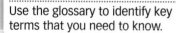

Answer and commentary

Option D (only one option is correct) – Marx used the term 'lumpenproletariat' to describe the lowest levels of the working class in the nineteenth century.

TIP ✓
Use the glossary to identify key terms that you need to know.

Question 2 (descriptive answer)

Describe one social area in which one group is able to control or influence the behaviour of another through power relationships. [3 marks]

Answer and commentary

The question requires you to describe one group that is able to control or influence the behaviour of another through power relationships. You need to develop an accurate and logical description of a relevant group that is clearly linked to the question. Remember to be concise and keep to the point.

You could write about:

- Social class, e.g. how Marx saw the bourgeoisie's ownership and control of the means of production enabled them to exploit the proletariat.
- Gender, e.g. how feminists see men can use patriarchy to oppress women in the home, workplace and public life.
- Sexuality, e.g. how members of the LGBTQ community can face prejudice and discrimination from members of society.
- Ethnicity, e.g. how some members of minority ethnic groups continue to experience prejudice and discrimination.
- Age, e.g. children and young people can be seen to be vulnerable to exploitation by adults or age discrimination in the workplace.
- Disability, e.g. individuals with physical or mental disabilities can experience prejudice and discrimination.
- Religion and belief, e.g. members of some religious communities can experience prejudice and discrimination.

Question 3 (short answer question linked to source material)

Item A

In 2015 Tamika Perrott undertook qualitative interviews with ten female firefighters in order to gain an insight into how they navigated their gender in a traditionally male-dominated workplace. She was exploring how, within the context of uniformed services, institutional practices account for a large proportion of the gendered barriers women face in historically masculinised workplaces. The aim of her research was to listen to women's everyday lived experiences in order to reveal significant insights into what employment as a fire fighter was like for them. Most of her interviews took approximately 20–30 minutes or longer to complete.

From Item A, examine one strength of the research method she chose. [2 marks]

Answer and commentary

It is important to identify a potential strength of the research method and to explain and justify why the use of this method enhanced the quality of her research.

You could write about:

- Interviews are an example of a qualitative research method which is associated with the collection of data that is high in validity. It should therefore be possible to gain an insight into the female firefighters' experiences and feelings.
- With interviews it is possible to gain a rapport with the respondent, thus encouraging a discussion which should encourage them to express how they really feel about their employment.

Question 4 (paragraph answer linked to the source material)

Identify and explain one practical factor that could be seen to impact on the research discussed in Item A. [4 marks]

Question 5 (essay question)

Discuss how far sociologists would agree that Britain is a meritocratic society. [12 marks]

Answer and commentary

Remember to think of your 'mini-essay' in three parts: an introductory paragraph in which you focus on the question and begin your argument, a second paragraph in which you develop your answer (consider one or more alternative sociological perspectives on the issue) and a final paragraph in which you reach a conclusion.

You could write about:

- The functionalist perspective on 'meritocracy'. Davis and Moore argued that people with the necessary talent, drive and ambition would be encouraged by higher rewards to compete for the most 'functionally important' positions in society with the most able rising to the top.
- The Marxist perspective on 'meritocracy'. Modern Marxist sociologists emphasise the inequalities in society and the way in which elite groups seek to retain and then pass on their wealth and privileges to their descendants.
- The feminist perspective on 'meritocracy'. Feminist sociologists argue that women experience disadvantages in a society which is still male dominated (patriarchal). They believe that laws designed to ensure gender equality have not removed the 'glass ceiling' limiting the careers of many women.
- In each case you will need to evaluate the extent to which a particular perspective represents a valid picture of contemporary British society as a 'meritocracy'. Try to reach a clear, logical, evidence-based conclusion and avoid contradictions in your argument.

Answer and commentary

It is important to identify a relevant factor that could be identified as applicable to the research discussed in the item.

You could write about:

- The interviews took 20–30 minutes or more each. Therefore, time to undertake all the interviews was a practical factor the researcher had to take into account. Given the insight the researcher wanted to gain about the female firefighters' work experiences, this method could be judged as an appropriate tool to investigate the complex area of gendered workplace relationships.
- Another practical factor might be gaining access to her sample. How easy was it for the researcher to gain access to the firefighters? Did she have to negotiate with a gatekeeper such as the fire brigade organisation or the person in charge of the fire station? Were female firefighters necessarily willing to talk openly about their experiences?
- Personal interest can be seen to impact as a practical issue. Did the researcher, perhaps as a feminist female, approach the study from a particular or personal perspective? It is important for researchers to be objective and retain an open mind that differentiates between evidence and opinion.
- A practical issue that underpins all research is the need to cover basic costs. In this case these would include the time to conduct the interviews, travel costs and the time to transcribe and collate her findings.

TIP
Take a few moments to develop an outline plan of your answer.

Glossary

Absolute poverty this exists when an individual cannot pay for the basic essentials of life, e.g. food, clothing and shelter

Achieved status social status gained by an individual as a result of educational qualifications and/or success in their career

Affluence having an abundance of money

Ageism the negative stereotyping and unfair treatment of individuals because of their age

Agencies of social control institutions that influence the process of social control, e.g. families, schools or the police

Alienation individuals who feel that they have become separated from the wider society are said to be alienated, e.g. they lack power and control over their lives

Anomie the breakdown of norms governing accepted social behaviour

Anthropology the scientific study of the origins and development of human society

Apartheid the institutionalised system of segregation between races that existed in South Africa from 1948 to 1994

Aristocracy an elite social group with inherited titles

Arranged marriage a matchmaking practice instigated through relatives or friends

Ascribed status social standing given to an individual on the basis of inheritance

Assimilation in migration terms the process of settling down and integrating into the host country's norms and values

Asylum seekers people who have left their home country as political refugees in order to seek asylum in another

Attrition rate the drop-out rate from a longitudinal study

Authority a form of power in which people willingly obey commands that they believe to be lawful

Average a measure of central tendency

Beanpole family a family whose living members come from many generations, but with few members in each generation

Bedroom culture the subcultures created by girls, which allow them to develop communication skills within their own home

Beveridge Report a report on future welfare provision to the wartime coalition government

Bias people's (often unconscious) values and preferences that shape their understanding and actions. Researchers' biases will affect how they conduct research and interpret their findings

Bourgeoisie the capitalist class who own the means of production

Bureaucracy when the administration of rules and procedures dominates the practice of organisations

Capitalism a system of economic organisation in which businesses are owned by private individuals who profit from the labour of the workers they employ

Case study a detailed examination of a single example providing qualitative in-depth data

Caste system a form of social stratification based on religion found in India

Census a government survey of the population of Britain conducted every ten years

Centre-left (social democrats) the political beliefs generally associated with the British Liberal Party and past Labour governments

Charismatic authority a type of authority based on the unusual personal gifts of a particular leader

Chattel slavery where enslaved people were property, bought, sold, traded or inherited

Chivalry factor/thesis the idea that a male-dominated police force and criminal justice system treats women offenders more leniently because of their gender

Class a type of social stratification based on economic factors

Class alignment when people vote out of loyalty for a particular political party

Class conflict the conflicting interests of socio-economic classes

Class dealignment when individuals become less loyal in terms of their support for a particular political party

Class identity this is the social class with which an individual identifies

Closed questions a questionnaire that only allows the respondent to choose from a predetermined set of answers

Closed society when social mobility is limited or absent altogether

Cluster sample a subject population grouped conveniently together in one place

Cohabitation partners who live together without getting married

Cohort an age-related group, e.g. research subjects born in the same year

Collective conscience the shared beliefs and values that bind communities together and regulate individual behaviour

Colonialism control and exploitation of another country

Commune a group of people living together and sharing possessions and responsibilities

Communism Karl Marx believed that a future ideal communist society would be one in which the community would own all property and there would be no social classes

Communist Manifesto a political pamphlet outlining the principles of communism

Comprehensive school a state secondary school that does not select pupils on the basis of ability

Compulsory state education in Britain, state education was first made compulsory in the late-nineteenth century (for children up to the age of ten); this was later extended to include children of secondary school age in the Education Act 1944

Confidentiality   the need for researchers not to publish the personal details of respondents (without their consent)

Conjugal relationships   the relationship between marital or cohabiting partners

Conjugal roles   the roles typically associated with male and female partners

Constituency   a geographical area where voters elect a representative to a legislative body

Consumerism   a desire to buy and use consumer products for their use and gratification

Content analysis   the analysis of documents or visual material, e.g. newspapers or television broadcasts

Control theory   the idea that people do not commit deviant acts because various factors control their impulse to break social norms

Controlled conditions   variables that can affect research data are recognised and taken into account

Correspondence principle   the idea that the education system is designed primarily to serve the needs of the capitalist economic system, e.g. by producing an obedient workforce, and mirrors/corresponds to the workplace

Crime   any form of behaviour that breaks the law

Crime rate   a measure of the level of criminal activity in society based on crimes recorded by the police

Cultural capital   the skills and values passed on to their children by middle-class parents, e.g. language skills and the motivation and support required to succeed in the education system

Cultural deprivation   the controversial idea that some groups, for example working-class children, lacked the cultural capital that helps achieve educational success

Cultural institutions   organisations that promote or preserve a particular culture, e.g. the media and the education system

Cultural reproduction   the process of obscuring the realities of social class inequality and exploitation of the working class in capitalism

Culture   customs, ideas and practices of a particular society or group

Culture of dependency the idea that social welfare systems encourage people to stay on benefits rather than support themselves through work

Culture of poverty   when poverty is seen as inevitable and becomes a way of life

Dark figure of crime   the unknown amount of criminal activity that is not reported to or recorded by the police

Data Protection Act   the law regarding the storage and use of personal information

Deindustrialisation   social and economic change resulting from the loss of manufacturing industry

Democracy   a political system that allows individual citizens to elect their representatives to parliament, used more generally to describe the right of citizens to participate in political debate

Demography   the study of population trends

De-schooling   the idea that schools should be abolished and replaced with some kind of informal education system

Deviance   any form of behaviour that does not conform to dominant norms, ranging from behaviours that are simply disapproved of to criminal actions

Deviancy amplification   the exaggeration of a particular social issue as a consequence of media coverage, e.g. antisocial behaviour by groups of young people

Deviant career   a process that develops over time as the individual progresses through various stages of deviant behaviour, accepting and adopting external social labels. For example, the young person who is labelled as a 'troublemaker' and who then goes on in later life to exhibit gradually more serious forms of criminal behaviour

Dictatorship   a political system where power is concentrated in the hands of a single individual or small group

Disablism   discrimination against disabled people

Discrimination   an action based on prejudice, e.g. racial discrimination

Dispersed extended family   where kin are geographically separated but still maintain frequent contact

Displacement   to shift blame to another

Division of labour   the separation of any form of work into various component parts, all of which are relatively simple. In industry, this allows employers to use cheaper unskilled or semi-skilled workers

Divorce   the formal (legal) ending of a marriage

Domestic division of labour   household tasks divided between different family members

Domestic violence   behaviour in any relationship that is used to gain or maintain power and control over an individual. This behaviour can be physical, sexual, emotional, financial or psychological

Double shift (dual burden) working   women who continue to perform the bulk of domestic labour are said to work a 'double shift' of paid employment followed by an unequal share of household work

Dual career families   a family in which both parents have careers

Dysfunctional family   a family which does not meet society's needs in socialising children and supporting adults. This may be a family in which conflict, neglect and even abuse are common experiences

Economic inequality   differences in income and wealth

Economics   the study of the production and consumption of goods and services

Edgework   behaviour at the edge of what is normally allowed or accepted; risky or radical behaviour, e.g. stealing and racing a car

Education   the process of giving and receiving knowledge, generally associated in contemporary society with schools and universities

Egalitarian   the principle of equality for all people

Elite   a minority group who have power and influence over the other members of society

Embourgeoisement the adoption of middle-class values and behaviours by prosperous members of the working class

Emigrant a person who leaves one country to live in another

Empirical facts knowledge gained through scientific observation

Empty nest family a stage in the life cycle of a family when children have reached adulthood and have left the parental home

Environmental policies governmental laws, regulations and policies concerning environmental issues

Equal pay and sex discrimination laws introduced in Britain in the 1970s to stop gender-based discrimination (now incorporated into the Equality Act 2010)

Establishment in sociology, the term is generally used to describe dominant elites (superior groups) who hold power and authority

Estate a type of social stratification based on the ownership of land and feudal duties

Ethical considerations the need for researchers to ensure that their work neither causes harm nor unnecessary offence to participants, e.g. anonymity, confidentiality and informed consent

Ethnic groups people within a particular society who share a distinct identity based on a common culture, traditions and history

Ethnicity a shared cultural identity, e.g. language and customs

Ethnocentric curriculum subjects taught within schools or universities that uncritically assume the superiority of certain customs and behaviours

Ethnocentrism judging other cultures relative to your own and where the other cultures will present as inferior

Ethnography the scientific study of different people and cultures (links to anthropology)

Eugenics a belief in the possibility of improving the qualities of the human species by selection

Evidence-based when findings are based on the data collected

Evolution the process by which living organisms have developed over time

Expressive role the family member who provides care and emotional support to other family members

Extended family parents, their children and other more distant relatives, e.g. grandparents, aunts and uncles

False consciousness the mistaken belief that capitalist society is basically fair and opportunities are open to all (see ruling class ideology)

Family a group of two or more people linked by birth, marriage, adoption or cohabitation based on a long-term relationship

Family diversity the many different types of family structure that exist in contemporary society

Fascism an extreme right-wing nationalistic ideology centred on dictatorial power

Feral child a child who has had no human contact and is in extreme cases raised by animals

Feudal system a form of social stratification based on the ownership of land

First past the post voting system in which the candidate who receives the most votes wins

Focus group a small group of people who are asked to consider a particular issue and discuss it in depth with an interviewer

Forces of production the materials, technology and knowledge required to produce the goods that society needs

Formal curriculum the timetabled subjects taught in school

Formal social control where our behaviour is controlled through organisations that exist to enforce order, e.g. the police, judiciary, prisons

FTSE the *Financial Times* Stock Exchange Index (top 100, top 250 companies, and so on)

Functional prerequisites the basic needs of society

Functionalism a sociological perspective that attempts to explain social structures by reference to the role that they perform for society as a whole

Gatekeepers (mass media) owners and editors who control the content of the media

Gender a culturally determined identity (masculine or feminine)

Genderquake fundamental change to society whereby young females are increasingly striving for a fulfilling career

Generic name in sociological research, a name used to conceal the real identity of a place or organisation, e.g. Cornerville

Genocide defined by the UN as 'acts committed with intent to destroy, in whole or in part, a national, ethnical, racial or religious group'

Gentry a group of landowners with social standing below the aristocracy

Glass ceiling (in relation to women in employment) an informal barrier that prevents women from achieving senior positions in their chosen career

Grounded theory a research method that allows theory to emerge from the data collected

Group closure establishing and maintaining boundaries between cultures

Group solidarity common interests that bind people together

Hereditary peer an inherited aristocratic title, e.g. duke or duchess

Hidden curriculum a set of values, attitudes and principles transmitted to pupils but not as part of the formal curriculum of timetabled subjects

Hierarchy the organisation of society into a rank order of importance

Holocaust the race murder (genocide) of the Jewish people and various other groups during the Second World War

Home schooling when parents take full responsibility for the education of their children rather than allowing them to attend school

Home secretary senior government minister in charge of the Home Office

Homophobia attitudes and behaviours (that can result in violence) based on negative stereotypes of homosexual people

Homosexuality sexual behaviour between members of the same sex

Hypothesis an idea that can be tested by research

Identical twins two identical babies of the same sex, born at the same time, from the same fertilised egg

Identity a sense of self (who you believe yourself to be)

Immigrant a person who enters a country from another

Immigration the movement of individuals or a group of people from one part of the world into another, e.g. people who leave their country of origin to live in another country

Industrial democracy involving employees in the management of an industry

Infanticide the intentional killing of infants

Informed consent respondents understand and agree to participate

Infrastructure the class structure that forms the basic foundation of society

Institutional racism organisational procedures, practices and attitudes that either intentionally or unintentionally discriminate against a minority ethnic group

Institutions important parts of the structure of society maintained by social norms

Instrumental role the family provider (usually associated with the traditional role of the adult male)

Instrumentalism describes the attitude of some working-class people towards their jobs and any form of collective action, e.g. work as simply a way of earning money and self-interest rather than traditional working-class collective values

Interactionism a theoretical perspective that focuses on small-scale everyday social interactions

Interest (or pressure) groups formally organised groups created to represent the interests of a section of society

Interpretivism an approach to research that aims to understand motives and meanings behind behaviour. It is particularly associated with collection of qualitative data

Interval data data presented on a scale, e.g. calendar years

Interview a research method where questions are asked using either a formal approach (a structured interview) or an informal approach (an unstructured interview)

Interviewer bias this occurs when interviewers influence the answers given by a respondent

Joint conjugal roles male and female partners share household tasks

Judiciary the system of courts that interprets and applies the law in a country

Key informant a knowledgeable participant in sociological research

Kibbutz a collective community in Israel that was traditionally based on agriculture

Kinship relationships of blood and marriage

Labelling a label as applied to an individual influences both their behaviour and the way that others respond to them

Left wing political beliefs that emphasise social equality, e.g. socialism

Legislation refers to the various laws that govern behaviour in society

LGBTQ lesbian, gay, bisexual, transgender and queer (or questioning)

Liberalism a political belief in systems of government in which the rights and freedoms of the individual are protected by laws and a constitution

Life chances the opportunities each individual has to improve their quality of life

Life histories qualitative research that provides an overall picture of an informant's or interviewee's life experiences

Life history research a type of qualitative research that uses life experiences to provide insights into the workings of society

Lifestyle the various ways in which social groups choose to use the resources that are available to them, reflecting the attitudes and priorities of the group

Literature review a critical review of previous work on the topic of your investigation

Local extended family where kin live in close proximity

Lone parent family a family with only a mother or father as a consequence of death, divorce or individual choice

Longitudinal (panel) study a research project that follows the same group of people over a long period of time, used to study trends over time and the impact of social change

Lumpenproletariat the lowest level of the working class in nineteenth-century society

Market capitalism an economic system that supports private business in a competitive market

Market situation Weber believed that socio-economic classes developed in market economies in which individuals compete for economic gain; those who achieve a similar share of available resources (e.g. access to education, ownership of housing and other forms of property) occupy a similar market situation

Marketisation of education refers to changes in the late 1980s that made the education system more business-like, based on competition and consumer choice

Marriage a cultural phenomenon that gives legal status to a union between two partners and any children they may produce

Marxism ideas based on an interpretation of the ideas of Karl Marx

Mass media any form of communication media that can reach a large audience, e.g. newspapers, television or various forms of social media

Master status a status which overrides all other features of a person's social standing; the characteristic that shapes how a person sees themselves and how others perceive them

Material deprivation refers to the inability of individuals or households to afford the goods and activities that are typical in a society at a given point in time

Mean   an arithmetical average

Means of production   the resources from which wealth is derived, such as land, factories, etc. Ownership of these defines the ruling class

Media amplification   media reporting that exaggerates the significance of an event

Median   a form of average associated with the middle value within a range of numbers

Member of parliament   person elected to represent the interests and concerns of their constituents

Meritocracy   a social system that is supposed to reward merit rather than inherited status

Minority ethnic group   a social group with a different ethnic identity from the majority population

Miscarriage of justice   when a failure occurs within the criminal justice system, especially one which results in the conviction of an innocent person

Mixed ability   in educational terms this refers to a group of students of all ability levels, taught together in the same class

Mixed methods   social research that combines a variety of methods, e.g. observation, questionnaires and interviews

Mode   the most frequently occurring value

Modern slavery   the harbouring of children, women or men through the use of force for the purpose of exploitation

Monarchy   a political system that has hereditary heads of state

Money management   the power relationship surrounding how finances are spent within the family

Monogamy   the practice of being married to one person at a time

Moral panic   heightened public concern created by media coverage of an event

Nation state   an independent geographically located state, whose citizens recognise a common nationalistic identity

National Curriculum   subjects that must be taught in all local-authority-maintained schools in England. Non-local-authority schools, such as academies and free schools, do not have to follow the national curriculum but do have to teach a 'broad and balanced curriculum', including English, mathematics, science and religious education

Nationalism   a strong belief in the importance of a particular nation state

Nature versus nurture   a debate about how far human behaviour is a result of life experiences (socialisation) as opposed to biology

Negotiation   the process by which an individual changes the reactions of others or shapes their own role

Neo-liberals and neo-conservatives   those who favour capitalism and the free market to allocate resources

Nepotism   the practice of favouring relatives or friends, especially by giving them jobs

New Right   economic and political ideas closely associated with the governments of Margaret Thatcher in Britain and Ronald Reagan in the USA; key features included support for free market economics, a reduced welfare state and a weakening of social democracy and trade unions

New social movements   an informally organised group (often very large and sometimes global in reach) who support a particular cause or promote certain interests, e.g. women's rights or environmentalism

New working class   home-centred members of the working class with instrumental attitudes (first described in the 1960s)

News value   the importance given to a particular event by newspaper editors or television producers

Nominal data   a simple count, e.g. the number of times a particular type of behaviour is observed

Non-participant observation   the researcher watches and observes without taking part in the activities of the group

Norms   informal rules that influence social behaviour

Nuclear family   a family group consisting of parents and their children

Nurture   to care for a child while it is growing up

Objective   judgements that are not influenced by personal prejudices

Objective approach   sociologists who attempt to study the social world without allowing their personal values to influence the outcome of their research

Observation   a research method involving either covert (hidden) or overt (open) observations of a social group

Observation schedule   a form used to record observations using predetermined categories

Observer effect   group members alter their behaviour because they are being observed

Official crime statistics   government statistics on crime based on official sources, e.g. police records

Official statistics   government statistics, e.g. the crime rate

Oligarchy   a small group of people having control of a country

Open questions   a questionnaire or unstructured interview that allows the respondent space to answer as they wish

Open society   when social mobility can occur within a society

Opinion poll   a sample survey of public opinion

Ordinal data   counting in categories arranged in rank order

Outsourcing   practice of firms to relocate manufacturing in countries with cheap labour

Participant observation   the researcher takes an active part in the activities of the group while observing it

Particularistic standards   subjective judgements based on individual characteristics – people are seen and judged as individuals

Patriarchal family   a male-dominated family group

Patriarchy   male domination of society and its institutions

Patrilineal   inheriting or determining descent through the male line

Peer group   a group of people of similar age and status

Personality test   a questionnaire that is supposed to reveal an individual's personality

Petty bourgeoisie   owners of small businesses

Pilot study   a small-scale trial to test a particular research method before using it in a research project

Plagiarism   pretending that the work of another is your own

Polarisation of social classes   increasing differences between the lives of different socio-economic classes

Police caution   a formal warning given by the police to anyone aged 10 years or over who has admitted that they are guilty of a minor crime

Political science   a branch of social science concerned with systems of government

Polyandry   the accepted practice in some societies of women having more than one husband at the same time (rare but found in the Himalayas)

Polygamy   the accepted practice in some societies of having more than one spouse at the same time

Polygyny   the accepted practice in some societies of men having more than one wife at the same time

Positivism   an approach to research that is based on the scientific method and particularly associated with collection of quantitative data

Postmodernism   theory that sees society as having distinctly different characteristics to the era of modernity which it replaced, with more diverse and less stable family structures and a blurring of family roles

Poverty line   a measure of minimum income required to meet the essential cost of living

Poverty trap   poor families in receipt of means tested welfare benefits become 'trapped' in poverty if their earnings marginally increase, resulting in the loss of benefits and, as a consequence, no improvement in their economic situation

Power   the capacity or ability to direct or influence the behaviour of others

Power relationships   the ability of one group in society to control or influence another

Pre-industrial tribal culture   a term used to describe cultures that existed before industrialisation or cultures isolated from the modern world, e.g. the Trobriand Islanders studied by anthropologists in the early twentieth century

Prejudice   to be hostile towards another individual or social group based on previously formed opinions, frequently refers to racial prejudice

Primary data   information gathered at first hand by a researcher

Primary socialisation   the process of social learning that takes place within the family during a child's early years

Prime minister   the head of the British government

Prison system   the deprivation of liberty is the ultimate punishment in British society; British prisons vary from open institutions for low-level offenders to high security institutions for offenders who are convicted of serious offences and are held to pose a risk to other members of society

Private school   a school run by a non-state organisation, where families have to pay for their children to attend

Private sector   part of the economy that is neither owned nor controlled by the government and that exists to create profits for shareholders

Probation system   Her Majesty's Prison and Probation Service (HMPPS) which supervises high-risk offenders released into the community, or community rehabilitation companies (CRCs) which monitors low and medium-risk offenders given community service rather than custodial sentences

Progress   belief in the continual improvement of society

Proletariat   a term used by Marx to describe all the workers who do not own the means of production

Proportional representation   a term that describes various systems that allocate seats in parliament based on a proportion of the votes cast

Protestant work ethic   the moral and spiritual virtue of individual effort and hard work

Pseudonym   in sociological research, a name used to conceal the identity of an individual informant

Public school   a high-status and expensive private school in Britain

Public sector   part of the economy that is owned or controlled by government

Pupil premium   additional funding granted to state-funded schools in England to raise the attainment of disadvantaged pupils

Qualitative data   information presented in a variety of forms that is rich in descriptive detail

Quantitative data   information presented in a numerical form

Questionnaire   a research method that uses a predetermined list of questions

Quota sample   subjects are selected because they represent groups in the total population (e.g. age, gender) often used in market research

Race   the classification of people based on apparent physical differences

Random sample   a group selected for research at random from a particular sampling frame. To be truly random everyone in the group must stand an equal chance of selection

Ratio data   data measured on a scale from absolute zero

Rational authority   rules and procedures that are generally believed to be fair and impartial

Rationalisation   the efficient organisation of society based on rational legal authority, technical and scientific knowledge

Raw data   numerical data that has not been processed or analysed

Reconstituted (or blended) family   when two adults with children from previous relationships remarry (or cohabit) to form a new family

Recorded crime   crime that is reported to and recorded by the police

Referendum   a national vote on a single issue

Relative poverty   when an individual lacks the resources to participate in activities that are widely available to the majority of people in the society in which they live

Reliability   data is reliable if research can be repeated and consistently produces similar results

Reported crime crime that is reported to the police – not all reported crime is recorded

Representative a researcher's data/sample is not biased but accurately reflects the wider population being studied

Resource allocation the control of economic resources

Response rate the number of people who complete a survey divided by the number who made up the total sample

Right-wing the political beliefs of the majority of the British Conservative Party and other right of centre politicians

Right of appeal the opportunity to challenge a judicial court's decision

Role patterns of behaviour expected by individuals in different situations, e.g. student and teacher

Ruling class ideology the ideas and beliefs of the ruling class

Russell Group the top ranked 18 universities in the UK

Same sex family families headed by a couple of the same sex

Sample a group selected for study by a researcher from a target population

Sampling frame a complete list from which the researcher selects their sample, e.g. all the students in a school

Sanction negative sanctions are any form of penalty for unacceptable actions of an individual or group, while positive sanctions (or rewards) are applied for good behaviour

Scapegoat an individual, or their community, who is blamed unfairly for a negative event

Secondary data data from pre-existing research, e.g. previously published research papers exploring the same social phenomena

Secondary labour market sector of the labour market characterised by low-paid, low-status and insecure employment

Secondary socialisation a process of social learning that takes place outside the family, e.g. school, employment and mass media

Segregated conjugal roles male and female partners perform different and clearly defined activities

Self-concept the idea an individual has of the kind of person that they think they are

Self-fulfilling prophecy when an individual accepts the label that has been given to them by others and acts accordingly

Self-report study a survey that asks respondents to identify crimes they have committed, but for which they have not been caught

Semi-structured interview this combines some of the features of structured and unstructured interviews

Setting dividing students into different groups for particular subjects based on their ability in those subjects

Slavery when individuals become the property of another

Snowball sample each member of a group of respondents is asked by a researcher to recommend someone who is known to them and who is in a similar situation

Social class a type of social stratification based on economic factors

Social cohesion a sense of belonging to the wider society

Social construct patterns of behaviour based on the norms and expectations of a society

Social control the process by which the members of a society are persuaded to conform to the rules of that society, e.g. the actions of the police who enforce the law (formal) and the disapproval of the other members of society (informal)

Social inequality differences between the members of society in terms of wealth, class, status and power

Social mobility the movement of an individual either up or down the social scale, e.g. the working-class student who obtains a university degree and enters a profession (upward mobility)

Social order how society is constructed and maintained

Social psychology an area of psychology concerned with human interactions

Social stratification the way in which a society is divided hierarchically on the basis of various factors, e.g. class, gender and ethnicity

Social theorists this term can be used to describe sociologists, economists, philosophers and others who think and write about society

Socially organised labour human activity intended to satisfy the economic needs of society

Society a group of people with a common culture – the term is often used to describe nation states, e.g. British society

Sociobiology the scientific idea that human behaviour has evolved

Socio-economic class a type of social stratification based on economic factors (different types of employment, e.g. manual and non-manual) and various social factors linked to an individual's economic position

Sociological debate discussions between sociologists about how to best understand the nature of society

Sociological research methods these include questionnaires, interviews and observation

Standard deviation the spread of data from the arithmetical mean

State school a school funded by the government

State standard of poverty definition of poverty when households have an income of 'less than 60 per cent of the national median'

Status frustration a sense of frustration arising in individuals or groups because they are denied status in society

STEM science, technology, engineering and mathematics

Stereotype an unfavourable simplistic image of a group based on the behaviour of a small number of individuals from within that group

Stock exchange a market in company shares (stocks)

Strategy a plan of action

Stratified sample a sample selected to represent groups within the total population (similar to a quota sample)

Streaming dividing students into different groups (usually referred to as streams or bands) based on a general assessment of their ability rather than their performance in a particular subject

Structured interview an interview using a predetermined list of tightly controlled questions

Subculture a group with a distinctive set of values and behaviours who set themselves apart from the wider society

Subjective judgements that are based on personal opinions

Subjective class the socio-economic position a person feels they are located in

Subjective poverty an individual's perception of their level of deprivation

Superstructure the cultural and political aspects of society built upon the foundation of the infrastructure, e.g. government and political systems

Survey a marketing technique used to judge customer satisfaction or purchasing preferences

Symbolic violence the term Bourdieu gives to the systematic undermining of working-class characteristics and confidence within schools

Symmetrical family a family where both domestic and economic responsibilities are equally shared between male and female partners

Systematic sample the systematic selection of names from a list, e.g. every tenth name

Target population the whole group that is being researched

Terrorism the unlawful use of violence and intimidation, especially against civilians

Trade union an organisation of workers designed to protect their common interests through negotiation and collective action

Traditional authority a form of power based on established customs and inherited status

Transcript a written version of the interview

Trend the general direction (either increasing or decreasing) as revealed by the data

Triangulation (corroboration) of data the accuracy of data gathered using one method can be compared with data gathered using alternative methods, e.g. questionnaires, interviews and secondary sources

Triple shift the three types of work that create a burden for women: paid work, domestic work and emotional work

Underclass a group of people at the very bottom of the social scale who are dependent on welfare benefits

Unit of consumption the family unit consumes the products of industrial society by purchasing goods and services

Universal standards attempts to provide objective judgements applied equally to all members of society, regardless of who they are, e.g. a teacher's objective assessment of a child's performance in school, based on test results, as opposed to a parent's subjective view of their child's abilities

Unstructured interview an informal conversation that allows the respondent to talk freely about the general theme agreed for the interview

Urban towns and cities; sociologists often refer to social groups such as the urban working class

Validity data is valid if it gives an accurate picture of the social world

Value consensus beliefs that are commonly shared by a particular social group

Values important beliefs held by individuals and social groups

Variable any factor that may differ and have an impact on the results of your research, e.g. gender, age, socio-economic class and ethnicity

Victim survey a survey that asks respondents about their experience of crime, regardless of whether or not those crimes have been reported

Violent crimes these are recorded as 'violence against the person', which covers more than 30 offences including grievous bodily harm (GBH), assault, kidnap, child abduction, harassment and threats to kill

Vocationalism education designed to provide the skills necessary for work

Wealth material resources owned by individuals, e.g. property, savings and businesses

Welfare state government systems for supporting the health and general well-being of the population. In Britain, this term is often used to describe post-1945 welfare reforms including the introduction of the National Health Service in 1948

White collar crime criminal activities typically of a financial nature such as fraud, embezzlement, forgery, etc.

White collar workers non-manual workers in offices and the service sector

Working class members of society who are engaged in some form of manual work

Youth crime crimes committed by individuals who are too young to be sent to an adult prison; in Britain, children aged ten and above can be held responsible for their actions

Index

A

absolute poverty 234
academies 135, 143, 144
adults' attitudes to education 140
affluent workers 232–3
age/ageism 203–5, 229–31, 249
alienation 225
alternative education 138–9
Althusser, Louis 147
anomie 11, 182, 186, 189, 194
anonymity 74, 75
appropriate aims 39
authority 15, 245–6, 250
average 68

B

bar charts 69, 70
Bastøy Prison 209
Becker, Howard 147–8, 153, 180, 183
bedroom culture 158, 197
Beveridge Report 243
Bourdieu, Pierre 147, 149, 152
bourgeoisie 13
British Sociological Association
    ethical code 74
business power 253

C

capitalism 13, 14–15, 23, 83, 100, 114,
    224–5
  and class exploitation 18–19
  and education 130–1
  market capitalism 24
case studies 56–7, 60
caste system 219
censuses 64, 65
centre-left (social democrats) 244
charismatic authority 246

chattel slavery 218–19
Chester, Robert 90, 92
childcare 143
child poverty 234
children 106–7
  effects of divorce on 118, 119
chivalry thesis 176, 196–7, 198
class alignment/dealignment 248
class conflict 12–13, 14, 19, 224–5
class exploitation 18–19
class identity 233
closed questions 49
cluster samples 43
cohort diversity 90
collective conscience 185
commercialisation of housework 109
communal living 93–4
communism 12
Communist Manifesto (Marx and
    Engels) 12
comprehensive schools 134, 144
compulsory state education 126
computer crime 195
Comte, Auguste 4–5, 41
confidentiality 74, 75
conflict theories 6–7, 18–19, 22–3
conformity 182
conjugal roles 84, 96–104
consensus 7
consumerism 7
contemporary families 106
corporate crime 176, 193, 194, 195
counter culture 148
court system 192
crime 11, 25, 64–5, 172–6
  age and 203–5
  corporate crime 176, 193, 194, 195
  definition of 172–3
  ethnicity and 200–2
  gender and 196–9
  mass media and 212–13
  perception of 211
  social class and 194–5
  social construction of 179

  as social issue 31
  sociological explanations for
      181–4
  theories of 185, 187–8
  violent crime 210–11
  white collar crime 176, 186, 187,
      194, 195, 197
crime statistics 174–6, 194, 196, 201,
    202
Crime Survey for England and Wales
    (CSEW) 177, 211
criminal behaviour: factors affecting
    194–205
criminal justice system 192–3
criminal responsibility: age of 206
cultural capital 149
cultural deprivation 152, 165
cultural diversity 89
culture 8, 32–3
culture of poverty 24–5, 235
curriculum
    ethnocentric curriculum 166
    hidden curriculum 145, 147, 158, 166,
        189
    National Curriculum 134, 136, 142,
        157
cycle of deprivation 235

D

dark figure of crime 175
Darwin, Charles 9
data
    interpretation of 68–71
    presentation of 69
Data Protection Acts (1998 and 2018)
    75
data sets 68
deindustrialisation 241
democracy 247–8
demography 64
deprivation
    cultural deprivation 152, 165

The Publishers would like to thank the following for permission to reproduce copyright material.

Text credits

p. 137 data in Table 4.4 reproduced from 'Elitist Britain 2019' by the Sutton Trust with permission; **p. 254** extract in Item A reproduced from the Economic and Social Research Council's Society *Now* magazine with permission.

Photo credits

p. 6 © Popperfoto/Getty Images; **p. 8** © BlueSkyImage/Shutterstock; **p. 10** © Bettmann/Getty Images; **p. 12** © Everett Historical/Shutterstock; **p. 14** © Hulton Archive/Getty Images; **p. 16** © Rawpixel.com/stock.adobe.com; **p. 18** © Colin Waters/Alamy Stock Photo; **p. 20** © Rawpixel.com/stock.adobe.com; **p. 22** © Matthew Chattle/Alamy Stock Photo; **p. 24** © Bettmann/Contributor/Getty Images; **p. 28** © Syda Productions/stock.adobe.com; **p. 30** © Photographee. eu/stock.adobe.com; **p. 32** © Stan Meagher/Daily Express/Hulton Archive/Getty Images; **p. 34** © Universal Images Group via Getty Images; **p. 36** © Caiaimage/Chris Ryan/Getty Images; **p. 40** © anyaivanova/Shutterstock; **p. 46** © Antonioguillem/stock.adobe.com; **p. 48** © Andrey_Popov/Shutterstock; **p. 50** © Monkey Business Images/ Shutterstock; **p. 52** © Happy Art/Shutterstock; **p. 54** © History and Art Collection/Alamy Stock Photo; **p. 56** © Jojje/ Shutterstock; **p. 58** © Plume Creative/Getty Images; **p. 60** © momentimages/Getty Images; **p. 62** © Rawpixel Ltd/ Alamy Stock Photo; **p. 64** © Patrick Ward/Alamy Stock Photo; **p. 66** © Cultura Creative (RF)/Alamy Stock Photo; **p. 72** © Kevin Fleming/Corbis via Getty Images; **p. 74** © leungchopan/Shutterstock; **p. 76** © Andrew Bret Wallis/ Getty Images; **p. 80** *l* © Monkey Business Images/Shutterstock, *m* © Ocskay Mark/Shutterstock.com, *r* © Caiaimage/ Paul Bradbury/Getty Images; **p. 85** © wavebreakmedia/Shutterstock; **p. 91** © Monkey Business/stock.adobe.com; **p. 95** © Tang Ming Tung/Getty Images; **p. 97** © topvectors/stock.adobe.com; **p. 101** © Dragon Images/Shutterstock; **p. 111** © Cultura RM Exclusive/Jason Butcher/Getty Images; **p. 112** © pixelheadphoto digitalskillet/Shutterstock; **p. 117** © Shelly Mantovani, Ruth D'Rozario and Paul McCabe; **p. 118** © andriano.cz/Shutterstock; **p. 121** © Stock-Asso/Shutterstock; **p. 128** © alexandre zveiger/Shutterstock; **p. 131** *l* © Monkey Business Images/Shutterstock, *m* © Caiaimage/Chris Ryan/Getty Images, *r* © aphichato/Shutterstock; **p. 139** © Rawpixel.com/Shutterstock; **p. 158** © highwaystarz/stock.adobe.com; **p. 160** © Stock Rocket/Shutterstock.com; **p. 172** *l* © Syda Productions/ Shutterstock, *m* © Syda Productions/stock.adobe.com, *r* ©Josep Curto/123RF; **p. 173** © GL Archive/Alamy Stock Photo; **p. 176** © Janine Wiedel Photolibrary/Alamy Stock Photo; **p. 179** *l* © PeopleImages/Getty Images, *r* © PRESSLAB/Shutterstock.com; **p. 182** © I-Wei Huang/stock.adobe.com; **p. 183** © Photofusion Picture Library/Alamy Stock Photo; **p. 209** © Caspar Benson/Getty Images; **p. 212** © spiral media/stock.adobe.com; **p. 218** © Mike Moore/ Evening Standard/Getty Images; **p. 224** © World History Archive/Alamy Stock Photo; **p. 226** © elenabsl/stock.adobe. com; **p. 228** © iLongLoveKing/Shutterstock.com; **p. 232** © Daily Herald/Mirrorpix/Mirrorpix via Getty Images; **p. 234** © Stavrida/Shutterstock; **p. 237** © Chris Morphet/Redferns/Getty Images; **p. 239** © motortion/stock.adobe.com; **p. 241** © paulprescott72/Getty Images; **p. 243** © Cover from a leaflet published by the Liberal Publication Department (Liberal Party – UK) in 1911 (Public Domain); **p. 246** © Keystone/Getty Images; **p. 252** © Ben Gingell/Shutterstock.com.

Every effort has been made to trace all copyright holders, but if any have been inadvertently overlooked, the Publishers will be pleased to make the necessary arrangements at the first opportunity.